JOHN WESLEY
AND THE
CHURCH OF ENGLAND

Frank Baker

JOHN WESLEY
AND THE
CHURCH OF ENGLAND

ABINGDON PRESS
NASHVILLE AND NEW YORK

TO THOSE STUDENTS
AT THE DUKE DIVINITY SCHOOL
WHO HAVE SHARED
AND WILL SHARE WITH ME
THE ADVENTURE OF STUDYING
'THE RISE OF METHODISM AND
ITS ANGLICAN BACKGROUND'

PREFACE

THIS book has been many years in the writing, having been shelved on three occasions because of urgent research and writing tasks connected with the *Oxford Edition of Wesley's Works*. During this process it has undergone considerable modifications in approach and depth of treatment, in response both to the advice of friends and to what seemed the demands of the material.

It deals with a problem which only the brash have been able to approach with any confidence, and where timid people such as I have feared to speak. Yet I have long been convinced that we need not only sweeping generalizations about Wesley's relations with the Church of England based on a few well-worn facts, but the setting of these facts in their context, and the introduction of other factors either forgotten or never considered—even though this might render facile generalizations more difficult, and introduce the danger of not being able to see the shape of the wood for the abundance of trees.

This study in depth has not been undertaken with a view to proving any point—except perhaps that in the long run truth is more important than propaganda. The evidence here set forth may indeed be used to prove that were John Wesley to return today his position about modern Anglican-Methodist relations would clearly be on this side or on that side—or possibly on neither side. Although I personally desire a fuller integration of the Church Universal, only indirectly is that my concern in this book. It is in no sense party propaganda, but an honest attempt to discover the truth and to present it as accurately and dispassionately as possible. My approach is factual rather than interpretative, but because cultural and ecclesiastical bias is almost certain to colour the necessary selection and arrangement and interpretation of the facts it may be well to state that I am a British Methodist minister permitted to serve as Professor of English Church History in a Methodist-oriented American theological seminary.

When so many facts remain obscure and so many motives are imperfectly comprehended, it would be folly to imagine that I had written the definitive book on this complex subject. Others will correct my mistakes, possibly as silently as in this book I have corrected scores of those made by previous writers. New facts will be adduced, based on further research, new documents discovered, and these may well modify some of my conclusions. They must be welcomed if they bring us nearer to a full understanding of one of the most remarkable and baffling love stories in modern church history, that of John Wesley's fluctuating and frustrated affections for the Church of England.

For sympathetic help and encouragement I am indebted to many friends and fellow-workers on both sides of the Atlantic, more especially to Dr. Robert E. Cushman of the Duke Divinity School for creating conditions conducive to research; to Dr. Charles A. Rogers and to my wife Nellie for constructive criticism and assistance with the chores of preparing the manuscript for the press; to Dr. Frank Cumbers and Dr. John C. Bowmer for making so fully available the matchless research resources of the Methodist archives in London, and to numerous other librarians and scholars throughout the English-speaking world. If the result is appreciated as much as the help given in making it possible I shall indeed be amply rewarded.

FRANK BAKER

The Divinity School
Duke University
9 September 1967

CONTENTS

INTRODUCTION

IT WOULD be impossible to write an adequate history of the Church
of England without devoting a chapter to John Wesley and the movement of which he was the centre. Nor can Wesley himself be understood
apart from the Established Church. It was not simply that he happened
to be born an Anglican, and from that base began to erect a new
denomination, founding Methodism in reaction against his mother
church. In thought and affection, in habit and atmosphere, his whole
being was inextricably interwoven with that of the church. This was
not so with many religious leaders of his own and other days. His
fellow-evangelist George Whitefield, for instance, was also reared in
the Church of England, received his education at church foundations,
and was ordained an Anglican priest. He sat so lightly to his heritage,
however, that his churchmanship is merely an incidental feature in his
religious background. For John Wesley, on the other hand, the Church
of England formed an indispensable part of life, a limb, a major organ:
it was just possible to imagine life without it, but only just. His religious
thought and practice were conceived in terms of loyalty or disloyalty to
the Church of England. The church formed a living part of his experience—along with the Holy Spirit. The sad thing was that frequently
the two seemed to be in opposition. Much of the fascination of John
Wesley's story is to see his inborn deeply-rooted prejudice in favour of
the church beaten down, broken, twisted, yet constantly struggling to
its feet in spite of the inexorable blows struck by a providence demanding other things of him: and at the end to see him, in the face of all
logic, still proclaiming, 'I live and die a member of the Church of
England!'

This book is neither a biography of Wesley nor a study of his peculiar brand of churchmanship in any static sense. For Wesley's churchmanship was never static, but constantly developing—a fact which has
too frequently been ignored. I am here attempting to trace this development through the years, not as a new 'Churchman's Life of Wesley' or
'The Founder of Methodism', but as a study in human reaction to
changing circumstances—a study of great importance when that

human being is probably the most significant religious figure in his century, and when those circumstances included the burgeoning of a growing industrial nation into an empire and the beginnings of a great world church.

Dr. Joseph Beaumont's description of Wesley's enigmatic relation to the Church of England is both vivid and apt: 'Mr. Wesley, like a strong and skilful rower, looked one way, while every stroke of his oar took him in the opposite direction.'[1] He was not Mr. Facing-Both-Ways, but he came uncomfortably close to it. Wesley himself explained his lifelong position in terms of tension between two principles: 'The one, I dare not separate from the Church, that I believe it would be a sin so to do; the other, that I believe it would be a sin not to vary from it in . . . cases of necessity.'[2]

Dr. Beaumont's analogy is especially useful in prompting us to distinguish between contemplation and action. Whatever deliberate separation from the Church of England took place during Wesley's ministry was primarily in the realm of deeds rather than of thought. Although Wesley did in fact revise his early views of church, ministry, and sacraments in some details, these revisions making it easier for him to alter his ecclesiastical ways and yet retain a clear conscience, there is little doubt that the original cause of most of his separatist actions was spiritual need rather than theological conviction. He did not attempt to formulate a new doctrine of the church but to remedy its decadence. Once intuitively embarked on some mission of ecclesiastical mercy, however, he was inclined to rationalize his irregularities so that his unorthodox relations with the church occasionally developed into a question of semantics: he 'consented' to preach in the open air, he 'permitted' lay preaching, he was ready to 'vary' from the church.

Wesley's views of the church owed little to the continental reformers, except indirectly through their presence in the climate of English thought. He firmly accepted the *via media* of the Church of England, as incorporated in Cranmer's *Book of Common Prayer*, and expounded in turn by Jewel as the fulfilment of Scripture and the Fathers and by Hooker as the crown of human reasoning. The 19th Article remained his lifelong definition of the church: 'The visible Church of Christ is a Congregation of faithful men, in the which the pure Word of God is preached, and the Sacraments be duly ministered according to Christ's Ordinance, in all those things that of necessity are requisite to the same. . . .' Like most of the Articles this was capable of multifarious interpretations, and Wesley squeezed the Methodist societies, lay preaching, lay administration of the sacraments, and even presbyterial ordination into this definition with very few twinges of conscience and with almost complete immunity from ecclesiastical censure.

A church which both needed and could permit these irregularities surely needed reform. Many heartening exceptions could be marshalled to counterbalance the general impression of decay, but the impression remains. The Church of England in Wesley's day was not only lax in the ordering of worship and in pastoral oversight. At the higher levels of church government there was little co-ordination of responsibilities; ecclesiastical authority had become an empty show, and spiritual initiative dissipated itself in political manœuvring. Preserving a different kind of middle way had become almost a religion in itself, though for the Scylla of Rome and the Charybdis of Wittenberg were substituted the two extremes of dogmatism and enthusiasm. There was some excuse for the church's seeking a quiet corner where she could lick her wounds. Gaping holes had been left by the loss of the Nonconformists on the left and the Non-Jurors on the right. How could a church soar after losing both wings? As the enfeebled church faltered, so did the power of the state grow, and during Wesley's long lifetime a maturing parliamentary government laid hands on many powers not only of the crown but of the church. The attempt to renovate the two Convocations as effective centres of co-ordinated ecclesiastical debate and discipline was shipwrecked on the rock of the Bangorian controversy, though Archbishop Wake had already issued the Erastian warning that the ancient vessel was no longer seaworthy.

Wesley came to see his own life's task as that of 'spreading scriptural holiness throughout the land', preferably through the agencies of a spiritually renewed national church, among which agencies he hoped would be gratefully included his own societies and preachers. This challenging task was to be carried out within the church is possible, but outside if necessary. Church or no church, the gospel must be proclaimed. More fully than his brother Charles, John Wesley was convinced that strict church order and evangelical efficacy did not always make an ideal couple, and was ready if called upon to officiate at their divorce, and to award custody of the spiritual children to the partner most capable of promoting their welfare. In his approach to both church and ministry he was alike the biblicist, the traditionalist, and the rationalist, but above all he was the religious pragmatist. He worshipped the God who answered by fire, and served Him intuitively, imaginatively, and fearlessly. One of the prices he was prepared if necessary to pay was that of being labelled a schismatic, though he continued to insist that the charge was unjust.

Throughout his sixty-five years' ministry John Wesley was constantly on the alert for spiritual need, and constantly responded in the manner he urged upon the multitudinous readers of his *Primitive Physic*, by using whatever remedies lay to hand, whether official or highly recommended or frankly experimental (so long as they were not obviously harmful), throwing aside those that did not work until he found one that did. The story of the separation of Methodism from the Church of England is one of the humble apothecary prescribing homely remedies for spiritual ills, so as to keep the church going and doing its job, rather than the carefully-planned blue-printing of diet and exercise by an Olympic trainer intent on fashioning the super-spiritual-athlete who is finally going to beat all records and achieve the imperishable crown of the perfect church missed alike by Paul, Gregory, and John Calvin. Methodism was the result not of the fulfilling of an ambitious dream, but of the constant frustration of hopes which we now see as fruitless. Possibly there was some unrecognized admixture of ambitious dross in the gold of Wesley's day-by-day response to the promptings of the Holy Spirit, but if so it was the merest grain. Constantly John Wesley acted, spoke, and thought to the glory of God, never to the glory of John Wesley. Yet time after time urgent spiritual needs prompted irregular action, and then reaction necessitated counter-action, until inch by inch Wesley was manœuvred into a position of actual though undeclared and unacknowledged separation.

The separation of Wesley's Methodism from the Church of England can perhaps most readily be visualized in terms of the relation of a branch to a tree, from which it is gradually being split, yet from which it continually draws the lifeblood of crude sap, and to which it continually returns its own contribution of elaborated sap. Meantime callus is forming both to protect and to heal the wound. This process may continue for many years, indeed for the life of the tree if the branch is so protected that it is not torn off or pulled down by its own weight. The analogy would be even closer with a woody plant like the azalea or the bramble, in which while splitting from the main growth at one end, at the other end a part of the branch in contact with the earth could develop its own root system by layering, and enjoy an independent existence if the split eventually became a complete rupture.

The widening breach between John Wesley and the Church of England is not readily amenable to any ordered summary which is completely convincing, whether based on chronology or on subject matter. Some of the 'firsts' can easily be assembled: his 'submitting to be more vile' by preaching in the open air at Bristol on 2 April 1739, his summoning of the first annual Conference at the Foundery in London on 25 June 1744, and especially the crucial events of that crucial year of 1784—the signing on 28 February of the Deed Poll which incorporated the Conference as a legal entity, and his ordination of preachers for America on 1 and 2 September. Some admittedly epochal events, however, like his acceptance of Thomas Maxfield as his first 'son in the gospel' can neither be accurately dated nor fully explained. Nor can the timing and manner and significance of Wesley's first ordinations be fully grasped apart from a study of the twenty years' growth of American Methodism, thirty years of status seeking by Methodist preachers, and forty years' development in Wesley's doctrine of the ministry. A rigid chronological survey of Wesley's split with the church would reveal a number of minor splits slowly combining during the stormy years 1739-44. There followed a lengthy period of apparent quiescence, during which healing tissue appeared to be forming, though occasionally the splits would widen because of atmospheric conditions or the sagging of the growing branch. In 1784 there came a combined effort by vigorous hands to pull the branch away from the parent tree, but still a tenuous connection remained, and the sap continued to flow in both directions.

Nor can the complex interplay of Wesley's 'variations' from Anglican normality be sensed from a mere classification of the categories into which they fall—though this is far from saying that such an approach has little value. One of the most useful summaries of this kind is contained in George Eayrs' *John Wesley, Christian Philosopher and Church Founder*. Mr. Eayrs lists eight of 'Wesley's acts as church founder' and four 'regulative principles'. The church founding acts are entitled:

   i. Unauthorized Religious Services.
   ii. A New Fellowship Instituted.
   iii. Separate Church Buildings Erected.
   iv. Church Workers Appointed.
   v. A Supreme Court Constituted.
   vi. Legal Acts to Secure Continuity.
   vii. A Church Constitution for American Methodists.
   viii. Ministers Ordained for British Methodism.

Although we must be grateful for this attempt to classify Wesley's schismatic tendencies in general terms with the aid of specific examples, we find ourselves dissenting from some points in this list, and wondering why others were not included. And it is possible to accept their tendency without agreeing that Wesley 'definitely and unmistakably' intended to found a separate church.[3]

Nor is this mild disagreement surprising. Even Wesley himself experienced difficulty in enumerating the steps by which he became 'irregular' and 'varied' from the church, though he undertook the task on several occasions. Sometimes, indeed, he makes demonstrable errors in chronological order, as when in his *Plain Account of the People called Methodists* he implies that Methodist 'classes' were organized before 'bands'.[4] Similarly in his 'Farther Thoughts on Separation' he speaks of field-preaching as his 'first irregularity' and 'extemporary prayer' as his second, whereas in fact the latter was deliberately undertaken a year almost to the day before the first.[5]

My own approach has been a combination of the chronological and topical methods which solves some of the problems of each and introduces others of its own. Within a biographical framework I have traced Wesley's relations with the Church of England at various stages, and when any major change occurs I have stopped to describe the steps leading to that change and (more briefly) its later developments and related features. I had originally planned a major section of printed documents to which reference would have been made, but the story itself has squeezed these out. As a minor atonement I have occasionally interwoven generous quotations into the narrative, and console myself with the pious hope that at least a few scholars will turn to the works cited for fuller information.

I have taken the liberty of using the term 'Anglican' throughout as a synonym for 'pertaining to the Church of England'; although it did not come into regular use until after Wesley's day it is found occasionally in the eighteenth century, and even in the seventeenth. Similarly I have used 'churchmanship' in a generic sense to mean 'the views and practices of a member of the church', and 'High Church' to imply a general emphasis both upon the authority of the church and of its ordained ministers, and also upon the importance of the sacraments and the other historical forms of worship.

ONE

A SON OF THE CHURCH

ALTHOUGH Nonconformity was in Wesley's blood, even his 'reversion to type' (as A. Skevington Wood calls it)[1] was not brought about by the direct influence of his dissenting forebears, of whose heroic stand he seems to have been unaware until his middle years when his own course had been clearly set. Indeed, it seems fairly certain that his parents deliberately withheld from him that part of his inheritance.[2] Coming from Nonconformity to the Church of England as convinced converts, both Samuel and Susanna Wesley had proved the more zealous in their Anglican allegiance, the more enthusiastic in impressing its values upon their children.[3] John Wesley himself realized that his father's influence had strongly predisposed him to become a Tory in politics, and told the Earl of Dartmouth in 1775: 'I am an High Churchman, the son of an High Churchman, bred up from my childhood in the highest notions of passive obedience and non-resistance.'[4] August Gottlieb Spangenberg saw Wesley's extreme ecclesiastical views in Georgia as the outcome of his early background and training: 'He has moreover several quite special principles, which he still holds strongly, since he drank them in with his mother's milk.'[5]

There is not the slightest doubt that Wesley's life at the Epworth rectory until he was ten years old was one of the most formative influences of his whole career, both directly and indirectly shaping the churchmanship that was to nurture the Methodist societies until they could do little else but separate from the Church of England. All the evidence shows that from his mother he inherited a studious, thoughtful disposition and a calm, stubborn patience under adversity; brother Charles took after their father's more tempestuous 'artistic' temperament. Both parents were painstaking and courageous, sincerely devout, methodical in their 'religious exercises', strict in morals, and confirmed believers in the spiritual as well as the social values of discipline. In all this the strong influence of their own puritanical upbringing persisted, to leave its mark on John.[6]

A firm yet affectionate discipline was undoubtedly what first impressed Wesley about his parents, strongly colouring his childhood views of the God to whom they early taught him to pray, and whose holy book they helped him to read. He himself testifies to a very strict upbringing in a home where obedience was expected and rewarded, and disobedience punished, and where this relationship between parent and child was regarded as typifying that between God and man.[7] It is easy to point the finger of scorn at Mrs. Wesley's insistence on conquering her children's wills and on their addressing each other as 'brother Charles' and 'sister Hetty', easy to forget that this was a fruitful means of teaching them to exercise the admirable quality of self-discipline, so essential to a happy life, as also of recognizing and respecting the dignity and rights of others. More especially it was a training for a lifetime's obedience to God. Susanna Wesley saw this spiritual discipline as making 'a child capable of being governed by the reason and piety of its parents till its own understanding comes to maturity and the principles of religion have taken root in the mind'.[8] John Wesley echoed her words in later years: 'The will of a parent is to a little child in the place of the will of God.'[9]

Small wonder that to young Jacky Wesley religion meant doing what God told you. Yet this was no grudging unthinking obedience, no more than was that which he gave his parents. They were both so strongly individualistic—and in many ways so different from each other—that marital peace was at times kept only with extreme difficulty. The right to hold different opinions was firmly maintained, the right even to disobey established authority at the call of conscience, and the duty if need arose to suffer for conscience' sake. The children's religious doubts were honestly discussed, and they were taught that although God's being and nature were known mainly through divine revelation in the Bible, His will for man could and should be discovered by human reason supplementing that revelation, and that when discovered it must be obeyed implicitly. This approach to religion through faith and reason and will alike was sincerely practised and strongly inculcated by both parents.

The Bible played a prominent part not only in church worship and in family prayers, but in their remarkable private education at their mother's knee. As soon as they could speak the Wesley children were taught the Lord's Prayer, 'which they were made to say at rising and bedtime constantly'. To this were soon added 'a short prayer for their parents, and some collects; a short catechism, and some portions of Scripture, as their memories could bear'. All this, of course, before they could read. Once taught their alphabet on their fifth birthday by Mrs. Wesley, the Bible furnished their 'First Reader'. They began at the opening chapter of Genesis, spelling out each verse, then reading it out 'over and over' till they could 'read it offhand without any hesitation'. Their mother kept them at their home schooling for six hours a day, and they soon knew many passages of their Bibles intimately, as well as some general literature.[10] The Bible remained their central study. Every morning they read a psalm and a chapter in the Old Testament, every evening a psalm and a chapter in the New Testament—the passages prescribed in the Calendar of the *Book of Common Prayer*, which became almost as familiar to them as the Bible itself. The four older children were enlisted to oversee the four younger ones in this discipline, and it seems almost certain that young Jacky's supervisor was Mary.[11] Such daily Bible reading Wesley maintained throughout his life.[12]

Partly through their similarity of temperament, partly because she was admired teacher as well as beloved mother, Susanna Wesley made far more impression upon John than did his father. She so won his affection that in later life he could say of this authoritarian education that he 'gladly received and often thought of' these parental instructions.[13] From birth there had been a peculiar bond between them. John Wesley was conceived after his mother's longest period of freedom from pregnancy during a long and fruitful childbearing life, conceived as the result of a reconciliation with her husband after his passionate response to her Jacobite refusal to pray for a widower king whose only right to the throne (in her view) was through his dead Stuart wife.[14] In 1709 the five-year-old boy was rescued from the rectory 'as a brand plucked out of the burning'. In May 1711, as he was approaching eight, she penned a special resolve to 'be more particularly careful of the soul of this child'.[15]

During the following winter Mrs. Wesley underwent a deep emotional and spiritual experience through reading Ziegenbalg's account of two Danish Moravian missionaries and their work in Tranquebar.[16] One result was that during her husband's long absence at Convocation she began what a handful of jealous people called a 'conventicle' in the parsonage: enormously enlarged family prayers, attended sometimes by as many as two hundred people. These were continued in face of Samuel Wesley's disapproval, and she dared him to command her to stop. One is tempted to think that the thoughtful boy of eight sensed the tension between his parents over these unorthodox gatherings, but he himself claimed that not until very much later did he realise their significance as precursors of his own religious societies.[17]

Another practice, inspired by this same spiritual quickening, left a permanent impression on young Jacky Wesley. His mother set aside an hour or so every evening for discussing spiritual and moral problems with each child in turn. Thursday evening was given up to Jacky, and even when he had become a grown man Wesley referred longingly to

these privileged occasions.[18] This routine must have suffered somewhat
in April 1712, when five of the nine children then at home were ill
with smallpox, but one is not surprised to find Susanna reporting to her
absent husband:

> Jack has bore his disease bravely, like a man, and indeed like a
> Christian, without any complaint, though he seemed angry at the
> smallpox when they were sore—as we guessed by his looking sourly
> at them, for he never said anything.[19]

When Samuel Wesley returned from Convocation later that spring
it was undoubtedly to find Jacky not only recovered from the smallpox
(though marked for life) but so matured, so clear and convincing in his
rational faith and spiritual dedication, that he had no hesitation in
admitting the boy to communion long before he had reached the
normal age of sixteen. It seems almost certain that John Wesley's nine-
year-old head was one of those eight hundred upon which William
Wake, Bishop of Lincoln, laid confirming hands on 15 July 1712 in the
Epworth parish church.[20]

'The child is father of the man,' and when ten-year-old John Wesley
left Epworth for the Charterhouse, London, in 1714, the guiding principles of his life had already been formulated. Carefully instilled habits
of religious discipline played their part so effectively that when removed
from parental oversight he continued faithfully to say his prayers, to
read his Bible morning and night, and to remain outwardly diligent
and respectable and inwardly devout.[21]

There can be no doubt that his parents, and especially his mother,
pursued him with letters. Twenty years later Wesley told her that their
Thursday evening sessions were mainly responsible for 'forming [his]
judgment'.[22] The process was continued by the less satisfactory method
of correspondence, and in default of the letters themselves we can
follow her advice and his response through the remnants of her correspondence with John's elder brother when he left for Westminster
School. Indeed, some passages in the long series of letters to Samuel
admirably describe John's own approach to life throughout most of his
youth and early manhood:

> Examine well your heart, and observe its inclinations, particularly
> what the general temper of your mind is; for . . . it is not a fit of
> devotion now and then speaks a man a Christian, but it is a mind
> universally and generally disposed to all the duties of Christianity.
> . . . The mind of a Christian should be always composed, temperate,
> free from all extremes of mirth or sadness, and always disposed to

hear the still small voice of God's Holy Spirit, which will direct him
what and how to act in all the occurrences of life, if in all his ways
he acknowledge Him, and depend on His assistance.[23]

Reduced to its simplest terms, this approach to life was a balance
between obedience to a final authority in fundamentals and the exercise
of freedom of opinion in non-fundamentals. This had operated in the
Epworth rectory more than in most households, for there Samuel and
Susanna Wesley were more interested in nurturing responsible Christians than on the one hand manufacturing religious robots or on the
other of being mere spectators watching the development of unco-
ordinated bundles of instinctive reactions. When removed from his
parents' personal insistence on both obedience and initiative a similar
process nevertheless continued. These two essential ingredients of
John's early upbringing were projected into his developing religion,
with God now as the supreme parent demanding obedience, but
expecting also respect for the rights of others, with its corollary of the
Christian's liberty to follow his personal judgement where no absolute
command of God intervened.

One major problem remained. Granted that the law of God must be
obeyed, how was it to be discovered? God was the final authority on
living, but what constituted the final authority in discovering His will?
The answer usually given by Anglican theologians was: 'The Bible,
interpreted by reason and the ancient church.' Wesley seems to have
reached this conclusion by a process similar to osmosis, absorbing the
Anglican spirit into his bloodstream without specific teaching or
reading—at least without any readily demonstrable instruction. Certainly he may have read, or at least dipped into, some of the treatises
condensed in the folio volume prepared by his father in 1692, *The
Young Students Library, containing extracts and abridgments of the most
valuable books printed in England and in the foreign journals.* If so he
was not yet ready for what they had to say about the source of religious
authority, no more than he had been for his mother's words about
'inward obedience or holiness', so that little conscious influence
remained.[24]

The foundation laid by his father and more especially by his mother
was built upon by the clergymen who taught him at the Charterhouse,
but even more (one suspects) by his brother Samuel, who was the
junior master at nearby Westminster School, and with whom he spent
Sundays and holidays. Like their father, Samuel was an ardent High
Churchman, a classicist, a patrologist, and a poet.[25] In spite of the
thirteen years difference in their age a warm friendship existed between

the two brothers, and it is certain that John's loyalty to the Church of England was both reinforced and developed during his adolescence by conversations with his elder brother, to whom he acknowledged his deep gratitude.[26] Samuel, for his part, kept the family at Epworth informed about John's progress, though only two fragments of his letters home in 1719 have survived. The news was good: 'My brother Jack, I can faithfully assure you, gives you no manner of discouragement for breeding your third son a scholar,' and 'Jack is with me, a brave boy, learning Hebrew as fast as he can'.[27]

The same kind of influence continued when at seventeen Wesley removed to Christ Church, Oxford, in the summer of 1720, taking with him an 'exhibition' of £40. Adolescence seems to have done little except extend the characteristics already evident in the child, the studious independence of thought, the devout respectability, the reverence for constituted authority, the conception of the perfect life as assured by following a set of divine rules. At Oxford the range of his studies widened, and he became more fully conscious of the opposite sex as an object of emotional stimulus, but memories of his sisters and of his paragon of a mother combined with the built-in restraints of his temperament and training to prevent any surrender of himself in an all-encompassing love affair. In the closing weeks of 1721 he seems to have made up his mind to exercise a more rigorous self-discipline in his use of time, thus returning consciously to the habits of Epworth from which he had somewhat relaxed. His brother Samuel warned him about his characteristic over-intensity of concentration in study as well as in religion, saying, 'your soul is too great for your body'.[28] At twenty-one Wesley seems still to have been an older version of the boy of ten who left Epworth for the Charterhouse, though undoubtedly a little more polished in manners, and able to meet the polite world upon its own terms. The simple religious faith of childhood had hardened into a conventional habit of religion, punctuated by moments of regret at allowing himself to become too much engrossed in 'the innocent comforts and pleasures of life'.[29]

Far too little attention has been paid to Wesley's formative years at Oxford, partly because of mistaken preconceptions about its lack of significance for his future ministry, partly because of the difficulty of handling the available manuscript material. The ground has now been cleared by Dr. V. H. H. Green's valuable *The Young Mr. Wesley*, and further studies will undoubtedly follow. No apology is made for devoting a considerable portion of this book to sketching in this background, though a full delineation of his developing churchmanship at Oxford remains a desideratum.

Wesley's tutor and father-in-God during his early years was Dr. George Wigan, both a learned biblical scholar and a sober disciplinarian who nevertheless commanded the respect and affection of his charges.[30] Wigan was succeeded after three years by Henry Sherman, and Wesley was also strongly influenced by the Christ Church Precentor, Jonathan Colley.[31] These men, like his father and elder brother, were conventional High Churchmen, whose conversation and recommendations for reading brought Wesley to a fuller understanding and more self-conscious acceptance of the general Anglican position, which he conceived something like this. The primary source of authority for discovering God's supreme law was the Bible, and where one scriptural passage was obscure or ambiguous others should be consulted to resolve the difficulties, always reading scripture in its plainest and most obvious sense. As a secondary authority for revealing his will, however, God had provided the church, and the Church of England had fallen heir through continuous connection to the wisdom and divine grace of the apostolic church—the nearest to the Bible, and therefore the best able to offer authoritative interpretations. God had also implanted an independent means of ascertaining His will in human reason; by reason a man could both instinctively recognize the divine law and make his own valid interpretations of scripture. According to this point of view the church's ordained ministers, in addition to being the custodians of sacred mysteries by whose due performance God nurtured His people, were also the authorized interpreters of the divine law as revealed in the Bible. They were not the sole interpreters, however: the law of God was naturally present in the consciences of all men, who by the light of reason were able to discern His law within themselves and to test, confirm, or reject other interpreters of the divine revelation.

In this was reflected the compromising spirit of English Protestantism, which imposed no cast-iron system upon its adherents, whether of church government or theology or philosophy, but provided a series of checks and balances designed to preserve what was seen to be good both in Roman Catholicism and in the continental Reformation, and at the same time to guard against what was feared: to maintain alike the primacy of scripture and a sense of continuity with the rites and government of the apostolic church; to preserve the dignity of the ancient episcopal order along with the validity of other types of ministry, and even in theory to accept the priesthood of all believers; to secure also the flexibility of varying personal judgements against any over-rigid systematizing of doctrine, especially in a predestinarian mould.

All this had been less a matter of action than of reaction, and not being fully thought out was vulnerable to challenges, which came from all sides. During the seventeenth century a working agreement had been reached, itself subject to interpretation and modification in accordance with the needs and the moods of each generation, each continent. This, indeed, was and is part of the genius of Anglicanism. Although a comprehensive system of church government was finally rejected in favour of an episcopal polity, the fact that comprehension was seriously considered meant that only among High Churchmen like those of Oxford was the hierarchy sacrosanct. Although the diocesan and parish system was in theory regarded as inviolable, in practice all kinds of modifications developed. The 141 *Constitutions and Canons Ecclesiastical* of 1603 formed a body of law which could in dire need be invoked against miscreants or annoying innovators, but they were neither devoid of ambiguity nor easy to enforce. Although Anglican doctrine was crystallized in 39 Articles and expounded in 33 Homilies, both these documents were subject to private interpretation, and from their eminence as important but occasionally ambiguous expressions of the spirit of Anglicanism they had shrunk into the dead and forgotten letter of the law. The net result was that although prestige and lucrative church office could be secured only by following a strict set of rules and conventions, the worship and witness of the church in general remained more open to the winds of the Holy Spirit than those of most European churches, whether Catholic, Lutheran, or Reformed.

Bishop H. R. McAdoo has put us greatly in his debt by demonstrating in detail how during the seventeenth century Anglican theologians of all altitudes and intensities agreed in a basic approach to this question of the final authority in the discovery of God's law. He takes as his text an adaptation of a discerning passage in Dean Paget's introduction to the fifth book of Hooker's *Ecclesiastical Polity*:

> Hooker's appeal in things spiritual is to a threefold fount of guidance and authority—to reason, Scripture, and tradition—all alike of God, alike emanating from Him, the one original Source of all light and power—each in certain matters bearing a special and prerogative sanction from Him, all in certain matters blending and co-operating. And in maintaining the rightfulness and the duty of thus appealing, Hooker rendered his highest service and did his most abiding work. For on equal loyalty to the unconflicting rights of reason, of scripture, and of tradition rest the distinctive strength and hope of the English church.[32]

That this approach was unique in Christendom is never claimed; that it was distinctive of seventeenth-century Anglicanism is now proven.

Bishop McAdoo steadily works his way through the writings of forty thinkers, from Hooker to Pearson and Tillotson, from Andrewes, Laud, and Jeremy Taylor to Cudworth and Locke, and even Boyle, Toland, and Isaac Newton. Although variously classified he shows that 'there is no essential difference' in their views. Each employs the same theological method of seeking final truth by means of scripture, reason, and tradition, their distinctive individuality appearing in the varying weight given to each essential ingredient.

It was into this theological heritage that Wesley entered, partly as the atmosphere breathed by his questing spirit in Epworth and London, and more consciously in his reading and academic relationships at Oxford. Indeed, it is somewhat strange how the influence of Hooker and Chillingworth and Laud and others appears to be so obvious an element in his thought without it being possible to give chapter and verse for his study or even possession of their writings. This is the more strange in view of the direct evidence of his knowledge of some thousands of volumes by other writers. There seems to be no evidence that he seriously studied Hooker's *Laws of Ecclesiastical Polity* after his ordination as deacon in 1725, but some acquaintance before that date is almost certain from the way in which it is commended in his father's *Advice to a Young Clergyman*, by which Wesley was directing his own preparatory studies, and which he later published: 'Hooker everyone knows, and his strength and firmness can hardly be too much commended; nor is there any great danger of his being solidly answered.'[33]

Wesley's personal commitment to his Anglican heritage became more conscious and concerned towards the end of 1724, while he was still twenty-one, for at that time he set his sights on entering Holy Orders. It seems clear that he still looked for nothing better than the quiet scholarly life of an Oxford don, and the gaining of some repute in languages and philosophy.[34] His decision to 'enter the church' was much more to further that end than to engage actively in the life of pastor and preacher and priest. Both universities were staffed by celibate clergymen, and ordination, like the Ph.D. in the U.S.A., was the open sesame to an otherwise closed world of secure scholarship and academic advancement. This is surely the significance of Wesley's seeking his father's reaction to his being ordained like Eli's sons 'to get a piece of bread'.[35] Indeed, Samuel Wesley's letter of 14 July 1725 implies as much, though he nevertheless urged devotional as well as academic and political preparation.[36]

The rector of Epworth encouraged his second son's desire to enter Holy Orders and thus to join his elder brother Samuel in the family's fourth successive generation of clergy.[37] He urged further doses of critical scholarship, and in January 1725 promised to send the lengthy treatise on clerical learning which he had prepared for a former curate.[38] During the early months of 1725 John Wesley may well have been studying some of the works recommended by his father which had so far not come under his eye, and looking again at others (like Hooker) which he had already perused, for it was characteristic of him fully to throw himself into a task which had won his attention. It is of value, therefore, to recollect at least a little of his father's annotated bibliography:

> The *Homilies* should be often and carefully read . . . Jewel's *Apology*, neat and strong . . . Laud against Fisher is esteemed unanswerable. . . . In the first rank stood Bishop Wilkins, who may be almost said to have taught us first to preach; as his kinsman, Archbishop Tillotson, to have brought the art of preaching near perfection. . . . Bishop Pearson all the world allows to have been of almost inimitable sense, piety, and learning; his critique on Ignatius, and his tract on the Creed, must last as long as time, and ought to be in every clergyman's study in England, though he could purchase nothing but the Bible and Common Prayer Book besides them. Bishop Bull comes next for their subject and way of thinking and arguing: a strong and nervous writer, whose discourses and directions to his clergy can scarce be too often read. Bishop Beveridge's sermons are a library, writ in the most natural, moving, unaffected style. . . . They are perhaps as like those of the apostolical ages as any between them and us. . . .[39]

Samuel Wesley's commendations are so numerous that his son could hardly have been expected to encompass more than a fraction of the works listed during the eight months before his ordination, even in the relatively leisurely life of Oxford. His diary proves, however, that he was indeed reading vigorously and methodically from April onwards, and reading works recommended by his father.

Susanna Wesley's advice differed somewhat from that of her husband. Far more prophetic as well as more influential, she urged John to study 'practical divinity', and continued to serve as his sounding-board as he read Thomas à Kempis and Jeremy Taylor and others during that crucial year of 1725. In the detailed diary which he undertook as a response to Taylor's advice about careful self-scrutiny in the use of time he later entered 14 April as a red letter day: on that day he 'Met V!' 'Varanese' or Sally Kirkham was surely the 'religious friend' mentioned in his *Journal*, who acted as another guide and stimulant to his reading programme, and who proved a spur to deepen his devotional life and to awaken a sense of call to spiritual service, so that Holy Orders now offered him a calling instead of a living. He deliberately 'set in earnest upon a new life', even though this was in effect an intensification of the same pursuit of holiness upon which he had been engaged more or less constantly since childhood, except that he now began to aim at inward holiness even more than outward rectitude.

Wesley's greatest literary debt during these months preceding his ordination was probably to Jeremy Taylor's *Holy Living* and *Holy Dying*. As noted above, this work had prompted his beginning of a diary on 5 April 1725–a diary which he continued for almost sixty-six years, making his last entry less than a week before his death. On this private diary was based his famous *Journal.* Although he had read Taylor's *Holy Living* before he met Sally Kirkham on 14 April that year, he seems to have discussed the work with her, just as he did the *Imitatio Christi*, though in the case of Taylor he found her enthusiasm tempered by great caution.[40] Taylor took the normal Anglican theological position, but laid greater stress than many upon the direct apprehension of God's will by a devout, expectant spirit, and on the joint authority of the Bible and the Holy Spirit. In *Holy Living* Wesley read (and later reproduced) Taylor's words about the Holy Spirit as the inspirer and interpreter of the Bible: 'The Holy Spirit is certainly the best preacher in the world, and the words of the Scripture the best sermons.'[41] Wesley also reproduced in his *Christian Library* the following passage:

> God is especially present in the hearts of his people by his Holy Spirit; indeed the hearts of holy men are temples in the truth of things, and in type and shadow they are heaven itself . . . God is especially present in the consciences of all persons, good and bad, by way of testimony and judgment.[42]

Even in 1725 Wesley was looking for the possibility of a personal assurance of salvation, but did not find it in Taylor, although to a limited extent this also was present.[43] Among the seventeenth-century Anglican theologians Taylor came nearest to being John Wesley's spiritual father. His best known spiritual classic exerted the major influence, but during his Oxford years Wesley became familiar also with others of Taylor's writings, and would undoubtedly react sympathetically to the general approach of his classic of casuistry, *Ductor Dubitantium*: 'I affirm nothing but upon grounds of Scripture, or universal tradition, or right reason discernible by every disinterested person.'[44]

John Wesley had not only become concerned about his spiritual life but about his doctrinal position. Although his initial motive in seeking Holy Orders was not purely religious, once having resolved upon this

course he went fully into its implications, and his providential association with Sally Kirkham deepened his seriousness in taking this step.
Clearly this meant a much fuller submission of himself to the authority
of the church. His sensitive conscience was uneasy about some aspects
of this, and he questioned his ability in good faith to accept the damnatory clauses of the Athanasian Creed and the church's seventeenth
Article—on Predestination.[45] Although Wesley's letter about the
Creed seems to have disappeared, his words on this particular point of
conscience would almost certainly be similar to those addressed to his
mother on 29 July that year, when he attacked the idea of predestination, claiming that 'to lie under either a physical or a moral necessity
is entirely repugnant to human liberty':

> As I understand faith to be an assent to any truth upon rational
> grounds, I don't think it possible without perjury to swear I believe
> anything unless I have rational grounds for my persuasion. Now that
> which contradicts reason can't be said to stand on rational grounds:
> and such undoubtedly is every proposition which is incompatible
> with the divine justice or mercy.[46]

The somewhat overscrupulous scepticism of this logic-chopping son,
indeed, frankly disturbed his father, whose own adjustment to traditional Anglican formulae had become much more complete:

> I like your way of thinking and arguing; and yet must say, I'm a
> little afraid on't. He that believes without or against reason is half a
> Papist, or enthusiast. He that would mete Revelation by his own
> shallow reason is either half a Deist, or a heretic. O my dear! steer
> clear between this Scylla and Charybdis. . . .
>
>   If you have any scruples about any p[oin]t of Revelation, or the
> scheme of the Church of England (which I think exactly agreeable
> to it) I can answer 'em.[47]

No matter how increased in thoughtful devotion, even when
approaching ordination, John Wesley was by no means prepared un-
critically to subject either his judgement or his conscience to the
authority of the church. He was still prepared, however, to be convinced by reason, and on 22 November 1725 acknowledged that his
mother had succeeded in changing his views on the relation between
reason and revelation:

> I am . . . at length come over entirely to your opinion, that saving
> faith (including practice) is an assent to what God has revealed
> because He has revealed it, and not because the truth of it may be
> evinced by reason.[48]

He continued, however, to uphold the right of even the heretic to his own opinion, for which he might be rebuked but not punished.[49] Yet John Wesley the rationalist was nevertheless not quite able to subdue John Wesley the mystic, even in these early days. He was ready to 'trace the wisdom and mercy of Providence' even in failures and disappointments, and to exclaim 'Is not this the finger of God!'[50]

His scruples about Article 17 and the Athanasian Creed removed, on 19 September 1725 John Wesley was ordained deacon by Dr. John Potter, Bishop of Oxford.[51] Already the possibility had been mooted that he might succeed to the Fellowship of Lincoln College which had become vacant on 3 May by the resignation of John Thorold. Only after much hesitation, however, apparently caused by Wesley's ultra-strenuous churchmanship, was he finally elected, on 17 March 1725-6.[52] The income from the fellowship gave him financial security, and the fact that Potter ordained him priest (on 22 September 1728) while he was a Fellow of Lincoln later furnished a defence, however tenuous, for preaching in parishes to which he was not licensed.[53] He completed the requirements for his M.A. in February 1726-7, but never proceeded to the B.D. which was expected of him.[54]

Wesley's removal to Lincoln College was the occasion of a further emphasis upon the methodical use of time, as well as upon more rigorous asceticism and deeper piety. To help in redeeming the precious hours, in January 1727 Wesley drew up a scheme of studies for himself and began those experiments in early rising which extended his working life by many years.[55] Looking back at this period through the haze of ten momentous years Wesley wrote:

> Meeting now with Mr. Law's *Christian Perfection* and *Serious Call*, although I was much offended at many parts of both, yet they convinced me more than ever of the exceeding height and breadth and depth of the law of God. The light flowed in so mightily upon my soul, that everything appeared in a new view. I cried to God for help, and resolved not to prolong the time of obeying Him as I had never done before.[56]

This sounds almost like a new conversion experience. More probably, however, it reflects the idealizing in memory of a lengthy ordeal of increasing self-discipline punctuated by moments of spiritual elation, so that these appeared like one supreme experience of illumination. Wesley seems not to have read Law's *Serious Call* until December 1730, but was so impressed that he went on to read *Christian Perfection*.[57] Similarly, his arrival at a rising hour of 4.0 a.m. was not achieved during a few days in 1727, but only in 1730 after many months of experiments and frustrations, nor even then was it maintained as steadily as in later years he came to believe.[58]

Long before his ordination as priest Wesley had begun to ponder hard the question of the authority both of the church and of the minister. On 6 October 1727 he transcribed a sermon on II Cor. 2:17, affirming the centrality of the Bible in Christian doctrine, and castigating those who abused its authority. By this time his lifelong method of approach to the Scriptures had been settled. This was the authoritative handbook of doctrine, but it must be handled with scrupulous honesty both to text and context lest the Word of God be corrupted. His summary was a challenge to himself as well as to others:

> If then we have spoken the Word of God, the genuine unmixed Word of God, and that only; if we have put no unnatural interpretations upon it, but taken the known phrases in their common, obvious sense, and when they were less known explained scriptures ['SS' in the manuscript] by scripture; if we have spoken the whole Word as occasion offered, though rather the parts that seemed most proper to give a check to some fashionable vice or to encourage the practice of some unfashionable virtue; and last, if we do this plainly and boldly, though with all the mildness and gentleness that the nature of the things will bear . . . here is all a preacher can do.[59]

Although the Bible constituted his final authority, he recognized quite clearly that 'scarce ever was any heretical opinion either invented or revived but Scripture was quoted to defend it'.[60] Therefore some secondary authority or authorities were needed to supervise the interpretation of the Bible. Reason had long served him as one such check, and now that he had entered Holy Orders he came to realize more fully the authority of the Church, stretching back in unbroken tradition to the days of the Apostles themselves. So strong was this conviction that during those long absences from Oxford in the years 1726 to 1729, while serving his father as a serious painstaking curate both at Epworth and Wroot, he later considered himself to have been a 'bigot' for the Church of England, 'believing none but the members of it to be in a state of salvation'.[61] This strong sense of loyalty was deepened on 22 September 1728 when Dr. John Potter ordained him priest at Christ Church, Oxford. Not only did the general solemnity of the occasion impress him, but one particular remark of the examining archdeacon, Dr. Hayward, stuck in his mind, echoing his own frequent preoccupation with persecution as the seal of a devout Christian's life:

> Do you know what you are about? You are bidding defiance to all mankind. He that would live a Christian priest ought to know that

whether his hand be against every man or no he must expect every man's hand should be against him.[62]

This foreboding was soon to be fulfilled, as the Oxford which had witnessed Wesley's maturing as a typical High Churchman also witnessed his sowing of the first seeds of separation from the Church of England.

TWO

THE OXFORD METHODIST

WE HAVE seen that Wesley's childhood religion was based on strict obedience to the laws of God, made known by divine revelation in the Bible (of which he read a chapter morning and evening), by the voice of conscience, and by the confirmation of informed reasoning. Reverence for the established authority of the church, as symbolized by his father, was not so important a stimulus or guide as the combined mystical-rationalist approach of his mother. From both parents, but again especially from his mother, he learned to value the Christian's liberty to make his own judgements where he could recognize no infallible rule of God, and never to flinch from the path of duty to which conscience clearly pointed him. As during his youth and early manhood he swung more into the orbit of the church, and especially as he prepared to enter Holy Orders, more and more he emphasized the role of the Church of England as the interpreter of God's Word for his own nation. During the intervals from 1726 to 1729 when he served as curate in Epworth and Wroot he proved himself an authoritarian priest and a conscientious pastor like his father. On 22 November 1729, in response to the request of Dr. George Morley, Rector of Lincoln College, he returned to share more fully the duties of the resident Fellows, becoming a full-time Oxford tutor. Earlier that year his younger brother Charles, who had come up to Christ Church in 1726, became more serious about his studies and began to meet regularly for joint study and devotions, as well as for weekly attendance at Holy Communion, with two other students, William Morgan and Robert Kirkham. On John's return his sympathy was enlisted, and he became the natural leader of this small religious study circle.[1]

John Wesley's somewhat rigid churchmanship at this time may be gathered from an open letter which he published sixty years later:

> In my youth I was not only a member of the Church of England, but a bigot to it, believing none but the members of it to be in a state of salvation. I began to abate of this violence in 1729. But still I was as zealous as ever, observing every point of Church discipline, and teaching all my pupils so to do.[2]

In fact there was little sign of abatement, though 1729 was indeed a turning-point in his relationship with the church. What did happen was that from his brief pastoral experience in a frustrating rural parish he graduated to the spiritual directorship of a small academic group. This proved a much more fruitful testing-ground for his proselytizing zeal, as he urged others to subject themselves to the spiritual discipline which he had in large measure learned from Jeremy Taylor's *Holy Living*. Although Wesley was never a dictatorial autocrat in the harshest sense, he was a born organizer, and the responsibility of setting rules, maintaining discipline, settling disputes, presiding over discussions, even the chore of keeping statistical records, seemed to satisfy some deep emotional need quite irrespective of the service which he thus believed himself performing for others.

An Oxford tutor was in any case expected to be the father-in-God to one or more students, and this duty Wesley took seriously. In the summer of 1730 he was allocated his first batch of pupils.[3] Already, however, he had been serving as a kind of unofficial spiritual director for his brother Charles and Charles's friends, though them he met as a group rather than as individuals. From June 1730 onwards he directed both official individual tutorials in (supposedly) mainly secular learning, and also unofficial group tutorials in mainly religious learning. Although all Wesley's pupils were subjected to his insistence upon method and piety, only the most responsive were invited to throw in their lot with the Holy Club, which grew slowly in numbers and reputation. Its inner circle of committed members was never more than forty, and rarely above fourteen or fifteen.

Wesley took his pastoral responsibilities for this select group so seriously that he regarded it as 'the work to which Providence so plainly calls me', and therefore as a valid reason for refusing other calls upon his time.[4] John Gambold, who joined the Holy Club in 1730, had observed John Wesley and his methods for five years or more when he wrote a somewhat idealized description of him, which is nevertheless worth quoting at length:

Mr. John Wesley was always the chief manager, for which he was very fit. For he had not only more learning and experience than the rest, but he was blest with such activity as to be always gaining ground, and such steadiness that he lost none. What proposals he made to any were sure to charm them, because he was so much in earnest; nor could they afterwards slight them, because they saw him always the same. What supported this uniform vigour was the care he took to consider well of every affair before he engaged in it, making all his decisions in the fear of God, without passion, humour

3

[i.e. caprice], or self-confidence: for though he had naturally a very clear apprehension, yet his exact prudence depended more on humility and singleness of heart. To this I may add that he had, I think, something of authority in his countenance; though . . . he never assumed anything to himself above his companions; any of them might speak their mind, and their words were as strictly regarded by him as his were by them.[5]

Perhaps it was at Oxford during the years 1730–1 that the strong pragmatic element in Wesley's churchmanship first began to develop as he grappled with the problems of his peculiar pastoral situation. The shepherding of the Holy Club, with its expanding activities, in ways that were unusual though not irregular, must have made him realize that the Christian's pilgrimage to heaven might occasionally proceed by an unmarked route through strange territory. True, he was seeking a churchly end in urging 'the necessity of private prayer and of frequenting the church and sacrament',[6] but in his innovations he wisely followed the prudential advice of first securing the agreement of his bishop and of any parish clergy upon whose toes he might be treading.[7] One of the criteria which he thus added to those of Scripture, antiquity and reason as tests of the will of God was 'experience', by which he usually meant not an instinctive feeling for a thing's rightness, but the findings of a series of tests. At Oxford, especially as the spiritual director of the Holy Club, he became an experimental Christian, and an experimental pastor. He defended the strictness and 'singularity' of his religious regimen in a thoughtful and sincere, even though somewhat stilted, letter to 'Aspasia' (Mrs. Mary Pendarves):

I was made to be happy: to be happy I must love God; in proportion to my love of whom my happiness must increase. To love God I must be like him, holy as he is holy; which implies both the being pure from vicious and foolish passions and the being confirmed in those virtuous and rational affections which God comprises in the word 'charity'. In order to root those out of the soul and plant these in their stead, I must use (1) such means as are ordered by God; (2) such as are recommended by experience and reason.[8]

Moving from the 'instituted means' of divine blessing he expounded the 'prudential means', for they formed the nub of criticism—'these are the points which I am said to carry too far'. Firmly Wesley set forth his own conviction: 'Whatever helps me to conquer vicious and advance in virtuous affections, that to me is not indifferent, but to be embraced, be it ever so difficult or painful'.[9] The same was true of every method of helping others, no matter how unorthodox it might seem. In all this Wesley was greatly under the influence of that pious Platonist, John Norris of Bemerton. Not only his thought, but even his language, is reminiscent of Norris's *Treatise on Christian Prudence*, which Wesley read in 1730 and abridged for publication in 1734.[10]

John Gambold was first attracted to Charles Wesley (and through him to John) by hearing of 'the whimsical Mr. Wesley, his preciseness and pious extravagancies'.[11] Both brothers were 'singular', and at times even appeared to take delight in being so, though in 1731 John tried to soften the charge of 'being too strict', at least in the eyes of 'Aspasia'; when she avoided his specific questions about this by referring in a flattering way to his holiness and wisdom he replied: 'Give me the censure of the many and the praise of the few'.[12] Dr. Hayward's challenge at his examination for priests's orders was etched upon his mind: 'He that would live a Christian priest ought to know that . . . he must expect every man's hand should be against him'. As Wesley's own definition of 'Christian' became more exacting so did the reactions of his critics gradually turn from mild amusement to scorn and contempt and hate, and eventually to outright persecution.[13] So inured to criticism did he become, however, even enamoured of the bitter-sweet joys of martyrdom, that when in 1734 his father argued that one as despised as he could do little good in Oxford, Wesley not only strongly disagreed, but claimed that without being despised no man was even in a state of salvation:

> I must therefore, with or without leave, . . . keep close to my Saviour's judgment, and maintain that contempt is a part of that cross which every man must bear if he will follow him; that it is the badge of his discipleship, the stamp of his profession, the constant seal of his calling; insomuch that though a man may be despised without being saved yet he cannot be saved without being despised.[14]

Although singularity is first cousin to separation, nevertheless it must be said in Wesley's favour that he rarely used the many nicknames that were flung at him and his group as in later years he did come to accept the term 'Methodist', though usually in the hesitant form of 'the people called Methodists'. These nicknames were many and varied, though all proved successful caricatures in exaggerating some genuine feature of the group they mocked. The first seems to have been 'Sacramentarians', gradually supplanted by 'Methodists' and then 'The Holy Club'. Other names arising at least as early as 1732 were 'The Godly Club' and 'The Reforming Club', 'Enthusiasts', and 'Supererogation Men'.[15] Wesley himself later recorded also the

derogatory titles of 'Bible moths' and 'Bible bigots', but the contemporary evidence for these (eminently suitable) names is not clear.[16]
The essential element in all these labels was the recurring 'club'
linked with varying pious adjectives. Wesley himself referred to 'The
Holy Club' as indeed a 'glorious title'.[17] The young men formed a
group of limited membership organized for specific religious purposes,
a 'society'—even though Wesley himself usually avoided this more
technical term in favour of 'our little company'.[18] Nevertheless neither
he nor his companions attempted to escape from the pattern of Anthony
Horneck's Religious Societies, so ably continued and described by Dr.
Josiah Woodward. John Wesley kept these societies in view in many
of the books which he commended to his students and friends.[19] In
later years he came to realize that this 'fellowship of kindred minds'
under a spiritual director was indeed the very essence of Methodism,
and therefore spoke of the formation of the Holy Club as 'the first rise
of Methodism'.[20] The solitary pursuit of holiness he eschewed, but a
company of like-minded devotees could both urge each other on to
better churchmanship by the benevolent rivalry of good example, and
also provide spiritual checks against any fanciful or misguided behaviour. Fifty years' experience had already shown, however, that such
societies as Horneck's and Woodward's, though originally founded as
spiritual auxiliaries to the Church of England, tended to become either
self-sufficient or disputatious, and in either case divisive in tendency.[21]
The second point which should be stressed about the Oxford Methodists was that they were associated for a disciplined pursuit of holiness,
underlined by the various adjectives applied to their 'club' and by the
word 'Methodist' itself. Holiness could only be achieved by obedience,
by discipline, by rules. Wesley's own rules for achieving holiness by
self-discipline became the norm for all conscientious members. Taylor's
Holy Living—the full title, be it noted, was *The Rule and Exercises of
Holy Living*—had insisted upon the importance of rules. From 1725
until the end of his life Wesley constantly amended and extended those
which he had learned from Jeremy Taylor and which had been
seconded by John Norris.[22] The earlier religious societies had similarly
embodied into their constitutions rules for members' private conduct,[23]
and Wesley followed the same principles in his own later societies,
though in their case he was influenced also by William Cave's *Primitive
Christianity*.[24] The general intentions, and to some extent the actual
phraseology, of Wesley's 1743 *Rules* find precedent, however, in the
questions for self-examination and in the resolutions for conduct
prepared for the pioneer Methodists at Oxford.
From the outset the Oxford Methodists emphasized attendance at

Holy Communion, thus earning the name 'Sacramentarians'. The parents of the Wesleys were also ardent advocates of frequent communion after devout preparation, and this emphasis remained equally true of the tentative beginnings under Charles Wesley and the later flowering under John. The university statutes enjoined three compulsory communions each year, although the 23rd Canon in fact required four 'in all colleges and halls within both the universities'.[25] The Prayer Book rubric, however, directed a weekly communion without 'a reasonable cause to the contrary', and this rubric John Wesley had followed since 1725.[26] He continued to communicate weekly or more frequently to the end of his life.[27] Upon his Oxford colleagues he urged not only the need for *frequent* communion, or even *weekly* communion, but *constant* communion.[28]

Strangely enough the aspect of the Holy Club which (according to John Gambold) drew most scorn was in many respects the most obviously praiseworthy, their 'charitable employments'.[29] The Wesleys began the scriptural task of visiting those who were sick or in prison on 24 August 1730, at the urging of their companion William Morgan.[30] John Wesley sought his father's advice, receiving both encouragement and the hint that he ought to obtain his bishop's approval, which he accordingly did.[31] In order to serve the poor, said Wesley, 'I abridged myself of all superfluities, and many that are called necessaries of life. I soon became a by-word for so doing, and I rejoiced that my name was cast out as evil'.[32]

The Rev. Samuel Wesley wisely warned his enthusiastic sons of the danger of spiritual pride to which they were exposing themselves by undertaking such 'unfashionable duties'.[33] Of this danger, indeed, John Wesley was aware. In the hierarchy of Christian virtues which he was zealously striving to inculcate in his spiritual charges humility ranked at the top with love. Both had been enforced by Thomas à Kempis and Jeremy Taylor, those key influences upon him in 1725. His own cult of humility may be seen from the periodic summaries and resolutions in his diary, such as that of 1 December 1725: 'Pride of my parts or holiness; greedy of praise; . . . disrespect of governors; desire to seem better than I am. Kyrie eleison.'[34]

Although the title of 'Enthusiasts' might well be applied to those so zealously combining rigorous asceticism and vigorous philanthropy, that particular nickname referred more correctly to what prompted these observances, the Methodists' conviction that they were in direct touch with God, 'possessed' by him, 'enthused' in the literal sense of the Greek word. Wesley's mother had urged her children to listen for 'the still small voice of God's Holy Spirit' directing them in all their conduct, though John Wesley later claimed that he 'neither understood nor remembered' what was said to him about 'inward holiness'; only on Samuel Wesley's death-bed did his testimony to 'the inward witness' make a major impact on John.[35] Kempis taught Wesley to seek 'inward holiness', and Jeremy Taylor to scrutinize his soul for 'purity of intention'.[36] His incipient mysticism was strengthened by the writings of William Law, reinforced by a personal interview at Putney in the summer of 1732, so that he deliberately began to pursue 'a union of the soul with God'.[37] His close study of the many writings of John Norris emphasized a similar point. Norris disliked the Quakers' notion of the inner light as an entity in itself, yet urged the search for the conscious indwelling of God, so that John Locke dismissed him as 'an obscure, enthusiastic man'.[38] Soon Wesley himself came to maintain the teaching castigated by Locke as the heresy of the enthusiasts:

> They see the light infused into their understandings and cannot be mistaken; it is clear and visible there, like the light of bright sunshine; shows itself, and needs no other proof but its own evidence; they feel the hand of God moving them within.[39]

On 28 October 1732, as rumours were circulating that by their ridiculous practices the enthusiastic Methodists had killed William Morgan,[40] Wesley declared publicly that it was indeed possible to have such a 'daily intercourse' with the Holy Spirit that 'we are more and more transformed into his likeness', and that the same Spirit 'assures our spirits that we have a title to eternal happiness'. It matters little that in fact it was William Tilly's sermon that Wesley thus borrowed for his own preaching: the thought was now his own.[41] His original sermon on 'The Circumcision of the Heart', preached before the assembled university on 1 January 1733, maintained the same position:

> The Spirit witnesses in their hearts that they are the children of God, . . . that they are now in the path which leadeth to life, and shall, by the mercy of God, endure therein to the end. It is He who giveth them a lively expectation of receiving all good things at God's hand. . . .'[42]

Wesley was quite explicit in telling his mother how he solved his problems as spiritual director: 'I depend upon the Holy Spirit to direct me.' Nevertheless the clause following recognized that this guidance was in part mediate as well as immediate—'in and by my own experience and reflection, joined to the advices of my religious friends'.[43] When in 1733 the fortune of the Holy Club and his own prestige as tutor slumped badly Wesley continued to seek guidance in providential signs (some might claim them as superstitious), informing his mother: 'If I have no more pupils after these are gone from me, I shall then be glad of a curacy near you: if I have, I shall take it as a signal that I am to remain here.'[44]

A little later in his Oxford career he fell victim to another flirtation with the mystical writers which came dangerously near an obsession. Though vigorously rejected as his supreme guide, they remained a pervasive though sometimes unrecognized and unacknowledged influence. He agreed that their 'noble descriptions of union with God and internal religion made everything else appear mean, flat, and insipid', and gave him 'an entire new view of religion'. But in spite of being elated he also became thoroughly confused, because mysticism seemed to substitute for normal Christian activities and Christian fellowship an unhealthy introspection which was only a refined form of works-righteousness.[45] Later he was able to pour scorn on the heavenly vision which supposedly came through renouncing religious activities, and upon 'holy solitaries', claiming:

> The gospel of Christ knows of no religion but social; no holiness but social holiness. 'Faith working by love' is the length and breadth and depth and height of Christian perfection.[46]

Nevertheless the mystics did reinforce his growing awareness of the possibility of the direct contact of the soul with God, and throughout his life he praised the best examples of Roman Catholic spirituality, especially the *Imitatio Christi*, with the result that he himself was occasionally dubbed 'Papist'.

We have already seen how from 1727 Wesley carefully studied the Holy Scriptures, not merely as a devotional aid, but as the authoritative handbook upon every aspect of life, both personal and social, both theological and moral.[47] The interpretation of doubtful texts was made more reliable as he enlisted others to explore with him the Greek and Hebrew originals. In later years, indeed, he claimed that the Holy Club was born in Bible study:

> From the very beginning, from the time that four young men united together, each of them was *homo unius libri*—a man of one book. . . . They had one and only one rule of judgment with regard to all their tempers, words, and actions, namely the oracles of God. They were one and all determined to be *Bible-Christians*. They were continually reproached for this very thing, some terming them in derision 'Bible-bigots', others 'Bible-moths' feeding, they said, upon the Bible as moths do upon cloth.[48]

The phrase 'from the very beginning', however, is another instance of events and dates being incorrectly fused in his memory, an error first made in 1765.[49] His contemporary account shows that the young men originally met on week evenings to study the Greek and Latin classics and on Sunday evenings 'some book of devotion', although it is quite possible that the Greek New Testament was from the outset a part of their 'classical' studies, as it certainly furnished the nucleus of the Greek studies of most of Wesley's pupils.[50] The manuscript records of some of those joint porings over the Greek New Testament still survive, as well as Gambold's account of Wesley's tutorial methods:

> After every portion of it, having heard the conjectures the rest had to offer, he made his observations on the phrase, design, and difficult places; one or two wrote these down from his mouth.[51]

Such an important place did the Scriptures play in his life from this period onward that even the practice of bibliomancy—the random opening of the Bible to find a word from God upon issues which would not yield to reason nor even to prayer—appears to have begun at Oxford rather than in Georgia, witness a resolution in his manuscript diary: 'May 30 [1732]: Try all doubtful occ[asion]s by the Test[ament]. Break off the moment y[ou] find [an answer].'[52]

One more significant Oxford Methodist title remains to be discussed, that of 'Supererogation Men'. Apparently this did not arise from those works of charity inspired by William Morgan, but because of their strict observance of the fasts of the ancient church.[53] In writing his spiritual autobiography Wesley said: 'The next spring [1732] I began observing the Wednesday and Friday Fasts, commonly observed in the ancient church, tasting no food till three in the afternoon.'[54] This must not be taken to imply that heretofore he had been a stranger to fasting: indeed, one of the resolutions made in December 1725 was 'to fast once a month'.[55] Nor was the adoption of a much more rigorous programme mainly ascetic or disciplinary in nature, but a deliberate attempt to seek spiritual union with the apostolic church. Wesley already knew Robert Nelson's *Festivals and Fasts*, wherein he read:

> The ancient Christians were very exact both in their *weekly* and *annual* Fasts. Their *weekly* Fasts were kept on Wednesdays and Fridays, because on the one our Lord was betrayed and on the other crucified. These fasts were called their *Stations*, from the military word of keeping their guard, as Tertullian observed. . . . Their annual fast was that of Lent, by way of preparation for the Feast of our Saviour's Resurrection.[56]

It was John Clayton, however, a devout young tutor from Brasenose College, who convinced Wesley and the Holy Club of the importance of thus linking themselves across the centuries with the church of the apostles. Nor to his life's end, did Wesley overlook the spiritual value of fasting though the 'stations' fell by the wayside.[57]

This emphasis upon both the ancient church and the keeping of the 'stations' was strongly reinforced during the summer of 1733. Accompanying Clayton to his home town of Manchester, where he was to serve as chaplain of the collegiate church, Wesley was introduced to Dr. John Byrom (whose shorthand he later learned) and Dr. Thomas Deacon, a leading Non-Juror. Deacon enlisted Wesley's services in preparing his *Complete Collection of Devotions, taken from the Apostolical Constitutions, the Ancient Liturgies, and the Common Prayer Book of the Church of England.* Wesley returned from this visit thoroughly fired with zeal both for the ancient church and for the 'stations', which he continually urged upon his friends and pupils, from time to time exultantly recording in his diary that one or other of them was 'convinced of Stations'. He spent much time in preparing 'An Essay upon the Stationary Fasts', from which Deacon included excerpts in his *Devotions.*[58]

Wesley instinctively warmed to the Non-Jurors whom he met, for they spoke his mother's language, though with a bolder accent. He was so impressed in 1727 by hearing Dr. George Coningsby's sermon on the Non-Juring principle of passive obedience that he made extensive notes about it in his diary.[59] Several Non-Jurors were personal friends of his own family, men like Robert Nelson, whose *Festivals and Fasts* and other writings he studied so avidly, and the Rev. John Hutton, Samuel Wesley's neighbour at Westminster, whose son James was one of John Wesley's later converts.[60] William Law's influence has already been noted. The writings of several other Non-Jurors were influential during his Oxford years—those of George Hickes, Jeremy Collier, John Kettlewell, Charles Leslie, as well as bishops John Cosin and Thomas Ken. Joseph Hoole he had himself known as vicar of Haxey, had sought his advice about the Holy Club, and visited him in Manchester.[61] Now through John Clayton he was able to establish warm personal relationships with Thomas Deacon and John Byrom.

It may well have been under the influence of the Non-Jurors that Wesley adopted a peculiar affectation about which too little is known, inscribing copies of books in his personal library with the letters 'E.A.P.J.' after his signature, a practice which his brother Samuel had been observing for a decade and which Charles also came to follow. The first three letters clearly stood for 'Ecclesiae Anglicanae Presbyter'

—presbyter of the Church of England. The fourth might represent any one of several words, of which the more likely are 'juramento' (by oath), 'juratus' (sworn), 'jure' (by right), 'jurejurando' (sworn), and 'justus' (proper). In any case it implied loyalty in a high degree, so that after John took it upon himself more than fifty years later to ordain some of his preachers Charles challenged him: 'Have the people of America given you leave to die E.A.P.J.?'[62]

Apart from the specific influence of Clayton and other Non-Jurors in turning Wesley's attention towards the 'stations', they greatly strengthened his interest in the primitive church, and especially in the Eastern Church. He would hardly have been his father's son without studying them already, of course. The first page of his Oxford diary may reveal him translating the early Fathers, and as he took over the direction of the Holy Club he was abridging William Wake's *Apostolic Fathers*.[63] Wesley's advisers and reading so far, however, though directing him to the early church as an authoritative interpreter of Holy Scripture, had failed to demonstrate the living unity of the church through the centuries.[64] This defect the Non-Jurors remedied by pointing him to 'a sure rule of interpreting Scripture, viz. "Consensus veterum: quod ab omnibus, quod ubique, quod semper creditum".'[65] This Vincentian Canon Wesley himself quoted, augmented, and defended, in his 'Essay upon the Stationary Fasts', as a test of apostolic authenticity:

> The celebrated rule of S. Austin has never yet been controverted, 'That which is held by the Universal Church, and was not instituted by Councils, but always was, is delivered down from the Apostles.' The same in sense is the golden rule of Vincentius Lirinensis (as it has been termed for many ages): That is Apostolical 'which has been observed by all men, in all places, at all times.' The reason is plain: whatever has been at any time received in all parts of the Church Universal must have been instituted either by some General Council or by the Apostles. But if it was so received from the beginning, before any such Councils were held, then it could not be instituted by any of them, and consequently must be of Apostolical institution.

He went on to insist that where there was apostolic authority for any practice, the governors of national and other churches had no more power to repeal such observance than had 'all the governors of the Church Universal together' in General Council.[66] Approvingly he quoted at some length the condemnation by the controversial Bishop of Ely, Dr. Peter Gunning, of those heretics and schismatics who disregard the tradition of the primitive church in interpreting scripture, and thus 'departing from the sense of the church, pervert the Scriptures to their own and others' destruction.'[67] Wesley found it easier to speak of 'the sense of the church' at this time because he accepted also the Non-Jurors' insistence that the ancient church was continuous with 'the one church at all times and in all places.'[68] Indeed he envisaged at first a uniformity of the Church Universal in the early Christian centuries which later study compelled him to discard in favour of a more fragmented development. By this time, indeed, Wesley had swung far away from his earlier position on the seat of authority in religion. On his return from Georgia he was to confess his error in 'making antiquity a co-ordinate rather than a subordinate rule with Scripture.'[69]

In the preface to his *Devotions* Deacon laid down two principles which had secured Wesley's eager acceptance:

1st. That the best method for all churches and Christians to follow, is to lay aside all modern hypotheses, customs, and private opinions, and submit to all the doctrines, practices, worship, and discipline, not of any particular, but of the ancient and universal church of Christ from the beginning to the end of the fourth century; which doctrines, practices, worship, and discipline, thus universally and constantly received, could not possibly be derived from any other than apostolical authority.

2ndly. That the Liturgy in the Apostolical Constitutions is the most ancient Christian Liturgy extant; that it is perfectly pure and free from interpolation; and that the book itself called the Apostolical Constitutions contains at large the doctrines, laws, and settlements which the three first and purest ages of the gospel did with one consent believe, obey, and submit to, and that as derived to them from apostolical men. . . .

Deacon added: 'If these two principles were once put in practice, all the ecclesiastical distractions which subsist at present would cease; and a truly catholic union would be restored among all Christian churches.' It was indeed to this end that he offered his *Compleat Collection of Devotions*.[70]

Later Wesley's faith in the authenticity of the Apostolic Constitutions was sadly shaken, so that he forsook Deacon's second principle. Throughout his life, however, he remained loyal to the first, as well as to Deacon's overall catholic purpose. He introduced extracts from the ante-Nicene Fathers in his *Christian Library*, with a lengthy encomium claiming that their writings were to be valued as only just below the Scriptures themselves, as 'containing the pure, uncorrupted doctrine of Christ', and so inspired 'as to be scarce capable of mistaking'.[71]

There was indeed, especially during these Oxford days, every reason why he should be awarded the friendly nickname of 'Mr. Primitive Christianity'.

On 15 June 1733 Wesley discovered *The Country Parson's Advice to his Parishioners*, originally issued in 1680, and republished in 1701. This reinforced not only his allegiance to the whole method of forming religious societies as 'the most effectual means for restoring our decaying Christianity', but his own high sense of privilege and responsibility as a spiritual director.[72] The 'country parson' advocated great care in the choice of a spiritual guide, but went on to insist upon the necessity of committing oneself unreservedly to his direction as the representative of Christ.[73] Wesley distributed the *Country Parson's Advice* in the Oxford prisons, took copies with him to Georgia, and later published an abridgement in his *Christian Library*. This book, together with the high churchmanship of the Non-Jurors, may have led to Wesley's interest in confession, rejected by his oldest sister Emily, who wrote to him:

> To lay open the state of my soul to you or any of our clergy is what I have no inclination to at present, and I believe I never shall. I shall not put my conscience under the direction of mortal man, frail as myself. To my own master I stand or fall. Nay, I scruple not to say that all such desire in you or any other ecclesiastic seems to me like church tyranny, and assuming to yourselves a dominion over your fellow creatures which was never designed you by God.[74]

In later years Wesley gradually came to question the value and validity of private confession to a priest, though he pointed out that group confession in the Methodist 'bands' and society meetings was a very different matter.[75]

John Gambold shows that as a spiritual director Wesley himself was authoritarian but not overbearing. He continued to insist upon the right of private judgement in all matters not specifically laid down in the Bible, with a corresponding emphasis upon the responsibility of every individual to inform his mind so as to be able to make a rational judgement even on matters concerning the divine revelation. He was convinced that Christians were neither spiritual automata nor the playthings of constituted ecclesiastical authority. It will be remembered that William Morgan, one of the original Oxford Methodists, had died mentally deranged. In 1733 his father, Richard Morgan, sent his second son, another Richard, to Oxford. In committing him to Wesley's tutorial care, however, he wrote stating that 'five able divines, some of them bishops', had warned him that this 'strict religious society' might well prove 'a dangerous experiment for young people', so that he only wished his second son to 'avoid sins of commission, that he may be ranked in the class of good Christians'. Because he was 'no divine', however, he was not prepared to enter into a debate as to what constituted a good Christian. Wesley's shocked reply implies a high view of the spiritual responsibilities of the laity, even though it by no means reaches the priesthood of all believers:

When both the glory of my Saviour and the safety of your soul so loudly require me to speak I may not, I dare not, I cannot be silent, especially when I consider the reason you give for my being so, viz. that it is not your province to manage this point of controversy. No! Are you not, then, in covenant with Christ? And is it not your province to know the terms of that covenant? 'This do, and thou shalt live', saith the Lord of life. Is it not your business to understand what this is? Though you are no divine, is it not your concern to be assured what it is to be a Christian?[76]

In helping Richard Morgan senior to make up his mind on this important issue Wesley unhesitatingly pointed to the Bible, which must be reverenced far more than bishops:

The question, then, must be determined some way; and for an infallible determination of it to the law and to the testimony we appeal: at that tribunal we ought to be judged. If the oracles of God are still open to us, by them must every doubt be decided. And should all men contradict them we could only say, 'Let God be true, and every man a liar'. We can never enough reverence those of the episcopal order. They are the angels of the church, the stars in the right hand of God. Only let us remember He was greater than those Who said, 'Though I or an angel from heaven preach any other gospel than that ye have received, let him be accursed'.

Wesley went on to describe the plan of salvation as he saw it, prefacing his outline with words of defiance for Morgan's five ecclesiastical advisers: 'Whether divines and bishops will agree to this I know not; but this I know, it is the plain word of God.'[77]

The summer of 1733 was made noteworthy by a further covenanting of himself to God in a document which exhibits both his devotional life and his churchmanship at this period, and also reveals the genesis of his amazing publishing career. The document is in abbreviated longhand and cipher, here extended:

July 19, 1733.

In the Name of God! Amen!

I do resolve to devote the remainder of my life to God my
Creator, God my Redeemer, and God my Sanctifier,

I. By immediate application to Him, either

    1. By Prayer, publick or private, or

    2. By Reading (1) The Fathers, (2) True, Affectionate Divinity,
    or (3) Absolutely necessary miscellanies.

    3. By Meditation, at least from 4 to [4] ½ every afternoon, unless
    company or absolutely necessary business [prevent].

II. By application to my fellow servants, either

    1. By Speaking to (1) Pupils, (2) Relations, (3) Friends, (4) Ac-
    quaintance, (5) The afflicted, (6) The wicked, or

    2. By Writing—either by Composing (1) Geneses and Letters
    for my Pupils, Relations, Friends, Acquaintance, (2) Prac-
    tical Treatises for the P[oo]r and Wicked, (3) Sermons
    for all:

    Or by Abridging (1) Uncommon treatises for Pupils and
    Acquaintance, (2) Plain ones (as Christian Monitor) for the
    Poor and Wicked:

    Or (1) By Translating True Divinity for all.[78]

Wesley's first venture into the publishing field was with *A Collection
of Forms of Prayer for Every Day in the Week*, culled from many authors,
but especially from Nathaniel Spinckes's *Church of England Man's
Companion in the Closet*, of which he had bought a copy in October
1732.[79] For this modest volume he wrote a preface at his brother
Samuel's on 26 November 1733, reading it to his father, who was also
visiting at Westminster.[80] In this preface he stated that the volume was
an expression of his devotion to 'our excellent church', and the early
editions also pointed out that it was especially designed for those who
had 'a sincere reverence for, if not some acquaintance with, the Ancient
Christian Church'.[81] Clayton may well have helped Wesley in the
early preparation of this volume, though by the time it neared publication he had left Oxford.[82]

This pioneer venture Wesley followed up in 1734 by two abridgements of treatises by John Norris of Bemerton. In 1735 he prepared
three more, an original sermon, the magnificent edition of Thomas à
Kempis's *Christian's Pattern*, and his father's *Advice to a Young Clergyman*. The manuscript of the latter had been entrusted to him ten years
earlier as he was on the verge of taking Holy Orders. As we have

already noted it stressed not only pastoral duties, Bible study, and sermonizing, but patristics and Caroline divinity. This publication was in part an evidence of John Wesley's own dedicated churchmanship, but it was no doubt also in part an act of homage to his father, who had died in April of that year, the pamphlet itself appearing in October.[83] Some might see in the publication of the *Advice* an attempt also at atonement for having refused to take over from his father the Epworth living.

The physical deterioration of his father in 1734, and the urge that he should relinquish his closely-organized academic and pastoral charge at Oxford for the heterogeneous demands of a parish ministry at Epworth, threw Wesley into a frenzy of study and debate. He was so fully committed to serve God that if this were indeed his duty he knew that he must answer the call, however reluctantly. He read many books and wrote many letters on 'Christian liberty', and his attempt to discover the roots of authority so as to arrive at and support a personal decision seemed still further to lessen the power of demands made upon him by others, and to increase his determination to follow the inner light—though it is somewhat unfair to dismiss the twenty-six points of his laboured letter to his father of 10 December 1734 as either smug hypocrisy or selfish rationalization. He was fully convinced that his spiritual task for others as well as for himself must anchor him at Oxford, at least for the time being, and in all probability for many years. He spoke of his own spiritual needs being there fulfilled because of those he felt himself best able to judge, and their fulfilment seemed the necessary means for his most fruitful service to others. The question extended into a general debate on Christian liberty in an authoritarian world.

Wesley's elder brother Samuel claimed that John was 'not at liberty' to refuse the Epworth living, urging that '*The order of the Church* stakes you down, and the more you struggle will hold the faster'.[84] Their mother also took the side of institutional authority. In 1725, forgetful of her lay defiance of her own husband a decade or so earlier, she had written to 'Dear Jacky': 'Prudence requires all persons . . . to keep within their own sphere of action, . . . neither should any secular person of what degree soever invade the province of a priest.'[85] On this occasion she went farther, warning her son how dangerous it was for a man to get out of step, to 'break his rank', for in so doing 'he breaks the eternal order of the universe and abuses his Christian liberty'. John, on the other hand, claimed that whatever might have been the case in a ritualistic theocracy such as that of the Jews, Christians might sometimes be justified in following their own consciences in defiance of established authority, claiming 'a liberty as to external ordinances, to set them aside *pro tempore* on extraordinary occasions'. This he elaborated by means of an extended rhetorical question:

> [Do not] Christians enjoy . . . a liberty as to rules, (1) to lay aside those prudential rules which we no longer need? (2) To suspend those we do need upon extraordinary occasions, and (3) to alter those we do not either lay aside or suspend continually, as the state of our soul alters?[86]

This was certainly the liberty of conscience which increasingly he was to claim for himself as his religious destiny unfolded. Meantime, in order to clear himself of family censure and personal uneasiness, Wesley inquired of Bishop Potter whether at his ordination there was any implication that he should accept a living when offered. The bishop confirmed his own views by replying:

> It doth not seem to me that at your ordination you engaged yourself to take the cure of any parish provided you can as a clergyman better serve God and His Church in your present or some other station.

When Wesley asked this question he was quite convinced that he was called of God to the task of spiritual director of the Oxford Methodists and to that only, apart from the enlarging of his circle of spiritual influence by religious publications. By the end of the summer, however, 'some other station' did indeed beckon him, and he was commissioned as a missionary of the Society for the Propagation of the Gospel, and began rounding up other members of the Holy Club to accompany him to Georgia.[87]

THREE

THE EXPERIMENTAL MISSIONARY

Sir John Perceval, first Earl of Egmont, accurately characterized Wesley for the Georgia Trustees as 'a very odd mixture of a man', though we would wish to modify the second part of his description—'an enthusiast, and at the same time a hypocrite'.[1] Wesley was genuinely zealous for the Church of England, yet deeply anxious to encompass her reform by the restoration of what he believed to be apostolic usages and a far stricter discipline. This anxiety appeared to his more placid fellow-churchmen very much like fanaticism. He was eager to serve the bodies as well as the souls of men, but this remained subsidiary to an over-powering urge to cultivate personal holiness both in himself and in others. Indeed, the 'Instructions for the Missionaries' handed to him as an agent of the Society for the Propagation of the Gospel in Foreign Parts might almost in his case have been deemed superfluous. He had indeed thoroughly acquainted himself with 'the doctrine of the Church of England as contained in the Articles and Homilies, its worship and discipline and rules for the behaviour of the clergy as contained in the Liturgy and Canons'.[2] He was determined to follow the letter of the law in order to keep faith both with his parishioners and with the Society.

The voyage out lasted two months, but because of lengthy delays off the shores of England and before disembarking at Savannah the *Simmonds* remained Wesley's home for over four months. During this time, as senior clergyman, he acted as chaplain for the ship's company. In order effectively to serve the large group of Moravian emigrants he learned German. The Moravians in turn introduced him to their deep spiritual resources of simple piety, and he was especially impressed by their joyful as well as tender hymns. He also continued to find fulfilment as the spiritual director of that segment of the Holy Club which was accompanying him to Georgia, his brother Charles and Benjamin Ingham, both ordained for that purpose. To them was added a young layman, Charles Delamotte, 'who had a mind to leave the world and give himself up entirely to God'.[3] These four formed a monastic cell, entering into a written pact to preserve 'an entire union' among themselves, undertaking nothing important without consulting each other agreeing to abide by a majority vote when disagreements arose, and to

settle tied votes by recourse to the lot.[4] They also resolved to rise early
and to spend the first hour in prayer, the second in Bible study, and the
third in reading 'something relating to the primitive church'.[5]

Wesley's own diary confirms this general pattern, though it is clear
that he remained the superior among equals, and his reading of books
relating to the early church was far from restricted to the hour before
breakfast. The bulk of his reading, indeed, seemed designed to prepare
him for transplanting not only the spirit but the specific methods of
the primitive church into the primitive pioneering colony of Georgia.
As he initiated his young protégé Delamotte into the mysteries of
Deacon's *Complete Devotions* and similar works[6] his own mind became
clearer about the liturgical patterns which it seemed important to
stamp upon this parish unspoiled by settled habits of worship. His
companions also were seized by the rich promise of this experiment,
even though it remained secondary to the anticipated joys of raising a
Christian harvest among the innocent Indian heathens. On 4 February
1736 they sighted land, and Wesley was greatly impressed by the providential fitness of the set Evening Lesson, which contained the words,
'a great and effectual door is opened'. To this he added a fervent: 'O let
no one shut it.'[7]

As they sailed into the river Savannah they discussed more specifically
their 'manner of living in this new country'.[8] Ingham decided to join
the two Wesleys in one of the ascetic practices which they had embraced at the outset of the voyage, on weekdays eating no meat and
drinking no wine.[9] It is probable that the three clergy also formally
pledged themselves to follow in their new parish responsibilities the
liturgical practices which after much research and thought John Wesley
had come to believe represented genuine apostolic procedure. These he
had embodied in a document which he may well have read to them
only a few days earlier.[10] At some stage he struck his pen through two
passages (here shown italicized in brackets):

> I believe [*myself*] it a duty to observe, so far as I can [*without
> breaking communion with my own Church*]:
> 1. To baptize by immersion.[11]
> 2. To use Water,[12] oblation of elements,[13] [and?] alms,[14] invoca-
>   tion[15] a prothesis,[16] in the Eucharist.[17]
> 3. To pray for the faithful departed.[18]
> 4. To pray standing on Sunday and in Pentecost.[19]
> 5. To observe Saturday Sunday and Pentecost as festival.[20]
> 6. To abstain from blood and things strangled.[21]
> I think it prudent[22] (our own church not considered):

1. To observe the stations.[23]
2. Lent, especially the Holy Week.[24]
3. To turn to the east at the Creed.[25]

These points clarified and decided, and probably agreed to by his companions, Wesley incorporated those which were applicable into the copy of the *Book of Common Prayer* which as a good Anglican priest he must use for public worship in Savannah. For nearly two hours on 5 March, according to his diary, he "revised Common Prayer Book". This would be similar and supplementary to the operation first suggested as an adequate explanation of this phrase by Mr. Frederick Hunter, namely bringing the 1662 Prayer Book into line with the First Prayer Book of King Edward VI, for the 1549 book included the 'four usages' of the Non-Jurors as well as trine immersion in Baptism and similar practices which had disappeared from the later book.[26] Two days later Wesley began his public ministry in Savannah.

Savannah, with five or six hundred inhabitants, was the only sizeable town in the infant colony, and indeed contained about one-half of Georgia's population.[27] It had been 'miserably neglected' by its first minister, Samuel Quincey,[28] and in succeeding him Wesley was bent on reform. He approached his task with devotion and courage. At the very outset he warned his rough pioneering parishioners that he intended to preserve strict ecclesiastical discipline such as would almost certainly antagonize some of them. He read to the congregation an outline of his principles and intended procedure:

(1) That I must admonish every one of them, not only in public but from house to house; (2) that I could admit none to Holy Communion without previous notice; (3) that I should divide the morning service on Sundays, in compliance with the first design of the church; (4) that I must obey the rubric by dipping all the children who were able to endure it; (5) that I could admit none who were not communicants to be sureties in baptism; (6) that in general, though I had all the ecclesiastical authority which was entrusted to any within this Province, yet I was only a servant of the Church of England, not a judge, and therefore obliged to keep to her regulations in all things.[29]

This document Wesley read in public once more eighteen months later, when his forebodings had been realized, and some of his parishioners summoned him before a Grand Jury to answer charges based almost solely on the fulfilment of this manifesto. The preamble to the charges claimed that at the outset of his ministry he 'omitted any public declaration of his adherence to the principles and regulations of the Church of England'. Nor indeed does he appear to have made the usual formal declaration customary at institution into an English parish, considering it inappropriate to his status as a missionary of the S.P.G. The implication of disloyalty to the church, however, was ludicrous. The minority report vehemently contradicts any suggestion that either his announced disciplinary practices or his omission of a formula implied any lack of respect for the church:

> Several of us have been his hearers when he has declared his adherence to the Church of England in a stronger manner than by a formal declaration, by explaining and defending the Apostles', the Nicene, and the Athanasian Creeds, the Thirty-Nine Articles, the whole Book of Common Prayer, and the Homilies of the said church; . . . we think a formal declaration is not required but from those who have received institution and induction.[30]

The Moravian leader August Gottlieb Spangenberg, who met Wesley on his arrival, and who had many conferences with him, was convinced that the new minister's episcopal churchmanship was very advanced, and his main diary entry to this effect should be quoted at length:

> He has moreover several quite special principles, which he still holds strongly since he drank them in with his mother's milk. He thinks that an ordination not performed by a bishop in the apostolic succession is invalid. Therefore he believes that neither Calvinists nor Lutherans have *legitimos doctores* and *pastores*. From this it follows that the sacraments administered by such teachers are not valid: this also he maintains. Therefore he thinks that anybody who has been baptized by a Calvinist or Lutheran pastor is not truly baptized. Further, nobody can partake of the holy meal without being first baptized: accordingly he baptizes all persons who come from other sects, although not those who have been baptized in Roman Catholicism. He considers Nitschmann's and Anton [Seifert]'s baptism valid.[31] Reason: they have an episcopal order from the apostolic church. . . . He will therefore not share the Lord's Supper with anyone who is not baptized by a minister who had been ordained by a true bishop. All these doctrines derive from the view of the episcopacy which is held in the Papist and English churches, and which rests upon the authority of the Fathers. Above all he believes that all references in

Scripture of doubtful interpretation must be decided not by reason but from the writings of the first three centuries, e.g. infant baptism, footwashing, fast days, celibacy and many others.[32]

It is quite clear that the authority of the Early Fathers was now almost if not quite as important for Wesley as the Scriptures themselves, and reason was a poor third. He was embarking upon an experiment in preaching the gospel to innocent heathens whose receptive and uncorrupted minds would surely welcome it, but also upon an experiment in legalistic churchmanship that made him more harsh and tactless than at any other period of his life. Perhaps influenced by Non-Juring Roger Laurence's *Lay Baptism Invalid*, he not only insisted on re-baptizing dissenters before admitting them to Communion, but even took this attitude (albeit regretfully) toward a Lutheran minister, Johann Martin Bolzius, leader of the Salzburgher settlement at Ebenezer.[33] The friendly Bolzius recognized that Wesley was infected with 'papistical leaven' in thus refusing to acknowledge the validity of Lutheran ordination and therefore of Lutheran baptism, but two days later charitably affirmed of him: 'He performs the duties of Christianity very earnestly, and visits his people industriously, and is well received by some.'[34]

According to his *Journal* Wesley exercised some caution in one major restoration from the 1549 Prayer Book which he had announced on 7 March. Not until 9 May did he record: 'I began dividing the public prayers according to the original appointment of the church (still observed in a few places in England). The morning service began at five; the Communion Office (with the sermon) at eleven; the evening service about three.' The previous Thursday he had embarked on what became another regular practice, brief morning prayers for his flock every week day, beginning at 5.0 a.m.[35]

When Charles Wesley returned to England later that year he presented the Georgia Trustees with a written report of his brother's activities and success:

17. That when he arrived at Savannah he found the people had been miserably neglected by our late minister, Mr. Quincey; that but three persons partook of the communion, and the people diverted themselves with shooting on Sundays; but before he came away his brother, who is minister now there, had forty communicants every Sunday and on great holy days; that he preaches by heart and has a full assembly; that prayers are said twice every day, in the morning and at nine at night, by reason the day is spent at labour in the fields.[36]

Although many questions still remain unanswered about Wesley's Georgia ministry, one thing is certain: he was too much of a churchman rather than too little. It would be far easier to imagine him deserting Canterbury for Rome than for Geneva. Even while founding what he later called 'the rudiments of a Methodist society' at Savannah he insisted that he and his brother Charles 'were as vehemently attached to the church as ever, and to every rubric of it'.[37] Fifty years later, however, he began an article on separation thus: 'Ever since I returned from America it has been warmly affirmed, "you separate from the church".' In a sense this was in fact true. In America were sown the seeds not only of non-divisive observances like the 5.0 a.m. preaching services but of Methodist separation from the Church of England. Similarly, the religious needs of America led to the maturing of the harvest.

Strangely enough Wesley was accused of leaving the Church of England by two opposite doors at the same time. Some of his practices in Savannah must have smacked to the uninitiated of Roman Catholicism, while others seemed the actions of a puritan separatist. Both were in large measure the results of his attempt to return to the spirit and behaviour of the primitive church.[38] Some of the ritualistic observances followed in Georgia were later discarded, though they remained as a liturgical colouring throughout his ministry. The emphasis upon strict ecclesiastical discipline was never lost, though in the Methodist societies its pattern was modified. On the other hand he saw in the early church an emphasis upon the pragmatic nature of religion as a personal relationship with God. This was the true spirit of Pietism, already present in Wesley's Epworth and Oxford background, and now reinforced by his Moravian and Salzburgher contacts. Ritualism, legalism, and Pietism alike might have been furthered within the ordered ways of the Anglican Church, but if not he must still embrace them, either outside the church or even in opposition to the church. At least a hint of this is to be found in two phrases in the resolutions quoted above—'without breaking communion with my own church' and 'our own church not considered'. Granted that both the phrases themselves and their particular application remain ambiguous, they at least imply that Wesley had foreseen the possibility that both his ritualistic and his reforming actions might be construed as separatist; in fact were so construed.

Patrick Tailfer was such an avowed antagonist of Wesley (largely because of the latter's firm opposition to slavery, spirits, and Sunday sports) that his evidence even in matters of fact is strongly suspect.[39] Nevertheless, even the perjured statements mingling with the authentic in his *True and Historical Narrative of the Colony of Georgia* retain some evidential value as indicating what he thought he could 'get away with':

> The reverend gentleman . . . frequently declared that he never desired to see Georgia a rich, but a religious Colony. [A footnote adds: 'According to his system'.][40] At last all persons of any considera-tion came to look upon him as a Roman Catholic, for which the following reasons seem pretty convincing:
>
> *1st.* Under an affected strict adherence to the Church of England he most unmercifully damned all Dissenters. . . .
>
> *2ndly.* . . . Persons suspected to be Roman Catholics were received and caressed by him as his First-rate Saints.
>
> *3rdly.* A third confirmation of this suspicion arose from his endeavours to establish Confession, Penance, Mortifications, mixing wine with water in the Sacrament . . .; by appointing Deaconesses,[41] with sundry other innovations, which he called Apostolic Constitu-tions.[42] (The colonists in general, including Tailfer, may be par-doned for not understanding their minister's constant references to the chief documentary authority for his ecclesiastical behaviour, the supposedly ancient Apostolic Constitutions.)

The widespread impression that he was a Roman Catholic was un-doubtedly strengthened by Wesley's occasional description of himself as the 'ordinary' for Savannah. Apparently this meant for him no more than 'priest-in-charge', though in combination with his patriarchal insistence on enforcing discipline it might well imply to the uninitiated almost papal powers.[43] At the outset of his Georgia ministry he had resolved: 'Never make yourself familiar, cheap,' and he refused to talk about trifles, insisting that his fundamental task was to prepare his parishioners for heaven.[44]

Without question Wesley was an assiduous as well as an authoritarian pastor, constantly reminding himself of his sacred commission.[45] He himself lived strictly by the strictest rules, and expected his flock to follow him at not too great a distance.[46] His daily diary had for some months become an hourly diary, recording almost without fail five, six, or seven minutes of private devotion at the end of every waking hour.[47] In order to converse with his widely-scattered and immensely varied flock he not only learned German on the *Simmonds* and per-fected it in Georgia, but added to this Spanish, and then Italian. (French he already knew, as well as Latin, Greek, and Hebrew.) He did not feel prepared, however, to tackle Dutch, even though this meant compelling the small group of Dutch settlers 'to be without public worship, and in effect to be without God in the world'.[48] He prepared wills, conducted baptisms, weddings, funerals.[49] He spent three hours a day visiting from house to house.[50] Every day he read public prayers morning and evening, and expounded the Second Lesson.[51] He conducted weekly catechism classes for children and adults, and prepared young people for Communion.[52] He administered Holy Communion every Sunday and Saint's day, and on every day (except Good Friday) in Holy Week; he also carried the elements to the sick and dying (whom he visited daily), and kept not only a regular tally of the number of communicants present on each occasion, but a register showing on which days each had attended.[53] Methodically he maintained mountains of statistics.[54]

Small wonder that John Wesley found his work in Georgia too much for him, even without the peculiar trials to which he exposed himself by his tactlessness, inflexibility, and occasional naiveté. Well might he say: 'A parish of above two hundred miles in length laughs at the labours of one man.'[55] He suffered constantly from frustration at not being able to prosecute his mission to the Indians.[56] Yet he did not throw up his hands in disgust or despair, though there were occasions when he seems to have been preparing himself for a martyrdom such as might furnish the seed for a future great church in America.[57] He retained a keen sense of a providential call, and of the possibility of discovering the divine will by special signs, as well as a readiness to sacrifice himself to God's commands thus discovered.[58] He remained conscious of a personal guiding providence:

> With the power of the Holy Ghost preventing, accompanying, and following me, I know that I (that is, the grace of God which is in me) shall save both myself and those that hear me.[59]

Sometimes his heart rejoiced at the evidence of spiritual fruit, such as the revival among the young people of Savannah.[60] He wrote impassioned letters pleading with the Oxford Methodists to 'come over and help us', and in the case of George Whitefield was successful—a truly momentous success.[61] Never did Wesley lose his deep pastoral concern, and his genuine distress at spiritual setbacks was expressed in sighing words such as 'Ah, my Frederica!' and his final echo of our Lord's lament over Jerusalem:

> I shook off the dust of my feet and left Georgia, after having preached the gospel there, . . . not as I ought, but as I was able, one year and nearly nine months. 'Oh that thou hadst known, at least in this thy day, the things which make for thy peace!'[62]

The first official charge of separation made against Wesley was sparked by his refusal to administer Communion to his own potential bride, now married to another, Sophia Williamson, niece and ward of the chief bailiff of Savannah, Thomas Causton, though he did this only after repeated and lengthy interviews with her, her guardian, and his colleagues and friends.[63] This spark set fire to a train of smouldering ecclesiastical grievances, drawn up by Causton for the packed Grand Jury which he assembled. Almost all the charges concerned Wesley's strict adherence to the Anglican rubrics, in other words his excessive zeal—though it is true that on one occasion he had so far forgotten himself as to baptize a child with only two godparents present instead of three. Several of the indictments in the original document were eventually dropped, including those of administering Communion to 'boys ignorant and unqualified', and not pronouncing the benediction until all but confirmed communicants had left.[64]

Two charges of special interest were those of 'changing or altering such passages as he thinks proper in the version of Psalms publicly authorized to be sung in the church', and 'introducing into the church and service at the altar compositions of psalms and hymns not inspected or authorized by any proper judicature'.[65] On 5 March 1736, when he spent nearly two hours revising the Prayer Book in preparation for his Savannah ministry, he went on to spend even longer (about three hours) in revising the New Version of metrical psalms by Tate and Brady attached to it. The nature of these revisions remains matter of conjecture, but the fact is important in itself.[66]

This was not enough, however. He was intent not only on reforming the old but on experimenting with the new. His unauthorized psalms and hymns were incorporated into *A Collection of Psalms and Hymns* published at Charleston, South Carolina, in 1737. Like Wesley's own churchmanship this small volume blended strangely diverse elements of Christian culture: adaptations of the Anglican priest-poet George Herbert rubbed shoulders with translations of mystical German poems from the Moravian *Gesangbuch*, and Non-conformist Isaac Watts' psalms stood side by side with the poems of the Roman Catholic John Austin, gleaned from his *Devotions* by way of the Non-Juror George Hickes; here and there were scattered original compositions by Wesley's father and by his brother Samuel.[67] This pioneer attempt at grafting hymn-singing on to the *Book of Common Prayer* was a presage of one of the outstanding features of the Methodist Revival, and was not without influence in Anglican worship.

The accusation that Wesley was leaving the Church of England by the right door of Roman ritualism could clearly not be pressed by anyone conversant with church lore. Back in England Wesley was warmly defended before the Georgia Trustees by the Rev. Dr. Richard Bundy. The Earl of Egmont reports:

> Dr. Bundy showed us out of the Liturgy that Mr. Wesley's refusal to christen the child without dipping, or to bury a person not of the Church of England unless satisfied that the person had been baptized, was no more than by law he was absolutely obliged to, and had he complied he would by law have lost his preferment.

Nor was his rejection of Sophy Williamson from Communion in the least out of order, however much his personal emotions may have become entangled in the affair. Bundy went on to explain that:

> By the same Liturgy and law of the land, any person intending to communicate must send his name the day before to the minister, who, if he knows any objection to the persons taking the Sacrament, is to admonish him of his fault, and the person must publicly declare [his] repentance of the same.[68]

Nor could a charge of leaving the church by the left door of sectarian 'enthusiasm' really be upheld. From the beginning Pietist influence upon Wesley met with a strangely mixed response. He was tremendously impressed both by Moravian spirituality and by what he could learn of their church order, yet puzzling questions remained. In a lengthy conversation with Spangenberg about the ministry on 27 February 1736, the Moravian apparently denied either the validity or the value of Apostolic Succession, but Wesley was nevertheless greatly moved by the actual election and ordination of Anton Seifert as a Moravian bishop on the following day:

> The great simplicity, as well as solemnity, of the whole, almost made me forget the seventeen hundred years between, and imagine myself in one of those assemblies where form and state were not, but Paul the tentmaker or Peter the fishmerman presided, yet with the demonstration of the Spirit and of power.[69]

Church order continued to engage his attention throughout his stay in Georgia. He discussed episcopacy with Dr. Tailfer on 20 March, 'lay baptism' (i.e. baptism by a minister not episcopally ordained) with the Germans on 27 March.[70] In May, with the aid of Töltschig, he studied the validity of Moravian orders, and was offered evidence (since disproved) that in them an unbroken succession from the apostles had in fact been maintained.[71] In September he read Archbishop Potter's treatise on church government.[72]

Of crucial significance was Wesley's study with Charles Delamotte that same month of William Beveridge's *Synodikon; sive Pandectae Canonum Apostolorum et Conciliorum ab Ecclesia Graeca Receptorum*. This weighty work (it actually tips the scale at over twenty pounds) was required reading for the S.P.G. missionaries, who were thus expected to make themselves familiar with early conciliar legislation in the original tongues. Wesley had owned a copy since 1731, and had certainly dipped into it in the winter of 1734–5 if not earlier, when he probably concentrated on the Apostolic Canons, which occupied the first fifty-seven pages of Volume I; text and ancient commentary were presented in parallel columns of Greek and Latin. This more careful reading in 1736, however, persuaded him of two things. First, that he had allotted Church tradition a higher place than it merited in relation to the Bible. The *Synodikon* convinced him that General Councils had erred, 'and that things ordained by Councils as necessary to salvation have neither strength nor authority unless they be taken out of Holy Scripture.'[73] Secondly, that the foundation upon which he had laid so much of his own ecclesiastical structure was unreliable. His ecclesiastical Bible had been the Apostolic Canons, the closing section of the Apostolic Constitutions. The *Synodikon* eventually showed him that the Canons were nothing like as ancient and as original as he had been led to believe, and this in turn cast doubt on the Constitutions themselves. Bitterness at wasted spiritual energy and initiative came out in angry comment because he had first discovered this on page 159, from an incidental reference in a commentary by Theodore Balsamon on a different subject, the second Canon of the Sixth General Council of 681 A.D.—'and why did he not observe it in the first page of the book?' This was more than a little unfair. Beveridge believed in, and his Prolegomena had asserted, the authenticity and early origin of the Apostolic Canons, and he could hardly have been expected to point out that the whole foundation of his work was shaky![74]

It was at this point that the possibility of Wesley's turning sectarian became more pronounced, though for some time it was far from obvious. His desire to imitate the primitive church was by no means lessened, but the emphasis upon observance gave way markedly before an emphasis upon spirit. Wesley's faith in the authentic documentation of those observances dwindled. He continued to follow some if not most of the same practices, but with diminished zeal. Although this swing of the pendulum from undue trust in church traditions to what seemed to many an equally undue emphasis upon the mystical experiences of religion took place (as Wesley described it) 'insensibly', there is little doubt that the pendulum reached the point of pause before changing direction with his closer study of Beveridge's *Synodikon*. Henceforth he had finished with 'making antiquity a co-ordinate rather than subordinate rule with scripture', with 'admitting several doubtful writings as undoubted evidences of antiquity', with 'extending antiquity too far, even to the middle or end of the fourth century', and with 'believing more practices to have been universal in the ancient church than ever were so', as also with the assumption that every practice of proven antiquity was equally applicable to every time and place.[75] Egged on by James Hutton, however, he did undertake further debates with the Moravians on their supposed maintenance of unspoiled primitive Christianity. Hutton wrote: 'Take care to inquire carefully and strictly concerning the mission of the Moravian bishop. I will make what inquiries I can. A great deal depends upon the validity of ordinations.'[76] Undoubtedly so. But by this time the impact of Moravian spirituality upon Wesley was of far more importance to him than the validity of their orders.

A visit to the Scots settlement of Darien in January 1737 softened even his prejudices against the Presbyterians. They taught him the value of extempore prayer, and introduced him to a Scots devotional classic which he later edited and published, the life of Thomas Haliburton.[77] Without any doubt Wesley's views of church order had reached a state of flux. That he was therefore amenable to further changes of mind is shown by some of the questions which he posed to the Moravians on 31 July 1737:

> 3. Ought we so to expect the Holy Ghost to convert either our own or our neighbour's soul as to neglect any outward means?
>
> 4. Ought we so to expect the Holy Ghost to interpret Scripture to us as to neglect any outward means? Particularly inquiring into the sense of the ancient church?
>
> 5. What is the visible church? . . .
>
> 9. Do you believe those called the Athanasian, the Nicene, and the Apostles' Creed to be agreeable to Scripture?
>
> 10. Do you believe the Mosaic precepts concerning unclean meats to be binding? . . .
>
> 16. Is celibacy a state more advantageous for holiness than marriage?
>
> 17. Are the ministrations of a man not episcopally ordained valid?
>
> 18. Does the wickedness of a man episcopally ordained make his ministrations invalid? . . .[78]

The following day he accompanied Spangenberg to New Ebenezer to confer with Bolzius, the Lutheran minister to whom two weeks earlier he had refused communion, and who had promised to demonstrate from Wesley's revered Early Fathers that episcopacy was not an essential mark of a true church. His zeal for episcopacy may well have been somewhat dampened on this occasion, though no details of the interview have survived.[79]

Certainly Wesley did try out in Georgia many unusual religious experiments, some of which later became regular features of British Methodism. As we have seen, he introduced the singing of hymns (as opposed to metrical psalms) into public worship, even sacramental worship, and his *Collection of Psalms and Hymns* was the first American hymn-book. He utilized the services of laymen in his parish work: Charles Delamotte was set not only to teach but to catechize, and in emergency even to exercise pastoral care of the parish, and possibly to preach;[80] Robert Hows, the parish clerk, led a communion class and a fellowship class.[81] At least three women carried similar responsibilities, and Wesley seems to have called them 'deaconesses': Margaret Bovey, whom he unsuccessfully tried to dissuade from becoming Mrs. James Burnside,[82] Mrs. Robert Gilbert,[83] and Mrs. Mary Vanderplank, widow of a seaman appointed Savannah's naval officer shortly before Wesley's arrival.[84] The infant society in Frederica depended heavily upon lay leaders: Will Reed, whose hut Charles Wesley shared, and whom during their absence John Wesley persuaded to read evening prayers,[85] Samuel Davison, the constable,[86] and Mark Hird, a young Quaker whom Wesley had baptized aboard the *Simmonds*.[87] Wesley himself tried various unusual types of ministry, partly because of the demands of a pioneering situation, but mainly because he was even then prepared to respond to realized need by any allowable method. Thus he undertook on board ship and in America some activities which later in England were to be labelled schismatic, such as extempore prayer, extempore preaching, preaching in the open air, and serving as an itinerant preacher with a 'round' of preaching places in the 'smaller settlements'.[88] In Georgia, also, he came to know and to admire the love-feast, though it does not appear that he himself conducted this form of Christian fellowship until his return to England.[89]

Most important of all, both in Savannah and Frederica, Wesley organized societies for religious fellowship quite apart from ordered public worship. In these gatherings the members spent about an hour in 'prayer, singing and mutual exhortation', naturally under the close supervision whenever possible of their spiritual director. This he later called 'the second rise of Methodism'.[90] Wesley even divided these societies into the 'more intimate union' of 'bands' after the Moravian pattern. It was this which readily fostered the charge of his having instituted a Roman Catholic confessional, for mutual confession was indeed one of the purposes of these small homogeneous groups.[91]

By themselves none of these 'Methodist' practices could be magnified into anything approaching a real separation from the Church of England. Even collectively all they provided was evidence of a burning desire to revitalize the church, or at least to conduct the experiment of building a model Christian community in one Anglican parish. Yet when a church reluctant to undergo a blood-transfusion handed the would-be physician his coat and hat, he became the more eager to cure the patient in spite of herself, using whatever methods might be devised by the ingenuity of himself or others, methods ancient or modern. This determination was increased when shortly after his return to England Wesley's own spiritual experience entered a new dimension. Already, however, a new warmth had crept into his personal devotions, his pastoral care, and into his evangelism, mainly through the example and advocacy of the Moravians, whom he considered living vestiges of primitive Christianity.[92] After lodging with some of them at the beginning of his Georgia ministry he marvelled at the Providence of God: 'From ten friends [the Holy Club] I am awhile secluded, and He hath opened me a door into a whole Church.'[93] At the close of that ministry, though he had learned that the Moravians were not without blemish, he still spoke of their church as 'a city which ought to be set upon a hill. Their light hath too long been hid under a bushel'.[94]

One indication of Wesley's growing spiritual fervour was the firm adoption shortly after his return to England of the practice of extempore prayer in public. On 2 January 1737 he had visited the Scots Presbyterian settlement at Darien, and was both surprised and somewhat shocked 'to hear an extemporary prayer and a written sermon', asking: 'Are not then the words we speak to God to be set in order at least as carefully as those we speak to our fellow worms?' His diary shows, however, that in the evening he himself was constrained to experiment with this unorthodox procedure: 'Mrs. Mackintosh's, supper and singing; I prayed extempore!'[95] On Sunday 24 April 1737, this time during public worship at Ponpon, South Carolina, Wesley again offered extempore prayer, at a dissenting minister's request.[96] Later that year he asked the Moravians, 'Do you prefer extempore to set forms of prayer in public?'[97] Thus softened up, shortly after returning to England, on Easter Saturday, 1738, he entered this record in his *Journal*, to which when he came to reprint it in his collected *Works* he added the asterisk which implied that the passage was of special importance:

April 1, Sat.—Being at Mr. Fox's society [in Oxford], my heart was so full that I could not confine myself to the forms of prayer which we are accustomed to use there. Neither do I purpose to be confined to them any more; but to pray indifferently with a form or without as I may find suitable to particular occasions.[98]

Charles Wesley also accepted this method of mingling prepared forms of prayer with what he usually termed 'praying after God'.[99] Word soon got around, and their mother was sufficiently disturbed to write to their elder brother Samuel, who thus took John to task:

My mother tells me she fears a formal schism is already begun among you, though you and Charles are ignorant of it. For God's sake take care of that, and banish extemporary expositions and extemporary prayers.[100]

In a letter to their sister Mrs. Martha Hall, Samuel restricted his complaints to the former innovation, claiming that 'the extemporary expounding of Scripture is a natural inlet to all false doctrine, heresy, and schism'.[101] John Wesley himself felt not the slightest qualm on this score. He had first preached without a manuscript in 1735, though apparently more by error than design.[102] *En route* to Georgia he undertook this practice deliberately, probably in this also avowedly following the early Christians. Benjamin Ingham's journal for Sunday 19 October 1735 records: 'Mr. John Wesley began to preach without notes, expounding a portion of Scripture extempore, according to the ancient usage.'[103] On board the *Simmonds* and in Georgia these extempore expositions were daily events, helping to make Wesley the great preacher that he became, though he continued to prepare manuscript sermons on set texts and themes. Charles Wesley reported to the Georgia Trustees that his brother 'preached by heart'.[104] Charles himself somewhat timidly followed John's example in October 1738.[105] Clearly extempore preaching was an invaluable handmaid to the evangelist, especially to the open-air evangelist, and to that extent Samuel's fears were justified. Samuel's former neighbour, the Rev. John Hutton of Westminster, similarly complained to John Wesley early in 1739 'about his preaching without notes, which he thought was wrong to do'.[106] Hutton was a Non-Juror, but Wesley was rapidly escaping from their spell, and remained unconvinced.

Extempore prayer, however, was a different matter, about which his conscience remained somewhat tender. It did seem to imply a rejection of the *Book of Common Prayer* which, after all, was the immediate reason for the ejection of the Nonconformists in 1662. In 1740, indeed, Wesley recorded that: 'A gentleman came to me full of goodwill, to exhort me not to leave the church, or (which was the same thing in his account) to use extemporary prayer.'[107] Some years later a responsible cleric seriously claimed in print that Wesley disobeyed the church 'by using extemporary prayer in public', reminding him that 'the church has strongly declared her mind on this point by appointing her excellent Liturgy, which you have solemnly promised to use, and no other'. He must surely have been thinking of the Act of Uniformity, but Wesley pleaded ignorance, replying, 'I know not when or where'.[108] Wesley himself introduced the subject in a letter to 'John Smith' in 1746, saying, 'I use the service of the church every Lord's Day, and it has never yet appeared to me that any rule of the church forbids my using extemporary prayer on other occasions'.[109] This also was one of the points at dispute in the 1750s, when the charge of separation was levelled more vehemently and seemed likely to stick. Wesley constantly maintained, however, that extempore prayer by itself was unsatisfying, stating in 1778: 'I myself find more life in the church prayers than in the formal extemporary prayers of Dissenters.'[110]

The Moravians had introduced Wesley to something much more explosive than this question of the propriety of adding extempore prayers to printed collects. This was their strangely fascinating claim to *know* that they were in a state of salvation, a claim supported by courageous and radiant lives. For years Wesley had diligently been seeking salvation along the path of holy living, his earlier fumblings after spiritual certainty thrown overboard along with the toils of ancient tradition and the snares of mysticism. He now became convinced that man could not pay for his passage to heaven, but must accept it humbly and freely from God at the hands of Christ his Saviour. On 24 May 1738 this growing conviction of his mind and burden of his prayers for a month became the experience of his heart. No longer did he hope that he might be saved by a faith that implied a rational assent to the truths of Christianity backed up by the most devout and scrupulous Christian conduct; now he was *assured* that his sins were forgiven because of a faith which implied simply a leaning on Christ alone for salvation—even though this kind of faith, the faith of a son rather than a mere servant of God, must also issue in good works. Henceforth he was never quite the same, though he did not experience the transports of joy which he had expected, and indeed passed through moods of depression. His concern now as a Christian minister was no longer the negative duty of insisting that salvation came only by means of 'a grievous set of penances, confessions, mortifications, and constant attendance on early and late hours of prayer', such as he had been charged with in Savannah.[111] It became the positive privilege of pro-

claiming good news, of 'offering Christ'. Wesley still retained, however, much of what he later termed 'the impetuosity of [his] High
Church zeal'.[112] Discipline and devotion were by no means forgotten,
but were regarded now more as the fruits than the roots of salvation.

In order to see 'the place where the Christians live', and thus learn
at first-hand the spirit and customs of the Moravians, he made a pilgrimage to Herrnhut. He was enormously impressed by all that he
saw, especially by the fact that this community was indeed modelled
on the Bible and the early church. He was convinced that 'this Christianity' should 'cover the earth'. Yet he retained his independence of
judgement, and even at that impressionable stage was not prepared to
swallow Moravianism whole:

> O that after I have proved all things I may be enabled throughly
> δοκιμάζειν τὰ διαφέροντα,[113] and, calling no man master, in faith,
> practice, and discipline to hold fast that which is good![114]

The Moravians themselves, indeed, reinforced this determination to
'call no man master'. When in his *Journal* for August 1738 Wesley
summarized their constitution, one of the passages asterisked in later
years as important was the following manifesto:

> In all things which do not immediately concern the inward, spiritual
> kingdom of Christ, we simply, and without contradicting, obey the
> higher powers. But with regard to conscience, the liberty of this we
> cannot suffer to be any way limited or infringed. And to this head
> we refer whatever directly or in itself tends to hinder the salvation
> of souls, or whatsoever things Christ and His holy apostles . . . took
> charge of and performed as necessary for the constitution and well-
> ordering of His Church. In these things we acknowledge no head but
> Christ; and are determined, God being our helper, to give up, not
> only our goods (as we did before), but life itself, rather than this
> liberty which God hath given us.[115]

Henceforward Wesley felt equally compelled to proclaim 'the
unsearchable riches of Christ' by every method which had scriptural
support, no matter what bishop might say or mob might do. He had
delved deeply into orthodox Anglican teaching, and especially into the
Articles and Homilies, and was convinced that what he now experienced was present there, hidden under the dust of disputes and deism
and prosy moralizing. He set out to proclaim the glorious possibility
of justification by faith through grace, of the direct witness of the Holy
Spirit that a man is a saved child of God, of the possibility of perfect
love as the outworking and proof of that sonship. This type of preaching itself seemed to offer the challenge of another form of separation,

5

indeed to present itself as heresy. Certainly it was no more familiar as orthodox church doctrine in England than his liturgical and disciplinary practices had been in Georgia. Yet both were the outcome of a genuine concerned allegiance to the Church of England, and both could be supported from her official publications. Wesley himself resorted to the printing press (among other means) both to clear himself from the charge of separation and to promulgate his orthodox but unfamiliar message.

In 1738, the year of his 'conversion' experience, he published three works: another *Collection of Psalms and Hymns*, a *Sermon on Salvation by Faith*, and *The Doctrine of Salvation, Faith, and Good Works, Extracted from the Homilies of the Church of England*. Strangely enough the account for the five hundred copies of the *Collection* was actually entered in William Bowyer's ledger on 24 May 1738, though there is no evidence that Wesley took any copies along to the society meeting in Aldersgate Street that evening.[116] The sermon on salvation by faith he preached before the University of Oxford in St. Mary's on the afternoon of 11 June, after trying it out in the morning on a smaller congregation at Stanton Harcourt. It was what E. H. Sugden terms 'the first trumpet-call of the Evangelical Revival', and Wesley himself gave it pride of place when he came to publish his doctrinal 'platform' in a collected edition of his sermons.[117] It was published in October of that year, and went through twenty-eight single editions during Wesley's lifetime quite apart from its many appearances in volumes of collected sermons.[118] Less well known is the other 1738 publication a deliberate attempt to discover and publish the authorized views of the Church of England on this central theme of the Methodist Revival. By fitting symbolism this was the last of Wesley's publications to be printed in Oxford, for it marked both the climax of the old ways of the pursuit of piety in semi-monastic seclusion or experimental evangelism, and the beginning of the new day of proclaiming salvation in the highways and byways. In both, however, as in this echoing of Cranmer's rhetoric (sadly diminished for the practical uses of the eighteenth century) Wesley saw himself as a loyal son of the Church of England.[119]

That this approach would not find favour with more conventional clergy was fairly certain, and this was made clear by the reactions of his elder brother Samuel. Samuel argued that the emotional conversions which John described could never take place within the consecrated walls of a church, nor under any other sermon than one on the new birth, though he was fairly confident that in that age of lax ecclesiastical discipline his brother would not be officially admonished for his unorthodox views and actions. Nevertheless, he expressed the fear that if

John remained tied to a fanatic like George Whitefield, 'though the church would not excommunicate you, you would excommunicate the church'.[120] John Wesley vindicated himself in what must have been the last letter that Samuel received from him before his death. He claimed that in fact such phenomena *had* occurred within 'consecrated walls', and while he was preaching on the Atonement rather than on the new birth. He announced, however, that church order was far from being his most important consideration, adding:

> O my brother, who hath bewitched you, that for fear of I know not what distant consequences you cannot rejoice at, or so much as acknowledge, the great power of God? How is it that you can't praise God for saving so many souls from death . . . unless He will begin this work within 'consecrated walls'? Why should He not fill heaven and earth? You cannot, indeed you cannot confine the Most High within temples made with hands. I do not despise them any more than you do. But I rejoice to find that God is everywhere. I love the rites and ceremonies of the church. But I see, well pleased, that our great Lord can work without them. And howsoever and wheresoever a sinner is converted from the error of his ways, nay and by whomsoever, I thereat rejoice, yea, and will rejoice![121]

An epochal change had now taken place in his views. The work of evangelism must be furthered, church or no church.

FOUR

METHODISM AND THE BISHOPS

SAMUEL WESLEY'S last letter to his mother embodied his grave fears about the venture upon which his younger brothers had embarked. Writing on 20 October 1739 he begged her not to countenance them in 'joining a schism', and frankly summarized the view of the situation which he had gathered from the reports of his former neighbours, the Rev. and Mrs. John Hutton of Westminster:

> They design separation. . . . They are already forbid all the pulpits in London, and to preach in that diocese is actual schism. In all likelihood it will come to the same all over England if the bishops have courage enough. They leave off the Liturgy in the fields. . . . Their societies are sufficient to dissolve all other societies but their own. . . . As I told Jack, I am not afraid the church should excommunicate him—discipline is at too low an ebb—but that he should excommunicate the church. It is pretty near it. . . . Love-feasts are introduced, and extemporary prayers and expositions of Scripture, which last are enough to bring in all confusion.[1]

It was true that Anglican discipline was very lax, that Convocation no longer met, and that the bishops were unlikely to move unless pushed very hard. All this, indeed, was part of the malady which the Methodists were seeking to remedy. Nevertheless the danger of an unexpected episcopal reaction which might destroy their effectiveness was always present.

During the early years of the revival Wesley showed himself most anxious to secure the support or at least the acquiescence of the Anglican hierarchy, both because this was his duty as a loyal churchman and because the work might otherwise be hindered. With each of the two most important members—the archbishop of Canterbury and the bishop of London—the brothers were in fairly close touch. The next most important for their immediate concerns was the bishop of Bristol, the third largest city in the kingdom, and their second headquarters. At that period the archbishopric of York was regarded as much more of a sinecure, nor was there any tradition that York was a stepping-stone to Canterbury.[2] Although the Wesleys had little contact with northern bishops the two successive archbishops of York who did move up to Canterbury were in fact sympathetic to the Methodist lieutenant in the north, the Rev. William Grimshaw of Haworth.[3]

It was the Wesleys' good fortune that at the outset of the revival the sees both of Canterbury and London were occupied by men who were by no means strangers to them. This was particularly true of Dr. John Potter, archbishop of Canterbury. Like John Wesley he had been a Fellow of Lincoln College in his youth, and was bishop of Oxford from 1715 to 1737, in which capacity he had ordained John Wesley both deacon (1725) and priest (1728), and Charles Wesley deacon (1735). Potter was remarkable both for the depth of his classical and ecclesiastical learning and the breadth of his sympathies. While bishop of Oxford he had been Wesley's understanding confidant in the affairs of the Holy Club; he had also reassured Count Zinzendorf about the validity of Moravian orders.[4] In 1737 he succeeded William Wake as primate, and filled that office for ten of the most formative years of Methodism. John Wesley read Potter's *Discourse of Church Government* (1707) in Georgia, as did Charles in the spring of 1739, speaking of it as 'a seasonable antidote against the growing spirit of delusion'.[5] On returning to England they secured his authority for rebaptizing adult dissenters on the understanding that first they notified the bishop of the diocese concerned, though the archbishop went on to warn them to stress fundamental spirituality rather than the letter of the religious law—advice which throughout their ministry they never forgot. Nearly half a century later John Wesley closed his sermon 'On attending the Church service' with this tribute:

> Near fifty years ago a great and good man, Dr. Potter, then archbishop of Canterbury, gave me an advice for which I have ever since had occasion to bless God: 'If you desire to be extensively useful, do not spend your time and strength in contending for or against such things as are of a disputable nature, but in testifying against open notorious vice, and in promoting essential holiness.'[6]

Potter believed that thus they might indeed 'leaven the whole lump' of the Church of England.[7] It was encouraging, to say the least, thus to have the confidence of the highest ecclesiastic in the land, no matter how the local clergy might sneer and the mob pelt stones.

The same was to a lesser degree true at first of the bishop of London, Edmund Gibson, who held that key position throughout the same crucial decade, in fact from 1723 to 1748. It was he who had ordained Charles Wesley priest in 1735. After returning from Georgia in December 1736 Charles waited on the bishop several times, and in February

1738 informed Gibson of his brother's return. The bishop, Charles records in his *Journal*, 'spoke honourably of him, expressed a great desire to see him, asked many questions about Georgia and the Trustees, forgot his usual reserve, and dismissed me very kindly'.[8]

Six months later both brothers were invited to appear before Gibson in order to answer complaints that had been made against them on grounds of doctrine and discipline. They spent most of Friday morning 20 October 1738 with him. He found nothing objectionable in their teaching upon justification by faith alone, especially as they freed themselves from any suspicion of antinomianism by maintaining that they had no sympathy for preachers who failed to counterbalance their proclamation of salvation by faith with an insistence upon good works as a necessary fruit of genuine faith. In discussing another controverted Methodist emphasis, the possibility of a personal assurance of salvation, the Wesleys disclaimed any 'absolute assurance' which might seem to imply no possibility of backsliding, but apparently did not insist that this experience which they preached was the direct work of the Holy Spirit, simply acquiescing in Gibson's own definition—'an inward persuasion whereby a man is conscious in himself after examining his life by the law of God, and weighing his own sincerity, that he is in a state of salvation and acceptable to God'. This was the truth, but hardly the whole truth, and either Charles Wesley's brief reporting of the occasion was at fault or they put a far wider interpretation than did Gibson on the phrase 'examining his life by the law of God'.[9] On the matter of Potter's authorization of rebaptism Gibson considered that the archbishop had let the side down, and complained that the bishops in general were suffering from the backwash of this unfortunate decision. John Wesley's own views on the matter had mellowed, perhaps partly because of Potter's counsel, and he seems no longer to have insisted on the rebaptism of dissenters, simply claiming that he could not in good conscience refuse 'if a person dissatisfied with lay-baptism should desire episcopal'.[10]

Wesley then turned defence into attack in a subject of far more crucial importance for the future of Methodism. Many religious societies existed in London and Westminster (and a few elsewhere) which had originally been founded under church auspices but were no longer under close clerical supervision. Many of them had quite lost their spiritual vitality, and Wesley believed it an important part of his mission to revitalise them by an infusion of what was generally coming to be termed 'Methodist enthusiasm', though in fact it owed much to Moravian pietism. After returning from his pilgrimage to Herrnhut, the Mecca of renewed Moravianism, Wesley immediately attempted to reform the religious societies, in general by encouraging them to deeper spirituality, and in particular by urging them to organize small 'bands' for intimate fellowship. It was while this process was in its formative stages that the interview with the bishop of London took place.

In addition to holding responsibility for the key area in this experimental deepening of religious fellowship, Gibson was universally acknowledged to be the greatest ecclesiastical jurist of his day. It was the more important to discover his position. Wesley accordingly asked, 'Are the religious societies conventicles?' Gibson promptly side-stepped the question, suggesting that Wesley was able to interpret the laws for himself. Wesley knew Canon 73, which prohibited clergy from meeting in a private house for any purpose which might 'any way tend to the impeaching or depraving of the doctrine of the Church of England, or of the *Book of Common Prayer*, or of any part of the government and discipline now established of the Church of England, under pain of excommunication *ipso facto*'.[11] Surely, he urged, the religious societies were not private conventicles in this sense? Gibson refused to give a firm ruling, but did venture an opinion, 'No, I think not'. Thus confirmed in his own stand, Wesley pressed his attack still farther with a request that in the future the bishop would pay no attention to hearsay evidence against his fellow clergy, to which Gibson replied: 'No, by no means. And you may have free access to me at all times.'[12]

Charles Wesley took advantage of this invitation by visiting the bishop less than a month later in order to inform him of a woman who requested rebaptism. On this occasion Gibson was angry: 'He immediately took fire and interrupted me, "I wholly disapprove of it: it is irregular!"' He went on to challenge Charles Wesley's ecclesiastical standing in London, pointing out that he had power to inhibit him. Charles dared him to exert that power, whereupon the bishop drew back: 'Oh! Why will you push things to an extreme? I do not inhibit you.' Thereupon Charles Wesley claimed that this was tacit approval of rebaptism and asked whether the bishop wished to be informed of such cases in the future. Once more Gibson refused to announce any decision, and dismissed this prickly character with the words: 'Well, sir, you knew my judgment before, and you know it now. Good morrow to you.'[13]

The following February both brothers again visited the archbishop at Lambeth Palace, and went straight from him to see the bishop in Whitehall. Charles Wesley's account of the occasion merits quotation in full:

Wed. February 21. . . . With my brother I waited on the archbishop.

He showed us great affection; spoke mildly of Mr. Whitefield; cautioned us to give no more umbrage than was necessary for our own defence; to forbear exceptionable phrases; to keep to the doctrine of the Church. We told him we expected persecution; would abide by the Church till her Articles and Homilies were repealed. He assured us he knew of no design in the governors of the Church to innovate; and neither should there be any innovation while he lived; avowed justification by faith only; and his joy to see us as often as we pleased.

From him we went to the bishop of London; who denies his having condemned or even heard much of us. G. Whitefield's *Journal*, he said, was tainted with enthusiasm, though he was himself a pious, well-meaning youth. He warned us against antinomianism, and dismissed us kindly.[14]

On the whole this was an auspicious beginning with the two most influential ecclesiastics in the country, both of whom were satisfied of the Wesleys' orthodoxy and were at least prepared to raise no obstacle to their efforts to secure fuller spiritual fellowship through religious societies no longer under the direct control of the parochial clergy. Many of the clergy themselves did not regard their venture so sympathetically, however, especially as the Wesleys constantly seemed to be extending the range of their extra-parochial ministry. In this widespread evangelism Charles Wesley was his brother's faithful helper, and frequently the pioneer. Both were always careful to seek the co-operation of the local parish minister before such ventures, even though with little hope of success. On 31 May 1739 Charles Wesley recorded: 'A Quaker sent me a pressing invitation to preach at Thackstead. I scrupled preaching in another's parish till I had been refused the church.' This 'till' surely implied an expectation of the refusal which in fact came, so that he preached to seven hundred people 'in the highways'. Another entry in his *Journal* for 25 August of the same year shows how in spite of rebuffs he still avoided by-passing the local clergy:

Before I went forth into the streets and highways I sent, after my custom, to borrow the church. The minister (one of the better disposed) sent back a civil message that he would be glad to drink a glass of wine with me, but durst not lend me his pulpit for fifty guineas.

Mr. Whitefield durst lend me his field, which did just as well. For near an hour and a half God gave me voice and strength to exhort about two thousand sinners to repent and believe the gospel.[15]

A former member of the Holy Club, James Hervey, voiced the widespread criticism of this invasion of other men's parishes. His rebuke was written a month after the Wesleys' interview with Potter and Gibson noted above, but it first saw partial publication three years later in John Wesley's *Journal*. In his reply Wesley introduced a favourite argument supported by quotations from St. Paul, and also a famous original phrase which became a familiar watchword for his evangelistic irregularities:

God in Scripture commands me, according to my power to instruct the ignorant, reform the wicked, confirm the virtuous. Man forbids me to do this in another's parish: that is, in effect, to do it at all, seeing I have now no parish of my own, nor probably ever shall. Whom then shall I hear, God or man? 'If it be just to obey man rather than God, judge you. A dispensation of the gospel is committed to me, and woe is me if I preach not the gospel.'[16] But where shall I preach it upon the principles you mention? Why, not in Europe, Asia, Africa, or America; not in any of the Christian parts, at least, of the habitable earth. For all these are after a sort divided into parishes. . . .

Suffer me now to tell you *my* principles in this matter. I look upon *all the world* as *my parish*; thus far I mean, that in whatever part of it I am I judge it meet, right, and my bounden duty to declare unto all that are willing to hear the glad tidings of salvation. This is the work which I know God has called me to, and sure I am that His blessing attends it.[17]

Thus did Wesley develop into an evangelistic dogma another fundamental principle of Methodism, the itinerancy of its preachers, whose territorial boundaries were set by God alone. At first this was applied to the ordained clergy only, but in a few years was extended to the lay preachers also.

Refusal to acknowledge territorial restrictions, whether of parish or of diocese, was allied to a somewhat cavalier attitude to the governing authority of the bishops. In a letter to his brother John Wesley enunciated an important principle which had been taking shape in his mind for some time, a principle implicit in his reminder both to Hervey and to Charles Wesley of Paul's phrase about obeying God rather than man. He claimed that he had both an 'ordinary call' conferred by the bishop at his ordination and an 'extraordinary call' whose validity was confirmed by the works which God accomplished through his ministry. The spiritual fruits of his non-parochial activities, he maintained, proved that they had the divine blessing: 'God bears witness in an *extraordinary* manner that my *thus exercising* my *ordinary call* is well-pleasing in his sight.'[18]

This approach may well have reflected Wesley's memories of Richard Hooker's *Laws of Ecclesiastical Polity*. In Book VII Hooker stated that in some respects both presbyters and bishops were the successors to the apostles, but that normally the bishop was superior to the presbyter, and alone qualified to ordain.[19] He insisted, however, that this could not be settled by Scripture, and that episcopal ordination, though supported by antiquity and reason and not contradicted by Scripture, was not uniquely valid.[20] Hooker went on to plead that God himself sometimes validated extraordinary exceptions to the ordinary rule:

> The whole Church visible being the true original subject of all power, it hath not ordinarily allowed any other than bishops alone to ordain; howbeit, as the ordinary course is ordinarily in all things to be observed, so it may be in some cases not unnecessary that we decline from the ordinary ways.
>
> Men may be extraordinarily, yet allowably, two ways admitted unto spiritual functions in the church. One is when God himself doth of himself raise up any whose labour he useth without requiring that men should authorize them; but then he doth ratify their calling by manifest signs and tokens himself from heaven. . . .
>
> Another extraordinary kind of vocation is when the exigence of necessity doth constrain to leave the usual ways of the church which otherwise we would willingly keep: where the church must needs have some ordained, and neither hath nor can have possibly a bishop to ordain; in case of such necessity the ordinary institution of God hath given oftentimes, and may give, place. And therefore we are not simply without exception to urge a lineal descent of power from the apostles by continued succession of bishops in every effectual ordination. These cases of inevitable necessity excepted, none may ordain but only bishops: by the imposition of their hands it is that the church giveth power of order both unto presbyters and deacons.[21]

Wesley believed himself to have received both an ordinary call conferred by episcopal hands and an extraordinary call validated by the testimony of the Holy Spirit.

As in the conferment of the ministerial calling, so in its exercise, Wesley found support in Hooker for his view that the bishop was only of the *bene esse*, not of the *esse* of the church, and that the bishop was the servant of the church as the church was the servant of God. Hooker went on:

> Now when that power so received is once to have any certain

subject whereon it may work and whereunto it is to be tied, *here cometh in the people's consent, and not before.* The power of order I may lawfully receive without asking leave of any multitude; but that power I cannot exercise upon any one certain people utterly against their wills; neither is there in the Church of England any man by order of law possessed with pastoral charge over any parish but the people in effect do choose him thereunto.[22]

Although this reasoning made against the congregational polity in ordination it supported it in the appointment of a minister, just as it gave at least a modicum of justification for Wesley's invasion of a parish by the request of the parishioners in spite of the incumbent's denial and the bishop's wrath. As the years went by Wesley could also use such arguments to justify the extraordinary call of his lay preachers[23] and eventually his own assumption of the power of ordination. Meantime they supported him as he recognized the possibility that the Anglican hierarchy might turn against him. In that case he was resolved not to separate himself from them by turning dissenting minister, but to obey them as far as in conscience he could. He was quite prepared to suffer the consequences of thus obeying the voice of God within if indeed it were eventually to urge him to ecclesiastical disobedience:

> But what if a bishop forbids this? I do not say, as St. Cyprian, *Populus a scelerato antistite separare se debet.* ['People ought to separate themselves from a wicked bishop' (i.e. 'presiding priest')]. But I say, God being my helper I will obey Him still; and if I suffer for it, His will be done.[24]

By this time popular opinion was turning against the Methodists. Although their preaching might be unfamiliar but orthodox, and although they sincerely and legitimately claimed that they intended no breach with the Church of England, the results of their preaching among the dispossessed proved very disturbing to the more comfortable, sedate, and formally religious churchgoers. As a Student of Christ Church Charles Wesley courteously waited on the Dean, Dr. John Conybeare, when he visited Oxford. His *Journal* entries from December 1738 to July 1739 reveal the dean's increasing perturbation. This was especially marked during the week-end of 30 June to 3 July, when Charles returned to preach the university sermon, taking as his subject justification by faith. On the 30th the dean 'spoke with unusual severity against field-preaching and Mr. Whitefield'. On the 2nd Wesley was requested to visit the Vice-Chancellor, who though he approved Wesley's account of the Methodists 'objected the irregularity of our doing good in other men's parishes'. On the Tuesday night Wesley held another conference with Dr. Conybeare, who tried his hardest to dissuade him 'from preaching abroad, from expounding in houses, from singing psalms'.[25] Uneasy tolerance gradually gave way to a furious outburst of charges of 'enthusiasm'—the eighteenth-century equivalent of religious mania. During the year 1739 the Methodists were subjected to a hundred such printed attacks.[26]

The chief target of this abuse was George Whitefield, much more of a showman than either of his older colleagues, as well as more tactless in his uninhibited piety. All three leaders kept journals, but Whitefield was far less cautious both in his over-hasty publication and insufficient editing both of subject matter and phraseology. Against the advice of Charles Wesley, who corrected the copy for the press, he had published the first instalment of his *Journal* in 1738, and three more in 1739.[27] Charles Wesley's journal was never published during his lifetime, and the first of John's remarkable twenty-one extracts did not appear until the summer of 1740. In 1740 Whitefield continued to draw the fire upon himself by attacks upon familiar idols such as Archbishop Tillotson and *The Whole Duty of Man* as well as by undue self-exposure in his *Short Account of God's Dealings with the Reverend Mr. George Whitefield*. Little wonder that Wesley felt it necessary to plead that those criticizing either the doctrines, conduct, or separatist tendencies of Methodism, should not base their judgments solely upon the public utterances of George Whitefield. Whitefield's incautious exuberance, however, may well have proved a salutary warning to the Wesleys. They continued avowedly to follow where the Holy Spirit led, even into innovations potentially sectarian, but they exercised greater restraint than their younger colleague.

It was Whitefield who drew the first episcopal visitation charge against the Methodists. In August 1739 Edmund Gibson published *The Bishop of London's Pastoral Letter to the people of his diocese . . . by way of caution against lukewarmness on one hand and enthusiasm on the other*, which went through four editions that year. Nearly two-thirds of its fifty-five pages were devoted to the attack on enthusiasm, with White-field's *Journal* furnishing the major exhibit. Within two weeks Whitefield published an *Answer*—one of his better writings. He took up exactly the same position that John Wesley was at the time defending against Joseph Butler, Bishop of Bristol: that Methodism did not pretend to any 'extraordinary operations of the Holy Spirit', but simply an expectant receptiveness to His normal presence in Christian believers. Again like the Wesleys, Whitefield protested his complete loyalty to the church in maintaining the possibility of regeneration:

My constant way of preaching is, first to prove my propositions by Scripture, and then to illustrate them by the Articles and collects of the Church of England. Those that have heard me can witness how often I have exhorted them to be constant at the public service of the church. I attend on it myself, and would read the public liturgy every day if your Lordship's clergy would give me leave.[28]

Whitefield's less co-ordinated activities may have been more culpable in the eyes of church leaders, but the Wesleys clearly associated themselves with him, and during his second absence in America from August 1739 to March 1741 public attention was naturally diverted to their societies. Strenuous opposition against the Wesleys was indeed no novelty. Most Anglican pulpits had been closed against them since 1738, even when sympathetic clergy attempted to keep them open. Driven from pulpit to field the Methodists aroused still further clerical antagonism. Again Whitefield had led the way, but speedily challenged his older colleagues to follow the example that he had apparently copied from the Welsh layman Howell Harris, and possibly others.[29] John Wesley himself found it extremely difficult to overcome his ingrained prejudice by becoming a regular 'field-preacher', even though he had on several occasions taken his stand in the open air before Whitefield was ordained as well as after. He prepared himself for this momentous occasion by expounding the Sermon on the Mount— 'one pretty remarkable precedent of field-preaching'—and by recalling how on board ship and in Georgia he had preached under the sky for lack of a church or a large enough house, and of that more recent occasion the previous November when his diary recorded that he 'preached to the mob' at a Tyburn execution.[30]

Occasional preaching in the open air was one thing, the deliberate acceptance of preaching outside parish churches as a normal method of evangelism quite another, especially for this staid little clergyman so prejudiced in favour of doing everything decently and in order and according to the rules and customs of his beloved church. It was the beginning of a new epoch not only for England but for John Wesley himself when on 2 April 1739 he 'submitted to be more vile, and proclaimed in the highways the glad tidings of salvation, speaking from a little eminence in a ground adjoining to the city [of Bristol], to about three thousand people'.[31] A generation later, again in Bristol, he still confessed: 'To this day field-preaching is a cross to me. But I know my commission, and see no other way of "preaching the gospel to every creature".'[32]

Meanwhile Whitefield, supported by Charles Wesley, had been

drawing great open-air congregations in London, one of his preaching-stands being a raised tombstone in the churchyard of St. Mary's, Islington. During this same month of April 1739 opposition against the Methodists drew to a head there. Although in this instance Charles Wesley was the main target, John Wesley also became involved in 'the Islington case', and indeed in the first part of his *Farther Appeal* took over the role of chief protagonist. In this incident may be discerned a pattern for future charges that the Wesleys broke the canon law by dis-regarding parish boundaries and by disturbing the ordered worship of the church.

The Rev. George Stonehouse, curate of St. Mary's, had frequently opened his pulpit to the Wesleys and Whitefield, but the protests of his church officers increased with the growing unpopularity of the Methodists. Some supporter of the Islington officials (possibly the bishop of London himself) directed their attention to a neat method of ridding themselves of the unwanted preachers and circumventing their minister's encouragement of the Wesleys. This involved invoking canon laws which were almost forgotten, universally neglected, and in any case of somewhat doubtful application.[33] Canons 47–54 of the *Constitutions and Canons Ecclesiastical* of 1603 dealt with preachers coming from outside the parish. Canon 50 was clear:

> Neither the minister, churchwardens, nor any other officers of the church, shall suffer any man to preach within their churches or chapels but such as by showing their licence to preach shall appear unto them to be sufficiently authorized thereunto, as is aforesaid.

Canon 48 showed that the licence must be in writing under the hand and seal of the bishop, and must specifically refer to the parish involved. Canon 52 provided that the churchwardens should maintain a book recording the names of such strangers so that 'the bishop may under-stand (if occasion so require) . . . who presume to preach without licence'.[34]

On 15 April 1739 the Islington churchwardens, after appropriate schooling, asked to see Charles Wesley's licence to preach in their parish. He had no such licence, of course, but duly inscribed his name in the book which they tendered him.[35] On Friday 27 April Whitefield was similarly asked to produce his licence; instead of forcing the issue he went outside and preached in the churchyard from a raised tomb-stone.[36] On the following Sunday Charles Wesley again came to preach. The wardens again demanded his 'local licence', and when this was not forthcoming forbade his preaching, to which he simply replied 'I hear you'. When he attempted to mount the pulpit after prayers the beadle forcibly held him back, and he submitted without a struggle, though he did assist at the Lord's Supper later. After the service the churchwardens summoned a vestry meeting, which recorded the following minute:

> Resolved, that it appears to this vestry that the Rev. Stonehouse is the real occasion of the frequent disturbances in this church and churchyard, by his introducing strangers to preach in this church, particularly Mr. Charles Wesley, Mr. Whitfield, and other unlicenced persons, by encouraging and promising to stand by and indemnify them in their preaching without producing their licences as the canon directs.
>
> Resolved, that it be referred to the churchwardens and others, or any five of them, to draw up a presentment to be exhibited by the churchwarden to the Bishop of London or his surrogate at the next visitation relative to the aforesaid facts.[37]

The following day Stonehouse waited on the bishop, found him 'sour', and was persuaded to sign an agreement that he would 'absolutely refuse the granting his pulpit to Mr. John Wesley, Mr. Charles Wesley, and Mr. George Whitefield, and that those gentlemen shall not officiate any more for him in the parish church or churchyard in any part of the duty whatsoever'.[38]

In this instance at least the archbishop seemed to support the bishop of London against the Wesleys, for a technical breach of canon law was indeed involved. When the Rev. Henry Piers of Bexley sought permission for the Wesleys to preach in his church, Potter forbade it on account of the Islington precedent. Charles Wesley protested to the archbishop that the Holy Spirit was at work in Methodism, and that possibly Gamaliel's advice was applicable in this instance—'let them alone: for . . . if it be of God ye cannot overthrow it'.[39] This touched a raw nerve, however, and Potter hinted at excommunication, whereupon Charles tactlessly reminded him that in his own book on church government he had claimed that unjust excommunication did not cut a man off from Christ. Small wonder that on this occasion at least the archbishop dismissed Wesley 'with all the marks of his displeasure'.[40]

Thus the year 1739 witnessed both increasing Methodist activity outside the parish churches and society rooms and increasing tension with the ecclesiastical authorities. The same was true in Bristol as in London. Here Whitefield had preached in the open air and had then been offered pulpits, only to have them speedily closed by order of the chancellor of the diocese. From the chancellor he appealed to the bishop himself, Joseph Butler of *Analogy* fame, but with little success.

It appears that the bishops had put their heads together, and the Islington strategy of enforcing outmoded canons was applied in Bristol. Even the prison was closed to Whitefield's ministrations, and the sky remained his ceiling.[41] It was to this ministry that he enlisted John Wesley's aid.

This year of 1739 was in many ways unique for Wesley. For the first and only occasion in his life he spent more time in Bristol than in London. He found it difficult to tear himself away from the fruitful opportunities for evangelism and society-building. Apart from a hurried week's visit to London in June he remained in Bristol for five months, preaching in the open air, organizing bands, settling disputes, even beginning to build his first chapel, prudently called a new 'room' or 'schoolhouse'. When Whitefield returned in July it was to acknowledge that 'Bristol had great reason to bless God for the ministry of Mr. John Wesley'.[42]

Ecclesiastical storm-clouds were gathering, however. Already Whitefield had been in trouble. Now again he was challenged. Being delayed by a shipping embargo from setting out on his second voyage to America he visited the west. He received a letter from the kindly bishop of Gloucester, Dr. Martin Benson (who had ordained him in 1736) affectionately advising him that he ought not to preach in the parishes of other men, and also warning him of the danger of being 'over-righteous' and of claiming special revelations from the Holy Spirit. Defending the preaching of himself and his colleagues Whitefield concluded: 'But, my Lord, if you and the rest of the bishops cast us out, our great and common Master will take us up.' Whitefield's *Journal* for 10 July records:

> Heard today that the town clerk of Bristol did my brother Wesley and me the honour to desire the grand jury at their Quarter Sessions to prevent our meetings and to have the Riot Act read; but they did not regard him, nay one . . . offered to subscribe to any fine rather than do anything against us, who, he said, were true servants of Jesus Christ.[43]

Later in the summer, after the bishop of Bristol had returned to his diocese from his parliamentary labours in London, Wesley had two interviews with him, when they discussed the orthodoxy and decorum of Methodist practices. At the longer interview on 18 August Wesley maintained that Methodist teaching was simply that of the Anglican *Homilies*, claimed that he had not administered the Lord's Supper in his societies, nor intended so to do, and responded to the bishop's charge that he was 'not commissioned to preach in this diocese' with the bold assertion that he would nevertheless continue to preach there, both because his divine commission was superior to any episcopal veto, and because as a Fellow of a college he was not restricted to any parish. This forthright challenge to Butler should be quoted in full:

My Lord, my business on earth is to do what good I can. Wherever therefore I think I can do most good, there must I stay so long as I think so. At present I think I can do most good here; therefore here I stay. As to my preaching here, a dispensation of the gospel is committed to me, and woe is me if I preach not the gospel wherever I am in the habitable world. Your Lordship knows, being ordained a priest, by the commission I then received I am a priest of the church universal: and being ordained as Fellow of a College I was not limited to any particular cure, but have an indeterminate commission to preach the word of God in any part of England. I do not therefore conceive that in preaching here by this commission I break any human law. When I am convinced I do, then it will be time to ask, 'Shall I obey God or man?' But if I should be convinced in the meanwhile that I could advance the glory of God and the salvation of souls in any other place more than in Bristol, in that hour by God's help I will go hence, which till then I may not do.[44]

However stubborn they might be, however difficult to fit easily into any conventional category, the Wesleys demonstrated that they were no dissenters. They supported the Church of England on every possible occasion, and continued to rebaptize converts from dissent. Butler also was subjected to notices of such rebaptism.[45] As a result the brothers found themselves equally in trouble with both Anglicans and dissenters. Bishop Gibson apparently felt at one time that the Wesleys ought to leave the church in order to prosecute their task unhampered, but their conscience forbade this step.[46] Constantly they tried to keep within the bounds of ecclesiastical law, though at the same time insisting that the law of God was superior to that of the church, and might sometimes conflict with it. They were forthright in defending this point of view in private interviews with the bishops, but tactful in keeping those interviews private—far more tactful in this than was their colleague George Whitefield.

Not until 1744 did either brother venture into print against any of the bishops, or even mention them in print, so that details of their episcopal contacts can be gleaned only from manuscript fragments and later reminiscences. Wesley claimed that Gibson acknowledged his obligation that the Methodist advantage had not been pressed unduly.[47] Other episcopal interviews followed, both with Potter and Gibson. Indeed it seems that Edmund Gibson was really responsible for the

6

publication of Wesley's sermon on *Christian Perfection* in September 1741. Several times in later years Wesley told the story with slightly varying details, the best-known narrative being that in his *Plain Account of Christian Perfection* (1767):

> I think it was in the latter end of the year 1740 that I had a conversation with Dr. Gibson, then bishop of London, at Whitehall. He asked me what I meant by perfection. I told him without any disguise or reserve. When I ceased speaking he said, 'Mr. Wesley, if this be all you mean, publish it to all the world. If anyone then can confute what you say he may have free leave'. I answered, 'My Lord, I will', and accordingly wrote and published the sermon on Christian perfection.

Not for a moment, however, did Wesley embarrass the bishop by the merest hint of his endorsement in the publication itself.[48]

The first notice in print of such episcopal interviews occurred in John Wesley's *Journal* under the date 12 May 1742, though in fact this extract was not published until 1749. Even so it was very circumspect:

> I waited on the archbishop of Canterbury with Mr. Whitefield, and again on Friday [the 14th], as also on the bishop of London. I trust if we should be called to appear before princes we should not be ashamed.[49]

The main topic of conversation may well have been the inexpediency of the large open-air gatherings which both Wesley and Whitefield had been addressing in London, and which were accompanied by extensive mobbing as well as numerous conversions. But this is only surmise.[50] Upon the evidence of a document preserved by Henry Moore, however, it seems that by 1741 the archbishop had begun to modify his support of the Methodists, especially in view of their widespread field-preaching. This document incorporates Wesley's brief answers to a number of questions from an overseas correspondent, and includes the following:

> 10. Why the bishops do not effectually inhibit them and hinder their field- and street-preaching?
> The bishops do not inhibit their field- and street-preaching: (1) Because there is no law in England against it. (2) Because God does not yet suffer them to do it without law.
> 11. Whether the Archbishop of Canterbury is satisfied with them, as we are told?

The Archbishop of Canterbury is not satisfied with them, especially since Mr. Molther, in the name of the Moravian Church, told his Grace their disapprobation of them and in particular of their field-preaching.[51]

The Wesleys appear to have maintained their defences carefully so as to forestall any outright episcopal attack on their free-lance evangelism. Nevertheless, it seems quite clear that from 1739 Edmund Gibson used his influence to close the pulpits of his diocese to the Wesleys and their colleagues.[52] Samuel Wesley had surmised that in spite of the lax discipline of the church any such example of repression might spread throughout the country. Casual conversations among bishops pursuing their duties in the House of Lords might well have furthered this, even if there were no deliberate concerted action, and this seems to have been the case in Bristol. At least one other example of episcopal obstruction, in Wales this time, was reported by Wesley in his *Journal* for 3 March 1742:

I rode to Llantrisant, and sent to the minister to desire the use of his church. His answer was, he should have been very willing, but the bishop [Dr. John Gilbert] had forbidden him. By what law? I am not legally convicted either of heresy or any other crime. By what authority, then, am I suspended from preaching? By bare-faced arbitrary power.

This direct attack on episcopal authority, be it noted, was not published until 1749.[53]

In later years John Wesley claimed that the various archbishops of Canterbury and bishops of London had been kept 'thoroughly acquainted with every step we took' without issuing any reprimand, except that 'Archbishop Potter once said, "those gentlemen are irregular; but they have done good, and I pray God to bless them".'[54] Old age may well have erased some of the minor emergencies from Wesley's mind, but it could hardly have transformed a picture of continual warfare into one of settled peace.

FIVE

SOCIETIES, PREACHERS, AND COMMUNION

IN 1781 John Wesley yielded to importunity by publishing in four volumes a *Concise Ecclesiastical History*, based mainly on Mosheim's work. This was supposed to take the reader 'to the beginning of the present century', but Wesley had a change of mind and described the eighteenth century also, appending to volume four a hundred-page 'Short History of the People called Methodists', dated at the end 'November 16, 1781'. The 78-year-old author was perhaps spurred to his task in part by the fact that Mosheim's English editor, Dr. M'Laine, had in his appendix listed the Methodists as heretics. Wesley looked back over the years and corrected this assertion by a summary of the more important events in the growth of his separatist movement. In addition he strove to point out the significance of those events. Especially does he enable us to see that in his opinion the differentiating feature of Methodism was the society. He distinguished three 'rises' or experimental beginnings for the movement:

> The first rise of Methodism, so called, was in November 1729, when four of us met together at Oxford; the second was at Savannah in April 1736, when twenty or thirty persons met at my house; the last was at London on [1 May 1738], when forty or fifty of us agreed to meet together every Wednesday evening, in order to a free conversation, begun and ended with singing and prayer.[1]

For Wesley the evolution of Methodism was the development of these groups of people meeting for Christian fellowship in addition to their normal worship in parish church or (occasionally) dissenting meeting-house. The first 'people called Methodists' in Wesley's day were Oxford students and dons, a group confined to one sex and one stratum in society. The second group was both larger and much more representative, including both men and women from a wider though lower stratum, and forming an integral part of the life of an Anglican parish of which either John or Charles Wesley was the minister. The third group was larger still, and much more cosmopolitan, including German Moravians as well as English churchmen, and recognizing one representative of each as their joint founders—Peter Böhler and John Wesley.

In spite of its mixed membership the Fetter Lane society was similar to most of the older religious societies which already existed in London and Westminster and Bristol and elsewhere, known from their original inspirers as Horneck's or Woodward's societies.[2] Even though clerical supervision by the parish minister had almost died out these religious societies were still recognized as an integral part of the Church of England. Any doubt about the allegiance of the Fetter Lane society caused by the omission from its orders of any reference to the Church of England is dispelled by the fact that they went in a body to communion at St. Paul's Cathedral, expelled two members 'because they disowned themselves members of the Church of England', and 're-admitted' another lapsed member after he had 'gladly returned to the church'.[3] At the same time this society was more flexible both in its membership and its programme, placing far greater emphasis upon personal spiritual experience than upon theological discussion. One most important innovation was the introduction of the tiny confessional cells known as 'bands'.[4]

Böhler left for America a few days after the founding of the society on 1 May 1738, and John Wesley remained its acknowledged spiritual director—though this term of Horneck's does not appear to have been used. Both Wesley brothers became so involved in their widespread evangelism, however, that the close supervision of the Fetter Lane society increasingly slipped from their grasp, and was taken over by their able young lieutenant James Hutton, in whose bookshop the group seems first to have met. The position deteriorated while John Wesley tasted the joys of the forbidden fruit of field-preaching during his lengthy absence in Bristol.

Bristol was the third largest city in the kingdom, exceeded only by London and Norwich. Wesley was welcomed so enthusiastically that Whitefield was able to say his 'Nunc dimittis'. Treading in Whitefield's footsteps Wesley preached in the open air (as well as from an occasional friendly pulpit) and visited the old religious societies, bringing to them new spiritual vigour. Two of the societies were especially receptive, those in Nicholas Street and Baldwin Street. Strangers eager to delve more fully into the spiritual truths outlined during the field-preaching pressed for admission when it was known that Wesley was continuing his scriptural expositions therein. Both rooms became overcrowded. Determined to make adequate provision for the tremendous influx of spiritual seekers, on 9 May 1739 Wesley secured a piece of land in the Horsefair to build a room 'large enough to contain both the societies of Nicholas and Baldwin Streets and such of their acquaintance as might desire to be present with them at such times as the Scripture was expounded'. Three days later the first stone was laid, and on Sunday evening 3 June, in view of difficulties at both the other rooms, Wesley 'made shift' to meet in the unfinished shell of the new room. For a time the landlord of the Baldwin Street room was placated, but Nicholas Street was lost for ever. The difficulties almost certainly arose from somewhat uproarious meetings such as that on 21 May, when Thomas Maxfield was converted, roaring and beating himself so much that six men had difficulty in holding him down. The 'New Room in the Horsefair', unfinished or not, rapidly became the headquarters for sympathizers with Wesley and Whitefield from all over the city. Another building was begun in Kingswood, three miles away, so as to give better service to the unchurched colliers. In both buildings, children were taught, so that both were often termed 'schoolrooms' as well as 'society-rooms'.[5]

Wesley continued to visit other religious societies in the Bristol area, but the focus of his energies as spiritual director was the New Room. During his absence for a week while he looked into the dissensions undermining the Fetter Lane society in London, the Bristol societies also showed signs of disintegrating into factions. The application of firm spiritual discipline upon his return established them once more. Gradually under his leadership they achieved both religious vitality, unity, and a sense of identity which distinguished them from the other religious societies. At some time during the summer of 1739 they began to call themselves 'The United Society', a term which might have arisen from the amalgamation of the two main groups, but which became a rallying title applied to all other societies throughout the country acknowledging allegiance to the Wesleys. Wesley himself seems first to have used the term in his diary for 30 October 1739, on the eve of his return to London. It remained in use for about thirty years.[6]

The example of a unified society under his own sole direction, meeting in premises for which he alone was responsible, had proved so fruitful in Bristol that Wesley welcomed the opportunity of a similar organization in the metropolis, especially as at the Fetter Lane society his choice seemed to lie between the new fad of silence and noisy disputes. Nor did he feel able to bulldoze his way through the mass of obstructions to genuine spiritual progress. The absence of his diary prevents us from following his actions this time as closely as we would wish. It seems, however, that on Sunday 11 November 1739 he preached in the ruins of the 'old foundery' where the king's cannon used to be made, and accepted an offer to secure the building on a lease. In December that year a new society was meeting there, and the building was rapidly being renovated and fitted up to provide not only a large society room but also a schoolroom, as well as living quarters for the Wesleys, their helpers, and even the widowed Susanna Wesley. The pioneer experiments in Bristol were repeated in London, with far greater assurance, and with a fuller realization of their significance. It was now clear that Wesley was not only providing for the religious needs of a new group of converts arising from his preaching, but a commodious headquarters for all those who sought his spiritual direction in whatever way. When in 1740 dissension at Fetter Lane developed into a rupture most members remained behind to form the first purely Moravian society in London. The rest followed Wesley and joined his 'Foundery' society, which by June 1740 thus became three hundred strong.[7]

When a few years later Wesley came to describe the origin of the Methodist society as distinct from the old religious societies, he gave pride of place to this far larger group in London, telling how 'in the latter end of the year 1739' he agreed to meet with a group on Thursday evenings and to act as their spiritual director. 'Thus arose,' he said, 'without any previous design on either side, what was afterwards called a Society—a very innocent name, and very common in London for any number of people associating themselves together.'[8] There was an important difference, however. These people owed their primary allegiance to Wesley and to Wesley alone, rather than to any church or closely church-related group. They too were given the title 'United Society' first used in Bristol, which now meant in effect 'Methodist Society'. Wesley defended this organization from charges of 'making a schism' or 'gathering churches out of churches' by pointing out that most of the members were previously heathens and knew no Christian fellowship elsewhere. Nevertheless he did speak of at least some of them as 'gathered out of . . . other congregations' for special fellowship, not at the cost of separating from those congregations, but rather so that they might return to them spiritually invigorated. Thus although his societies had some affinities with the 'gathered church' of Nonconformist tradition this affinity must certainly not be construed as either dependence or equivalence.[9]

As with the older Anglican religious societies and the new Fetter Lane experiment, Wesley had implanted in his own 'Methodist' societies the 'bands', each cell consisting of four or five persons only, of the same sex and marital status. At Bristol in February 1742 a new subdivision of the society originated—the 'class'. The story is well known of how this began with Captain Foy's suggestion of a penny-a-week fund to wipe off the debt on the New Room, he himself volunteering to collect from about twelve members living in his own neighbourhood. Wesley speedily realized the pastoral significance of this expedient, and soon these groups of twelve people of both sexes were meeting weekly for fellowship of a somewhat less searching kind than that of the bands. For both bands and classes Wesley appointed lay leaders who were responsible under him for the spiritual oversight of these members. It was a close-knit family system which made so many demands and maintained so many checks on deed and word and even thought that it is remarkable that most Methodists had time not only for normal parish activities but in fact attended to them more faithfully than did the non-Methodists.[10]

In his *Journal*, published seven years later, Wesley described how he came to transplant the same class system into the much larger London societies. When this account was eventually reprinted in his collected *Works* he prefixed it with the asterisk which showed that he regarded this paragraph as of peculiar importance:

Thur. 25 [April, 1742]. I appointed several earnest and sensible men to meet me, to whom I showed the great difficulty I had long found of knowing the people who desired to be under my care. [There were now well over a thousand in London alone.] After much discourse they all agreed there could be no better way to come to a sure, thorough knowledge of each person than to divide them into classes like those at Bristol, under the inspection of those in whom I could most confide. This was the origin of our classes at London, for which I can never sufficiently praise God, the unspeakable usefulness of the institution having ever since been more and more manifest.[11]

Wesley was careful that no meetings were held in the Foundery and the Bristol New Room during the hours of public service at the local parish churches, and in fact led his followers to church in a troop for divine worship and Holy Communion. Nevertheless, the Methodist premises were under no Anglican oversight but his own, and he was quite prepared to welcome dissenters there without any stipulation that they first become good churchmen, provided that they acknowledged themselves in spiritual need.[12] Although it was assumed that the bulk of the members were or would become loyal Anglicans no credal or ecclesiastical test was imposed. In this respect Wesley's societies were less rigid than the original Fetter Lane society.

In order to preserve the good name of his society, however, as well as to confirm the sincerity of the members' Christian professions, he did find it necessary to impose some ethical tests. As visible tokens of approved membership tickets were given four times a year to those whose daily living supported their professed desire of salvation. The withholding of the ticket proved an efficient means of discipline for those who fell short in this respect. This method was first used for the Bristol bands in February 1741, and later for those in London. Soon it spread to the more heterogeneous classes, and in 1743 became universally binding on Methodists by the publication of the most famous of Wesley's many sets of 'orders' or 'rules'. This formed an important landmark in the self-identification of the Methodist societies, one similar to that which had been taken a year earlier by the Welsh Calvinistic Methodist societies.[13]

The publication of *The Nature, Design, and General Rules of the United Societies in London, Bristol, King's-wood, and Newcastle upon Tyne* was urged upon Wesley by the disappointing results of a tour of his northern societies. This revealed not only a lack of discipline but even of common morality, which was bringing Methodism into disrepute. The chief purpose of the pamphlet was to lay down general principles of conduct and to illustrate these by specific examples. Henceforth all new members were handed a copy of this handbook of Methodist *mores*. Applicants were still admitted into membership upon a mere profession of 'a desire to flee from the wrath to come, to be saved from their sins', but they could only be *continued* in membership as they proved the sincerity of their professed desire by translating words into deeds. Three critical areas of conduct were mapped out—avoiding evil, doing good, and 'attending upon all the ordinances of God', namely 'the public worship of God; the ministry of the Word, either read or expounded; the supper of the Lord; family and private prayer; searching the Scriptures; and fasting, or abstinence'.[14]

Wesley had accepted without qualm the idea of laymen serving as leaders in the various bands and classes, and also as stewards of the societies in general, responsible for the collection and disbursement of money and for maintaining accounts. Already in some instances he had gone further. While in Georgia he had committed pastoral responsibility to Charles Delamotte during his own absence from Savannah, and reposed a similar trust in John Cennick in Bristol, and James Hutton in London. A newly-rising layman, Thomas Maxfield, thus served him as sub-pastor both in Bristol and London. In that capacity these men might deliver an address to the assembled society, relating their own religious experience and challenging their hearers with the need for spiritual awareness and decision. Wesley remained sufficient of a high churchman, however, to be convinced that only a deacon ordained to the ministry of the Word was entitled to venture upon the authoritative exposition of Holy Scripture.

Both John and Charles Wesley knew that the danger of separation from the church threatened if once these laymen sought an enhanced status by advancing from the occasional exhortation to the regular sermon, for the next step would be their administration of the sacraments. Thus the lay assistant might first trespass upon the functions of the ordained deacon and then upon those of the ordained priest. John Wesley sought to nip this danger in the bud while he was absent in Oxford during the winter of 1738. On that occasion he warned James Hutton against appointing permanent lay officers responsible for the general spiritual oversight of the Fetter Lane society, which was the minister's prerogative: 'If we should begin with appointing fixed persons to execute *pro officio* one part of the pastoral office I doubt it would not end there.'[15] The problem arose again almost as soon as John Wesley left London for Bristol, so that his return was urgently requested. His brother Charles reported on 18 April 1739 that John Shaw, one of the original members of the society, 'insisted that there is no priesthood, but he himself could baptize and administer the other sacrament as well as any man'. Charles spoke to the whole society on this issue, and 'warned them strongly against schism, into which Shaw's notions must necessarily lead'.[16] On 16 May, he recorded, 'at Fetter Lane a dispute arose about lay-preaching', and on the anniversary of his brother's conversion, Charles was chided by his old friend John Bray 'for checking the course of the Spirit'—in general by his stand against lay preaching and in particular by his opposition to Shaw, whom Charles termed 'the self-ordained priest'.[17] At a meeting of the society on 6 June 'Shaw pleaded for his spirit of prophecy' and charged Charles Wesley with 'love of pre-eminence'. Both he and a supporter 'declared themselves no longer members of the Church of England', whereon Charles admitted that he was relieved at thus being freed from pastoral responsibility for them: 'Now am I clear of them. By renouncing the Church they have discharged me.' A week later the society 'consented *nem. con.* that their names should be erased out of the society-book because they disowned themselves members of the Church of England'.[18] For the time being the danger of separation had been averted by the self-exclusion of over-enthusiastic (and perhaps over-ambitious) laymen. The possibility of laymen preaching as well as assuming pastoral responsibilities within the religious societies, however, was far from settled. In August 1739 Charles Wesley asked William Law's opinion on the matter, and found that he also was 'fully against the laymen's expounding as the very worst thing both for themselves and others'.[19]

Much of the evidence for John Wesley's eventual acceptance of the institution of lay preaching is either obscure or conflicting. The uncertainties have been compounded by the frequent assumption that the Methodist movement was something quite unique or at least quite distinct from the evangelical revival which was already in progress in 1739, and which continued alongside that element of it which John Wesley himself directed. This wave of spiritual renewal probably began with the Pietist movement in Germany, and had already spread to the British Isles and America. The Welsh movement under Howell Harris and the Rev. Daniel Rowlands and others, first independently, then in co-operation, had been in progress for some years. Revival came to the Highlands of Scotland in 1739, and to Cornwall as early or even earlier. Both in London and elsewhere the Moravians were now making a direct Pietist witness. In Bristol the Rev. William Morgan had preached in the open air a year before Whitefield came. Each evangelist raised not only enemies but supporters and converts. Some of these in their turn became focal points for free-lance evangelism, like Whitefield's convert Robert Seagrave. The preaching of the Wesleys also brought to birth evangelists who owed only a passing allegiance to the Methodist societies, or none at all. In the spiritual ferment of the day other local leaders arose apart from any cause now determinable, made their brief mark, and vanished.

It seems fairly clear that most of these evangelists were like each other and different from the Wesleys in two things—their preaching tended strongly towards Calvinistic predestinarianism, and even if nominally members of the Church of England they refused to be hampered by its conventions, and frequently ended up as pastors of independent congregations. In the early years of the revival the Wesleys moved fairly freely in and out of these intersecting circles of evangelical activity, and preachers who eventually made their spiritual homes elsewhere (or who remained religious gypsies) appeared for a time in the Methodist societies. Gradually two factors distinguished Wesley's followers from the remainder—their Arminian teaching and their firm resolve to stay within the Church of England. One added factor (setting aside for the moment considerations of divine guidance and assistance) assured the Methodists of growth into a national movement and a mistaken reputation as the sole originators of the revival—John Wesley's organizing genius.

Neither the spread of the Methodist societies nor their proliferation into a connected network of evangelical pockets throughout the land would have been possible without the itinerant lay preacher, Wesley's 'helper', 'assistant', other self. The story of how the brothers came to accept this kind of help on a regular basis has not yet been told in any detail, nor is this the place to embark on such an essay, however interesting and important. Wesley's own testimony about how he accepted Thomas Maxfield as his first 'son in the gospel' was set down long after the event and contains elements which conflict among themselves and with some contemporary evidence. It is quite impossible to assign priority to any one person as Wesley's 'first lay preacher' without first sub-dividing that broad category in some way, and even then being content to speak somewhat tentatively.

Certainly Charles Delamotte functioned in some such capacity for Wesley in Georgia. Howell Harris embarked on his remarkable career as a lay pioneer of the Welsh revival as early as 1735, and although his relations with the Wesleys blew first hot, then cold, he was on very friendly terms with them in 1739, and in the summer of 1740 both joined the Foundery society and served as Charles Wesley's assistant there. More remarkable still, when they moved to Bristol Charles Wesley actually asked this layman to preach in the presence of a minister, witness Harris's own diary: 'June 25 [1740] . . . I was persuaded by Brother Charles to discourse in the New Room, and so did on I Cor. xiii.'[20] A little later that same year Charles Wesley invited another layman to address the Kingswood colliers, although William Seward's few words on this occasion aroused some doubt in Wesley's mind about the authenticity of his call to preach. This was on 23 September 1740. A month later Seward was mobbed so severely while preaching that he died of his injuries, the first Methodist martyr.[21]

One of Charles Wesley's early converts was Joseph Humphreys, who preached his first sermon on 18 June 1738, and while still a student training for the dissenting ministry at a private academy founded a religious society in Deptford. In 1790 John Wesley spoke of him as 'the first lay preacher that assisted me in England in the year 1738'.[22] After being given time to amend his ways, at Christmas 1739 Humphreys was expelled from his academy for preaching before ordination. John Wesley welcomed his help even in the Methodist headquarters on at least a temporary basis, and Humphreys' autobiography fills in some of the details: 'On September 1st, 1740, I began to preach at the Foundery, in London, to Mr. Wesley's congregation.'[23]

Far better known as a pioneer Methodist lay preacher is John Cennick. Converted in 1737, before Cennick met Wesley in March 1739 he had begun a religious society in Reading. Accepted by Wesley as a teacher for his new school at Kingswood, Cennick also preached to the colliers there on 14 June that year. For over a year Wesley countenanced his preaching as a supplement to his teaching, until along with his growing Calvinism developed a strongly critical tendency, which the

Wesleys came to believe that he exercised in such an underhand way as to merit his dismissal in March 1741.[24]

It is interesting to note that in his letter to Cennick (which John Wesley failed to deliver) Charles Wesley referred to Cennick's having 'served under [John Wesley] in the gospel as a son'.[25] The term 'son in the gospel' seems certainly to have been used in later days by the Wesleys as a technical term to distinguish the full-time itinerant lay preachers from those whose services were accepted only occasionally and locally. John Wesley maintained that Thomas Maxfield was the first to occupy this specific position, though it seems likely that had Cennick remained within the fold his name would have replaced that of Maxfield. In Welsh Calvinistic Methodism such men were known as 'public exhorters', and it is interesting to note that the first three names listed under this heading in the minutes of the first recorded Welsh Association (for 5 and 6 January 1743) are not unfamiliar: 'Mr. Howell Harris, Mr. Joseph Humphries, Mr. John Cennick.'[26]

Thomas Maxfield gave undivided allegiance to Wesley for nearly twenty years, and thus came to be regarded as his first 'son in the gospel'. Wesley's first description of the rise of itinerant lay preaching within Methodism appeared in the annual *Minutes* of the 1766 Conference—three years after Maxfield also had separated from Wesley on a doctrinal issue:

After a time a young man came, T. Maxfield, and said he desired to help me, as a Son in the gospel. Soon after came a second, Thomas Richards, and a third, Thomas Westall. These severally desired to serve me as Sons, and to labour when and where I should direct. Observe, these likewise desired *me*, not I *them*. But I durst not refuse their assistance.[27]

The romantic story surrounding Wesley's reluctant acceptance of Maxfield's aid did not appear in print until after Wesley's death, though its general authenticity need not be doubted. Storming into the Foundery after a hurried ride from Bristol, Wesley cried 'Thomas Maxfield has turned preacher, I find!' To which his mother calmly replied: 'John, you know what my sentiments have been. You cannot suspect me of favouring readily anything of this kind. But take care what you do with respect to that young man, for he is as surely called of God to preach as you are. Examine what have been the fruits of his preaching: and hear him also yourself.' As John did so he would recall a childhood memory of his own mother discoursing to a crowd of parishioners in the rectory at Epworth. The result could hardly be in doubt: 'It is the Lord: let him do what seemeth him good.' Elsewhere

I have given detailed reasons for believing that this incident could hardly have taken place earlier than January 1741, after Wesley had gathered considerable experience of lay preaching in general.[28] In assigning priority to Maxfield, however, he was surely thinking of the deliberate acceptance of lay preachers as his full-time assistants, supported financially for an itinerancy similar to his own, with the exception that these 'sons in the gospel' were commissioned as prophets only, not as priests. Even their preaching seems at first to have been considered by Wesley more as a means of building up the established societies than of general evangelism: they were sub-pastors who also preached rather than preachers who also exercised pastoral care.

More and more the Methodist societies were becoming self-sufficient. To a limited extent this was true even in the sphere of worship. The Wesleys strongly emphasized the importance of Holy Communion, and helped to bring about a sacramental revival in the eighteenth century. Their sacramentarian principles, indeed, eventually proved the major factor in bringing about a separation. The members of the societies were urged to communicate frequently at their parish churches, and the Wesleys themselves led organized groups of Methodist communicants to St. Paul's or St. Luke's in London or to the Temple or St. James's in Bristol, and were happy to share in the administration of the Lord's Supper whenever invited so to do by sympathetic Anglican colleagues. In London, to avoid embarrassment to the local clergy, a kind of shift system was developed, whereby groups of about two hundred Methodists communicated at St. Luke's in rotation. In many parishes the clergy made it awkward for them to communicate by alleging some technical disqualification—much as Wesley himself had done in Georgia. To some extent Wesley was able to circumvent the problem of expecting constant communion in an unsympathetic churchly environment by the expedient of extending private communion for the sick to a large company of the sick person's friends, as also by following the practice of private communion which had been allowed to develop among some of the earlier religious societies.[29] Nevertheless he remained uneasy about this, and in his interview with Bishop Butler in 1739 denied the rumour that he administered the Lord's Supper in his societies, adding, 'I believe [I] never shall.'[30]

Not for many years did John Wesley feel able to administer Holy Communion in a Methodist preaching-house, nor was it realistic to expect a bishop—certainly not Edmund Gibson!—to consecrate Methodist premises for this purpose. A neat solution offered itself through a temporary expedient which became available for a time in 1741. The minister of a Huguenot chapel in Great Hermitage Street,

Wapping, Dr. J. L. Deleznot,[31] had 'long importuned' Wesley to preach for him, and apparently stated that Wesley's followers would also be welcome both to the service itself and to communion afterwards. Accordingly on Sunday 2 August 1741 and the four succeeding Sundays Wesley both preached for Deleznot and shared in administering communion to the thousand members of the London Methodist societies, who attended in batches of two hundred each Sunday. This was heavy physical labour—Wesley's diary shows that he did not return from a 10.0 a.m. service until 2.30 p.m.—but it satisfied the longings both of Methodist pastor and flock to share the sacred mysteries together in circumstances which were ecclesiastically regular, for the Huguenot chapel was episcopally consecrated.[32] Before eight months had passed, however, this arrangement was upset under circumstances which we can only suspect.[33]

A permanent solution along similar lines offered itself in 1743, when Wesley obtained the lease of another Huguenot chapel, now disused, in West Street, Seven Dials. This also was episcopally consecrated. West Street Chapel was a larger building, but the Methodist community had doubled, so that again Wesley arranged for them to attend in relays. The first Methodist communion there was celebrated on 29 May 1743, and it is worthy of note that Wesley was sufficiently a churchman to describe the day in his *Journal* as Trinity Sunday. The arduous exhilaration of this opening service, protracted from 10.0 a.m. until 3.0 p.m. because of the large number of communicants, marked also the many other communion services which he conducted there throughout the remainder of his lifetime. Perhaps it should be pointed out that West Street was the sacramental centre not only for the Foundery society but for other societies which had meantime been formed in the London area. Even after additional consecrated Huguenot buildings came into Methodist hands, West Street retained a peculiar place in their affections as '*the* chapel'. The designation 'chapel' (which Wesley normally spelt 'chappel') was in any event restricted to such consecrated buildings, the others being termed 'preaching-houses' or 'society-rooms'—almost anything, in fact, that would soften the charge of sectarianism by distinguishing them from an Anglican 'church' or 'chapel' on the one hand or a dissenting 'meeting-house' on the other.

At West Street Chapel the Anglican Orders for morning and evening worship were read, and here the Lord's Supper was administered, by Methodists for Methodists, with none to say them nay. Once again, however, Wesley was careful to secure the agreement of Archbishop Potter that this did not constitute separation from the Church.[34] Thus in London at least the Methodists were offered something almost like an alternative to the parish church, even though the hours of worship usually remained distinct, so that attendance at both was possible.

Not that Methodist communion was an exact replica of the Anglican order. It may indeed be claimed that Wesley offered an enrichment of the rite in a form of choral communion, as well as by the occasional use of extempore prayer. As we have seen in Georgia, Wesley added hymns to the communion office, and this practice became even more helpful in the crowded and therefore protracted English services; short hymns or groups of stanzas were sung during the communion of the people as a devotional background for their movement to and from the communion rail. Some of these hymns had been included in Wesley's first *Collection of Psalms and Hymns* of 1737, and others are to be found in later publications, the classic source being the *Hymns on the Lord's Supper* of 1745.[35] The whole approach of Wesley to Holy Communion furnishes a remarkable blend of loyal allegiance to the order and rubrics of the *Book of Common Prayer*, supplemented on the one hand by greater spontaneity and on the other by a deliberate attempt to recapture the liturgy of the apostolic church, as in the use of the mixed chalice of wine and water, and even (by way of the hymns) of the epiclesis or prayer for the descent of the Holy Spirit, otherwise preserved only by the Eastern Church.[36]

London, with its many episcopally-consecrated buildings available to Wesley, remained always a special case. In Bristol and elsewhere the situation was different. As late as the 1760s he continued to use the expedient of extending the practice of sick communion to friends and neighbours gathered in an invalid's home. Howell Harris's *Journal* for 2 November 1762 records defending him for this practice in Bath: 'When Mr. [William] Chapman came in he was warm against the Methodists for giving sacrament in houses. I said that was not more irregular than lay- and field-preaching.'[37] Even in 1766 Wesley still claimed that there was no administration of the Lord's Supper in Methodist preaching-houses.[38] Eventually, however, he felt able to offer communion even there without qualms.[39]

The provision of Methodist sacramental opportunities was clearly an important step in the development of Methodism from a society to a church, nor must it be thought that this occurred only or even mainly in response to pressure from without by unsympathetic clergy who denied the Lord's Supper to Wesley's followers. There existed in any case a pressure from within the societies themselves to extend their communal activities to the inner sacramental mysteries, and this preferably under the ministrations of their Methodist leaders. For many

Methodists, indeed, sacramental spirituality was a by-product of the rich and vigorous fellowship into which they had been introduced by the Wesleys' preaching, and this fellowship tended to overshadow for them the ordered worship of the parish church or (in the case of a few) their dissenting meeting-house. Even though they might formally be members of a parish church and attend more frequently than their non-Methodist neighbours, they had an increasing sense of 'belonging' to a true family of God in their Methodist society. The growth of this corporate feeling was gradual, but it had been given tangible form by the institution of membership tickets in 1741 and was enormously strengthened by the inauguration of class meetings in 1742. The development of an itinerant preaching order, whose services were shared in turn by most societies, provided a bond of union sometimes more powerful than that of Wesley himself. In London at least the fellowship of the Lord's Table tended to unify the neighbouring societies, and the same was true to a lesser extent as members from scattered societies in other areas congregated in the nearest parish church which rejoiced in an evangelical ministry. Other forms of specifically Methodist worship increased their self-identification, though emphasis upon these observances never approached the singularity of a Quaker 'concern'. Such were the love-feast, borrowed from the Moravians, the watchnight, a prudential adaptation of the vigils of the early church, and the covenant service, which owed its origin to English Puritanism.[40]

7

SIX

APOLOGIAE FOR METHODISM

WESLEY had tried to enlist the sympathy of the bishops for the work
to which he believed himself called, with a modest amount of success.
Their more generous reactions ranged from Archbishop Potter's 'You
are irregular, but God bless you!' to Gibson's 'Why can't the Wesleys
get out of the church and do no more harm!' In the spring of 1743
Wesley undertook a major attempt to break down the prejudice of
thoughtful leaders of public opinion both in church and state by the
publication of *An Earnest Appeal to Men of Reason and Religion*. The
main purpose of this 64-page pamphlet was to expound and defend
Methodist principles and practices in view of the many uninformed
rumours and published criticisms.[1] Two-thirds of it was in effect an
evangelical appeal, a proof by logical demonstration that the Methodists
were playing a valuable part in society by proclaiming justification by
faith and by living holy lives. From this Wesley turned to the charges
that they were undermining the Church of England.

Wesley reminded his readers that Article XIX, in a similar manner to
Article VII of the Confession of Augsburg, defined the church as 'a
company of faithful or believing people among whom the pure word
of God is preached and the sacraments duly administered'. (This was in
fact a paraphrase, not an exact quotation.) All his supposedly unorthodox and harmful practices were in fact designed to defend the true
church against other men who were secretly undermining or openly
destroying it. The true church, after all, consisted of 'the faithful people,
the true believers'. In order that they should be gathered into a visible
church in accordance with Article XIX, three things were essential:
living faith, 'preaching (and consequently hearing) the pure word of
God', and a due administration of the sacraments. In none of these three
things did the Methodists undermine the church. Rather, they served to
increase the number of faithful people and to swell the attendance at
preaching and communion.

The charge that he did not observe the laws of the church Wesley
dealt with under two headings: the rubrics, and the canons. He pointed
out that he had always observed the rubrics of the *Book of Common
Prayer* 'with a scrupulous exactness'. He instanced fasting during Lent,
Ember days, Rogation days, and Fridays. He emphasized many rubrics

which he knew were commonly neglected yet which in his own parochial ministry he had carefully followed, such as those about announcing fast days, avoiding private infant baptism, and catechizing children
in church. He concluded:

> Now the question is not whether these rubrics *ought* to be observed
> . . . but whether in fact they *have been* observed by *you* or *me* most.
> Many can witness I have observed them punctually, yea sometimes
> at the hazard of my life; and as many, I fear, that *you* have not
> observed them at all, and that several of them you never pretended
> to observe. And is it *you* that are accusing *me* for not observing the
> rubrics of the church!²

Turning to the canons, Wesley pointed out that they were 'never
legally established by the church, never regularly confirmed in any full
Convocation'. Nevertheless, he was prepared to accept the challenge
on this ground also, and claimed that he had been more obedient than
most clergy in obeying Canons 29, 59, 64, 68, and 75. These covered
similarly marginal territory to the rubrics noted earlier, though the last
struck a stern puritanical note: 'Can. 75. No ecclesiastical persons shall
spend their time idly by day or by night playing at *dice*, *cards*, or *tables*.'
Wesley closed:

> Now let the clergyman who has observed only these five canons for
> one year last past, and who has read over all the canons in his con-
> gregation (as the King's ratification straitly enjoins him to do once
> every year), let him, I say, cast the first stone at us for not observing
> the canons (so called) of the Church of England.³

What was generally implied by this charge, however, was that the
Wesleys could not be friendly to the church because they did not 'obey
the governors of it and submit . . . to all their godly admonitions and
injunctions' in accordance with their ordination vows. Wesley firmly
laid down the principle that he must obey God rather than the bishops,
setting the *Acts of the Apostles* over against the Anglican Ordinal:

> In every individual point of an indifferent nature we do and will (by
> the grace of God) obey the governors of the church. But the 'testi-
> fying the gospel of the grace of God' is not a point of an indifferent
> nature. 'The ministry which we have received of the Lord Jesus' we
> are at all hazards to fulfil. [Cf. Acts 20:24.] It is 'the burden of the
> Lord' [Jeremiah 23:33] which is laid upon us here; and we are 'to
> obey God rather than man'. [Cf. Acts 5:29.] Nor yet do we in any
> ways violate the promise which each of us made when it was said

unto him, 'Take thou authority to preach the word of God. . . .' We then promised to 'submit' (mark the words) 'to the *godly admonitions and injunctions of our ordinary*'. But we did not, could not promise to obey 'such' injunctions as we know 'are contrary to the word of God'.[4]

Wesley dismissed as nonsense the charge that the Methodists left the church:

What can you mean? Do we leave so much as the *church walls*? Your own eyes tell you we do not. Do we leave the *ordinances of the church*? You daily see and know the contrary. Do we leave the *fundamental doctrine of the church*, namely, salvation by faith? It is our constant theme, in public, in private, in writing, in conversation. Do we leave the *practice of the church*, the standard whereof are the ten commandments?—which are so essentially in-wrought in her constitution (as little as you may apprehend it) that whosoever breaks one of the least of these is no member of the Church of England. I believe you do not care to put the cause on this issue.[5]

At last he came to the meat of the objections: by their societies the Methodists divided the church. Here he chopped logic in his most sardonic vein:

Remember, the church is the 'faithful people', the true believers. Now how do we *divide these*? 'Why, by our societies.' Very good. Now the case is plain: 'we *divide* them', you say, '*by uniting them together*'. Truly a very uncommon way of *dividing*. 'O, but we divide those who are thus united with each other from the rest of the church.' By no means. Many of them were before 'joined to all their brethren' of the Church of England (and many were not, until they knew us)[6] by 'assembling themselves together' to hear the word of God and to eat of one bread and drink of one cup. And do they now *forsake that assembling* themselves together? You cannot, you dare not say it. You know they are more diligent therein than ever; it being one of the fixed rules of our societies 'that every member attend the ordinances of God', i.e. that *he do not divide from the church*. And if any member of the church does thus divide from or leave it he hath no more place among us.[7]

On the basis of all this evidence Wesley pleaded that reasonable men of the world ought to heed the advice of Gamaliel: 'Let them alone: for if this work be of men it will come to nought. But if it be of God, ye cannot overthrow it.'[8] Truly religious men, he believed, should 'wish us good luck in the name of the Lord'.[9]

The *Earnest Appeal* went through two editions in 1743, another in 1744, and six more during Wesley's lifetime as well as many thereafter. Although by no means a fabulous best-seller it did soften some of the opposition to Methodism, and even resulted in a few conversions, such as that of the musician John Frederick Lampe, who quickly set some of Charles Wesley's hymns to somewhat florid tunes.[10] Wesley's public apologia, however, also rallied some noteworthy churchmen to the ranks of the opposition. Believing that he had explained and defended his evangelical theology at least adequately, Wesley was genuinely surprised to discover that the archbishop of York, Dr. Thomas Herring, had circulated a letter among the clergy of his diocese criticizing the 'great indiscretion' of regarding the 'enthusiastic ardour' of the Methodists as 'the true and only Christianity'. Wesley felt compelled to answer the charges therein, but only in 1772 (long after Herring's death) did he in print reveal their source.[11]

Herring's leaflet was in fact a covering letter for a much more forceful attack by a much more doughty opponent, the bishop of London himself. Anonymously Edmund Gibson had published a folio pamphlet of twenty-four pages entitled *Observations upon the conduct and behaviour of a certain sect usually distinguished by the name of Methodists.* This was speedily reprinted in quarto, and copies were circulated by bishops in different parts of the country in such a way as to confirm Wesley's own certainty that Gibson was at least the publisher, and almost certainly the author.[12] The focal point of the attack on the Methodists in general was the question upon which Wesley had unsuccessfully sought Gibson's firm ruling in 1738—whether his societies were conventicles, and therefore illegal.[13] With the added experience (and frustrations) of a few more years behind him, the bishop now pronounced that in holding separate assemblies for worship without qualifying themselves as dissenters under the Toleration Act the Methodists had increasingly been breaking the law:

> They began with evening-meetings at private houses; but they have been going on for some time to open and appoint *public places* of religious worship, with the same freedom as if they were warranted by the Act of Toleration. And not content with that they have had the boldness to proceed to preaching in the *fields* and other open places, and by publick advertisements to invite the *rabble* to be their hearers, notwithstanding the express declaration in a Statute (22 Car. II.c.l) against assembling in a field, by name.

The author seemed genuinely shocked that such men could pretend to be loyal churchmen:

But notwithstanding these open inroads upon the national constitution the teachers and their followers affect to be thought members of the national church, and do accordingly join in *communion* with it, though in a *manner* that is very irregular and contrary to the directions laid down in our great rule, the Act of Uniformity.[14]

These societies, the writer maintained, had gone far beyond the practices of the former religious societies, some of which still happily existed and were '*countenanced* and *encouraged* by the bishops and clergy' so long as they furthered their desire for spiritual fellowship 'in a private inoffensive way'.[15]

The same press (and in all probability the same publisher) issued a four-page folio pamphlet entitled *The Case of the Methodists briefly stated; more particularly in the point of field-preaching*. This attacked Methodism in terms similar to those of the *Observations*, urging especially that field-preaching was a dangerous contravention of the Act of Toleration, and noting examples in Whitefield's *Journals* of crowds numbering from four to eighty thousand people.

John Wesley had by no means fully 'delivered his own soul' in his *Earnest Appeal*, and in view of these official attacks readily responded to those colleagues in his first Conference of June 1744 who urged him to 'write a farther Appeal'—which in fact he took as its title. The *Farther Appeal* was divided into three parts, Part I being published separately in December 1744 and Parts II and III jointly in December 1745.[16]

Part I of the *Farther Appeal* followed in general the pattern of the *Earnest Appeal* in expounding Methodist teaching and answering objections to the doctrines themselves, to his manner of teaching them, and to the effects which followed such teaching. Wesley rebutted an attack on the *Earnest Appeal* entitled *The Notions of the Methodists fully disproved by setting the doctrine of the Church of England concerning justification and regeneration in a true light*. He deliberately set down a series of passages from the *Book of Common Prayer*, from the Articles, and from the *Homilies*, which supported his teaching, appending a summary:

From the whole tenor then of her Liturgy, Articles, and Homilies, the doctrine of the Church of England appears to be this:

1. That no *good work*, properly so called, can *go before* justification.

2. That *no degree* of true sanctification can be previous to it.

3. That as the *meritorious cause* of justification is the life and death of Christ, so the *condition* of it is faith, faith alone; and

4. That both inward and outward holiness are consequent on this faith, and are the ordinary, stated condition, of final justification.[17]

Wesley then ventured upon his first public criticism of bishops, by referring to three of their attacks: 'a kind of circular letter which one of those whom the Holy Ghost hath made overseers of his church, I was informed, had sent to all the clergy of his diocese,' the accompanying pamphlet 'generally supposed to be wrote by a person who is every way my superior', and a recent *Charge* by the bishop of Lichfield and Coventry, Dr. Richard Smalbroke. Wesley seems to have been just as certain as was Whitefield that Gibson was the author of the *Observations*, but respected his desire for anonymity. Whitefield had immediately attacked the work as 'a notorious libel', and in two open letters challenged the bishop of London with being the author. Wesley remained the peacemaker, attempting to meet the accusations but not unduly to embarrass the anonymous accuser. (This was contrary to his later practice: normally he refused to answer anonymous letters in periodicals.) Not until 1748, in answering an official charge published over Gibson's name, did Wesley refer to the bishop's responsibility for the *Observations*, and even then in such a way as to acknowledge some measure of value in the pamphlet's anonymity.[18]

Having replied at length to the doctrinal arguments put forward in Gibson's *Observations* and *Case*, and to his criticism of the strange revival phenomena that sometimes accompanied Methodist preaching, Wesley turned in section five of the *Farther Appeal* to Smalbroke's attack. Faced with this instance of an avowed episcopal author Wesley had to choose between letting a serious challenge remain unanswered or refuting a bishop by name. As the lesser evil he chose the latter course.[19] Smalbroke had delivered the charge to his clergy in 1741, but it was not published until 1744. In it he distinguished between the extraordinary operations of the Holy Spirit, which he claimed were limited to apostolic times, and His less dramatic ordinary influence, which was still available. The Methodists, in his view, were guilty of 'enthusiastical pretensions' in supposing that the personal assistance of the Holy Spirit could still be experienced. Wesley rebutted the bishop's argument at some length, both from the Scriptures and from the early Fathers, turning eventually to extensive quotations from 'a modern writer'—who was eventually unveiled as Bishop Pearson on the Creed. He went on to marshal the *Book of Common Prayer* and the *Homilies* among his allies. Having once decided to come out into the open against a bishop who attacked his beloved movement, Wesley was restrained neither by fear of retribution nor hope of favour, nor even by undue reverence for a dignitary thirty years his senior.[20]

Section VI of the *Farther Appeal* took up the question of Methodist irregularities raised by Bishop Gibson's *Observations* and *Case*. Wesley strongly defended the necessity of field-preaching as an expedient to meet a desperate need, pleading once more 'a dispensation of the gospel':

> Wherever I was now desired to preach, salvation by faith was my only theme. . . . [This] I explained and enforced with all my might both in every church where I was asked to preach and occasionally in the religious societies of London and Westminster, to some or other of which I was continually pressed to go by the stewards or other members of them.
>
> Things were in this posture when I was told I must preach no more in this, and this, and another church. The reason was usually added with reserve: 'Because you preach such doctrine.'[21] So much the more those who could not hear me there flocked together when I was at any of the societies. . . .
>
> But after a time, finding those rooms could not contain a tenth part of the people that were earnest to hear, I determined to do the same thing in England which I had often done in a warmer climate, namely when the house would not contain the congregation to preach in the open air. This I accordingly did, first at Bristol, where the society rooms were exceeding small, and at Kingswood, where we had no room at all; afterwards, in or near London.

He summarized the situation in a paragraph which in his collected *Works* he asterisked as of special importance:

> Be pleased to observe: 1. That I was forbidden as by a general consent to preach in any church (though not by any judicial sentence) 'for preaching such doctrine'. . . . 2. That I had no desire or design to preach in the open air till long after this prohibition. 3. That when I did, as it was no matter of choice, so neither of premeditation. There was no scheme at all previously formed which was to be supported thereby, nor had I any other end in view than this—to save as many souls as I could. 4. *Field-preaching* was therefore a sudden expedient, a thing submitted to rather than chosen, because I thought preaching *thus* better than *not* preaching *at all*.[22]

One statute cited by his opponents (22 Car. II.c.1) did indeed specifically forbid field-preaching, but here he turned their own argument against them. They stated that it 'was evidently intended, not only to suppress, but also to prevent sedition':

> With what justice then, with what ingenuity or candour, with what shadow of truth or reason, can any man cite this Act against us? whom you yourself no more suspect of a design to raise sedition (I appeal to your own conscience in the sight of God) than of a design to blow up the city of London?[23]

Wesley turned to the more formidable charge that Methodist preaching was illegal because neither their preachers nor their preaching-houses had been registered under the terms of the Toleration Act. Again when reprinting the *Farther Appeal* in his collected *Works*, Wesley believed that this reply merited an asterisk to indicate its importance:

> 1. That Act grants toleration to those who *dissent* from the Established Church. But we do not dissent from it. Therefore we *cannot* make use of that Act. 2. That Act exempts dissenters from penalties consequent on their *breach of preceding laws*. But we are not conscious of *breaking any law at all*. Therefore we *need not* make use of it.[24]

Registration of the older religious societies, which had been sponsored by bishops and clergy, had not been deemed necessary under the Toleration Act, and their defence applied equally to the Methodists:

> They are not *dissenters* from the church, therefore they *cannot use* and they do *not need* the Act of Toleration. And their meetings are not seditious, therefore the statute against seditious meetings does not affect them.
> The application is obvious. If our meetings are illegal so are theirs also. If this plea be good (as doubtless it is) in the one case, it is good in the other also.[25]

Wesley went on to consider Gibson's criticism of his own itinerancy. Again he emphasized his ordination as a Fellow. He could similarly have pointed to his brother Charles's ordination as a Student of Christ Church, which amounted to the same thing and in like manner had been adduced by Charles in his own defence.[26] Wesley claimed also that the general right to preach wherever an incumbent invited him was the prerogative of every priest, and insisted that persecution of Methodist clergy such as had occurred at Islington was merely dressing up a prejudice in a pretext.

Wesley was also charged with disloyalty to his ordination vows because when quoting in justification the bishop's words 'Take thou authority to preach the word of God' he had omitted the following clause, 'where thou shalt be lawfully appointed'. He refused to acknowledge this implied restraint, drawing attention to the bishop's prior commission in the Ordering of Priests:

> But before those words . . . were those spoken without any *restraint* or *limitation* at all, which I apprehend to convey an indelible character: 'Receive the Holy Ghost for the office and work of a priest in the church of God. . . .'[27]

Wesley thus maintained that in ordination an indelible character was conveyed to a minister by the Holy Spirit, and this was not subject to any restrictions imposed by the church or its governors. When Gibson went on to decry Wesley's *Journal* declaration that God had called him to look upon all the world as his parish Wesley pointed out that this call came 'by the laying on of the hands of the presbytery' (I Timothy 4:14). This may just possibly have implied even at that time some hesitancy about the unique validity of episcopal ordination, but it seems almost certain that the term 'presbytery' was used simply because it was scriptural. In any event ordination by authorized representatives of the church implied a recognition that the Holy Spirit had already called him, a fact prior to and more important than the laying on of episcopal hands.

To Gibson's further challenge that Wesley should either obey the church or leave it he answered:

> As to your next advice, 'To have a greater regard to the rules and orders of the church', I *cannot*, for I now regard them next to the word of God. And as to your last, 'to renounce communion with the church', I *dare not*. Nay, but let them thrust us out. We *will not* leave the ship. If you *cast us* out of it, then our Lord will take us up.[28]

Parts II and III of the *Farther Appeal*, published almost exactly a year after Part I, approached the subject from a new angle, deserting the particular case for the general principle, and that principle the spirit of true religion as exemplified in other bodies, beginning with 'the Jews, the ancient church of God'. In Part II Wesley reminded his readers in some detail how the Chosen People had rebelled against God. As with the Jews, so with the proud but decadent English nation, he claimed: they have rebelled against God, and only disaster can be ahead for them unless they undertake a drastic reformation. He pointed to the moral corruption rampant at various levels of society, ripe for the judgement of God. Not even the church was guiltless, and Wesley scathingly denounced the hypocritical, ineffective religion of 'this Christian nation'. Especially he criticized the laxity and worldliness of the Anglican clergy in general, though castigating also the various dissenting denominations (including the Roman Catholics) for having lost the spirit and power of their ancestors.[29]

In Part III Wesley went on to propose Methodism as an antidote for the spiritual sickness at large in the country. He pointed out that Methodist doctrine was remarkably free from heresies: 'Those of the Church of England, at least, must acknowledge this. For where is there a body of people in the realm who, number for number, so closely adhere to what our church delivers as pure doctrine?' Methodism, he claimed, was not only free from heresy but from superstition, from enthusiasm, from bigotry, from vice, and from the persecuting zeal which marred the continental reformers.[30]

In spite of their sincere and successful allegiance to 'an unusual work of God', however, the Methodists had themselves been visited with worse persecution than that meted out to 'Popery, infidelity, or any heresy whatsoever!' He went on to describe in some detail the shameful anti-Methodist riots in Staffordshire during 1743 and 1744, about which a month or so earlier he had published a thirty-page tract under the satiric title of *Modern Christianity exemplified at Wednesbury and other adjacent places in Staffordshire*. Even from his early Oxford days, as well as in Georgia, Wesley had expected persecution, indeed had almost welcomed it as a sign that he could not be far wrong if he were stirring up hatred in some as well as support in others. It might even be claimed (unjustly, we believe) that he suffered from a martyr complex. He did indeed seriously maintain that 'though a man may be despised without being saved, yet he cannot be saved without being despised'.[31] Accordingly one of his favourite works was August Herman Francke's *Nicodemus: a treatise on the fear of man*, which exhorted Christians constantly to be prepared for persecution. Wesley published an extract of this work in 1739, and it went through five editions in ten years. Yet Wesley did not *seek* persecution, but claimed that it ought to be avoided if at all possible.[32]

The Wednesbury riots crystallized Wesley's fearful attraction towards physical persecution and confirmed his convictions about the validity of a cause which thus entailed suffering for righteousness' sake. *Modern Christianity* had consisted almost solely of factual reports by sufferers, recorded simply and without emotional flourishes. Appended was a moving prayer of dedication to God's service even in persecution. A brief preface explained why after preparing this tract in the spring of 1744 he had first laid it aside, and now at length published it:

It was our desire and design that the following accounts, drawn up long since, should have slept for ever, but the gross misrepresentations of these facts which are still spread abroad from day to day constrain us at length to speak the naked truth in as plain a manner as we are able. And now let any man of common humanity judge whether these things ought to be so.[33]

The few pages in the *Farther Appeal* devoted to these riots contained a brief résumé in the third person of *Modern Christianity*. Wesley made it clear, however, though without labouring the point, that the riots in the summer of 1743 were instigated by a band of hooligans on the pretence of persuading the general populace to 'keep from these men that went preaching about, and go to the church'. Jonas Turner, a Methodist, asked for trouble by replying, 'I do go to the church, but I never see any of you there'. The rioting in January and February 1744, on the other hand, was fired by something much more official, a document drawn up by a local clergyman calling for signatories to declare that they 'would never read, or sing, or pray together, or hear these parsons any more'. The town crier went round announcing publicly 'that all the people of the society must come to Mr. Forshew's and sign it, or else their houses would be pulled down immediately'. Wesley noted that 'several signed this through fear', and went on to record the fate of those who did not.[34]

Against this background of persecution, Wesley continued, the clergy who showed any sympathy towards the Methodists had been threatened and disowned, so that their mantle was falling upon a despised handful of lay preachers. His defence of these lay preachers formed a major part of the work. He showed how the pressure of circumstances had forced him to accept 'this surprising apparatus of Providence' which ran quite counter to his own strong prejudices, though on this occasion he did not deal in particular names and events. He agreed that some of these 'plain men' might not know Greek and Latin, but insisted that in an examination in 'substantial, practical, experimental divinity' they would fare better than most candidates for Holy Orders, even those in the universities. After all, the Scribes were laymen, the Apostles were laymen, Calvin was a layman, and 'in all Protestant churches it is still more evident that ordination is not held a necessary prerequisite of preaching'. Even in England the parish clerk read one of the Scripture lessons, which was certainly 'publishing the word of God' and in some sense at least akin to preaching.[35] Wesley reiterated his claim that the clergy would not help but only hinder this great work of God, therefore he *must* turn to laymen, the validity of whose labours had been proved by their manifest spiritual fruits. He made it quite clear, however, that his preachers had made neither claim nor attempt to administer the sacraments, which was 'an honour peculiar to the priests of God'.[36]

Turning once more to field-preaching, Wesley answered criticisms by the same general method: there were neither evangelically-minded ministers nor churches enough to cope with the multitudes who heard the Methodist preachers. He evinced little sympathy for those 'tender-hearted Christians' whose attitude to the unchurched masses was: 'It is their own fault; let them die and be damned.' Field-preaching from its very novelty aroused the interest of these 'poor wretches' who were utterly inaccessible every other way, even to a parish minister who 'preached like an angel'. 'But when one came and said, "Yonder is a man preaching on the top of the mountain!" they ran in droves to hear what he would say; and God spoke to their hearts.' 'Surely', he continued, 'it should rejoice the hearts of all who desire the kingdom of God should come that so many of them have been snatched from the mouth of the lion by an uncommon though not unlawful way.'[37]

Wesley moved to another charge, defending his position by the dialectic of dialogue:

'Why, I did once myself rejoice to hear', says a grave citizen, with an air of great importance, 'that so many sinners were reformed, till I found they were only turned from one wickedness to another; that they were turned from cursing or swearing or drunkenness into a no less damnable sin, that of schism.'

'Do you know what you say? . . . What do you mean by schism?'

'Schism! schism! why, it is separating from the church.'

'Ay, so it is. And yet *every* separating from the church to which we once belonged is not schism; else you will make all the English to be schismatics by separating from the Church of Rome.'

'But we had just cause.'

'So doubtless we had; whereas schism is a causeless separation from the Church of Christ. So far so good. But you have many steps to take before you can make good that conclusion, that a separation from a *particular national* church . . . comes under the scriptural notion of schism. However, taking this for granted, will you aver in cool blood that all who die in such a separation, that is every one who dies a Quaker, a Baptist, an Independent, or a Presbyterian, is as infallibly damned as if he died in the act of murder or adultery? Surely you start at the thought!'[38]

In any case the Methodists did not in fact separate from the Church of England: some never attended it before but did go now; others went previously but now attended three times as often. 'Will common sense allow anyone to say that these are separated from the church?' Even more important was the fact that now they 'live according to the directions of the church, believe her doctrines, and join in her ordinances'. Wesley contrasted the attitude of the Methodists with that of self-acknowledged dissenters such as those of the four denominations previously mentioned:

> We were born and bred up in your own church, and desire to die therein. We always were and are now 'zealous for the church'—only not with a blind, angry zeal. We hold and ever have done the same opinions which you and we received from our forefathers. But we do not lay the main stress of our religion on any opinions, right or wrong; neither do we ever begin or willingly join in any dispute concerning them. The weight of all religion, we apprehend, rests on holiness of heart and life. And consequently wherever we come we press this with all our might. How wide then is the difference between our case and the case of any of those that are above mentioned! They *avowedly separated* from the church: we utterly *disavow* any such design. They severely, and almost continually, inveighed against the doctrines and discipline of the church they left: we approve both the doctrines and discipline of our church, and inveigh only against ungodliness and unrighteousness.[39]

Published shortly before the *Farther Appeal* was the fourth extract from Wesley's *Journal*, which was designed as religious propaganda rather than autobiography. In this Wesley deliberately set out to identify the Methodists as true members of the true church in contrast to other groups. He singled out for especial criticism the quietist Moravians, separatists seeking to 'raise a church' on insecure foundations.[40] He dissociated himself from the predestinarianism of Whitefield and his Calvinist friends. The Methodists, on the other hand, insisted both on doctrinal purity and disciplined living, stressing the necessity of using the means of grace offered by the church, especially the Lord's Supper, which he maintained was a converting ordinance.[41]

Wesley was careful to show not only that Methodists were true churchmen rather than dissenters, but also that many supposed churchmen in fact were truly dissenters—the immoral, the sceptics, the unworthy ministers. The entry on this subject under 6 February 1740 was sufficiently important for him to append an asterisk to it in his collected *Works*, and was surely one of the main reasons for dispatching a complimentary copy to at least one bishop, and probably to all.[42] He recorded that when visiting Newgate prison in London the Ordinary 'told me he was sorry I should turn dissenter from the Church of England. I told him if it was so I did not know it, at which he seemed a little surprised'. Wesley went on to quote once more the nineteenth Article (which he incorrectly noted as the twentieth) defining 'a true church' as 'a congregation of faithful people, wherein the true word of God is preached and the sacraments duly administered'. On the basis of this definition he pointed out those who constituted the worst 'dissenters' from the Church of England:

(1) Unholy men of all kinds: swearers, Sabbath-breakers, drunk-ards, fighters, whoremongers, liars, revilers, evil-speakers; the pas-sionate, the gay, the lovers of money, the lovers of dress or of praise, the lovers of pleasure more than lovers of God. All these are dissenters of the highest sort, continually striking at the root of the church. . . .

(2) Men unsound in the faith: those who deny the Scriptures of truth, those who deny the Lord that bought them, those who deny justification by faith alone, or the present salvation which is by faith. These also are dissenters of a very high kind, for they likewise strike at the foundation, and were their principles universally to obtain there could be no true church upon earth.

Lastly, those who unduly administer the sacraments: who (to instance but in one point) administer the Lord's Supper to such as have neither the power nor the form of godliness. These too are gross dissenters from the Church of England, and should not cast the first stone at others.[43]

In view of all that he had set forth about his country, his church, and his Methodist societies, in the *Appeals* and in his *Journal*, Wesley was compelled to regard Methodism as offering God's last chance of repent-ance to a sinful nation. Here was a faithful remnant through whom there still remained a chance of salvation at the eleventh hour:

If we will not turn and repent, if we will harden our hearts and acknowledge neither his judgments nor mercies, what remains but the fulfilling of that dreadful word which God spake by the prophet Ezekiel: 'Son of man, when the land sinneth against me by tres-passing grievously, then will I stretch forth my hand upon it. . . . Though Noah, Daniel, and Job were in it, as I live, saith the Lord God, they shall deliver neither son nor daughter; they shall but deliver their own souls by their righteousness. . . . Yet, behold, therein shall be left a remnant that shall be brought forth, both sons and daughters. . . . And ye shall know that I have not done without cause all that I have done in it, saith the Lord God.'[44]

During the years following his *Appeals* criticism nevertheless continued. In 1746 Edmund Gibson, the aged bishop of London, entered the fray openly. In a charge delivered during his visitation of the diocese he accused the Methodists of 'breaking in upon the peace and good order of the church, and giving shameful disturbances to the parochial clergy'.[45] Wesley's *Letter* in reply was courteous but unequivocating: 'Give me leave, my Lord, to say you have mistook and misrepresented this whole affair from the top to the bottom.'[46] For over twenty years Wesley was constantly being forced to cover the same ground again and again because of attacks which ignored his previous public statements. Frequently such uninformed criticism was ignored, but some of his clerical opponents demanded attention because their standing lent credence to their charges. Twenty or thirty times he was thus drawn into what he thought of as the 'sad work' of controversy.

One opponent in particular he regarded as a genuine representative of those 'men of reason and religion' for whom his *Appeals* had been written. This was the Rev. (later Dr.) Thomas Church, vicar of Battersea and prebendary of St. Paul's, whom Wesley described as 'a gentleman, a scholar, and a Christian'.[47] In his *Farther Appeal*, Part I, Wesley acknowledged Church's *Remarks on the Rev. Mr. John Wesley's Last Journal*, and replied to his charges of doctrinal error, enthusiasm, and ecclesiastical innovations in *An Answer to the Rev. Mr. Church's Remarks* (1745). Of far more moment was a 150-page book whose title was an essay in itself: *Some Farther Remarks on the Rev. Mr. John Wesley's Last Journal, together with a few considerations on his* Farther Appeal; *shewing the inconsistency of his conduct and sentiments with the constitution and doctrine of the Church of England, and explaining the Articles relating to Justification. To which is annexed, A Vindication of the* Remarks, *being a Reply to Mr. Wesley's* Answer, *in a second Letter to that Gentlemen.*

This elicited Wesley's *The Principles of a Methodist Farther Explained*, published in July 1746.[48] In addition to rebutting Church's charges of doctrinal error and enthusiasm along similar but more ample lines to those of his first *Answer*, Wesley devoted one important section to the charge that he was disloyal to the Church of England and therefore should in honesty resign from the ministry. In this defence of his own standing as an Anglican priest, Wesley dealt one by one with the charges of irregularity. He stated that he knew of no church rule against his practice of extempore public prayer. He reiterated his readiness to obey his ecclesiastical superiors—though only, of course, in the absence of 'some particular law of God to the contrary'. His irregular preaching he defended as the necessary working out of his ordination vows. He insisted that the 'sacerdotal powers' conferred upon him at ordination were not expressly limited to any one congregation but were to be employed at large until such time as he renounced or was cast out of the Church of England. The Methodist societies, he maintained, were private organizations not directly subject to church law, and his authority therein was bestowed by the societies themselves, so that expulsion therefrom could not fairly be described as excommunication. Summarizing his position, he claimed:

> I dare not renounce communion with the Church of England. As a minister I teach her doctrines, I use her offices, I conform to her rubrics, I suffer reproach for my attachment to her. As a private member I hold her doctrines, I join in her offices, in prayer, in hearing, in communicating. . . . Nothing can prove I am no member of the church till I either am excommunicated or renounce her communion. . . . Nor can anything prove I am no minister of the church till I either am deposed from my ministry or voluntarily renounce her, and wholly cease to teach her doctrines, use her offices, and obey her rubrics for conscience' sake.[49]

It seems likely that Wesley continued to apprise the bishops of his activities and to solicit their sympathy by sending them copies of his *Appeals* and similar apologiae. Certainly on its publication in 1744 he dispatched a copy of Part IV of his *Journal* to the bishop of Durham, Dr. Edward Chandler, who was somewhat surprised to receive it. Nor did Chandler prove very sympathetic, especially as his diocese was now one of the focal points of the movement. He was prepared to overlook Wesley's field-preaching, but invasion by lay preachers was another matter. To Archdeacon Sharp he wrote in 1747 about one young preacher, possibly Christopher Hopper:

> I did hope the Methodists were wearing off in my diocese, but this mission of *exhorters* under age, and purely laicks, is a new thing, and may be of dangerous consequence. There is not the same indulgence due to such as to Mr. Wesley and persons episcopally ordained. If this man teaches in a congregation without licence, or reads prayers, he should be p[unished?] by the justices of peace according to the Act of Uniformity.

Two months later, however, he confessed that he was in some difficulty, for his legal advisers had pointed out that the Act of Uniformity did not apply to 'these miscreants', and if the Conventicle Act were pressed

8

into service against their meeting-places the cry of persecution might well be raised, and martyrdom 'knit them closer' and increase their numbers. He suggested, however, that when crowds gathered around a preacher in a market-place it was worth trying the experiment of dispersing them as riotous assemblies under the terms of the Riot Act of 1714—an expedient which had been successfully tried in Cheshire.[50]

The most notorious episcopal attack on the Methodists was by George Lavington, bishop of Exeter, almost twenty years Wesley's senior. It was sparked by a practical joker who circulated a supposed extract from Lavington's primary visitation charge, in which he was represented as favouring Methodist practices. By some innocents this document was taken literally, was reprinted, prompted a supporting pamphlet by a clergyman, and was eventually repudiated in newspaper advertisements taken out by the bishop. Later Lavington apologized for his mistaken implication that this was a deliberate fraud perpetrated by the Methodists, but the publication of this apology by the Countess of Huntingdon caused him to lose face to such a degree that the stage was set for a massive onslaught on this 'sect . . . actuated by a spirit of enthusiasm and delusion'. His work appeared anonymously in three parts published in 1749, 1751, and 1752 under the title of *The Enthusiasm of Methodists and Papists compar'd*. Several replies were published, and Wesley's own open letters to the anonymous author pulled no punches, though he was temperamentally incapable of the poor grammar, poor taste, and acrimonious inaccuracy of his opponent. In general, Lavington's attack was directed against the 'new dispensation' of Methodist spiritual experience, which he ridiculed rather than refuted as 'a composition of enthusiasm, superstition, and imposture'. Although roundly accused of being a sectarian, Wesley felt it necessary to reply only briefly to a handful of specific charges coming under this head, such as field-preaching, maligning the clergy, allowing lay preaching by women and boys (which Wesley claimed was news to him), and teaching justification by faith alone—for which the bishop was referred to the *Homilies* and Articles XI and XII.[51]

Not only did Wesley defend himself against attacks, but sought to expound the positive side of Methodism. This also was an important step in the growing self-consciousness of his societies as a distinct ecclesiastical entity. The most important of these expositions was written for the Rev. Vincent Perronet of Shoreham in 1748 and published the following year as *A Plain Account of the People called Methodists*. Although this was mainly an account of Methodist organization, including its ventures in social service, Wesley made it quite clear both at the outset and as he described each particular phase of

Methodist activity that there had been no blueprint for a new sect, but that 'everything arose just as the occasion offered'.[52] He also pointed out how in the very early days the objection had been raised against his societies: 'Is not this making a schism? Is not the joining these people together gathering churches out of churches?' To this he had answered:

> If you mean only gathering people out of buildings called churches, it is. But if you mean dividing Christians from Christians, and so destroying Christian fellowship, it is not. For (1) These were not Christians before they were thus joined. Most of them were bare-faced heathens. (2) Neither are they Christians from whom you suppose them to be divided. You will not look me in the face and say they are. What! drunken Christians! cursing and swearing Christians! lying Christians! cheating Christians!

In fact, he contended, the Methodists were introducing true Christianity where it was utterly destroyed or in danger of destruction—reviving the church, not separating from it.[53]

It was too much to expect that either this or any other of Wesley's numerous apologiae would meet with universal approval. One anonymous clergyman termed it 'as weak a performance as ever I met with'. In a reasoned theological argument he claimed that in fact Wesley was making a schism, and that 'corruptions in the church are better amended by living in communion of the church, and thereby exhorting, admonishing and showing good example to reclaim'.[54]

SEVEN

THE METHODIST ESTABLISHMENT

By THE year 1744 the Wesleys and their societies had weathered the initial storms raised by persecuting mobs and unsympathetic clergy on the one hand, and from the tension between their own evangelical urge and ecclesiastical loyalty on the other. Both men had come to accept certain integral features of their work as no more than necessary irregularities, which might indeed be set aside if and when the church was spiritually renewed, but which meanwhile must be developed to their full capacity, and carefully co-ordinated to ensure the fullest efficiency. This was in effect creating a church within a church. Every attack and every defence, every new method, every fresh success, every added preacher and society and service and sermon and hymn supported the growing sense of Methodist identity.

An apparently inconsequential step proposed by his brother in 1744 was seen by Charles as another brick in the wall rising between the Methodist society and the Established Church. In view of the troubled political state of the nation, and the fact that Methodists were often identified—no matter how ludicrous this seemed—with the Jacobites, on 5 March 1744 John Wesley prepared a loyal address to King George II. This assured the king that 'the Societies in England and Wales, in derision called Methodists', were 'steadily attached' to His Majesty's 'royal person and illustrious house'. In his preamble Wesley stated that a second consideration had prompted this address: 'in spite of all our remonstrances . . . we are continually represented as a peculiar sect of men, separating ourselves from the Established Church'. Charles Wesley realized better than did John, however, that even such a protest, especially when coupled with a phrase such as 'if we must stand as a distinct body from our brethren', could only serve to reinforce the independent status of Methodism. He complained to John: 'My objection to your address in the name of the Methodists is that it would constitute us a sect—at least it would *seem to allow* that we are a body distinct from the national church, whereas we are only a sound part of that church.' Under this pressure John Wesley decided to 'lay it aside'.[1]

Of much more lasting and far-reaching significance was a step under-taken three months later, the summoning of the first Methodist conference. Not that this was a completely new idea, for the Welsh Calvinistic Methodists had been holding their 'Associations' for four years, though these were for different localities only and usually met monthly or quarterly like the monthly and quarterly meetings of the Quakers.[2] It is highly probable, indeed, that Wesley absorbed this idea from Howell Harris, or from Whitefield, who had presided over the first such gathering whose minutes have been preserved. The mingling of clergy and lay preachers in these Welsh assemblies was another feature which commended itself. Wesley himself did not force the issue of the attendance of laymen beyond the point of no return. He simply invited a group of five sympathetic clergy to confer with him, and then asked them to co-opt four of the 'lay brethren'—whom he had also summoned, and who were waiting outside in anticipation of their invitation to share in the deliberations.[3]

Henceforth a similar group met annually for a few days by Wesley's invitation, with the proportion of laymen increasing rapidly during the first few years, and the total number of participants growing fairly steadily throughout the century. The Conference long remained a consultative body whose function was to help Wesley arrive at decisions in his administration of the Methodist societies, though it steadily increased in stature and eventually became the supreme legislative and administrative organ of Methodism. From the first there was an implicit understanding that Wesley would be guided by the clearly expressed desire of the majority, though never during his lifetime was there a straightforward government by a majority vote.[4] The results of the early deliberations were published by him in 1749 in two documents with identical titles: *Minutes of some late Conversations between the Rev. M. Wesleys and others.* These pamphlets followed the question-and-answer pattern of the conferences themselves, with Wesley posing the questions on the agenda (to which others might be added), and Wesley summarizing the discussion with his answer, the recorded decision of the Conference. The first printed document summarized the debates in the gatherings of 1744, 1745, 1746, and 1747, which codified the basic theological emphases of the Methodist preachers, from which it has been popularly known as the 'doctrinal minutes'. The second comprised the decisions of other sessions of those same conferences, together with that of 1748, but dealt mainly with matters of polity and administration, from which it has come to be known as the 'disciplinary minutes'.[5]

The first task for which Wesley sought his colleagues' aid was that of defining their evangelical message in as explicit terms as possible. From the outset it was considered quite unnecessary to lay down a

general theological framework. The Methodists accepted almost without question the historic creeds and their interpretation in the Articles,
Homilies and Liturgy of the Church of England, although in 1744 eight
of the Articles were indeed summoned for examination before the
tribunal of Scripture.[6] Their main task was to explore the problems
both implicit and explicit in the theology of salvation, what within a
decade Wesley was calling 'the Methodist doctrine', and even 'the old
Methodist doctrine'—known to later generations as 'our doctrines',
implying those upon which the Methodists placed peculiar emphasis, not
those about which they held peculiar views. A few of the thirty-six
questions on the agenda of the first conference furnish a key to the
whole range of these special emphases: 'What is it to be justified? . . .
Are works necessary to the continuance of faith? . . . In what sense is
Adam's sin imputed to all mankind? . . . In what sense is the righteousness of Christ imputed to believers, or to all mankind? . . . What is
implied by being made perfect in love?'[7] These and similar doctrines
were thoroughly debated not only in the light of the Bible but also of
the writings of the early Fathers, of later Anglican theologians, and
of 'serious dissenters'. They were also tested against specific examples of
actual Christian experience. Not only were the doctrines themselves
discussed, but the best methods of preaching them.[8]

Even before the series of conferences had dotted all the theological I's
and crossed all the casuistical T's, Wesley had begun to codify Methodist
doctrine by collecting his own sermons. This was probably precipitated
by the need to secure legal protection for his preaching-houses. Clearly
buildings were necessary for the varied activities of the societies, especially during the colder months, and buildings had been leased, and
bought, and built. In order to make quite sure that these were used for
Methodist purposes John Wesley had himself carried the financial and
administrative burden for this property, and to that end (at the urgent
recommendation of George Whitefield and others) had even cancelled
a deed conveying the Bristol headquarters to trustees.[9] With the increasing magnitude and complexity of the task, however, he was
convinced that some means must be devised for devolving this responsibility upon others in such a way as to ensure both the purity of the
doctrine proclaimed on Methodist premises and their legal security for
Methodist purposes. By Methodist purposes Wesley understood, of
course, not the formation of distinct congregations each choosing and
maintaining its own minister—a real danger when property was vested
in local trustees—but a nation-wide spiritual fellowship meeting in
distinct groups but linked by itinerant preachers whose chief aim was to
evangelize and sustain the spiritual glow rather than to serve and

administer settled churches. The itinerancy and the connexional principle were inextricably interwoven, and both were essential in the task for which Wesley believed Methodism had been raised up, the spreading of scriptural holiness throughout the land. It became more and more clear that some legal settlement was necessary to secure these spiritual ends, and in this he clearly must envisage the possibility that the need for the Methodist societies might continue long after his death, whether these societies remained in the church or outside it.

In the spring of 1746, therefore, after taking legal advice, Wesley settled three of his chief properties, at Bristol, Kingswood, and Newcastle, on model trust deeds. (The Foundery at London, like West Street and other chapels in the metropolis, was a leased building, and therefore in a different category.) These deeds contained no mention of the Church of England, and their main purpose was simply to secure the continuance of evangelical preaching under the direction of John Wesley, after his death of Charles Wesley, and after the death of both of them by preachers nominated by the trustees themselves. In 1750 the Rev. William Grimshaw's name was added as the designated successor of the Wesleys in control of the Methodist societies, and in 1784 the conference of preachers was named to discharge this function.[10]

The necessary task of defining the kind of preaching for which the premises were held in trust proved very difficult, and Wesley's eventual solution was to insist on the teaching contained in his *Explanatory Notes upon the New Testament* and the first four volumes of his *Sermons*. Neither of these standard publications, of course, prescribed anything contrary to the Articles or *Homilies* of the Church of England, but simply concentrated upon and made more explicit certain areas of teaching in those Anglican documents. Nevertheless, it was clear that defining the doctrinal bases of a society which was supposedly an integral part of a church without specific reference to that church could be interpreted as tantamount to the formation of a new sect.[11]

Neither *Notes* nor *Sermons* were available when these first model deeds were prepared, and Wesley tried to ensure continuity of teaching after his death and that of his brother by stipulating that the trustees should appoint persons 'to preach and expound God's holy word in the said house in the same manner, as near as may be, as God's holy word is now preached and expounded there'.[12] This unavoidable lack of precision must surely have formed one of the most pressing reasons why towards the end of 1745 Wesley began producing a definitive statement of Methodist doctrine in his sermons. The first volume of what was originally projected and announced as a three-volume work was published in 1746. Volumes 2 and 3 were issued in 1748 and 1750. Ten years later Wesley issued a supplementary volume which consisted largely of tracts on Christian duties. In effect, however, by 1750 he had fulfilled his intended purpose, which was thus explained in the preface to Volume 1:

> The following sermons contain the substance of what I have been preaching for between eight and nine years last past. . . . Every serious man who peruses these will therefore see, in the clearest manner, what those doctrines are which I embrace and teach as the essentials of true religion. . . .
>
> I have accordingly set down in the following sermons what I find in the Bible concerning the way to heaven. . . . I have endeavoured to describe the true, the scriptural, experimental religion, so as to omit nothing which is a real part thereof and to add nothing thereto which is not. And herein it is more especially my desire, first, to guard those who are just setting their faces toward heaven . . . from formality, from mere outside religion . . .; and, secondly, to warn those who know the religion of the heart, the faith which worketh by love, lest at any time they make void the law through faith, and so fall back into the snares of the devil.[13]

Although the title of the four volumes was *Sermons on Several Occasions*, these were by no means miscellaneous hortatory utterances, but a carefully planned body of doctrine, a creed in solution, presented as 'plain truth for plain people'.[14] To illustrate this we may draw attention to some facts revealed by tracing some of his favourite texts through his sermon register for the years 1747 to 1761.[15] Two unique Marcan texts appear frequently: Mark 1:15, on which he preached 129 times, was published in Volume 1 of the *Sermons* under the title 'The Way to the Kingdom'; but a sermon on a companion text, 'Thou art not far from the kingdom' (Mark 12:34), although used on 51 occasions, was never published. Similarly, Wesley preached from I Kings 18:21 on 38 occasions and from II Kings 5:12 on 19 without publishing a sermon on either text, but his sermon on 'Catholic Spirit' from II Kings 10:15 was published in Volume 3 of the *Sermons* even though he had preached from that text only twice, at Newcastle on 8 September 1748 and at Bristol on 3 November 1749. It is quite clear that these volumes were deliberately prepared as a body of preached doctrine rather than a collection of favourite sermons. This very deliberateness was yet another means of identifying the Methodists, and became another instrument for securing their independence of the church.

The 1744 conference laid a foundation not only for the establishment of Methodist doctrine but of Methodist discipline. The very first disciplinary subject discussed was that of the relationship of the societies to the Church of England. Wesley and his colleagues confidently asserted that they were not separating from the church, though they did differ from some of its clergy and were prepared to obey the bishops only 'in all things indifferent'—i.e. where no conscientious scruple was involved. The possibility of an eventual schism was frankly faced. Wesley believed that after his death most Methodists would remain true to the church unless they were thrust out, and pledged himself to take whatever steps he could to prevent any such eventual schism. He was convinced, however, that the spiritual needs of the contemporary situation demanded that he take such a risk: 'We cannot with good conscience neglect the present opportunity of saving souls while we live, for fear of consequences which may possibly or probably happen after we are dead.'[16]

The 1745 conference elaborated this point about obedience to ecclesiastical authority. Wesley would submit to the discipline of the rubrics, but not to that of individuals: 'If any bishop wills that I should not preach the gospel, his will is no law to me.' The justification pleaded for this attitude was, of course, the same apostolic one that he had claimed before the bishops face to face: 'I am to obey God rather than man.'[17] He went on to consider the basic forms of church polity then in existence, in response to the question, 'Is Episcopal, Presbyterian, or Independent church-government most agreeable to reason?' In this instance, where scriptural evidence was almost negligible, reason and antiquity furnished his main criteria, though in fact he did not provide a real answer to the question, but instead a summary of early church history. Whether by accident or by design this unduly simplified (and therefore inaccurate) account could have served almost equally well as an outline of the early history of Methodism:

The plain origin of church-government seems to be this. Christ sends forth a preacher of the gospel. Some who hear him repent and believe the gospel. They then desire him to watch over them, to build them up in the faith, and to guide their souls in the paths of righteousness.

Here then is an *independent* congregation, subject to no pastor but their own, neither liable to be controlled in things spiritual by any other man nor body of men whatsoever.

But soon after some from other parts who are occasionally present while he speaks in the name of Him that sent him, beseech him to

come over and help them also. Knowing it to be the will of God he
consents, yet not till he has conferred with the wisest and holiest of
his congregation, and with their advice appointed one or more who
has gifts and grace to watch over the flock till his return.

If it please God to raise another flock in the new place, before he
leaves them he does the same thing, appointing one whom God has
fitted for the work to watch over these souls also. In like manner, in
every place where it pleases God to gather a little flock by his word
he appoints one in his absence to take the oversight of the rest, and
to assist them of the ability which God giveth. These are *Deacons*,
or servants of the church, and look on the first pastor as their common
father. And all these congregations regard him in the same light, and
esteem him still as the shepherd of their souls.

These congregations are not absolutely *independent*: they depend
on one pastor, though not on each other.

As these congregations increase, and as their deacons grow in
years and grace, they need other subordinate deacons or helpers, in
respect of whom they may be called *Presbyters* or Elders, as their
father in the Lord may be called the *Bishop* or Overseer of them all.[18]

The conference of 1746 examined more fully the question of the
ministry, stressing the call of God as more important than the call of
man, yet also maintaining the right of a congregation to choose its own
pastor, which had been adumbrated in 1745.[19] As for his lay preachers,
Wesley claimed that both he and they should be considered as 'extraordinary messengers, designed of God to provoke the others to jealousy'.[20] He went on to formulate tests of the genuineness of their
divine call and regulations for their growth in efficacy. In reply to some
who would have preferred 'more form and solemnity in receiving a
new labourer', Wesley used weighty words that revealed his reluctance
to undertake anything that might imply the founding of a new sect,
though at the same time they proved his readiness to follow that
sectarian path if God were eventually to summon him that way: 'We
purposely decline it: (1) Because there is something of stateliness in it:
(2) Because we would not make haste. We desire barely to follow
Providence, as it gradually opens.'[21]

The opening session of the 1747 conference heard Wesley's version of
Luther's *Freedom of the Christian Man*:

Q.5. It was then inquired, How far does each of us agree to submit
to the unanimous judgment of the rest? And it was answered: 'In
speculative things each can only submit so far as his judgment shall

be convinced, in every practical point so far as we can without wounding our several consciences.'

Q.6. Can a Christian submit any farther than this to any man or number of men upon earth?

A. It is undeniably plain he cannot: either to Pope, Council, Bishop, or Convocation. And this is that grand principle of every man's right to private judgment in opposition to implicit faith in man on which Calvin, Luther, Melanchthon, and all the ancient Reformers both at home and abroad, proceeded: 'Every man must think for himself, since every man must given an account for himself to God.'[22]

Once more the question of schism was discussed, and Wesley reiterated his loyalty to the Established Church, enunciating the principle guiding that loyalty: 'We will obey the rules and the governors of the church whenever we can consistently with our duty to God: whenever we cannot we will quietly obey God rather than man.'[23] Wesley agreed that in the New Testament the three orders of deacons, priests, and bishops were described, but not that they were prescribed, insisting that 'necessary variety' in church order was God's intention. He claimed that the 'divine right of episcopacy' was first asserted in England during the reign of Queen Elizabeth, and that the idea of a national church was 'a mere political institution'.[24] Thus, during the first decade of the revival, Wesley had formulated views of church and ministry that were charismatic rather than authoritarian, and therefore held within them the seeds of sectarianism.

Long after the doctrinal and disciplinary foundations of Methodism had been securely laid the Conference continued to fulfil another important function—to unify the Methodist societies throughout the nation. To unify, be it noted, not to petrify. New ideas were constantly being suggested, examined, tried out, rejected or accepted, and then applied in different areas with varying degrees of success and with accumulating modifications. Methodism was a growing organism whose every limb, every cell, was connected to the head by the nervous system of the preachers and the life-blood of a disciplined evangelical impulse. The Wesleys were quite clear that they must follow the leadings of the Holy Spirit, but equally clear that they must do it both scripturally and rationally—to 'try the spirits whether they are of God' (I John 4:1) and to 'prove all things; hold fast that which is good' (I Thess. 5:21). They were even ready to make the experiment of preaching without the arduous follow-up work of organizing societies —what might be called Whitefield's method. This did indeed offer the opportunity of accepting more invitations to preach, but proved such a dismal failure that it provided a salutary warning of where their real strength lay.[25]

Gradually the general pattern of the connexional system became clear: a Methodist society in each evangelized community, subdivided into classes and (usually) bands, each with lay leaders who assured the flow of inspiration and information between the individual members, each supervised by lay itinerant preachers who visited them frequently, as did the Wesleys occasionally; a network of itinerant preachers moving from society to society throughout the nation, preaching in the open air, forming new societies, keeping in constant touch with the Wesleys, and meeting with them annually in conference in order to settle problems, to consider new openings for evangelism, new ideas for improving its efficacy, and to station the preachers during the coming year. At the 1746 conference England was subdivided into seven rounds or circuits, with two or three preachers assigned to travel in each circuit, both the location and composition of each group of preachers changing monthly. In spite of the advantage of ensuring variety this plan proved unduly cumbersome, and in 1747 the preachers were performing two-monthly stints in nine circuits, with Ireland added.

Bit by bit the growth of the societies both in number and in size necessitated more concentration in order to avoid wasted effort, so that three or four preachers were assigned to remain in a circuit for a year at a time. These men really earned their title of itinerant or travelling preachers. Within their circuits they were constantly on the move, making a series of rounds of different towns and villages lasting six or eight weeks at a time, during which they hardly ever slept in the same bed twice: after a week-end in the main centre of population back they went to their regular itinerary. Each year they were moved to a new circuit to follow a similar pattern. This principle of itinerancy was dear to Wesley, however irksome to the flesh and however productive of desertions by preachers who wanted to settle down in a quiet little pastorate. Without any doubt, quite apart from its value in preserving both variety and expectancy in both societies and preachers, the itinerant system linked Methodism into a living unity, a 'connexion', in a way which the inspiring travels of Wesley alone could never have done. The Established Church was a national machine, with many cogs broken and badly in need of overhaul. The Methodist societies were much more a national *body*, exuberant with life, tensing young muscles and rapidly developing into a mature, co-ordinated individual. All this was happening in the name of infusing new spiritual life into the Establishment, but in effect it was creating a Methodist establishment.

Nor did the closer unification of the societies simply happen. In this matter at least Providence was given a push. Unity was deliberately planned as a means to efficiency. This planning came to a focus in the 1748 conference:

> Q.8. Would it not be of use if all the societies were more firmly and closely united together?
>
> A. Without doubt it would be much to the glory of God, to the ease of the ministers [i.e. the Wesleys], and to the benefit of the societies themselves both in things spiritual and temporal.[26]

At least one step was taken immediately towards this end by instructing all the preachers to co-operate with the stewards of each society in securing membership lists and spiritual reports to bring to the annual conference.

Arising experimentally out of this expressed desire for a more tightly-knit organization came the circuit quarterly meeting, first suggested by two members of that 1748 conference (John Bennet and William Darney) to Wesley's lieutenant in the north, the Rev. William Grimshaw of Haworth. The first Methodist quarterly meeting was held, with Grimshaw presiding, on 18 October 1748—strangely enough not in his own parish, but in one where he had formerly served as curate. This quarterly assembly for both mutual encouragement and administrative purposes brought together the preachers and the lay leaders of all the societies within a circuit, and proved of immense value. By its aid the rapidly growing Methodist connexion was divided into manageable larger units which were able to bridge the gap between the individual society and the conference. Although some years passed before it arrived at maturity the circuit quarterly meeting proved as valuable for fostering the connexional spirit of Methodism as the class meeting had in forging the larger societies into inter-related groups of members with an enhanced sense of belonging to each other.[27]

The year 1749 was epochal in this coming of age of Methodism as a national entity. The doctrinal emphases and overtones of Methodist preaching had been hammered out on the anvil of debate, and the general patterns of Methodist polity had been refined. Summaries of both had been published. At this year's conference the first subject on the agenda was 'the general union of our societies throughout England'. It seems possible, indeed, that an additional one-day conference was summoned later in the year for the specific purpose of discussing this question.[28] Various proposals were put forward to encompass the desired end of making the societies 'as one body, firmly united together by one spirit of love and heavenly mindedness'. It was agreed that quarterly meetings should be organized in every circuit and that one of the itinerant preachers should be named Wesley's 'Assistant', responsible on

his behalf for all the societies therein. Each Assistant should 'make diligent enquiry at every quarterly meeting concerning the temporal as
well as the spiritual state of each society', and 'put them into a regular
method of keeping their accounts and transacting all their temperal
affairs'. The activities of the different circuits should be co-ordinated by
regular correspondence between the assistants and the stewards of the
Foundery in London.

In all this planning, Wesley approached as near as he ever came to
drawing up a blue-print of an ideal organization instead of solving
individual problems as they arose. In his enthusiasm he even allowed a
word to slip into the recorded minutes which so far he had firmly
rejected, at least as applied to his societies: 'Might not the [society] in
London be accounted the mother church? And the stewards of this
consult for the good of all the churches?'[29] Elsewhere in the manuscript
minutes of this conference the normal word 'society' was used, but in
this passage 'church' re-appeared in the printed editions of the 'Large
Minutes' published in 1753 and 1763. From subsequent editions the
whole section was deleted. By that time the close union of the societies
had been accomplished, and the separatist tendencies of the word
'church' doubtless pointed out by brother Charles.[30] After thus outlining the substance of his scheme for a Methodist establishment
Wesley closed: 'Being thus united together in one body of which Christ
Jesus is the head, neither the world nor the devil will be able to separate
us in time or in eternity.' Then he seemed to come down to earth,
realizing that this was after all a dream, and that they must deal with
what was immediately practicable: 'Q.2. How may we make some
advances towards this?'[31] After all, his personal dreams of marital happiness with Grace Murray had been shattered only a few weeks earlier by
his own brother marrying her off to one of his trusted lay preachers—
the same one who had been mainly responsible for introducing the
institution of the quarterly meeting. An imperfect world indeed, in
which it was best not to be carried away by one's dreams, especially
when those dreams seemed at variance with one's settled convictions!

By this time Wesley was not only prepared but felt compelled to
support his family of societies by any means which were not demon-
stratively contrary to Scripture, and was ready to suffer whatever disciplinary measures might be inflicted by the governors of the church. If
necessary he would face being cast out of the Church of England, and so
being forced to found a new denomination, in which case his conscience
would be quite clear of any charge of schism. He maintained that he
would never voluntarily separate from the church, though he had in
fact separated *within* the church. Already the Methodist societies formed

an *ecclesiola in ecclesia*, a little church with its own organization and leadership and ethos, even with its own doctrinal emphases—although Wesley's teaching was certainly not (for the most part) new, but a forgotten part of the orthodox heritage of the parent body.

What Wesley had brought into being was a new form of church polity, a 'connexion' which corresponded neither to congregationalism nor presbyterianism nor diocesan episcopalianism as it existed in his own day, but was perhaps nearer to the formative formlessness of the primitive church with its dominant notes of evangelism and pastoral care, and its loose affiliation of varied groups linked by apostolic labours. Wesley described this as a 'society', though it differed alike from the old Societies for the Reformation of Manners, from the Horneck/Woodward Religious Societies, all of which formed more or less independent parochial groups, and from the Society for the Propagation of the Gospel and the Society for Promoting Christian Knowledge, which though like Methodism organized on a national basis were almost solely administrative in character, in effect committees of church leaders sponsoring worthy causes outside themselves. We might claim, indeed, that what Wesley had founded was a new S.P.C.K.—a Society for Promoting Christian Koinonia. Or those realizing his strong ties with the primitive Greek tradition might suggest that Methodism was a new attempt at creating a Pilgrim Community of the Holy Spirit, dedicated to Sobornost, 'a community distinguished by unity in freedom and creating out of many races and nations the family of the redeemed'.[32] Certainly the Methodist societies were more flexible in character, more adaptable to varying circumstances, more united around common spiritual aims and a common leader, than any others in Wesley's England: they also came much nearer to offering something like a complete substitute for the parish church and its ordained ministry.[33]

In all this Wesley deliberately avoided any kind of rigidity either in teaching or organization. All was to be responsive to the needs of the moment and the workings of the Holy Spirit. True, he sought to define the essential ingredients of the message which he proclaimed, but he made no attempt to provide a systematic theology. Nor was this simply from exigencies of time or talent. His fundamental concern was not with a *Summa Theologica* nor a *Christianae Religionis Institutio* but with the *Imitatio Christi*. He knew that this needed to be translated afresh into the terms of each generation, and so provided, not only a best-selling printed *Christian's Pattern*, but a thriving society adapting itself 'to serve the present age'. For John Wesley any theology which dealt only with a transcendent God, like any church which remained merely an institution, was little more than empty speculation, fruitless organization. He must present a God who was immanent and active in the fellowship and evangelism of a living Christian community alert to the needs and opportunities of its secular environment.

Wesley's over-all purpose was not consciously to found a new church or sect, but to revive the old one from within by proclaiming the doctrines of personal salvation and by gathering groups together for the practice of Christian fellowship. Although this was more fully articulated in later years the fundamental approach never changed. One of the best known sections of the 'Large Minutes' of 1763 summarized Methodism's function in church and nation:

> Q[uestion]. What may we reasonably believe to be God's design in raising up the preachers called Methodists?
> A[nswer]. To reform the nation, and in particular the church; to spread scriptural holiness over the land.[34]

Wesley constantly emphasized that this was his sole purpose, nor until 1789 did he deem it necessary to prefix the phrase, 'Not to form any new sect, but . . .'

Writing to the Rev. Samuel Walker of Truro on 3 September 1756, Wesley began:

> Reverend and Dear Sir,
> I have one point in view—to promote, so far as I am able, vital, practical religion; and by the grace of God to beget, preserve, and increase the life of God in the souls of men. On this single principle I have hitherto proceeded, and taken no step but in subserviency to it.

He went on to show that all the methods of Methodism—its societies, its lay preaching, its itinerant system, its complex connexional organization—arose piecemeal through the necessary demands of this spiritual principle:

> With this view, when I found it to be absolutely necessary for the continuance of the work which God had begun in many souls (which their regular pastors generally used all possible means to destroy) I permitted several of their brethren, whom I believed God had called thereto and qualified for the work, to comfort, exhort, and instruct those who were athirst for God, or who walked in the light of His countenance. But as the persons so qualified were few, and those who wanted their assistance very many, it followed that most of these were obliged to travel continually from place to place; and this occasioned several regulations from time to time, which were chiefly made in our Conferences.

He added: 'So far as I know myself, I have no more concern for the reputation of Methodism or my own than for the reputation of Prester John.'[35] This was a slight exaggeration, but Wesley had made his point. What concerned him was that the *work of God* committed to Methodism should continue, whether in the church or out of it, whether through the Methodist societies or through some other organization, whether under his own leadership or that of someone else. He was prepared to sacrifice not only himself but his preachers, his societies, even the church itself, if he were convinced that thus he might advance the cause of God.

The peculiar and unique tension between the Methodist societies and the Church of England throughout most of Wesley's lifetime undoubtedly arose from his peculiar brand of churchmanship, and especially from this urgent thrust for evangelizing and forming societies in accordance with methods framed bit by bit to meet spiritual emergencies. The continuity of the gospel was far more important to him than the continuity of the church, though he would dearly have loved to preserve both. Charles Wesley seconded John's aspirations most of the way, and when eventually he could no longer wholly agree slipped into the background without creating too much trouble apart from an occasional pained complaint flung at his brother from the wings.

It became increasingly apparent that the new wine was going to burst the old bottles, and that Wesley was going to find it extremely difficult both to secure the permanence of the Methodist witness and to avoid forming a new denomination. He undertook a few not very hopeful inquiries about co-operation with other religious groups, he sought to secure a union of the evangelical clergy, he even felt compelled to make at least tentative plans for the possible continuance of Methodism as a distinct body after his death. These varied experiments continued simultaneously from 1749 onwards, the year which to a large extent marked the maturing of Methodism as an entity, and the complete throwing aside of Wesley's narrower churchmanship, as heralded by his sermon *Catholic Spirit*.

EIGHT

A CATHOLIC SPIRIT

WITH the identity and unity of the English Methodist societies securely established, Wesley paid a closer attention to other Christian groups who were seeking similar ends. One of his early ecumenical adventures took place in Anglesey, nominally Anglican, but poised between the enthusiastic Dissent of North Wales and the predominant Catholicism of Dublin. Methodism had been introduced to Dublin in 1747, and John Wesley had followed up his brother Charles in visiting Ireland that year, *via* Holyhead. He had little direct interest in North Wales, and no interest at all in learning the peculiar language spoken by the majority of its inhabitants. This was the territory of his good friend and colleague Howell Harris. Being held up in Holyhead by fickle weather and frail sea-transport, however, he used his time to advantage by distributing copies of his printed sermons, and even venturing to preach.

In Anglesey Wesley found a strange intermingling of Anglicans and Dissenters, as well as a readiness to co-operate in evangelical enterprise once mutual trust had been established. At first Methodism in Anglesey had been identified with the militant dissent which had invaded from Carnarvonshire. As a result of the prejudice thus aroused, Howell Harris and company had found it almost impossible to gain any favour in spite of fair speeches and self-denying ordinances not to fraternize with avowed dissenters. One of the strongest opponents of Methodism, thus imperfectly understood, was the Rev. Thomas Ellis of Holyhead, who had published an attack on the Methodists as 'schismatics' which went through two editions. During Wesley's visits to Holyhead in August 1747 Ellis missed him, otherwise (says William Morris) 'there would have been a scuffle perhaps'.[1] In February 1748 Wesley was delayed in Holyhead for a week, and preached at the inn there. Ellis came in towards the close of the sermon and began 'speaking warmly' to the landlord. Wesley's preacher-companion Robert Swindells managed to intervene with the clergyman, and even to soften his wrath sufficiently for 'a long and friendly conversation'. The result was described in Wesley's *Journal* for 27 February:

> Mr. Swindells informed me that Mr. Ellis would take it a favour if I would write some little thing to advise the Methodists not to leave

the church, and not to rail at their ministers. I sat down immediately
and wrote 'A Word to a Methodist', which Mr. Ellis translated into
Welsh and printed.[2]

This statement (set down much later) apparently needs revising in so far
as it implies that Ellis himself published Wesley's pamphlet. Certainly
this was not the original intention, as appears from Wesley's letter to
Howell Harris written the following day:

> I presume you know how bitter Mr. Ellis (the minister here) used to
> be against the Methodists. On Friday he came to hear me preach. I
> believe with no friendly intention. Brother Swindells spoke a few
> words to him, whereupon he invited him to his house. Since then
> they have spent several hours together, and I believe his views of
> things are greatly changed. He commends you much for bringing the
> Methodists back to the church; and at his request I have wrote a little
> thing to the same effect. He will translate it into Welsh, and then I
> design to print it both in Welsh and English. I will send you some as
> soon as I can, that you may disperse them when you see occasion.
> I thought it good to apprise you of this before. I know your heart is
> herein as my heart.[3]

'I know your heart is herein as my heart.' This Old Testament phrase
in a letter tactfully informing Harris of what might possibly have been
construed as another invasion of territory reappeared in the pamphlet
which Wesley had prepared for Ellis, and the following year furnished
the text for one of Wesley's most fruitful sermons on ecumenical co-
operation—'Catholic Spirit'. F. E. Stoeffler refers to this phrase as a
characteristic emphasis of Pietism.[4] Although Wesley was indeed prepared to work with all who earnestly sought to proclaim Christ as
Saviour, he still believed that this could best be done in hearty co-
operation with the Church of England, as also did Ellis and Harris.
Hence his *Word to a Methodist*, prepared at Ellis's request. When at last
the packet-boat set off for Dublin, Wesley carried with him Ellis's
translation of this pamphlet, entitled *Gair I'r Methodist*. He published
this Welsh version from a Dublin press, and it was reprinted with minor
corrections in 1751. It was long thought to have disappeared completely,
but in fact one copy of each edition has survived, though it appears
never to have been published in English as Wesley planned. In order to
reconstruct what Wesley wrote, therefore, we need to re-translate back
from Ellis's Welsh and adjust the result to Wesley's known stylistic
preferences.[5]

Wesley opened his *Word to a Methodist* by asking whether his readers believed in a string of Pauline texts which he presented as a summary of the evangelical faith, and added: 'Then thy heart is as my heart: give me thy hand.' Challenging them to be sure that this faith was not unfruitful in their own lives he instanced some of the dangers they faced:

> Some of you have turned away from the Church of England in which you were brought up, you have forsaken the sacrament and the church service. Why was this necessary? Without leaving the church you can adhere to all the great and glorious truths of the gospel; and without turning your backs on either the sacrament or the church prayers you can certainly be holy in your conduct. Why then did you have to leave the church? I cannot understand this.

To their arguments that they were jeered at and called by nicknames for going to church, Wesley replied, 'Endure it for Christ's sake'; to the plea that they were more comfortable when they stayed away, 'That may be, but the less your comfort, the greater your blessing'. He pressed home his point: 'There is no reason for you to leave the church, but there are many strong reasons to the contrary.' These he enumerated:

> 1. Have you not received a blessing there from God more than once in times past?
> 2. Have not many others received the same thing in the prayers and the Lord's Supper? . . .
> 3. If there are but two or three in the whole congregation who know God, Christ is there in their midst, and where He is should not his servant be also?
> 4. Were He not there previously, go you who know God, and take his blessing there with you.
> 5. If you are Christians you are 'the salt of the earth' (Matt. 5:13); but how can you season others unless you move in their midst? If you are Christians you are like the little leaven which leavens the whole lump (I Cor. 5:6). But if you do not come in contact with the dough how will it be leavened? . . .
> Lastly, do you not by leaving the church bring ridicule upon the truths you hold or profess? Yea, and harden people's hearts against the truth, those who but for that might accept it in love. O think on this! If these are counted lost in their sins, will not their blood be on your heads?

If some of the Welsh-speaking Methodists nevertheless continued reluctant to return to the Church of England he pleaded that they should at least avoid harmful criticism of her:

I beg of you do not scorn or belittle her, do not offer her reproach or disrespect or abuse; for that is no less than bringing a 'railing accusation' against her, which the archangel would not bring against the devil himself (Jude 9). How much less should any one of us bring an accusation against the Church of England, all of whose doctrines we subscribe and hold, whose Common Prayer Book we love, and in communion with which we have received so many blessings from God.

Wesley even asked reverence for the '*building* commonly called the church'. More especially he pleaded for respect towards the clergy:

Allow me to give you one further advice: 'Behave courteously towards ministers'; yea, even to those who are not as they should be; yea, unto the worst of them—even if you suppose that one of them is not only wicked, but also opposes the truth he should be preaching. ... Whatever he does your rule is clear: 'Dearly beloved, revenge not yourselves, but rather give place unto wrath, for it is written, Vengeance is mine, I will repay, saith the Lord' (Rom. 12:19). ... If possible think not of them except in prayer. Do not speak of them at all. If anyone tells you about their conversation or their misdeeds silence him with this answer: 'Let them alone.' If you yourself should happen to see them doing wrong or hear them speaking ill, take care not to tell anyone else. Rather let that word of our Lord's be engraved on your heart, 'What is that to thee? Follow thou me' (John 21:22).

In Anglesey at any rate this publication, combined with the advocacy of Howell Harris, bore fruit. Anglican visitation inquiries undertaken in 1749 showed that there were a few Methodists in nearly every parish, but that most of them came 'regularly and zealously' to church.[6]

Narrow-mindedness and bigotry in religion were by no means confined to Wales, and Wesley saw them among the Methodists as well as among both dissenters and churchmen. Indeed, with the increasing tempo of the revival there seemed to be an increase in the ill-informed antagonism of both clergy and rival sectarians alike, and a corresponding increase in the self-righteous indignation of the Methodists. It was as an appeal to all Christians in danger of regarding others as rivals that Wesley prepared his sermon on 'Catholic Spirit', hanging it upon the text which apparently gripped his mind in Anglesey: 'And when he was departed thence he lighted on Jehonadab ... and he ... said to him, Is thine heart right, as my heart is with thy heart? And Jehonadab answered, It is. If it be, give me thine hand' (II Kings 10:15). This sermon marked the discarding of most of the narrower prejudices of Wesley's earlier churchmanship, though he was still only feeling his way to a matured catholicity. He seems first to have preached from this text in Newcastle on 8 September 1748, and used it again at Bristol on 3 November 1749. It first appeared in print in the third volume of his *Sermons on Several Occasions* in 1750.

Even a lengthy extract hardly does justice to this important ecumenical pronouncement, but it seems best nevertheless to let Wesley speak for himself, however briefly.

10. Although . . . every follower of Christ is obliged by the very nature of the Christian institution to be a member of some particular congregation or other, some 'church' as it is usually termed, . . . yet none can be obliged by any power on earth but that of his own conscience to prefer this or that congregation to another, this or that particular manner of worship. I know it is commonly supposed that the place of our birth fixes the church to which we ought to belong, that one (for instance) who is born in England ought to be a member of that which is styled 'The Church of England', and consequently to worship God in the particular manner which is prescribed by that church. I was once a zealous maintainer of this: but I find many reasons to abate of this zeal. I fear it is attended with such difficulties as no reasonable man can get over. Not the least of which is that if this rule had took place there could have been no Reformation from Popery, seeing it entirely destroys the right of private judgement on which that whole Reformation stands.

11. I dare not, therefore, presume to impose my mode of worship on any other. I believe it is truly primitive and apostolical: but my belief is no rule for another. I ask not, therefore, of him with whom I would unite in love, 'Are you of my church, of my congregation? Do you receive the same form of church government, and allow the same church officers, with me? Do you join in the same form of prayer wherein I worship God?' I inquire not, 'Do you receive the Supper of the Lord in the same posture and manner that I do?' Nor whether in the administration of baptism you agree with me in admitting sureties for the baptized, in the manner of administering it or the age of those to whom it should be administered. Nay, I ask not of you (as clear as I am in my own mind) whether you allow baptism and the Lord's Supper at all. Let all these things stand by: we will talk of them, if need be, at a more convenient season. My only question at present is this: 'Is thine heart right, as my heart is with thy heart?'[7]

To make it quite clear that this was no flash in the pan but a deliberate re-orientation of his thought we may quote the closing section of Wesley's *Letter to the Reverend Doctor Conyers Middleton*, written in January 1749. This closing section was reprinted under the title *A Plain Account of Genuine Christianity*, and went through six separate editions during Wesley's lifetime. Wesley claimed that the true Christian was a man full of love to his neighbour, of universal love, not confined to one sect or party, adding:

> Away with names! Away with opinions! I care not what you are called. I ask not (it does not deserve a thought) what opinion you are of, so you are conscious to yourself that you are the man whom I have been (however faintly) describing.

He added later that this universal love was 'the strongest evidence of the truth of Christianity', far more important than any traditional evidence, and that it was this spirit of humble love which characterized the best of the primitive Fathers, more than cancelling their limitations and short-comings. These he carefully listed: 'Clemens Romanus, Ignatius, Poly-carp, Justin Martyr, Irenaeus, Origen, Clemens Alexandrinus, Cyprian, to whom I would add Macarius and Ephraim Syrus.'[8]

A companion-piece to 'Catholic Spirit' was another sermon published in the same 1750 volume, 'A Caution against Bigotry', This was in part an appeal that those bigoted against a lay preacher should not forbid him as the disciples forbade the man who did not belong to their group but who was nevertheless casting out devils (Mark 9:38,39). Wesley also directed his message at all party spirit in Christian belief and practice:

> Suppose, then, a man have no intercourse with us, suppose he be not of our party, suppose he separate from our church, yea and widely differ from us both in judgment, practice, and affection; yet if we see even this man 'casting out devils', Jesus saith 'Forbid him not'. . . . Beware how you attempt to hinder him either by your authority or arguments or persuasions. Do not in any wise strive to prevent his using all the power which God has given him.[9]

In order to put the case as strongly as possible he continued:

> What if I were to see a Papist, an Arian, a Socinian, casting out devils? If I did I could not forbid even him without convicting myself of bigotry. Yea, if it could be supposed that I should see a Jew, a Deist, or a Turk, doing the same, were I to forbid him either directly or indirectly I should be no better than a bigot still . . . If he forbids *you*, do not you forbid *him*. . . . Imitate herein that glorious saying of

a great man (O that he had always breathed the same spirit!) 'Let Luther call me an hundred devils; I will still reverence him as a messenger of God.'[10]

That very year of 1749, indeed, Wesley had sought a measure of reconciliation also with the Roman Catholics, in his *Letter to a Roman Catholic*. In this he pared down the basic minimum of Christianity to love of God and love of man:

> My dear friend, consider, I am not persuading you to leave or change your religion, but to follow after that fear and love of God without which all religion is vain. I say not a word to you about your opinions or outward manner of worship. But I say, all worship is an abomination to the Lord unless you worship him in spirit and in truth; with your heart as well as your lips; with your spirit, and with your understanding also. Be your form of worship what it will. . . . Use whatever outward observances you please. . . . But honour his holy name and his Word, and serve him truly all the days of your life.[11]

On this basis he urged:

> In the name, then, and in the strength of God, let us resolve: First, not to hurt one another. . . . Secondly, God being our helper, to speak nothing harsh or unkind of each other. . . . Thirdly, resolve to harbour no unkind thought, no unfriendly temper, towards each other. . . . Fourthly, endeavour to help each other on in whatever we are agreed leads to the kingdom.[12]

In accordance with the spirit of these publications, Wesley had striven for co-operation between the Arminian and Calvinist wings of the revival. He readily responded to a request from the Welsh Calvinistic Methodists that he should attend one of their Associations in order to prevent the building up of undue rivalry between the two arms of the movement. Accordingly on 22 January 1747 he and four of his assistants met with Harris and his colleagues in Bristol. In addition to remedies suggested for specific problems it was agreed in general:

> That wheresoever we might occasionally preach among each other's people we would endeavour to strengthen rather than weaken each other's hands, and particularly to labour to prevent separations in the societies.[13]

It was in the spirit of this agreement that Wesley had informed Harris of his Anglesey labours and their outcome. In 1749 another attempt was made to secure a rapprochement. On 2 and 3 August the two Wesley brothers met with Howell Harris and George Whitefield at Bristol. John Wesley's memorandum of their conversations is still extant. The purpose and agenda were summarized thus: 'How far can we unite with each other? Either in affection? In judgment? Or in jointly carrying on the work of our common Master?' As for the first heading, they unanimously agreed 'not willingly to speak of each other's opinions in such a manner as to make them either odious or contemptible'. In matters of judgment they frankly discussed their wide doctrinal differences, and decided never to preach controversially; when they could not avoid incidentally touching upon some controversial topic they would attempt amicably to blend each other's favourite expressions with Scripture. As for a joint organization the document was not too hopeful, but suggested the prerequisites for such a scheme:

> III. In order to facilitate an union in carrying on the Work of God it was agreed:
> 1. Each of us to take a copy of the preceding minutes.
> [2. To read] these, as we find occasion, to some of our preachers.
> 3. And to a few prudent persons of our flock,
> 4. But to suffer no copy thereof to be taken, nor our own copy ever to go out of our hands.[14]

Howell Harris's journal shows that one of their decisions was also 'to abide in the communion of the Established Church and to look upon the bishops as fathers till thrown out'.[15]

Both Harris and Whitefield were somewhat afraid of John Wesley's overpowering personality and administrative competence, which might lead to his predominance. Harris recorded: 'I mentioned my fears lest he [Wesley] should ask to be head and form a party. Mr. Whitefield mentioned his objection to his monopolizing the name of Methodist to himself only.'[16] Charles Wesley's journal noted: 'August 3. Our conference this week with Whitefield and Mr. Harris came to nought; I think through their flying off.'[17] To his own copy of the minutes John Wesley added the endorsement, 'Vain agreement!'

In fact, however, it was not quite in vain. A measure of evangelical co-operation between the Wesleys and Whitefield had once more been achieved to complement their never-quite-broken friendship. Not until the year of Whitefield's death did the Calvinist-Arminian tension once more break out into open war. Whitefield was personally introduced by the Wesleys to their chief followers, and remained an evangelist welcome to rove throughout the Methodist societies until his death. It must be realized, of course, that most of the concessions in this instance were made by the Wesleys, because Whitefield had very few societies to offer, and in fact proved himself somewhat hesitant in introducing Wesley to those few, and in the case of Harris downright obstructive. Harris found Wesley much easier to get along with, and much more amenable to frank criticism. The projected union of Harris's Welsh societies with Wesley's did not in fact mature, though in 1750 they did hold yet another conference on the subject. One suspects that a major reason was that in his wide charity Harris had urged that he was 'for a full union, not as a party, but so as to be open to invite too the Dissenters and Moravians'.[18] This was still a little too much for the Wesleys' catholic spirit.

Minor dissensions continued to disturb the co-operation between the Wesleys, Whitefield, and Harris, especially on the matter of preaching extreme Calvinist doctrine in Wesley's societies. The 1753 Conference tried to counteract the 'predestinarian preachers' by barring Methodist pulpits to them, and by asking Whitefield in particular 'not to declare war anew'.[19] In 1758 Whitefield felt able to write to Professor Francke in Germany in optimistic terms:

> Mr. Wesley has societies in Ireland and elsewhere; and though we differ a little in principles yet brotherly love continues. When itinerating I generally preach among his people as freely as among those who are called our own.[20]

Preaching interchanges continued through the years.[21] A disruption between Daniel Rowlands and himself drove Harris into semi-retirement at Trevecka in 1751, from which he was only gradually coaxed by the Wesleys and others. Not until 1759 did he return to itinerating, and from that time maintained wide contacts with evangelicals from several denominations, and even tried to engineer a union between the Wesleys and the Moravians.[22] The last major conference to secure continued preaching interchange between the Wesleys and Whitefield (representing also the Countess of Huntingdon's chapels) took place in August 1766, and the countess herself sought to keep this alliance both alive and active until the sad controversies of 1770.[23] Whitefield and Harris attended Wesley's 1767 Conference as honoured guests, and the Wesleys preserved a warm friendship with both men until their deaths in 1770 and 1773 respectively.[24] Both Harris and Wesley preached funeral sermons for Whitefield, Wesley being welcomed to Whitefield's London Tabernacle for this purpose. Wesley also paid public tribute to Harris's memory on the occasion of his first visit to Trevecka after his death.[25]

Until the bitter doctrinal dissensions of 1770 and onwards there were other examples of co-operation between the Arminian and

Calvinist wings of the revival. One of the most interesting occurred at Norwich, where the Tabernacle had been built with the aid of the Countess of Huntingdon by James Wheatley, one of Wesley's preachers who had been expelled for immorality, but who had since reformed. In 1758 Wheatley invited Wesley to this Calvinist pulpit, and soon the Tabernacle and Wesley's Foundery society in Norwich were sharing joint evangelism and worship. Wesley conducted joint communion services and organized 'classes without any distinction between them who had belonged to the Foundery or the Tabernacle'.[26] He remained sensitive about the dissenting scruples of many of the Tabernacle congregation, noting in his *Journal* for 18 March 1759:

> I administered the Lord's Supper to near two hundred communicants. So solemn a season I never remember to have known in the city of Norwich. As a considerable part of them were dissenters, I desired every one to use what posture he judged best. Had I required them to kneel probably half would have sat. Now all but one kneeled down.[27]

This co-operation lasted until 1765, though it proved a constant source of embarrassment. One Sunday evening in September 1759 Wesley told the united congregation that they were 'the most ignorant, self-conceited, self-willed, fickle, untractable, disorderly, disjointed society' that he knew in the British Isles, and in 1763 claimed: 'For many years I have had more trouble with this society than with half the societies in England put together.'[28]

From the outset the Tabernacle worshippers had been accustomed to receive the Lord's Supper from their own preacher, William Cudworth, and it was almost certainly upon their insistence that Wesley's preachers administered communion here in 1760, and thus almost precipitated a separation from the Church of England.[29] Similarly the Tabernacle society had normally held services at the same time as the parish church, and Wesley experienced great difficulty in ridding them of this separatist tendency. In 1763 he first stated that he 'would immediately put a stop to preaching in the time of church service', and then persuaded a large body of the members to attend church worship with him.[30] All this reinforced Wesley's convictions about the dangers of independent congregations and the values of a unified connexion with a firm central control. He was not prepared to purchase union with any group, large or small, no matter how evangelical, at the expense of worsening Methodist relations with the Church of England. Possibilities for ecumenical enterprise without any danger of breaking with the Church of England, however, continued to attract his attention.

Benjamin Ingham, one of the Oxford Methodists who had accompanied the Wesleys to Georgia, had become a successful pioneer evangelist and organizer of religious societies in the north of England. He had handed over his first group of societies to the care of the Moravians. In 1749, however, he declared that he was 'neither Methodist nor Moravian but a lover of mankind, and that his design in going about was to bring souls to a saving knowledge of Jesus Christ'.[31] He continued to raise societies which paid at least lip service to the Church of England, though like Wesley's they were completely independent of any Anglican control except that exercised by Ingham himself, an ordained deacon of the church. In 1749 William Grimshaw initiated an attempt to link Ingham's societies with Wesley's, and enlisted Whitefield's aid to this end. On this occasion, however, although Charles Wesley was sympathetic, John would have nothing to do with the proposal. At the Conference of 1753 it was asked: 'Can we unite, if it be desired, with Mr. Ingham?' The answer was cautious: 'We may now behave to him with all tenderness and love, and unite with him when he returns to the old Methodist doctrine.'[32] An equally cool reception awaited Ingham and his colleagues at the 1755 Conference, so that later that year he summoned a conference of his own preachers and leaders. This settled a constitution and rules for the Inghamite societies, and Ingham took the drastic step of ordaining two of his preachers. After a few years the Inghamite movement largely disintegrated, and most of the preachers and societies joined the dissenters.[33] There seems little doubt that John Wesley thus felt vindicated for his refusal of Ingham's overtures, having sensed the undoubted separatist tendencies to which he would have been exposing his own already infected followers.

The Moravians presented an even more promising yet also more difficult and dangerous possibility of organic union. Charles Wesley always remained sympathetic to 'the Germans', and especially to their English leader James Hutton.[34] John Wesley had been far less forthcoming ever since their doctrinal embroilment in 1740–41, and in particular had come to entertain an increasingly low opinion of Count Zinzendorf. For his part Zinzendorf seems to have frustrated a Moravian move towards reconciliation with the Methodists during 1746 and 1747.[35] In 1749 the Moravians gained recognition by the British Parliament as an ancient Protestant episcopal church, though they still needed to license their preachers and premises under the Toleration Act.[36] Zinzendorf was fired with an ecumenical vision of all devout Christians constituting a universal community overriding all denominational differences, a 'Congregation of God in the Spirit'. Within this

each distinct communion would form a 'Tropus' with its own particular 'Jewel' of Christian experience to contribute to the common
pool, which would include all forms of polity and worship. In 1749
John Gambold, another Oxford Methodist who had thrown in his lot
with the Moravians, suggested that an Anglican tropus might be
formed, and Dr. Thomas Wilson, Bishop of Sodor and Man, agreed to
serve as President. To make the bonds even closer, in 1754 John Gambold was elected the first English Moravian bishop.[37] John Wesley
remained unconvinced.

On 16 May 1760 Zinzendorf died. Later that year John Wesley at
last made overtures to the British Moravians to discuss the possible
union which he had been pondering for at least four years, and there is
no doubt that Zinzendorf's removal triggered his action. Our inform-
ant about this venture is Howell Harris, who in fact served both as
encourager and go-between.[38] John Wesley told his preachers, assembled in conference at Bristol, that the Moravians would no longer
look to one man as their head—they were in fact in a similar position
to that which the Methodists would experience after his own death.[39]
At a later stage in the Conference he 'proposed taking some steps
toward a union with the Moravians', namely 'to offer a Conference, he
and his brother with Mr. Gambold and Nyberg, and then for them to
propose it to as many as they please, then to meet six or more on a
side'.[40] The following day Harris went to see Laurentius Nyberg, a
Moravian then living in Bristol, who 'rejoiced in it and was willing
and would write to Johannes [i.e. Bishop Johannes de Watteville] and
to Mr. Gambold'.[41] Harris urged that it was a misconception among
the Moravians that the Methodists took people away from the church,
'not allowing any fellowship except coming plump to their plan and
under their care'.[42] In spite of his warm advocacy, however, this move
came to nothing. Harris himself took the initiative in bringing the two
Wesleys together with Nyberg again in 1763—which he termed
'striving for universal union and for the clergy to meet each other'—but
still to no effect.[43]

Organic union, of course, was not the only means of expressing a
catholic spirit. Sympathetic understanding was itself a potent force,
whether or not it led to occasional active participation in joint Christian
ventures. On one point Wesley was quite clear. He roundly condemned
all persecution on religious grounds, witness his scathing remarks about
the treatment of the original Nonconformists when he first read
Edmund Calamy's account of their sufferings:

In spite of all the prejudices of education, I could not but see that the poor Nonconformists had been used without either justice or mercy; and that many of the Protestant bishops of King Charles had neither more religion nor humanity than the Popish bishops of Queen Mary.[44]

He was quite prepared to defend the victims of religious persecution even when he strongly disagreed with the opinions for which they had been persecuted. Thus he defended the Reformed and Lutheran churches, maintaining that they had been 'violently thrust out of' the Church of Rome because they would not subscribe to 'all the errors of that church'. They did not *separate*, for separation is a voluntary removal, whereas the Reformation was 'not a matter of choice but of necessity'.[45] Wesley agreed that the Reformed churches of Europe formed a part of 'the Catholic Church, that is, the whole body of men, endued with faith working by love, dispersed over the whole earth, in Europe, Asia, Africa, and America'. With these he contrasted the Church of Rome, maintaining that it was neither 'founded by Christ himself', 'one', 'holy', nor 'secured against error'.[46]

In common with most English Protestants of his age, Wesley was unable to regard the Roman Catholics dispassionately, and his prejudice against them was increased by reaction against being himself mistaken for the Young Pretender during the 1745 Rebellion, and in more recent years hearing Methodism seriously likened to Roman Catholicism. Although appreciative of Catholic piety, he was at pains to point out the many fundamental differences in doctrine and polity, and even in morals, between the Methodists and Rome. In 1753 he published *The Advantage of the Members of the Church of England over those of the Church of Rome*, and in 1756 reprinted Bishop John Williams's *A Roman Catechism, with a reply thereto*.[47] Thomas Walsh, a devout and eminently capable Irish preacher who had been converted to Methodism from Roman Catholicism, was distressed that Wesley refused to allow his Irish preachers to administer the sacraments as a means of securing the convinced allegiance of Roman Catholic converts. This was the burden of his dying expostulations:

> Sir, they must have the ordinances of Christ, but they will not go to church. They will not hear the men whose ungodly lives they daily behold; but they will joyfully communicate with those by whom they have been brought to God. You may open the kingdom of heaven to those multitudes who have hitherto walked in the way to hell, as they have been led. Beware how you shut it against them.[48]

Wesley nevertheless remained obdurate, unready to stretch his catholic spirit to these limits at the cost of precipitating a separation from the Church of England.

It was one thing to recognize the validity of non-episcopal churches in Europe and America, and even in Scotland and Ireland, where the argument of 'necessity' could be used in their favour. In England and Wales, however, there existed a national episcopal church whose ministrations were almost universally available. Those denominations, therefore, that set up in opposition to it, as dissenters from its constitution and worship, were clearly on a different footing from those in other lands who knew no better and were forced to frequent the only churches accessible to them. Wesley remained intent on renewing and supplementing the national church, not on supplanting it. He therefore found it almost impossible actively to second the efforts of English dissenters from the church, difficult even to tolerate them:

No sinful terms of communion were imposed upon them; neither are at this day. Most of them separated either because of some opinions or some modes of worship which they did not approve of.[49]

In other words they had left the church by choice rather than necessity. In his *Farther Appeal*, Part II (1745), he castigated the various dissenting bodies in some detail for their separation over inessential points:

The people called Quakers spent their main strength in disputing about opinions and externals rather than in preaching faith, mercy, and the love of God. . . .

In these respects the case was nearly the same when the Baptists first appeared in England. They immediately commenced a warm dispute, not concerning the vitals of Christianity, but concerning the manner and time of administering one of the external ordinances of it. . . .

The same occasion of offence was in a smaller degree given by the Presbyterians and Independents; for they also spent great part of their time and strength in opposing the commonly-received opinions concerning some of the circumstantials of religion; and, for the sake of these, separated from the church.[50]

Wherever dissenters continued to wrangle over opinions about church order or theology Wesley was exceedingly cautious about committing himself to any kind of co-operation with them. Just as most of his *Christian Library*, however, had been given over to the devotional writings of the Puritans, and just as he excepted from his condemnation of the Nonconformists men of irenic piety like Philip Henry, so he was always ready to collaborate with the dissenters of his own day who gave themselves to practical religion rather than to controversy. In this he was much more tolerant than his brother Charles, who in a moment of panic in 1760 wrote to John Nelson: 'Rather than see thee a dissenting minister I wish to see thee smiling in thy coffin.'[51] In Part II of his *Farther Appeal* John Wesley marvelled that he had so far been cured of religious bigotry that he could now think of the dissenters as his 'brethren', though in varying degrees of remoteness from the Church of England at its spiritual best. The Presbyterians and Independents were 'the smallest distance from us', the Anabaptists 'one step farther', and there was 'a still wider difference in some points between us and the people usually termed Quakers'. Not even the Church of Rome was completely disenfranchised, though in her case there was 'an abundantly greater difference still'.[52]

As might be expected, the extent of Wesley's collaboration with ministers of these bodies was in the same order as this list.[53] His embracing of Presbyterians is most worthy of note. His friendship with Dr. Philip Doddridge is well known. As early as 1745 he visited Doddridge's academy at Northampton, and by invitation delivered a Bible exposition to the students. Doddridge, indeed, afforded Wesley important help in preparing for his *Christian Library*.[54] In April 1753 Wesley accepted an invitation from Dr. John Gillies of Glasgow to stay in his home and preach in his church. Wesley inserted a surprised comment in his *Journal*:

> Surely with God nothing is impossible! Who would have believed five-and twenty years ago either that the minister would have desired it or that I should have consented to preach in a Scotch kirk!

In 1755 Wesley was able to return the compliment by offering the pulpit of the Newcastle Orphan House to Gillies. They remained good friends for life.[55] From time to time Wesley shared the hospitality of other Presbyterian pulpits, especially in Scotland and Ireland, but also in England, as at Swalwell, County Durham, where in 1759 he preached in the Presbyterian meeting-house when pouring rain prevented his usual open-air gathering.[56]

To Presbyterianism Wesley was much more sympathetic than to any other English denomination, though he saw and bemoaned the tendency of many English Presbyterians to slide by way of speculative theology into Unitarianism. The connexional system of Methodism was closer to theirs than to that of any other denomination. Presbyterianism was also the polity of the national church of Scotland, and therefore deserving of a special kind of tolerance and respect. Wesley reproached the Presbyterians chiefly for their often extreme Calvinism. This charge was levelled also against both Independents and Baptists, who were in addition much more guilty of sheep-stealing. Many of Wesley's preachers, having tasted the intoxicating fruits of public status, bec am pastors of Independent congregations.[57]

Wesley became more and more convinced, however, that the spirit of Methodism could be preserved only as the Methodists avoided the dissenters in general: 'I see clearer and clearer, none will keep to us unless they keep to the church. Whoever separate from the church will separate from the Methodists.'[58] Indeed, he told Samuel Walker that any group of Methodists who deliberately separated from the church was therefore debarred from the Methodist connexion, instancing a group at Falmouth in 1755. He confessed, however, to 'want of more resolution and firmness of spirit' in applying this policy.[59] In any event, the true focal point for evangelical dissenters was not Wesley but Whitefield.

From the early days dissenters had been allowed into membership of the Methodist societies on equal terms with churchmen. The comparatively few who availed themselves of this opportunity for deep spiritual fellowship were expected to keep any peculiarities of doctrine to themselves, and especially to eschew controversy. For many, however, this proved too difficult, and at one Conference the propriety of their admission was therefore the subject of debate among the preachers. Wesley closed the discussion with the words:

I have no more right to object to a man for holding a different opinion from me than I have to differ with him because he wears a wig and I wear my own hair; but if he takes his wig off and begins to shake the powder about my eyes I shall consider it my duty to get quit of him as soon as possible.[60]

To the end of his days Wesley continued to insist on an ecumenical approach, even if on occasion it thus needed to be modified. The preface to his important *Explanatory Notes upon the New Testament*, written in January 1754, well represents this irenic outlook:

I cannot flatter myself so far . . . as to imagine that I have fallen into no mistakes in a work of so great difficulty. But my own conscience acquits me of having designedly misrepresented any single passage of Scripture, or of having written one line, with a purpose of inflaming the hearts of Christians against each other. God forbid that I should make the words of the most gentle and benevolent Jesus a vehicle to convey such poison! Would to God that all the party names and unscriptural phrases and forms which have divided the Christian world were forgot, and that we might all agree to sit

10

down together, as humble, loving disciples, at the feet of our common Master, to hear his word, to imbibe his spirit, and to transcribe his life in our own![61]

So far did he remain from party spirit that forty years after its first utterance he was still echoing his sermon on *Catholic Spirit*:

One circumstance more is quite peculiar to the people called Methodists: that is, the terms upon which any person may be admitted into their society. They do not impose, in order to their admission, any opinions whatever. Let them hold particular or general redemption, absolute or conditional decrees; let them be Churchmen or Dissenters, Presbyterians or Independents, it is no obstacle. Let them choose one mode of worship or another, it is no bar to their admission. The Presbyterian may be a Presbyterian still: the Independent or Anabaptist use his own mode of worship. So may the Quaker; and none will contend with him about it. They think and let think. One condition, and one only, is required—a real desire to save their soul. Where this is, it is enough. They desire no more. They lay stress upon nothing else. They ask only, 'Is thy heart herein as my heart? If it be, give me thy hand.'[62]

WESLEY'S CHANGING CHURCHMANSHIP

THE first quarter-century of Wesley's ministry witnessed changes both in his religious practices and his doctrine of the church, the ministry, and the sacraments. Already it has become clear that these things were mutually influential: his practices modified his theology, and his changed theology led him into new practices. Most of his ecclesiastical innovations were forced upon him by emergencies, when he clutched at the likeliest expedient to further the work to which he firmly believed that God had called him. Each of these breaches made in the defences of his orthodoxy made him the more prepared for further innovations, and his mind the more receptive to unconventional views of the church and ministry. In other instances, however, innovations were first prepared for in the realm of thought, and were translated into ecclesiastical action later. Our purpose in this chapter is to summarize the changes which had taken place in his thinking about the nature and authority of church and ministry by the year 1755, including those which so far had not been put to the test of action.

Throughout his adult life Wesley responded with varying degrees of enthusiasm to two fundamentally different views of the church. One was that of an historical institution, organically linked to the apostolic church by a succession of bishops and inherited customs, served by a priestly caste who duly expounded the Bible and administered the sacraments in such a way as to preserve the ancient traditions on behalf of all who were made members by baptism. According to the other view the church was a fellowship of believers who shared both the apostolic experience of God's living presence and also a desire to bring others into this same personal experience by whatever methods of worship and evangelism seemed most promising to those among them whom the Holy Spirit had endowed with special gifts of prophecy and leadership. The first view saw the church in essence as an ancient institution to be preserved, the second as a faithful few with a mission to the world: the first was a traditional rule, the second a living relationship. In the church as an institution Wesley had been born and reared and ordained: into the church as a mission he was gradually introduced, in part by his parents, but increasingly by a widening circle of colleagues, and especially by a growing awareness of God's calls upon him as an individual. In this process every inch of institutional loyalty reluctantly yielded at the challenge of providential openings led to the demand for another yard. Nevertheless, just as something of the Pietist sectarian approach was present in his youthful upbringing, so to his life's end he retained several Catholic convictions, and although his ecclesiastical odyssey was in general from one pole to the other he was subject to occasional fluctuation.

Wesley himself later summarized the springs of his churchmanship on the eve of his Aldersgate experience and his mission to England:

> From a child I was taught to love and reverence the Scripture, the oracles of God: and next to these to esteem the Primitive Fathers, the writers of the three first centuries. Next after the Primitive Church I esteemed our own, the Church of England, as the most scriptural national church in the world. I therefore not only assented to all the doctrines but observed all the rubrics in the liturgy, and that with all possible exactness, even at the peril of my life.
>
> In this judgment and with this spirit I went to America, strongly attached to the Bible, the Primitive Church, and the Church of England, from which I would not vary in one jot or tittle on any account whatever. In this spirit I returned, as regular a clergyman as any in the three kingdoms.[1]

This was the classical Anglican approach, entailing obedience to God's will as revealed in the Bible, interpreted by the church both ancient (especially) and modern, and recognized by reason, God's light in all men. Already for Wesley there had been an addition to this board of directors mediating God's will, as well as some shifting of power among them. Already he was convinced that in some instances God made His will known also through the Holy Spirit speaking directly to the educated and responsive human conscience, at least when dire spiritual need was frustrated in its search for some clear word of guidance from Scripture. Already during his Oxford years there had been a strengthening of the mystical element in his life, as also a temporary heightening of his dependence upon Christian antiquity, and during his Georgia years a pragmatic preparedness for experimentation in ministerial method, wedded to a waning enthusiasm for reproducing antiquity in liturgical detail. The pietism of the Lutheran Salzburghers and the Moravians had injected a doubt into his own Caroline pietism about the absolute necessity of episcopacy to a true church, and his study of Beveridge had disillusioned him about the transmission of true doctrine and practice by Church Councils and the Post-Nicene Fathers. Mainly under the spell of these German pietists, whom he saw as living patterns of the Spirit-directed primitive Christians, Wesley came to place less importance on speculative theology and ritualistic practice, much more on a conscious personal experience of a living God. Testing their teaching by Scripture, reason, and experience, he himself had sought in prayer, along with the continued use of the divinely appointed means of grace, a personal assurance of salvation by faith in Jesus Christ as 'the one thing needful'. This once experienced all else took on a supporting rather than a determining significance, and he *knew* by the immediate authorization of the Holy Spirit that at that moment he was right with God, and that his time and talents must all be devoted to introducing others to this same rich experience. This he wished to do within the ordered ways of the Church of England, but if that proved impossible he would be ready to accept any method that was not contrary to the Scriptures, reason, and the voice of God within, and would be ready also to suffer whatever ridicule, censure, or persecution, official or non-official, which this personal following of Providence might generate.

In seeking solutions to the many problems posed by his unfolding prophetic ministry in a missionary movement, Wesley continued to turn to his old authorities. Uncorrupted antiquity was the co-ordinate with reason in interpreting or supplementing Scripture; these also revealed new insights into the nature of a pragmatic church and ministry far different in some respects from the idealized apostolic preconceptions which he had hoped to transplant in eighteenth-century England or an unspoiled pioneer community in America. The apostolic *spirit* became the important thing, and this was still available through direct spiritual contact with God. The promptings of this spirit he tested rationally, and then applied them by a process of trial and error, thus determining whether and how far what he had heard with his spiritual ear was indeed the voice of God.

Wesley continued to follow a system of checks whenever he thought to venture on ecclesiastical experiments of doubtful orthodoxy. One test was to find Scripture that approved his conduct—or at least to be assured that no Scripture condemned it. Another was to see if it was in tune with the spirit (and better still the letter) of practice in the primitive church. Again he would examine the proposed expedient to see if it made sense when compared with his own experience of a God-guided, man-governed world. If it passed all these tests, he would try it. If it actually brought about the spiritual ends to which he believed himself divinely guided, or even others of obvious value of which he had never dreamed, then clearly this was a method approved by God, and he had no hesitation in pursuing it in spite of persecution by hooligans or criticism by more orthodox churchmen. Always, however, he tried as far as possible to secure the support of church authorities, deliberately cultivating tact and discretion, though not always successfully. He still believed that the Church of England was the nearest national approach to the apostolic church that could be found in an imperfect world, and still wished to reform her from within rather than to set up a rival institution.

All too briefly we have summarized Wesley's conception of theological authority and method by which he sought guidance as he approached one of the great ecclesiastical watersheds in his life. This was his agreement to share Whitefield's extra-parochial ministry in Bristol, with its corollary of going to the fields. This was undertaken only after much prayer, added to extensive bibliomancy and sortilege. In his *Journal* for 28 March 1739 Wesley spoke of himself as entering upon a 'new period' in his life.[2] What was his view of the church at this turning-point, based upon these authorities and formulated (or at least arrived at) by these methods? In what respects was this view later modified? By what influences, and in what stages? To these questions we now turn.

The major change which occurred gradually during the years 1739-45 was a relaxing of Wesley's views on valid church government. It is important to trace this change step by step. Even at the beginning of the revival Wesley was no blindly dogmatic episcopalian. His Georgia experience of ministering to a parish of mixed denominations had helped to soften some of his prejudices. The Salzburghers and Moravians in particular were influential in this, but so also were the Scots Presbyterians, and even the Spanish-speaking Jews, some of whom, he said, seemed 'nearer to the mind that was in Christ than many of those who call Him Lord'.[3] At least subconsciously Wesley was inclined at this time to Richard Baxter's vision of a church comprehending all sincere Christians, whatever their church polity. He had discovered Baxter's *Saints' Everlasting Rest* in 1732, and even then would surely have endorsed a passage in Baxter's dedication which later he omitted from his own drastic abridgement of the work because it was irrelevant to his theme of the moment. Baxter was discussing the duty of Christians of varying traditions and convictions:

To agree upon a way of union and accommodation, to come as near together as they can possibly in their *principles*; and when they cannot, yet to unite as far as may be in their *practices*, though on different principles; and where that cannot be, yet to agree on the most lovable peaceable course in the way of carrying on our different practices, that so . . . we may have *unity* in things necessary, *liberty* in things unnecessary, and *charity* in all.[4]

Wesley's famous sermon on 'Catholic Spirit', preached in 1749, might well have taken this passage as its inspiration rather than wresting Jehu's words out of their context. Wesley said:

Although a difference in opinions or modes of worship may prevent an entire external union, yet need it prevent our union in affection? . . . May we not be of one heart, though we are not of one opinion? . . . Every wise man, therefore, will allow others the same liberty of thinking which he desires they should allow him. . . . He bears with those who differ from him, and only asks him with whom he desires to unite in love that single question, 'Is thy heart right, as my heart is with thy heart?'[5]

It took ten years for Wesley to reach that position of what may be considered extreme catholicity. Even in 1738, however, he believed that his churchmanship had been modified towards far greater tolerance of denominational differences and less rigidity of priestly authority and sacerdotal ritualism. Nevertheless, he remained too much a loyal son of the Established Church to stomach readily either a congregational polity or laymen taking over the functions of the clergy. Gradually, however, he became reconciled in a measure to both.

On Wesley's return from his pilgraimage to Herrnhut he had enthusiastically advocated the system of 'bands' for all the religious societies in London, including that in Fetter Lane, which he and Böhler had founded on 1 May 1738. Lay leaders or 'monitors' for those bands were desirable, but he was very doubtful about the idea of permanent 'general monitors' to supervise the others, even when proposed by his trusted convert and friend James Hutton, in whose home the society met. He was prepared to accept such a general monitor *pro tempore* in the absence of a minister, but shrank from any *ex officio* supervision, saying, 'A General Monitor commissioned by God to reprove every one of his brethren you have so long as you have any Priest or Deacon among you'.[6]

Wesley's letter of 27 November 1738 exhibits to perfection the caution of a loyal though catholic churchman when faced with the possibility of laymen taking over the functions of the clergy and introducing something very like a congregational polity:

I believe Bishops, Priests, and Deacons to be of divine appointment. . . . Therefore I am tender of the first approach towards 'pastors appointed by the congregation'. And if we should begin with appointing fixed persons to execute *pro officio* one part of the pastoral office, I doubt it would not end there. . . . I believe you don't think I am (whatever I was) bigotted either to the ancient church or the Church of England. But have a care of bending the bow too much the other way. The national church to which we belong may doubtless claim some, though not an implicit, obedience from us. And the primitive church may thus far at least be reverenced, as faithfully delivering down for two or three hundred years the discipline which they received from the Apostles, and [they] from Christ.[7]

A few years were to pass before Wesley perforce accepted this kind of lay supervision by assistant preachers over his own proliferating societies, and it was not long thereafter that these same preachers did in fact seek the kind of ministerial status which he foresaw and feared. Wesley went on to urge Hutton that the religious societies must come second to the Established Church which they were designed to invigorate, and not set up as independent congregations: 'Are we members of the Church of England? First then let us observe her laws, and then the by-laws of our own society.'[8]

Strand by strand the ties of doctrine and practice binding Wesley to the English establishment frayed or were loosened. Within a year or so he changed his mind on the matter about which he had been so tender in his correspondence with Hutton, the acceptance of the right of congregations to choose their own pastors. This development was certainly possible under the episcopal polity. Richard Hooker had acknowledged the merit of the principle by indulging in some special pleading designed to show that in effect Anglican congregations exercised their democratic rights through the patrons who in many parishes had inherited the rights of nomination or presentation of clergy for the bishop's institution. Here Hooker was making a virtue out of necessity, for the patronage system was one of the targets for the reformers' scorn. Hooker also insisted that a clergyman could not exercise his ministry among his flock 'utterly against their wills'— though in fact almost their only practical recourse was to stay away from church.[9] The position had worsened in Wesley's day, and he himself complained that the bishop often tied a minister's hands, as by forbidding him to let Wesley preach in his parish church.[10] In spite of the theoretical rights of congregations to choose their pastors, and of pastors to exercise an unrestrained ministry under episcopal rule, the whole theory of a mutual pact between pastor and congregation smacked of nonconformity, and was therefore suspect to the Anglican hierarchy in general.

Wesley's own position on this matter remained delicately balanced. As a convinced episcopalian, in August 1740 he criticized the Moravians for being in effect congregational rather than episcopal in their polity, even though they held 'neither this nor any other form of church government to be of divine right'.[11] He claimed, in fact, that their church order was only an imitation of the real thing:

> Your church discipline is novel and unprimitive throughout. Your bishops as such as mere shadows, and are only so termed to please those who lay stress upon the threefold order. The Eldest is (in fact) your bishop. . . . The ordination (or whatever it is termed) of your Eldest plainly shows you look upon episcopal ordination as nothing.

Although this may in part be discounted as a somewhat peevish reaction to the trouble the Moravians had caused him in the Fetter Lane society, it confirms the fact that for him at this time the episcopal was the ideal and almost the only conceivable system of church government. When in 1744 Wesley came to publish this lengthy document in his *Journal*, however, he completely omitted the two sections dealing with Moravian polity.[12] In the interval his views had been greatly modified. Appreciating his sensitivity at this point, we realize that the breaking down still further of his prejudices was a minor ecclesiastical landmark. This came about through a correspondence with the Rev. Ralph Erskine, the Scots Presbyterian who with his brother Ebenezer in 1739 had formed an 'Associate Presbytery' and was formally deposed by the General Assembly of the Church of Scotland in May 1740.

There were several close parallels between the brothers Erskine and Wesley. Both pairs were poets as well as preachers. Both reverenced the Articles of their church but complained that the clergy in general were not loyal to those Articles. In attempting spiritual reform from within both engaged in field-preaching. Neither pair wished to separate from their parent body, but insisted that they would continue in their reforming behaviour until they were thrust out—which in the case of the Erskines came to pass speedily.

In his *Fraud and Falshood discover'd* (Edinburgh, 1743), Ralph Erskine published his correspondence with John Wesley. This does indeed support Erskine's contention that Wesley 'was in a reforming way, not only as to doctrine, but even as to presbyterian discipline and government'. Although they had chiefly been comparing notes on revival phenomena, Erskine had deliberately sought to indoctrinate Wesley as he had done Whitefield, and to that end sent him some Presbyterian literature, at the nature of which we can only guess. Wesley replied on 26 June 1740: 'I delayed answering your welcome letter till I could have time to read over and consider the tracts you was so kind as to send me.' He continued: 'Of one point which I knew not before it has pleased God to convince me by them, *viz.* that every Christian congregation has an indisputable right to choose its own pastor.'[13] Erskine's reply hailed this as a notable victory for Reformation principles, though he was unhappy that Wesley was not prepared to fence the Lord's Table and still regarded the Lord's Supper as a converting as well as a confirming ordinance.[14] Their correspondence withered, but Erskine had been responsible for inserting yet another wedge between Wesley and the Church of England. In later years this point was confirmed by other reading, and when in 1745 Wesley came to formulate his theories of church polity for the Methodist Conference he insisted on the theoretical right of a congregation to choose its own minister.

Q. 6. Is mutual consent absolutely necessary between the pastor and his flock?

A. No question: I cannot guide any soul unless he consents to be guided by me. Neither can any soul force me to guide him if I consent not.

Sheep were therefore free to leave their shepherd or the shepherd his flock whenever 'one or the others are convinced it is for the glory of God and the superior good of their souls'.[15] This position was confirmed by the 1746 Conference. In fact this was the kind of mutual agreement into which Wesley himself had entered with the Foundery society a few months before reading Erskine's tracts, and this kind of practical relationship would make him the more ready to alter his doctrinal views.

Admittedly this seems somewhat strange while Wesley himself continued to be the sole arbiter of the stationing of Methodist preachers. This apparent discrepancy between theory and practice he would doubtless have explained by pointing out that Methodist societies were neither churches nor independent congregations. His general conviction in this matter certainly remained firm, witness his important letter of 19 September 1757 to Rev. Samuel Walker:

Does Mr. Conon or you think that the King and Parliament have a right to prescribe to me what pastor I shall use? If they prescribe one whom I know God never sent, am I obliged to receive him? If he be sent of God, can I receive him with a clear conscience till I *know* he is? And even when I do, if I believe my former pastor is more profitable to my soul, can I leave him without sin? Or has any man living a right to require this of me?[16]

This extension of Christian liberty to the principle of 'mutuality' in the relations between pastor and flock may well have increased the tendency of many Methodists to become spiritual gypsies, and it certainly edged them nearer to the dissenting fold, where this principle was an axiom.

It is common knowledge that Wesley was eventually led to assume powers of ordination because of his early reading of two books, Stillingfleet's *Irenicum* and Lord Peter King's *Enquiry*. What these books in fact did was to continue the slow transformation in his thought about the church which had already been taking place in response to other reading, and more especially to the demands of his personal faith and his vocation as evangelist and pastor.

No one knows when Wesley first met *The Irenicum, a Weapon Salve for the Church's Wounds*, first published in 1659 by Edward Stillingfleet, later bishop of Worcester. It was a Latitudinarian attempt to prove that no form of church government was divinely ordained. Stillingfleet wrote as one striving to accommodate religion to philosophy and science, and viewed church government not only in its ecclesiastical context but as an expression of the eternal laws of nature. His more specific purpose was to heal the ecclesiastical controversies of his own day by pointing out that no one was wholly right, no one wholly wrong. Neither the New Testament nor the primitive church actually *prescribed* either congregational, presbyterian, or episcopal forms of church government, though all seem to have existed in apostolic times and to have enjoyed God's blessing. The important thing was not to dispute about polities but to accept whatever promised most spiritual fruit. Stillingfleet himself favoured some form of comprehension:

All parties may retain their different opinion concerning the primitive form, and yet agree and pitch upon a form compounded of all together as the most suitable to the state and condition of the Church of God among us: That so the people's interest be secured by consent and suffrage, which is the pretence of the congregational way; the due power of presbyteries asserted by their joint concurrence with the bishop;... and the just honour and dignity of the bishop asserted, as a very laudable and ancient constitution for preserving the peace and unity of the Church of God.[17]

A copy of the second edition of 1662 at Kingswood School carries

Wesley's inscription on the title page, 'I think he fully proves his point. J.W. 1760. Kingswood.' The volume was already an old friend, however. Although neither the arguments from silence nor those from influence are conclusive, it seems almost certain that Wesley first read Stillingfleet's work a year or two after Erskine had made his impact, between August 1741 (from which date his diaries are no longer available as a guide to his reading) and August 1745, when Stillingfleet's views seem to colour the deliberations of the second Methodist Conference. Possibly his influence had indeed made it easier for the first Conference of 1744 to discuss so calmly the possibility of separation. Certainly in 1756 Wesley wrote to the Rev. James Clark:

> I still believe 'the episcopal form of church government to be both scriptural and apostolical': I mean, well agreeing with the practice and writings of the apostles. But that it is *prescribed* in Scripture I do not believe. This opinion, which I once heartily espoused, I have been heartily ashamed of ever since I read Bishop Stillingfleet's *Irenicon*. I think he has unanswerably proved that 'neither Christ nor his apostles *prescribed* any particular form of church government, and that the plea of the divine right for diocesan episcopacy was never heard of in the primitive church.[18]

A second major transformation took place over a longer period, and much more slowly, in Wesley's views of the ministry. These may be considered apart from even though they are inextricably interwoven with his views of the church. We have seen earlier that Wesley refused to accept the authority of any bishop to silence his divine call to preach.[19] This position was confirmed at the 1744 Conference, where in response to the question, 'How far is it our duty to obey the bishops?' the answer was given: 'In all things indifferent. And on this ground of obeying them we should observe the canons, so far as we can with a safe conscience.'[20]

The authority of a bishop as spiritual governor was one thing, his uniqueness as the transmitter of spiritual grace in ordination another. Wesley seems to have retained his belief that in at least this respect bishops were of the *esse* rather than of the *bene esse* of the church until as late as 1745. His brother-in-law the Rev. Westley Hall had pressed him to 'renounce the Church of England', triggering an instinctive reflex action to a position probably more conservative than the liberal one which in general Wesley had by then accepted. In replying on 30 December 1745 he affirmed that the 'threefold order of ministry ... is not only authorized by its apostolical institution, but also by the written Word', and stated explicitly:

We believe it would not be right for us to administer either Baptism or the Lord's Supper unless we had a commission so to do from those bishops whom we apprehend to be in a succession from the apostles.[21]

Even here, however, Wesley did not claim that episcopal ordination was uniquely valid for all men, even though it was authoritative for him as a member of the Church of England. He admitted that the Anglican episcopate derived from the Church of Rome, and continued:

We believe there is and always was in *every* Christian church (whether dependent on the bishop of Rome or not) an 'outward priesthood' ordained by Jesus Christ and an 'outward sacrifice' offered therein, by men authorized to act as 'ambassadors of Christ and stewards of the mysteries of God' (I Cor. 4:1).

This does seem to allow for the validity of other than episcopal orders as well as for the dignity of churches other than those in the catholic tradition. Wesley did not come right out and say either that episcopal ordination only was valid or that there were other valid types of ordination, but the ambiguous silence probably indicated a more tolerant approach even in this statement than has been generally admitted. Certainly Wesley kept himself open to receive further light on the necessity of the threefold order: 'Yet we are willing to hear and weigh whatever reasons induce you to believe to the contrary.' We find a similar insistence on the antiquity and validity of episcopal ordination in his *Letter to a Clergyman* (1748): 'I believe bishops are empowered to do this, and have been so from the apostolic age.' Again, however, we notice the absence of the word 'only' on the one hand, as of 'and presbyters' on the other.[22] Wesley seems to have been cautious about committing himself to any extreme position. In fact this tolerance of non-episcopal orders had been characteristic of many Anglican divines of the previous century, who insisted that episcopacy was 'not of dominical but of apostolic appointment', and that its absence did not deprive a church of a valid ministry and sacraments.[23]

Later Wesley claimed that Stillingfleet had also convinced him that episcopal ordination was not essential to the valid administration of the sacraments.[24] In fact, however, his letter to Westley Hall shows that even though the message may have been accepted by his mind and will he was not yet fully and firmly convinced of the point. One more book was needed to weight the balance conclusively on the liberal side of the scales. Three weeks after writing to Hall, on the road from London to Bristol he read Lord Peter King's *Enquiry into the Constitution, Discipline, Unity, and Worship of the Primitive Church*, first published in 1691. In his *Journal* he entered this comment:

In spite of the vehement prejudice of my education, I was ready to believe that this was a fair and impartial draught. But if so it would follow that bishops and presbyters are (essentially) of one order, and that originally every Christian congregation was a church independent on all others![25]

In fact (as Edgar W. Thompson has pointed out) Wesley somewhat overstated King's case, perhaps because his own mind was already so strongly swayed in that direction. Although King maintained that presbyters and bishops were of the same order, and that there were clearer proofs that presbyters ordained than that they administered the Lord's Supper, he also claimed that there was an important difference in the degrees of their authority, so that the ecclesiastical acts of the presbyter were carried out only by the permission of the bishop: 'Presbyters were different from the bishops *in gradu* or in degree; but yet they were equal *in ordine* or in order.'[26]

Wesley acknowledged King's influence upon his doctrine of the church as well as of the ministry: King convinced him 'that originally every Christian congregation was a church independent on all others'. In fact he had maintained something very similar to this at the 1745 Conference, before he read King, but the *Enquiry* apparently reinforced this opinion, based largely on Stillingfleet. King had been pleading that the typical primitive diocese was in fact a large city parish served by several clergy, where all members could meet to discuss church matters with their ministers, and were in fact consulted about the appointment of a superintending bishop from among the presbyters serving groups in that municipal area. King claimed that bishops might be chosen by neighbouring bishops and approved by the local congregation, or chosen by the congregation and approved by the neighbouring bishops; in any case both were involved in such an appointment. This, he pointed out, was the practice of the apostles, 'who in the first plantation of churches ordained bishops and deacons with the consent of the whole church'.[27] Wesley certainly agreed that a congregation should thus share in the choice of their ministers—witness his reaction to Erskine in the light of Hooker's teaching—but this did not affect his belief that any *ordination*, even though it was not a sacrament, remained the prerogative of the clergy themselves.

In spite of the extreme youthfulness of the authors of both the *Irenicum* and the *Enquiry*, in spite of any later modifications which they made in their own theories, in spite of Wesley's misreading of what they wrote, an important point had been made. Henceforth Wesley could regard bishops only as specialized clergy, possibly of the *bene esse* of the church, but certainly not of its essence. This, at least, was the impression left on his mind when in 1753 he published the reference to King in his *Journal*. It cannot be claimed that King converted Wesley from episcopalian to Baxterian views, but he confirmed him in them. Erskine had played his own part in 1740 by convincing Wesley of the validity of the congregational principle; Stillingfleet a year or two later had made him the more certain that no one form of church government uniquely possessed divine right; early in 1746 he witnessed the elevation of the presbyterial chair to a place by the side of the episcopal throne, so that in 1747 he was prepared to assert before his preachers that any rigid scheme of uniformity in church government, whether episcopalian or other, was unscriptural, non-apostolic, and an absurd human folly.[28] Clearly this strengthened his defence of his own irregularities, and paved the way for possible further innovations.

Already by 1746 Wesley saw the essence of the church and its ministry as functional rather than institutional. This appeared clearly in his important correspondence with 'John Smith'. One of his most careful summaries of the true function of the church is to be found in his letter of 25 June 1746, which merits quotation at some length. Wesley was answering the familiar charge of 'breaking and setting aside [church] order':

What do you mean by order? A plan of church discipline? What plan? The scriptural, the primitive, or our own? It is in the last sense of the word that I have been generally charged with breaking or setting aside order, that is, the rules of our own church, both by preaching in the fields and by using extemporary prayer.

I have often replied: (1) It were better for me to die than not to preach the gospel of Christ, yea, and in the fields either where I may not preach in the church or where the church will not contain the congregation. (2) That I use the service of the church every Lord's Day, and it has never yet appeared to me that any rule of the church forbids my using extemporary prayer on other occasions.

But methinks I would go deeper. I would inquire, 'What is the end of all ecclesiastical order?' Is it not to bring souls from the power of Satan to God, and to build them up in His fear and love? Order, then, is so far valuable as it answers these ends: and if it answers them not it is nothing worth. Now I would fain know where has order answered these ends? Not in any place where I have been: not among the tinners in Cornwall, the keelmen at Newcastle, the colliers in Kingswood or Staffordshire; not among the drunkards, swearers, Sabbath-breakers of Moorfields, or the harlots of Drury Lane. They could not be built up in the fear and love of God while they were open barefaced servants of the devil: and such they continued notwithstanding the most orderly preaching both in St. Luke's and St. Giles's Church. One reason whereof was, they never came near the church, nor had any desire or design so to do till by what you term 'breach of order' they were brought to fear God, to love Him, and keep His commandments.[29]

This Wesley expressed still more dramatically a year later: 'I did far more good . . . by preaching three days on my father's tomb than I did by preaching three years in his pulpit.'[30]

Similarly, the institution of lay preaching was embraced under the exigencies of the evangelical situation, but confirmed by Wesley's reading. One obscure clue mistakenly connects this change in Wesley's churchmanship with Stillingfleet, but although the interpretation is somewhat difficult the clue itself should be recorded. In his manuscript journal Howell Harris recorded the proceedings of the Methodist Conference of 1760, when the two Wesleys argued that although the office of a preacher was legitimate for a layman, that of administering the sacraments was not. According to Harris's testimony:

> Mr. John Wesley said how he was convinced of a layman preaching by reading Bishop Stillingfleet's *Liberty of Prophesying*, and that the Council of Trent said that anyone called by the Spirit of God might preach.[31]

It seems likely that Harris conflated references to two books which had influenced Wesley in different ways, one being Stillingfleet's *Irenicum* and the other the *Liberty of Prophesying*. This title does not appear among Stillingfleet's publications. On the other hand Jeremy Taylor's well-known work of that title, which Wesley may well have read (though of this we have no other direct evidence) dealt mainly with the question of authority in religion and with religious toleration. Although there was no major section on lay preaching, however, two or three minor passages might well have been combined with a sudden illuminating flash to convince Wesley that the activities of men like Humphreys and Cennick and Maxfield were divinely authorized, though by themselves these passages could hardly be considered formidable arguments.[32] Perhaps some other work bearing that title was intended (though none appears in Watt's *Bibliotheca Britannica*); perhaps Wesley himself was confused. We would dearly like to know what work (apart from the Bible) convinced Wesley of the validity of the institution that was the most influential in the spread of Methodism.

The year 1749 seems to have formed another way-station in Wesley's churchmanship. In that year, having thrown over much of the influence of the Non-Jurors, he pointed out in print that the so-called 'Apostolic Constitutions' were spurious.[33] In that year he wrote a public apology for his former high church zeal in denying communion to Bolzius in Georgia because he had not been baptized by an episcopally ordained minister.[34] Later in the same year he preached his sermon on 'Catholic Spirit', published in 1750 as part of the doctrinal manifesto of his *Sermons on Several Occasions*.[35] By 1749 he had come to recognize the cumulative effect of the many seemingly small concessions to unorthodoxy that he had made over the years in order to further the Methodist cause. His own standards of religious authority had been clearly settled: the Anglican triad of Scripture, reason, and antiquity, strongly reinforced by an intuitive individualist approach deriving in part both from Pietist and mystical influence. The appeal to reason, however, had developed into an urgent pragmatism, by which he was able in good conscience to confirm both his main spiritual aims and the methods which served those aims. Whether or not it fitted into any known ecclesiastical pattern the Methodist connexional polity *worked*, and therefore must be accepted as part of the divine plan.[36]

Tradition had become of far less importance to him than spiritual success. The church and its hierarchy no longer held the keys of the kingdom. Originally he had accepted the traditional view that the Anglican bishops were in succession from the apostles themselves, probably accepting also (though this is less certain) the interpretation that this was tactile through the imposition of hands rather than historic through the occupancy of office. His letter to Westley Hall in December 1745 had been quite explicit: the right to administer the sacraments derived from the commission received 'from those bishops whom we apprehend to be in a succession from the apostles'.[37] This was his last known testimony in favour of apostolic succession, and he seems soon thereafter to have come over to Stillingfleet's view. Stillingfleet maintained that the whole period of early church history was so obscure that it was often impossible to be sure whether churches were governed by a bishop or by a college of presbyters, and that in the case of the Roman church 'the succession is as muddy as the Tiber itself'.[38] Wesley doubtless threw apostolic succession overboard along with the divine right of episcopacy, upon which he poured scorn in 1747 as a modern political invention.[39] Although in 1749 he defended Cyprian against Conyers Middleton's attacks he passed in silence over Cyprian's insistence that the essence of the church was episcopacy in succession from the apostles

—though in the context too much must not be made of this argument from silence.[40]

Wesley's earliest published denial of this doctrine did not appear until 1760, in a reply to the Roman Catholic bishop Richard Challoner's *Caveat against the Methodists*: 'I deny that the Romish bishops came down by *uninterrupted succession* from the apostles. I never could see it proved, and I am persuaded I never shall.'[41] By his italicizing Wesley rejected, not the idea of a spiritual succession resting in those who responded to God's call from age to age, but that this was 'uninterrupted', as was demanded by the theory of direct transmission by the imposition of episcopal hands upon episcopal heads. True apostolic succession for him consisted in having the apostolic spirit, a possibility and a responsibility not only for every preacher, but even for every Christian.[42]

Although Wesley had thus altered his views of the church and of the apostolic succession of the episcopacy, his view of the priesthood as the peculiar vehicle of sacramental grace persisted, to be modified later in the fires of controversy. In this respect also, however, he was already more liberal than he had been in the early years of his own ministry, as may be seen from a pamphlet written in 1753, *The Advantage of the Members of the Church of England over those of the Church of Rome*. He had long been familiar with and repudiated much of the Canons and Decrees of the Council of Trent, and in 1745 had attacked its teaching in *A Word to a Protestant*.[43] In the *Advantage* he went into more detail, and among the Tridentine dogma which he condemned as unscriptural (and therefore un-Anglican) were the following from Session 23 on the ministry:

> that ordination is a true and proper sacrament, instituted by Christ; that an indelible character is given thereby; . . . that the proper business of a priest is to consecrate and offer the body and blood of Christ and to remit or retain sins in the chair of confession.[44]

It might be claimed that this was little more than orthodox Anglican criticism of the Roman position, but it is extremely doubtful whether Wesley would have spoken thus while he was strongly under the influence of the Non-Jurors. It seems to mark an important though subtle and gradual change in his conception of the Anglican priesthood. He could no longer see it as mainly mediatorial, but as representative, so that along with confession he threw away absolution.[45] His view of the sacerdotal character of the ministry was certainly weakened, and although he never discarded the terms 'outward sacrifice' and 'outward priesthood' he came to interpret the Lord's Supper as a corporate spiritual action performed by one whom the church had appointed for that purpose. Eventually he used 'presbyter' or 'elder' in preference to 'priest' because of the latter's sacerdotal overtones.[46] Nevertheless, he continued to refer to his own 'sacerdotal office', and at the 1755 conference insisted that there was a New Testament priesthood and sacrifice, though this was not a propitiatory sacrifice: 'He that offers ["the Christian sacrifice of bread and wine"] as a memorial of the death of Christ is as proper a priest as ever Melchizedek was.'[47]

By 1755 Wesley was quite convinced that in essence there were two orders of ministry, with the higher order (which alone was empowered to administer the sacraments and to ordain) subdivided into bishops and presbyters. He completely rejected the notion that there was only one order authorized both to preach and to administer:

> Nor is there now any one Christian Church under heaven, Greek, Latin, Lutheran, Calvinist, or any other, that affirms or allows every preacher as such to have a right of administering [the Lord's Supper]. Because the supposition absolutely destroys the different orders of Christian ministers and reduces them to one, contrary both to the New Testament and to all antiquity. It is evident these always describe, if not more, at least two orders distinct from each other: the one having power only to preach and (sometimes) baptise; the other to ordain also and administer the Lord's Supper.[48]

The year 1755, indeed, forms another landmark in Wesley's churchmanship. In that year he published his *Explanatory Notes upon the New Testament*, in which he frequently took the opportunity to demonstrate how his fundamental principles were not inconsistent with Scripture even if they were not originally prescribed therein.[49] This volume was later added to his sermons to constitute the official doctrinal standards of Methodism. In 1755 also he was compelled to formulate his ecclesiastical position more carefully in order to meet a vigorous attempt by his preachers to sever Methodist ties with the Church of England. Wesley summarized his position in a lengthy paper read before the conference, from which his *Reasons against a Separation* was later extracted.[50] This therefore affords a convenient vantage point from which to survey rapidly the position he had reached in his struggles with evangelical circumstances to arrive at a practicable definition of the true church, ministry, and sacraments.

When in his comment on Acts 5:11 Wesley went out of his way to define the church he did not desert his favourite 19th Article, but still further spiritualized it:

> *The Church*. This is the first time it is mentioned. And here is a native specimen of a New Testament Church: called by the gospel, grafted

into Christ by baptism, animated by love, united by all kind of fellowship, and disciplined by the death of Ananias and Sapphira.

On Acts 9:31 he added the note: 'The Church—the whole body of Christian believers'; on Gal. 1:13 he described it as 'the believers in Christ', and on Heb. 12:23, 'the whole body of true believers, whether on earth or in Paradise.'

Although in the 1780s Wesley frequently lamented the secularization of this spiritual body, stemming from Constantine's embracing of Christianity,[51] he nevertheless approved of national churches, and applauded the spirit of patriotism even in religious allegiance. In 1755 he claimed that Methodists ought to feel 'a kind of natural affection for our country, which we apprehend Christianity was never designed either to root out or impair', and especially to the Church of England as their 'first and chief regard'. He flatly opposed those of his preachers who desired the disestablishment of the church.[52] He himself frequently spoke approvingly of 'the Established Church', and his important letter to the Earl of Dartmouth in 1761 reaffirmed his duty to the joint authority of church and state—though at the same time he claimed the right of conscience to disobey their laws and suffer the consequences. He allowed without a quibble the right of the state to enforce obedience to the church, criticizing only the abuse of such power.[53] He was not, however, prepared unhesitatingly to swallow crown and state whole, objecting against calling King Charles II 'our most religious king', and against the assumption that membership of the national church was mandatory.[54]

We have already seen that by 1755 Wesley's mind had undergone a change in his views of the ministry. This related not only to possession of valid authority to ordain, but to the spiritual content of ordination. He no longer believed that divine grace was necessarily conferred by or even during ordination, thus stamping upon the priest an 'indelible character'.[55] True ordination, the conferring of spiritual grace, was the work of God alone; the church could only through its authorized officials acknowledge this divine call and divine empowering, adding the seal of its own commission so that the minister would generally be recognized as such. Normally the divine conferment of grace would occur at some stage of the ordination service, but it might occur long before. With John Williams, bishop of Chichester, he repudiated the teaching of the Council of Trent that ordination was a sacrament.[56] This comes out clearly in his comments on Acts 13:2–3, the so-called 'ordination to the apostolate' of Paul and Barnabas. Wesley's comment is unambiguous:

V.2 *Separate me Barnabas and Saul, for the work to which I have called them.*—This was not ordaining them. St. Paul was ordained long before, and that 'not of men, neither by man'. It was only inducting him to the province for which our Lord had appointed him from the beginning, and which is now revealed to the prophets and teachers. In consequence of this they fasted, prayed, and laid their hands upon them: a rite which was used, not in ordination only, but in blessing and on many other occasions.[57]

Paul himself told the elders whom he had appointed at Ephesus (the πρεσβύτεροι): 'take heed therefore to yourselves, and to the whole flock over which the Holy Ghost hath made you overseers' (ἐπίσκοποι, Acts 20:28). Here Wesley's comment became even stronger by his deletions in the proof copy of the first edition (here shown italicized in brackets):

V.28 . . . *over which the Holy Ghost hath made you overseers.*—[*by Paul as an Instrument.*] For no man or number of men upon earth can constitute an 'Overseer', Bishop, or any other Christian Minister, [*unless as a bare instrument in God's hand.*] To do this is the peculiar Work of the Holy Ghost.[58]

It is fully in accordance with this position that Wesley regarded 'ordain' and 'appoint' as almost synonymous, and as early as 1755 confessed that he himself had already in some sense ordained, by commissioning his preachers, occasionally by handing them as they knelt a New Testament, and charging them, 'Take thou authority to preach the gospel'.[59]

In 1749, in his sermon 'Catholic Spirit', Wesley not only allowed that the modes or incidental circumstances of Baptism and the Lord's Supper were of relative unimportance, but even that he was prepared to recognize as good Christians those who had no use for either sacrament. One of his arguments against ordaining his preachers in 1755 was that not one soul would perish for lack of the sacraments if he refrained, though the same could not be said of their preaching.[60] Nevertheless, he remained quite clear in his own mind that for him and his followers, so closely linked to the Anglican church, both infant baptism and constant communion were axiomatic. Indeed, he attacked with vigour and almost vehemence the usual arguments against receiving communion.[61]

Baptism in infancy Wesley supported because it was instituted by Jesus and because it was the successor of the Old Testament rite of infant circumcision. He continued to believe that in some way objective grace was conferred upon the child by God, so that in a sense it was regenerated, or at least the process of regeneration was begun. At the same time he insisted that another form of regeneration was possible in adult experience quite apart from any sacramental rite. These two aspects of regeneration he never quite reconciled, but continued to insist on both. The classical summary of Wesley's teaching on baptismal regeneration remains his *Treatise on Baptism*, and on non-baptismal regeneration his sermon on 'The New Birth', first published in 1760, though probably preached much earlier.[62]

The *Treatise on Baptism* was his authorized abridgement of the appendix to his father's *Pious Communicant*, which he prepared for publication in 1756 and published two years later as a section in his *Preservative against Unsettled Notions in Religion*. We are fortunate in having for comparison his original draft of this document, which contains an important addition to his father's text:

> Before I begin to treat of baptism I would just observe that three things are essential to Christian baptism: 1. An episcopal adminis- trator. 2. The application of water. 3. That it be administered in the name of the Trinity. The two latter need no proof: and our Lord's commissioning his apostles only, and those who should derive their authority from them, to baptize, proves the former. And if so it necessarily follows that the baptism—I ought to call it the dipping— of the Anabaptists, as much stress as ever they lay upon it, is no bap- tism at all. For they want episcopal administrators, which are essential to Christian baptism. And indeed this invalidates the baptism of all who have formally separated from our church. But of this I need say no more to you. For there is no great danger of your employing any of them to baptize either yourselves or your children.

This seems to imply that when Wesley prepared this abridgement, which is dated at the end 11 November 1756, he still accepted the necessity to a valid sacrament of episcopal ordination, and his omission before actual publication that in the interval his mind had changed. This remains a puzzle, probably to be solved only by accepting Wesley's facility for embracing at the same time apparently contradictory con- cepts and responding chameleon-like to the environment of the moment without any sense of betraying his principles. He probably continued still to accept both the view that episcopal ordination was necessary and that it was not, though the omission would represent his dominant position in 1758 and later.[63]

Wesley was a pioneer in urging sprinkling as a permissible and indeed desirable method of infant baptism, and had reached this position by 1755.[64] He regarded 'the superstitious use of the sign of the cross in baptism' as one of the earliest abuses to creep into the Christian Church, and the first issue of his 1784 *Sunday Service* omitted the rubric enjoining the signation; it seems, however, that the omission was on Coke's initiative, and that Wesley once more changed his mind and replaced it.[65] Wesley was quite clear that only in the most exceptional circumstances should baptism be performed by a layman.[66]

Baptism Wesley regarded as the appropriate qualification for partaking of the Lord's Supper, thus by-passing confirmation as an optional rite of doubtful value. Widespread neglect during Wesley's day meant that the infrequent confirmations were tumultuous and disorderly, which in turn led to further depreciation. Wesley himself had apparently been confirmed before taking his first communion, and the Non-Jurors favoured the rite, but in Georgia no bishop was available to confirm, so that baptism followed by catechizing and conscious discipleship was perforce a sufficient qualification for communicants. This seems to have remained Wesley's position; proven spiritual desires were of far more importance than the touch of a bishop's hands.[67]

That Wesley's views about the Lord's Supper were subject to no more change throughout his ministry than was his practice of at least weekly communion may be seen from the fact that in 1787 he published a sermon on 'The Duty of Constant Communion' substantially as he had written it for his Oxford pupils fifty-five years earlier, claiming, 'I have not yet seen cause to alter my sentiments in any point which is therein delivered'.[68] The emphasis in this sermon was upon practice rather than doctrine, and this is characteristic of his whole approach, as of his text—'Do this in remembrance of me' (Luke 22:19). This was something a Christian must *do*, whatever his opinions about how God achieved His purposes in this sacrament. The Lord's Supper was for Wesley a memorial, yet not a mere memorial, but an ordained means whereby the grace of God was especially made available to the expectant soul. Nor did this depend at all upon the worthiness of the administrator, but upon the communicant's 'design to follow Christ'.[69] Christ Himself was the one and unique sacrifice whose benefits were made available to the believer in the rite which He instituted and commanded, though in joyous thanksgiving the communicant also offered himself as a willing sacrifice to God. Wesley continued to regard communion as a converting as well as a confirming ordinance. Although he welcomed penitent sinners to his own communion services, however, he was not prepared to admit all and sundry.[70] He continued to approve of some Non-Juring practices like the mixture of water and wine, and prayers for the dead, but these were mere accidental circumstances with only symbolic importance—the essential element was the spiritual preparedness of the worshipper, converted or unconverted.[71] Wesley never shook off his conviction that for the sake of decency and order, if not for validity and effectiveness, the Lord's Supper must be administered by an ordained clergymen.[72]

Thus several changes, both major and more subtle, took place over the years in Wesley's concepts of the nature and function of the church, the ministry, and the sacraments. Already by 1755 he had swung over into a position quite different from that of the majority of the Anglican bishops and clergy. Early this century Ernst Troeltsch divided Christian groups into two species, the church-type and the sect-type, though he realized that the whole of Christendom could not be apportioned between these two handy containers. Subsequent sociologists and historians have offered a number of modifications, either as sub-species or as intermediate species between the two wings of the institutional body accommodating itself to the world and the voluntary group separating itself from both the world and from institutional religion.[73] Troeltsch himself traced the course of Methodism from one pole to the other and back again, thus emphasizing the peculiar difficulties which face those who seek to affix simple labels and expect them to stick.[74]

It is impossible to fit John Wesley into any neat category except by Procrustes' somewhat drastic method—though I find myself agreeing with John Kent, that Wesley does sometimes strike sympathetic as well as non-sympathetic observers as being a 'charismatic leader with the will to separate'.[75] Only sometimes, however. If we seek to understand Wesley's churchmanship rather than to attach labels to it, we will be wise to return to a consideration of the two over-simplified and over-generalized views of the church and the two related views of the ministry which were mentioned at the beginning of this chapter, leaving the other differentia of the sociologists out of our account. The one view, clearly allied with Troeltsch's church-type, would see the church as an institution aspiring to represent and include all humanity, on whose behalf its ministers discharge a mainly sacerdotal function. The other, correspondingly allied with the sect-type, regards the church as a company of like-minded people who believe themselves called apart by God for some special purpose, and whose ministers (if indeed they recognize a separated ministry) are regarded as prophets rather than priests. Both concepts of church and ministry can and do and should co-exist in most major denominations, which are usually considered 'high' or 'low' (or right or left) in accordance with the proportion of emphasis placed on the one or the other aspect of their churchmanship.

In Wesley's case we find almost from the outset of his ministerial career a strong missionary element at work, so that he could not be content with the church as it was. He firmly believed in the validity and necessity of the church as a sacramental institution, yet was unable to offer implicit obedience to its governors because he constantly found their voice or their actions at variance with the injunctions of God written in Scripture or upon his own mind and heart. This strongly critical tendency sought expression, however, not in going out and being separate, but in forming a series of societies within the church, societies intended to reform by their example as well as to nurture spiritual life among their members. As his initial set of spiritual values was gradually reshuffled in a different order of importance, and new values incorporated, his view of the ideal church as a sacramental institution with an evangelical mission was slowly transformed into that of a missionary society performing sacramental functions, with the Church of England fulfilling the one task and the Methodist societies the other. Unlike a settled institution, such a missionary society was compelled by the changing character of spiritual needs constantly to adopt expediencies. An extraordinary task committed to a minister prepared to assume extraordinary powers was almost certain to issue in extraordinary methods—extraordinary, yet carrying their own validation in the form of spiritual efficacy. Eventually a part of Wesley's mind recognized that Methodism was in fact rapidly taking over both functions, whether the Church of England liked it or not, whether he himself liked it or not, and however he might attempt to justify it as an increasingly long-term yet still 'temporary' expedient adopted to renew the Established Church from within. This realization was clear before 1755, a climactic year. The rest, including his ordinations of 1784, was a lengthy and complex dénouement.

TEN

SEPARATION NARROWLY AVERTED

A FEW of the Methodist lay preachers had revealed themselves as unstable. James Wheatley brought Methodism into disrepute by his amatory adventures and was expelled.[1] John Bennet, who had stolen John Wesley's bride from under his nose in 1749, was apparently itching to become an independent minister, and there were more like him, restive under the clerical autocracy of the Wesleys. On 17 August 1751 John wrote to Charles: 'C[harles] S[kelton] pleads for a kind of aristocracy, and says you and I should do nothing without the consent [of] all the preachers; otherwise we govern arbitrarily, to which they cannot submit. Whence is this?' To which Charles replied: 'I am told from Bristol, "You rule the preachers with a rod of iron: they complain of it all over England, etc., etc." '[2] Worse still, along with rebellion against the Wesleys went rebellion against the church. A month earlier John had told Charles: 'I fear for Ch. Skelton and J. Cownley more and more. I have heard they frequently and bitterly rail against the church.'[3] John asked his brother to undertake a careful inquiry into the gifts and grace of all the preachers, and to dismiss those who proved unsatisfactory.[4] Unfortunately this tended to enhance the status of those who were continued in service. They were undoubtedly becoming much more self-conscious about themselves and their important task of evangelism. Soul-seeking occasionally became confused with status-seeking, enthusiasm was too easily transformed into ambition, and the eager rivalries of spiritual devotion sometimes took on unhappy overtones of suspicion and jealousy.

It was with this in mind that on 29 January 1752 John Wesley persuaded a group of the preachers to enter with their two leaders into a pact of mutual trust and unity. Six weeks later Charles Wesley persuaded his brother to extend this agreement to incorporate a resolution 'never to leave the communion of the Church of England without the consent of all whose names are subjoined'.[5] Nevertheless, Charles remained far from happy, writing to the Countess of Huntingdon on 4 August 1752: 'Unless a sudden remedy be found, the preachers will destroy the work of God.' He wanted most of them to return to their trades, or at least to prove that they could maintain themselves. One reason, as he confided to the countess, was that this might break his brother's power. 'If he refuses', Charles added, 'I will give both preachers and society to his sole management; for this ruin shall not be under my hands.' Unfortunately a copy of this letter was intercepted and passed on to John, doing little to ease the tension between the two brothers.[6] The 1752 agreement may well have been reiterated at the 1753 Conference, as it certainly was in 1754, 1755, and 1756.[7]

Agreements not to separate from the Church of England were perhaps impressive gestures of loyalty, but what in fact did they imply? What indeed was the separation therein envisaged and repudiated? Individual bishops, higher clergy, lower clergy (including both John and Charles Wesley), Methodist sympathizers, opponents of Methodism, including a varied host of laymen, might all draw the lines of demarcation differently. This lack of a clearly defined, universally accepted formula for separation allowed John Wesley continually to protest his loyalty while others proclaimed his treason. This ambiguity still makes it impossible to fix upon any historical moment when Methodism can definitely be claimed to have consummated a separation from the Church of England, still complicates ecumenical debates covering the area of unity versus uniformity.

John Wesley himself clearly believed that only complete and deliberate repudiation either of the church or by the church could truly fill the definition, and that a minimum of physical attendance at public worship, and especially at Holy Communion, was quite sufficient as a defence against the charge. He told the Rev. Thomas Church: 'Nothing can prove I am no member of the church till I either am excommunicated or renounce her communion.'[8] Repeatedly Wesley defied his opponents to prove that the Methodists were guilty of making a schism. The 1747 Conference addressed itself deliberately to this question:

Q. 1. What is schism in the Scripture sense of the word?

A. The word only occurs twice in the New Testament: I Cor. i:10, where St. Paul exhorts them, that there may be no schisms among them (*schismata* is the word which we render divisions); and xii:25, 'God hath mingled the body together, having given the more abundant honour to that part which lacked, that there may be no schism in the body', i.e. in the Church, the Body of Christ. In both these places the word undeniably means (which consequently is the true spiritual notion of *schism*) a causeless breach, rupture, or division, made amongst the members of Christ, among those who are the living body of Christ, and members in particular.[9]

Q. 2. Are not the Methodists guilty of making such a schism?

A. No more than rebellion or murder. They do not divide

themselves at all from the living body of Christ. Let any prove it
if they can.

Q. 3. But do not they divide themselves from the Church of
England?

A. No: they hold communion therewith now in the same manner
as they did twenty years ago, and hope to do so until their lives' end.[10]

This continued to be Wesley's position, and in 1755 he wrote:

At present I apprehend those and those only to separate from the
church who either renounce her fundamental doctrines or refuse to
join in her public worship.[11]

Strangely enough no one seems to have charged that Wesley's somewhat legalistic attitude was reminiscent of the stratagem by which
many dissenters had managed to retain their qualifications for public
office, which the Occasional Conformity Act of 1711 was powerless
to stop, so that in 1718 it was repealed; from 1727 annual Indemnity
Acts were passed to assist scrupulous dissenters. Even though Wesley
intended that Methodists should attend their parish church weekly,
occasional attendance at communion would technically exonerate
them also from the charge of separation.

How far was it possible to push this view? Continual straws had
been loaded onto the back of this sturdy camel: a sectarian type of
religion, independent societies, an itinerant ministry, informal worship
and field-preaching, the authorization of lay preachers, the institution
of a sacramental community, of a deliberative assembly, the erection of
Methodist buildings and the undertaking of legal provisions for their
security and continuity. During the years following the turn of the
century attempts were made to hoist the final bale that would bring the
long-suffering beast to its knees. This was either the administration of
the Lord's Supper by the unordained Methodist preachers or their
ordination at the hands of Wesley as a presbyter. Although delayed for
thirty years by the intransigence of Charles Wesley, in 1784 John
Wesley finally committed this outrageous breach of Anglican church
order, though characteristically he then refused to acknowledge that
even this constituted a technical separation from the church.[12]

The issue came to a head in the winter of 1754–5. Although John
Wesley's *Journal* records very little for this period—nothing at all
between 28 October 1754 and 16 February 1755—we are able to fill in
some of the gaps from the manuscripts of his brother Charles. In his
shorthand diary for 17 and 18 October 1754, Charles recorded that
two lay preachers, Charles Perronet and Thomas Walsh, had adminis-

tered the Lord's Supper, the one in London, the other in Reading. On
19 October he noted:

> I was with my brother, who said nothing of Perronet except, 'We
> have in effect ordained already.' He urged me to sign the preachers'
> certificates; was inclined to lay on hands; and to let the preachers
> administer.

After a further conversation five days later Charles Wesley felt that he
had gained some ground: 'He is wavering, but willing to wait before
he ordains or separates.'[13]

Three interrelated and progressively divisive issues were here involved: the registration of the Methodist lay preachers under the
Toleration Act, their administration of the sacraments without ordination, or their ordination by John Wesley himself in order to confer a
fuller semblance of authority to their administration. John Wesley
seemed ready to give way on all three fronts.

The Toleration Act of 1689 afforded legal protection to preachers
and congregations 'dissenting from the Church of England', provided
that they first registered themselves as such either at their bishop's
registry or county court. A certificate of registration could be secured
for sixpence, and the preacher's licence was valid in any county. In
1745, in his *Farther Appeal*, Part I, Wesley had stated explicitly that
because they were not dissenters from the church, Methodists could
not make use of the Act of Toleration.[14] Ten years later he was clearly
prepared to make two compromises, first to accept the technical designation of 'dissenter' even though disavowing its implications, and
second to regard such dissenting preaching licences as authorizations to
administer the sacraments. Charles Wesley was strongly opposed to
both these steps towards legitimizing the administration of the sacraments by Methodist lay preachers. He was equally opposed to the third
alternative, being quite convinced that any attempt at ordination by his
brother would constitute a final breach with the Church of England,
an opinion later confirmed by a friend of his old Westminster School
days, Lord Chief Justice Mansfield, who agreed that 'ordination is
separation'.

Charles Wesley began marshalling an opposition. He wrote to the
Rev. Walter Sellon, formerly one of Wesley's masters at Kingswood
School, and now an ordained parish priest. He told Sellon that when
the Countess of Huntingdon heard that the preachers were administering communion she was convinced that John Wesley must first have
ordained them. Charles foresaw grave danger:

> What a pity such spirits should have any influence over my brother!

They are continually urging him to a separation: that is, to pull down all he has built, to put a sword in our enemies' hands, to destroy the work, scatter the flock, disgrace himself, and go out—like the snuff of a candle.

May I not desire it of you as a debt you owe the Methodists and me, and the church, as well as him, to write him a full, close, plain transcript of your heart on the occasion?[15]

On 14 December he renewed his appeal:

Write again, and spare not. My brother took no notice to me of your letter. Since the Melchisedeckians[16] have been taken in I have been excluded his Cabinet Council. They know me too well to trust him with me. He is come so far as to believe a separation quite lawful, only not yet expedient. They are indefatigable in urging him to go so far that he may not be able to retreat. He may 'lay on hands', say they, without separating. I charge you to keep it to yourself, *That I stand in doubt of him.*[17]

Charles Wesley's own solution to the problem was clear: 'We must among us get the sound preachers qualified for Orders.' On 4 February 1755 he reported to Sellon:

Your letters (and some others wrote with the same honesty) have had the due effect on him, and made him forget he was *ever inclined to their party*. He has spoken as strongly of late in behalf of the Church of England as I could wish, and everywhere declares he never intends to leave her.

This has made the Melchisedeckians draw in their horns and drop their design. *Sed non ego credulus illis.*[18] We *must* know the heart of every preacher, and give them their choice of the Church or Meeting. The wound can no longer be healed slightly. Those who are disposed to separate had best do it while we are yet alive. . . .

Write to him again and urge it upon his conscience whether . . . he should not take the utmost pains to settle the preachers, discharging those who are irreclaimable, and never receiving another without this previous condition, that he will never leave the Church.[19]

In this same letter Charles Wesley announced that his brother John was 'writing an excellent treatise on the question whether it is expedient to separate [from] the Church of England', which he hoped to print by the summer. This was in preparation for their annual Conference in May, at which Charles had urged Sellon to be present.

En route to this crucial Conference, John Wesley stayed for a weekend with his lieutenant in the north, the Rev. William Grimshaw of Haworth. Grimshaw proved himself strongly against 'the lay preachers' new scheme' of taking upon themselves 'the office of administering the Lord's Supper', and claimed that this would entail 'a manifest rupture with the Established Church. We must then be declared Dissenters.' In such an event his own course would be clear:

> I can harmoniously, as matters have hitherto been carried on, be a minister of our church and a Methodist preacher, and thus I could wish to live and die. But if my fellow labourers will needs be innovating, I must adhere to the former capacity and decline the latter.

He felt fairly confident, however, that 'the espousers of this scheme will be obliged to drop it, or be cashiered by us'.[20]

From Haworth, Wesley went on to Leeds and Birstall, where Charles joined him. They spent a few days together studying the issue, partly in the light of Micaiah Towgood's classic presentation of the Nonconformist position, *A Dissent from the Church of England fully justified*, partly by a scrutiny of John Wesley's own treatise on the subject. John summarized their reading of Towgood thus:

> It is an elaborate and lively tract, and contains the strength of the cause; but it did not yield us one proof that it is lawful for us (much less our duty) to separate from [the church]. . . . In how different a spirit does this man write from honest Richard Baxter! . . . Surely one page of that loving, serious Christian weighs more than volumes of this bitter, sarcastic jester.[21]

Charles reported to his wife that 'in reading over the dissenter's book [John] found and showed me many flaws in his arguments against the church, which he interweaves and answers in his excellent treatise on that question'.[22]

John Wesley's 'excellent treatise' seems to have disappeared. Two parts of it were probably used three years later in his *Preservative*, one being a 'Letter to the Rev. Mr. Toogood [sic] of Exeter', the other his well-known 'Reasons against a Separation'. This latter was an abridgement, however, of a lengthy document which Wesley presented before the Conference, which assembled at Leeds on Tuesday 6 May 1755. Three Anglican priests were present (the two Wesleys and Grimshaw) along with sixty lay preachers—the largest and most crucial gathering so far held, meeting for the primary purpose of discussing their possible separation from the Church of England in order to form a new denomination. After Wesley had read his paper, entitled 'Ought we to separate from the Church of England?' the matter was debated for the better part of three days. Charles asked John Nelson to transcribe the address on to forty-five pages of a notebook which he henceforth reserved for transcriptions of other documents relating to this matter of separation.[23]

After an introduction John Wesley defined the terms used in his argument. The church he described as usual in the words of Article 19, appending as corollary what may be construed as a summary of Article 20: 'Perhaps some would add, "And to submit to the Governors of the Church, and obey the laws of it".' As church law, he accepted only the rubrics of the *Book of Common Prayer*, not the Canons, whose authority he regarded as doubtful. He affirmed that the Methodists separated neither from the people, the doctrine, nor the worship of the church, and submitted to its laws and governors 'in all things not contrary to Scripture'. In pondering whether they should 'refrain from the public service of the church', he maintained: 'This would amount to a formal separation from the church. This properly constitutes a dissenter.'[24] He completely discarded Towgood's argument that Christ was the only lawgiver for the church, claiming that there were other lawgivers subordinate to Him, who ought to be obeyed—the King, the magistrates, the bishops, though he agreed that the spiritual courts called aloud for a reformation, and that several of the Canons were indefensible.[25] He was highly critical even of some parts of the *Book of Common Prayer*—a fact which underlay his revision some thirty years later.[26] He could not, therefore, declare his 'unfeigned assent and consent to all and everything prescribed and contained in that book', though he salved his conscience by pointing out that such a declaration in his case was not applicable, being only legally necessary for those clergymen who were actually inducted to benefices. He and the Methodists could therefore continue as they were without separating from the church.

In Section III Wesley turned to the question whether he should 'appoint persons to baptize and administer the Lord's Supper'. Although he agreed that this would 'answer many good ends' he insisted that it was not expedient. The argument that in appointing men to preach he had *ipso facto* appointed them to administer the sacraments he answered in two ways: (a) *God* had appointed them, and having recognized that the finger of God was at work he had simply *permitted* them to serve with him; (b) he only permitted this preaching because otherwise 'numberless souls must have perished', whereas there was no such urgent necessity for their administering the sacraments. He emphasized that from the beginning of the church there were two orders, one for preaching, the other for sacramental functions. Therefore, even if it had been necessary for him to ordain his preachers it would probably not have been lawful, amounting to 'little less than a formal separation from the church'. The twelve reasons which he marshalled against such a breach formed the heart of his 'Reasons against a separation from the Church of England', included in his *Preservative* of 1758.[27]

Section IV dealt with the objection 'that till we do separate, at least so far as to *ordain* (that our helpers may administer the sacraments), we cannot be a compact, united body'. In spite of his former labours to this very end he maintained that he did not desire such unity if it meant becoming 'a body of people distinct from and independent on all others'. Nevertheless (as he urged in Section V) he did seek true unity of spirit among the Methodists as living witnesses to the Christian gospel, and desired for them a special affection toward their fellow-countrymen, and especially toward the clergy. To this end he urged all his preachers to set a good example to their people by regularly attending public worship at the parish church, and avoiding attendance at dissenting meetings. This latter in fact entailed actual separation because it prevented attendance at church, whose public worship was normally held at the same hour, while Methodist gatherings were deliberately arranged out of church hours.

Seven or eight sessions of the Conference were devoted to debating whether separation was lawful, and only when agreement could not be reached on this point was attention turned to the question of its expediency.[28] Here Wesley's arguments carried the day, especially when the dissident preachers found that Grimshaw also was against them. John Wesley claimed in his *Journal*:

> Whatever was advanced on one side or the other was seriously and calmly considered; and on the third day we were all fully agreed in that general conclusion—that (whether [separation] was *lawful* or not) it was no ways *expedient*.

This major issue thus settled, Charles Wesley left, and the members turned to more routine matters. Like Grimshaw, however, Charles Wesley saw that what they had done was to shelve the question, especially by the frequent use of the word 'expedient': what was inexpedient today might well prove expedient tomorrow. In his *Epistle to the Reverend Mr. John Wesley*, actually written before the Conference, Charles publicly built up an image of his brother as unshakeably loyal to the church, though the private question mark can be discerned even in this public utterance.[29] Certainly Charles continued to fear the worst. He confided to the Countess of Huntingdon that John Wesley's banker friend Ebenezer Blackwell had refused to have him in the house, and mused:

12

It *seems* as if God was *warning* me to prepare for some great change. What He does with me or by me I know not now, and never see two steps before me.[30]

His news on 9 June was more alarming:

Mr. Jones assures me that others of our preachers are swiftly following the separatists through my brother's dissimulation—unless he sincerely meant what he said: 'We agree not to separate from the church *as yet*', 'I allow, that presbyters have a right to ordain', and that 'T. Walsh, and a *few more*, may be called in an extraordinary way to administer sacraments without any ordination at all'.

I advised him to divide and scatter them: but he had sent them in a body to Ireland. I intreated him to try whether the most simple and last-perverted [? 'least-perverted'] preachers might not be set right. He took no farther thought about it. . . . I shall continue to honour him before the people, and *do him all the service in my power* for Christ and the work's sake. But no quarter do I expect from him or his implicit followers.[31]

On 11 June Charles added:

He still extols 'the unity, nay and unanimity, and the excellent spirit of the preachers at our late Conference'. I am astonished at his art of putting out his own eyes, and healing a wound slightly. But I think it safest not to trust him with my thoughts. . . .

My way is plain, *to preach everywhere* as a supernumerary if not independent. My brother, I foresee, will treat me as a deserter; but he has cured me of my implicit regard to him.[32]

John Wesley himself suspected that things were coming to a head, as Charles reported to the countess, paraphrasing for her benefit John's Latin:

My brother sends strange news, as follows: 'My turn is next![33] The good Bishop of London has excommunicated Mr. Gardiner for preaching without a licence.[34] It is probable the point will now be speedily determined concerning the Church. For if we must either *dissent* or *be silent*, the matter is over with us. We have no time to trifle.'[35] His preachers, I well know, would be overjoyed at a separation—and he would not be sorry.[36]

Nevertheless, John continued to calm Charles's fears, expressed in letters which for the most part seem to have disappeared. On 28 June he agreed that sometimes he had asked preachers to share a burial service with him, but protested that that constituted no 'breach of the sacerdotal office'. The preachers who had administered had made amends, and there was no need for Charles to follow them to Ireland to save that land from contamination. Nor would he accept the criticism that separation was being delayed only for the time being:

> 'Not yet' is totally out of the question. We have not one preacher who either proposed or desires or designs (that I know) *to separate from the church* 'at all'. Their principles, in the single point of ordination, I do not approve. But I pray for more and more of their spirit, in general, and their practice.[37]

The really important thing for John, however, overriding every question of ecclesiastical propriety, was the spiritual health of the nation, and especially of Methodism:

> Wherever I have been in England the societies are far more firmly and rationally attached the church than ever they were before. I have no fear about this matter. I only fear the preachers' or the people's leaving, not the church, but the love of God, and inward or outward holiness. To this I press them forward continually. I dare not in conscience spend my time and strength on externals. If (as my lady says) all outward establishments are Babel, so is this Establishment. Let it stand, for me. I neither set it up nor pull it down. But let you and I build up the City of God.[38]

He returned to this same practical issue in a letter of 16 July:

> *Some time* you may spend in recommending outward modes of worship, 'but not *all*, not the *most*, not *much* of it'. There are many greater things and more immediately necessary for our people. Holiness of heart and life they want most, and they want it just now.[39]

John complained that his brother was in a panic, and therefore losing his sense of proportion:

> Whoever is convinced or not convinced, ordination and separation are not the same thing. If so, we have separated already [presumably by his commissioning men to preach]. . . . Your gross bigotry lies here—in putting a man on a level with an adulterer because he differs from you as to church government.[40]

Meantime, in the course of his preaching tour through Cornwall, John Wesley met the Rev. Samuel Walker of Truro, an evangelical clergyman who in 1754 had organized a religious society after the pattern of Woodward's societies. Recognizing a kindred spirit, Wesley asked his advice about publishing his treatise on the possible separation of the Methodists from the church. After studying the manuscript, Walker wrote: 'I verily think the publishing it can do no good, and will probably do much hurt.'[41] He urged Wesley to reconsider his definition of separation, warning him that in appointing preachers he had in fact already made a partial separation from the Church of England, for the essence of the national church was not its doctrine and worship, which were common to the Church Universal, but its peculiar orders and laws. In some honourable way, therefore, Wesley ought either to rid himself of the institution of lay preaching or admit publicly that he had separated from the church.[42]

Walker's advice was sufficient to convince Wesley that he should not venture into print on the subject, though in accordance with Walker's recommendation he did send the manuscript to the Rev. Thomas Adam of Wintringham for a second opinion. To Adam, as also to Walker, Wesley pointed out that he was not prepared to silence his lay preachers if indeed this did involve separation. Surely, however, he protested, there should be some lawful method by which a presbyter like himself might not only *permit* preachers but authorize and *appoint* them, and thus 'reduce the constitution of Methodism to due order, and render the Methodists under God more instrumental to the ends of practical religion'. Although he listed three other points for which he was prepared to separate, namely 'preaching abroad', praying extempore, and forming societies, more and more the pivotal point had become that of authorizing lay preachers.[43]

Thomas Adam replied briefly on 10 October, hinting at some 'disingenuity' in Wesley's quibble about only 'permitting' lay preachers, and seconding Walker's view that they already constituted 'a manifest breach upon the order of the church, and an inlet to confusion'. In his view it would be better for Wesley to return to a closer union with the church. To this Wesley replied on 31 October protesting that he had moved as cautiously as possible:

> We have done nothing rashly, nothing without deep and long consideration (hearing and weighing all objections) and much prayer. Nor have we taken one deliberate step of which we as yet see reason to repent. It is true in some things we vary from the rules of our church: but no further than we apprehend is our bounden duty.

He defended his use of the word 'permit', implying that the next step after permission was to 'appoint or ordain', about which he hesitated— it seems likely, in fact, that his previous use of 'appoint' was as a synonym for 'ordain'. He then turned defence into attack by claiming that many of his preachers had *more* right to preach than some of the clergy, and really wondered whether he had been over-cautious about offending the Establishment: 'Soul-damning clergymen lay me under more difficulties than soul-saving laymen!' He knew of only one clergyman (Walker of Truro) who saved souls without in some way becoming irregular. Wesley felt, however, that he must not retreat by giving up his lay preachers, though he could not advance by ordaining them; therefore for the time being at least he must reluctantly preserve the *status quo*.[44]

Walker's next letter to Wesley in effect accused both Wesley and his preachers of rationalization—and did so with some cogency. It was not the defects in the liturgy nor the canons nor the spiritual courts, not even those in the clergy, which pushed them to the brink of an avowed separation, but on the one hand the preachers' 'ambition of being ministers', and on the other Wesley's own urgency to preserve the valuable work of Methodism. Wesley's reply of 20 November 1755 advanced the matter no further, and Walker came to feel that Wesley's mind was too fixed for him to hope for any change. It seems possible, indeed, that Walker did not sufficiently read between the lines and realize that in effect Wesley was seeking some support for his ordination of the lay preachers: for this, however, he could be excused, for Wesley never asked this question in set terms, simply trembled on the brink of it. On 3 July 1756 Wesley maintained: 'I do not separate yet, and probably never shall.'[45]

Charles Wesley enlisted Walker's advocacy once more in preparation for the Methodist Conference of 1756, seeking especially support for his own panacea: purge Methodism of the 'unsound, unrecoverable preachers', and prepare the remainder for Holy Orders, after securing the co-operation of the archbishop of Canterbury, Thomas Herring, who was apparently sympathetic.[46] Walker accordingly wrote warning John Wesley of the danger that after his death the Methodists would fall apart by separation or by disputes unless he took a firm stand at the forthcoming Conference. He commended a solution to the problem similar to that of Charles, with the added suggestion that the preachers who were retained but not ordained might serve as 'inspectors or readers' restricted to service in individual societies. Not that Walker really expected Wesley to make the clean break recommended, however, knowing that he was subject to so much tension from two directions at once.[47] In fact Wesley did not reply until after the Conference.

The 1756 Conference was again preceded by consultations between the two Wesley brothers, to whom were added Grimshaw and Henry Venn.[48] Again most of the preachers were present, and again the clergy succeeded in restraining the more ambitious of them, even managing to arrive at a decision on the legality of separation. John Wesley reported:

> My brother and I ended the Conference with a strong declaration of our resolution to live and die in the communion of the Church of England. We all unanimously agreed that whilst it is lawful or possible to continue in it it is unlawful for us to leave it.[49]

More preachers' signatures were added to the agreement not to separate, and Charles exulted, 'My brother seems farther from a separation than ever'.[50]

In his eventual reply to Walker, Wesley did not mention the Conference, but simply addressed himself to Walker's proposals, insisting that to restrict the preachers to individual societies would ruin the work as well as the preachers themselves—whether ordained or unordained. He waxed so enthusiastic about the Methodist system, indeed, that he ventured on declaring the principle of the Divine Right of the Itinerancy:

> I know, were I myself to preach one whole year in one place I should preach both myself and most of my congregation asleep: Nor can I believe it was ever the will of our Lord that any congregation should have one teacher only. We have found by a long and constant experience that a frequent change of preachers is best. This preacher has one talent, that another: No one whom I ever yet knew has all the talents which are needful for beginning, continuing, and perfecting the work of grace in an whole congregation.[51]

Transforming itinerant lay preachers into settled ministers, no matter how evangelical, offered no solution to Wesley. He even tried to tempt Walter Sellon to leave his circumscribed parish ministry in order to return to 'those who have more experience in the ways of God', because 'so little good is done in a *regular* way'.[52] Clearly he sought to preserve, not only the fellowship of his societies and spiritual outlets for his preachers' talents, but the whole Methodist system as a proven component of the Church Universal.[53]

Charles Wesley remained vigilant, constantly reminding his brother of his professions of loyalty to the church, undertaking preaching tours and extended correspondence with the express purpose of preventing separation.[54] In a shorthand addition to one of his lengthy journal-letters informing John of his activities Charles added: 'The short remains of my life are devoted to this very thing, to follow your sons . . . with buckets of water and quench the flame of strife and division which they have or may kindle.'[55] The year 1757 passed peacefully, with a 'little Conference' held at Keighley in May for Grimshaw and the northern preachers, and a regular one in London in August, when 'all was harmony and love'.[56]

A month after the 1757 Conference, the danger apparently passed, John Wesley wrote what turned out to be his last letter to Walker of Truro, who died four years later. Although similar in their piety and evangelism and concern for Christian fellowship, they found it difficult to communicate with each other on this matter of loyalty to the church. Having failed in his suggestions for organizing the lay preachers, Walker now recommended that Wesley should hand over his societies to sympathetic parish clergy. Again Wesley demurred. For one thing there were simply not enough such clergy—not even in Cornwall! The withdrawal of trusted lay preachers from the societies might precipitate rather than prevent a separation. Wesley continued to plead, 'tell me what [to do], and I will do it without delay', but each well-meant suggestion was swiftly vetoed. It seemed that he was determined to maintain Methodism intact, even though for what appeared to him the best of reasons. Walker's answer has disappeared, but it must have recognized that the usefulness of their correspondence was at an end. Nor is there any indication that the two met during Wesley's visit to Cornwall that month, though they did meet again in 1760.[57]

It is somewhat ironic that it was from Walker's Truro that on 29 September 1757 Wesley wrote a letter describing in detail 'the unspeakable advantage which the people called Methodists enjoy, . . . even with regard to public worship, particularly on the Lord's Day'. This letter apparently used the term 'church' of the Methodist preaching-house, implied that the Lord's Supper was regularly administered there, and spoke of the Methodist societies as if they were both independent of and preferable to the Established Church![58] It seems likely, however, that the letter was in fact originally written to a London Methodist, and that Wesley spoke only of West Street Chapel, to which he elsewhere referred as 'the little church (in the vulgar sense [of the word]) . . . wherein I read prayers, preach, and administer the sacrament every Sunday when I am in London'.[59] Twenty years later when he came to publish it the conditions described were more widespread, and he therefore deemed it unnecessary to point out its originally very limited application.

Charles Wesley was still torn between hope and fear. On 18 November 1757 he wrote to Howell Harris:

Our *friend* has agreed with me *to call in his licences*: I mean, to stop the preachers from qualifying themselves for dissenting teachers. I believe *the only way* to keep them steady is the prayer of faith.[60]

Strangely enough, the first extant example of a preaching licence taken out by one of Wesley's preachers is dated 11 January 1758. This was made out to Jacob Rowell of Barnard Castle—of whom Charles Wesley least suspected it.[61] The evidence of Charles's voluminous correspondence in 1760 on the issue of separation, however, shows that from about this period many preachers similarly

> did take repeat and subscribe the oaths of Allegiance Supremacy and Abjuration . . . the Declaration against Transubstantiation and also the Declaration . . . for disabling Papists from sitting in either House of Parliament . . . [and] did likewise then and there subscribe the Thirty-nine Articles of Religion save and except the words [']The Church hath power to decree Rites ceremonies and Authority in controversies of Faith and yet['] in [the] Twentieth Article and also save and except the Thirty Fourth, Thirty Fifth and Thirty Sixth Articles.[62]

From about the same period registration of Methodist preaching-houses became fairly normal, the more so as the procedure was much simpler than that for the preachers, except for the collecting of several signatures of the worshipers. The society in John Pawson's birthplace of Thorner, near Leeds, was thus registered in 1754, as was one in East Cottingwith in the East Riding of Yorkshire. Others followed in the late 1750s and 1760s, and the trickle turned to a torrent in the 1770s and later.[63] The same was true in Lincolnshire, where the first Methodist meeting-place was registered for Horncastle in 1758.[64]

In 1758 John Wesley's long-pondered treatise on loyalty to the church appeared, but appeared in such a way that it was very unlikely to become a focal point of controversy. Not only was it drastically reduced. It was not published separately but as the last of thirteen items in a volume entitled *A Preservative against unsettled notions in religion*.[65] The Conference in August 1758 hardly touched on the matter of separation except indirectly by urging the preachers to recommend to their people the *Preservative*.[66] Relative harmony continued throughout 1759, the Conference that year being mainly occupied with 'examining whether the spirit and lives of our preachers were suitable to their profession'. Wesley recognized, however, that there were some who 'hoped or feared the contrary' of the peace that prevailed.[67]

What seemed to Charles Wesley the prelude to disaster broke in

February 1760, when he heard that three trusted preachers at Norwich had been administering the Lord's Supper. John Wesley, who was preparing for his biennial preaching tour in Ireland, did not appear to be unduly concerned, probably because of the very peculiar ecclesiastical situation at Norwich.[68] Indeed, according to one of the Norwich preachers, John Murlin, they had been administering the sacraments for many months.[69] Now that the matter was brought to light, however, John asked Charles to visit Norwich and investigate the situation on his behalf. This Charles was quite prepared to do, but only if he carried a letter of condemnation from his brother. The outcome Charles bitterly reported to his wife:

> My brother's final resolution (or irresolution) is not to meddle with the Sacred Gentlemen at Norwich *till* the Conference, i.e. *till* they are confirmed in their own evil of pride and practice, and till they have poisoned all the preachers and half the flock.
>
> At the Conference, I presume, he will put it to the vote whether they have a right to administer. Then by a large majority they consent to a separation.
>
> Five months' interval we have to do whatever the Lord directs by way of prevention.[70]

Vigorously Charles set about his five months' task, pursuing his brother with vigorous letters:

> Upon the whole I am fully persuaded *almost all* our preachers are corrupted already: more and more will give the sacrament and set up for themselves, even before we die: and all except the few that get Orders will turn Dissenters before or after our death.
>
> You must wink very hard not to see all this. You have connived at it too, too long.[71]

Many letters were written to the preachers, pointing out that the three Norwich preachers had taken this step without consulting either of the Wesleys, and had done it on the sole authority of the sixpenny licence that they had taken out for the sake of legal protection. Charles urged restraint, followed by the securing of episcopal ordination after the pattern of Maxfield, Haughton, Richards, Sellon, and others.[72] Many leading London Methodists were 'scandalized at [the preachers'] licensing themselves, that is, coming to the people with *a lie in their pocket*'. In response to his wife's inquiry Wesley interpreted this phrase:

> We have allowed our lay preachers to take out licences *as dissenting Protestants*. To the government they therefore say, 'We are dissenting

ministers'; to the Methodists they say, 'We are not dissenters, but
true members of the Church of England'. To a press warrant or
persecuting justice they say again, 'We are dissenters'; to me at our
next Conference they will unsay it again. This is their sincerity; and
my brother applauds their skilfulness—and his own.[73]

Charles Wesley had promised that he would reprint his brother's
'Reasons against a separation from the Church of England', and this
first appeared as a distinct publication in March 1760. William Strahan
printed two editions that month, totalling the then huge number of
10,000 copies. Charles spared no pains, adding seven challenging
'Hymns for the use of the Methodist preachers', and an appended note:

> I think myself bound in duty to add my testimony to my brother's.
> His twelve reasons against our ever separating from the Church of
> England are mine also. I subscribe to them with all my heart. Only
> with regard to the first, *I* am quite clear, that it is neither expedient
> nor LAWFUL for *me* to separate. . . .[74]

Perhaps the most important letter sent by Charles Wesley, at least
in its immediate results, was that to the Rev. William Grimshaw:

> Our preaching-houses are mostly licensed, and therefore proper
> meeting-houses. Our preachers are mostly licensed, and so dissenting
> ministers. They took out their licences as *Protestant Dissenters*. Three
> of our steadiest preachers give the Sacrament at Norwich with no
> other ordination or authority than their sixpenny licence. My
> brother approves of it. All the rest will most probably follow their
> example. . . .
> I publish the enclosed [*Reasons*] with my brother's concurrence.
> He persuades himself 'that none of the other preachers will do like
> those at Norwich. That they may all license themselves, and give the
> Sacraments, yet continue true members of the Church of England.
> That no confusion or inconvenience will follow from these things.
> That we should let them do as they please till the Conference.'
> When I suppose it must be put to the vote whether they have not a
> right to administer the Sacraments: and they themselves shall be the
> judges. . . .
> I am convinced things are come to a crisis. We must now resolve
> either to separate from the church or to continue in it the rest of our
> days.[75]

Grimshaw's passionate response was what Charles had expected and
hoped. He himself had been complaining about the number of preachers

and preaching-houses being licensed in the north, but the matter had clearly gone farther than he realized. Nor could the preachers bear all the blame, for the people wanted a settled ministry of their own: 'The Methodists are no longer members of the Church of England. They are as real a body of dissenters from her as the Presbyterians, Baptists, Quakers, or any body of Independents'. His own course was therefore clear. As an Anglican priest he could no longer continue to superintend the extensive Methodist circuit known as the 'Haworth Round', could no longer indulge in itinerant preaching among the Methodists, for it seemed certain that John Wesley was leading them into a separation from the Church of England:

> I little thought that your brother approved or connived at these things, especially at the preachers' doings at Norwich. If it be so: 'To your tents, O Israel!' It's time for me to shift for myself—to disown all connection with the Methodists, to stay at home and take care of my parish, or to preach abroad in such places as are unlicensed and to such people as are in no connection with us. I hereby therefore assure you that I disclaim all further and future connection with the Methodists.[76]

This was just what Charles Wesley needed. The public reading of Grimshaw's letter to the London society, he told his wife, 'put them in a flame':

> All cried out against the licensed preachers: many demanded they should be silenced immediately; many, that they should give up their licences; some protested against ever hearing them more. . . . The lay preachers pleaded my brother's authority. I took occasion from thence to moderate the others, . . . and desired the leaders to have patience till we had had our Conference. . . . They all cried out that they would answer for ninety-nine out of a hundred in London that they would live and die in the church. My business was to pacify and keep them within bounds.[77]

John Wesley was still in Ireland, and would remain there until the end of August, but the vociferous opposition mustered by Charles persistently reached him. Almost certainly he would hear from the lips of his unpolished but loyal itinerant John Johnson, stationed in Dublin, the gist of the latter's reply to Charles Wesley:

> As for their licenses, it gives no authority to administer the sacraments. I am persuaded there always was some ordination before any person was suffered to give it. . . . As for baptizing and administering

the sacrament, I judge it separation at once, or else what is it? . . . I am fully persuaded in my mind we shall not do much good either in the meeting or church. It seems clear to me that God at present designs us to go into the highways and hedges to call sinners to repentance. If I could be ordained on these terms tomorrow I would.

To which Johnson's colleague added his endorsement: 'I say the same, R. Swindells.'[78]

At length John Wesley was convinced that the spiritual health of Methodism, for which he had been prepared to acquiesce in a kind of tacit ordination for his preachers, now demanded their unfrocking. He seems to have issued a gentle rebuke to the men at Norwich, and meekly asked his brother whether the Conference should be held at Leeds (which would suit Grimshaw best) or at Bristol (which was most convenient for Charles).[79] Bristol was agreed on, and Charles was present, summoning Howell Harris from Wales to his support. Harris preserved a full account of the occasion:

29 Aug., 1760. . . . Mr. John Wesley shewed from the practice of the Church of England, the Kirk of Scotland, Calvinists and Lutherans and the Primitive Churches, that they all made preaching or prophesying or evangelising and administering the ordinances two distinct offices. When they proposed to him to ordain them, he said it was not clear to him that he had a power so to do except they were wholly cut off from the Church by a public act, and also that it would be a total renouncing of the bishops and the Established Church, which he could not do and stumbling thousands. Many spake well on the opposite side, shewing they were already dissented from the Church, and by their being ordained and licensed they would remove the prejudice of the Dissenters. If they owned they were sent to preach, why not to administer the sacraments? . . . Mr. John and Charles Wesley spake their opinion strong of the unlawfulness of a layman administering the ordinances. . . .

On the following day Harris exclaimed triumphantly:

Sure the Lord has made a stand against a breach going to be made in the work by introducing licensing and even ordination, and so a total separation from the Church. Charles and I were the rough workers, and John more meekly, and said he could not ordain, and said if he was not ordained he would look upon it as murder if he gave the ordinances. He struck dumb the reasoners by saying he would renounce them in a quarter of an hour, that they were the most foolish and ignorant in the whole Conference.[80]

None of this went on public record in Wesley's *Journal* or elsewhere, and even the minutes which circulated among the participants have disappeared.[81] John Wesley had been saved in spite of himself, and the tide of an avowed separation from the Church of England had been stemmed. In spite of Charles Wesley's protests preachers and preaching-houses continued to be registered under the Toleration Act, but the preachers stopped their administering and their pressure for Wesley to ordain them. Grimshaw did not leave the Methodist fold after all, and had been dead for twenty years when the issue of separation reached its next major crisis in 1784.

ELEVEN

UNITING THE EVANGELICAL CLERGY

FOR ten years from 1758 Thomas Secker was archbishop of Canterbury. This was a period of growing Anglican distrust of the Methodists, and of a last ditch effort by Wesley to secure the position of Methodism as an integral part of the Church of England. According to information picked up by Howell Harris, writing in 1762, Archbishop Secker 'offered to Mr. Onslow, late Speaker, a scheme against the Methodists, and he [the elder Pitt, Leader of the House of Commons] said he did not like persecution'.[1] Wesley undoubtedly heard something of the same kind, and was confident also of royal support. Many years later he wrote:

> God stirred up the heart of our late gracious sovereign to give such orders to his magistrates as being put in execution effectually quelled the madness of the people. It was about the same time that a great man applied personally to His Majesty begging that he would please to 'take a course to stop these run-about preachers'. His Majesty, looking sternly upon him, answered without ceremony, like a king, 'I tell you, while I sit on the throne, no man shall be persecuted for conscience' sake.'[2]

Among the many attacks on Methodism which Wesley deemed worthy of individual rebuttal during this period were several by clergymen. Full of 'senseless, shameless falsehoods' was *Methodism Examined and Exposed* (1759), by the Rev. John Downes, a London clergyman.[3] Dr. John Free of East Crocker, Somerset, was scurrilous as well as ill-informed, and Wesley spoke of him as 'the warmest opponent I have had for many years'[4]. Similar, though not so formidable, was the Rev. Robert Potter of Rymerston, Norfolk, later Prebendary of Norwich.[5] Of much higher calibre was Dr. (later bishop) George Horne, whose sermon on 'Justification by Works' was preached before the University of Oxford in 1761.[6] More formidable still was Bishop William Warburton's *The Doctrine of Grace: or the Office and Operations of the Holy Spirit vindicated from the insults of infidelity and the abuses of fanaticism* (1763). Wesley, of course, came in the latter category, being accused of 'laying claim to almost every apostolic gift in as full and ample a manner as they were possessed

of old'.[7] 'Enthusiasm', indeed, was the main burden of most of these
recurring attacks on Methodism; this was true also in the case of Dr.
Thomas Rutherforth, archdeacon of Essex, whose charges to his clergy
Wesley did not answer until 1768, some years after they had first been
delivered.[8]

Wesley continued to proclaim that Methodism was a bona fide agent
of the Church of England, perhaps the most loyal segment, and that her
function was to revive that church from within. This claim was obviously unacceptable to those ecclesiastics who saw the essence of the
church as her episcopal government, but Wesley defined the church in
terms of doctrine and worship—and in this view found some support
in Article XIX.[9] As a means of building up the church, therefore, he
continued to advocate Methodist activities which the more legalistic
clergy claimed were undermining her.

One of his noblest apologiae designed to counteract Anglican misunderstanding at the highest levels was a lengthy letter published in his
Arminian Magazine in 1781 but written twenty years earlier. The
recipient was the Earl of Dartmouth—William Cowper's 'earl who
wears a coronet and prays'. Unsettled by the criticisms of his chaplain,
the Rev. George Downing, Dartmouth was exercised in conscience
about his support of the Methodist societies. Mr. Downing had raised
troubling questions, which the earl passed on for Wesley's comments:

> Is it a law of the Church and State that none of her ministers shall
> 'gather congregations' but by the appointment of the bishop? If any
> do, does not she forbid her people to attend them? Are they not
> subversive of the good order of the Church? Do you judge there is
> anything sinful in such a law?

To this Wesley replied:

> 1. If there is a law that a minister of Christ who is not suffered to
> preach the gospel in the church should not preach it elsewhere, I do
> judge that law to be absolutely sinful.
> 2. If that law forbids Christian people to hear the gospel of Christ
> out of their parish church when they cannot hear it therein, I judge
> it would be sinful for them to obey it.
> 3. This preaching is not subversive of any 'good order' whatever.
> It is only subversive of that vile *abuse* of the good order of our church,
> whereby men who neither preach nor live the gospel are suffered
> publicly to overturn it from the foundation: and in the room of it
> to palm upon their congregation a wretched mixture of dead form
> and maimed morality.[10]

Downing had also pointed out that the nobleman was committed by his rank to defend the constitution of the Church of England. Wesley replied:

> And is not her doctrine a main part of this constitution? A far more essential part thereof than any rule of external order? . . . But have you deliberately engaged to defend her *order* to the destruction of her *doctrine*? Are you a guardian of this *external circumstance* when it tends to destroy the *substance* of her constitution? And if you are engaged at all events to defend her *order*, are you also to defend the *abuse* of it?

He insisted that the fundamental principles of the Methodists were those of the Established Church, and continued: 'So is their practice too, save in a very few points wherein they are constrained to deviate.' The critic, however, regarded forming societies and employing lay preachers as 'oppositions to the *most fundamental principles* and *essentially constituent* parts of our Establishment'. Here Wesley waxed allegorical:

> 'The most fundamental principles!' No more than the tiles are 'the most fundamental principles' of an house. Useful, doubtless, they are: yet you must take them off if you would repair the rotten timber beneath. 'Essentially constituent parts of our Establishment!' Well, we will not quarrel for a word. Perhaps the doors may be 'essentially constituent parts' of the building we call a church. Yet if it were on fire we might innocently break them open, or even throw them for a time off the hinges. Now this is really the case. The timber is rotten—yea, the main beams of the house. And they [the Methodists] want to place that firm beam, salvation by faith, in the room of salvation by works. A fire is kindled in the church, the house of the living God, the fire of love of the world, ambition, covetousness, envy, anger, malice, bitter zeal—in one word, of ungodliness and unrighteousness! O who will come and help to quench it? Under disadvantages and discouragements of every kind a little handful of men have made a beginning. And I trust they will not leave off till the building is saved or they sink in the ruins of it.

Finally, Wesley compared the Methodist movement to the Protestant Reformation itself, and put the exact words of the earl's chaplain upon the lips of a German priest:

> Suppose one had asked a German nobleman to hear Martin Luther preach, might not his priest have said . . .: 'My Lord, in every nation there must be *some settled order* of government, ecclesiastical

and civil. There is an *ecclesiastical order* established in Germany. You
are born under this establishment. Your ancestors supported it, and
your very rank and station constitute you a formal and eminent
guardian of it. How then can it consist with the duty arising from all
these to give *encouragement, countenance, and support* to principles and
practices that are a direct renunciation of the *established constitution*?'
Had the force of this reasoning been allowed, what had become of
the Reformation?[11]

Increasingly Wesley had come to believe that the secret of a revived
Church of England lay in securing the co-operation of the evangelical
clergy.[12] Of these there were far more than has generally been recognized, for the most part orthodox ministers serving quietly in obscure
parishes, like Vincent Perronet and James Hervey; occasionally they
introduced religious societies into their parishes, as did Samuel Walker,
or like John Baddiley employed lay assistants,[13] or even like Henry
Venn built non-Anglican chapels for their flock, or ventured upon a
widespread itinerant ministry like that of John Berridge; at least one
man was sufficiently unconventional to engage in all these activities—
William Grimshaw. For the most part these men had little official contact with each other, though in 1750 Samuel Walker had begun a
'Parsons' Club' for sympathetic clergy in Cornwall: the members met
for eight hours at a time during 'seven months of the year, on the first
Tuesday after every full moon, at their several houses by turns'.[14] The
Independent minister Risdon Darracott of Wellington followed
Walker's example in 1755, forming a similar organization for Somerset.[15] John Fletcher of Madeley also proposed establishing 'A Society
of Ministers of the Gospel in the Church of England' in Worcestershire,
and drew up for this organization an undated set of rules.[16]

John Wesley dreamed of a much more far-reaching scheme—a
national union of evangelical clergy who might keep in touch with
each other by correspondence and occasional itinerancy, and who
could both serve Methodism and be served by it in ensuring a continuing evangelical witness within the Established Church. This seems first
to have been adumbrated at his Conference in 1757, as reported in a
letter to Samuel Walker:

I proposed that question to all who met at our late Conference,
'What can be done in order to a closer union with the clergy who
preach the truth?' We all agreed that nothing could be more desirable. I in particular have long desired it: not from any view to my
own ease or honour or temporal convenience in any kind, but

13

because I was deeply convinced it might be a blessing to my own soul and a means of promoting the general work of God.[17]

This project Wesley discussed with others of the Cornish clergy, but apparently with little success.[18]

Already Wesley had been attempting to take under his wing promising young evangelical clergy like Francis Fetherston,[19] Samuel Furley,[20] Martin Madan,[21] Walter Shirley,[22] Henry Venn,[23] Thomas Waterhouse,[24] and especially John Fletcher, who so fully threw in his lot with Wesley that he rushed immediately from his ordination in 1757 to help with a crowded London communion service, and remained as Wesley's ordained helper for three years before entering on his parish ministry at Madeley in 1760.[25] Wesley unsuccessfully opposed Fletcher's forsaking of the full itinerancy for the parish, calling it 'the devil's snare' —'others may do well in a living; you cannot; it is not your calling'.[26] Wesley was already in touch to a greater or lesser degree with some of the older evangelicals like Samuel Walker and the others in Cornwall,[27] Thomas Adam of Wintringham,[28] John Baddiley of Hayfield, Derbyshire,[29] James Rouquet of Bristol,[30] Henry Crook of Hunslet,[31] William Grimshaw of Haworth, and William Williamson of York,[32] though he does not seem to have known Joseph Jane and James Stillingfleet of Oxford.[33]

In December 1757 Wesley dropped a broad hint to his former schoolmaster Walter Sellon that he would find a more fruitful field in the Methodist itinerancy than in the parish ministry.[34] During 1758 and 1759 he courted a number of evangelicals or potential evangelicals: John Berridge, the eccentric vicar of Everton, and his neighbour William Hicks, vicar of Wrestlingworth, of whom Wesley said 'about two thousand souls seem to have been awakened by Mr. B. and him within this twelvemonth'[35]; Dr. Richard Conyers of Helmsley[36]; George Downing, rector of Ovington, Essex, as well as a somewhat disturbing chaplain to the Earl of Dartmouth[37]; Thomas Goodday of Sunderland[38]; Thomas Jones of Southwark[39]; John Newton, who had unsuccessfully sought episcopal ordination, and remained in limbo;[40] Francis Okely, a Moravian minister attracted to the Anglican ministry, who toured with Wesley in 1758, and attended the Conference that year[41]; Augustus Toplady, then in training at Trinity College, Dublin[42]; and William Romaine, removed from his position at St. George's, Hanover Square, because his preaching was too popular for the pewholders.[43]

This was only in small part coincidental. Mainly it was evidence of a deliberate attempt by Wesley to enlist the sympathies of evangelical clergymen, and to make himself and his brother a major focus of liaison between them. Charles Wesley's boyish boastfulness may be pardoned by remembering that it was to his wife that he wrote in 1759, 'The converted clergy will be multiplied by the time my brother and I finish'.[44] In fact they were far from alone in this effort. Their greatest ally was without doubt the Countess of Huntingdon, who in the winter of 1758-9 was seized by a powerful urge to wrestle for the soul of the nation, particularly in view of the parlous international situation half-way through the Seven Years' War, with the threat of imminent invasion from France. It was probably at some of the gatherings of clergy for prayer in her Downing Street home that Wesley first met some of the evangelical clergy, particularly Thomas Jones of South-wark, and possibly William Romaine.[45]

Whitefield's dramatic piety had always been welcome to his fellow-Calvinists at the Countess's frequent spiritual jamborees, and now there seems to have been a more general appreciation of the quieter qualities of the Wesleys. On one notable occasion the two Wesleys were accom-panied by Thomas Maxfield, their former lay preacher, who at the instance of the Countess had been ordained by the bishop of Derry, who said, 'Sir, I ordain you to assist that good man [Mr. Wesley], that he may not work himself to death'.[46] These three went to breakfast at Lady Selina's in Downing Street, and after breakfast were joined by Whitefield, Jones, Downing, Venn, Romaine, Lord and Lady Dart-mouth, and others.[47] Afterwards John wrote to the Countess in the vein of one reminiscing about the good old days:

> The agreeable hour which I spent with your Ladyship the last week recalled to my mind the former times, and gave me much matter of thankfulness to the Giver of every good gift. I have found great satisfaction in conversing with those instruments whom God has lately raised up. But still there is I known not what in them whom we have known from the beginning, and who have borne the burthen and heat of the day, which we do not find in those who have risen up since, though they are upright of heart.

Wesley thought he detected a certain brashness in the emphasis of these young evangelicals upon justification by faith, a lack of realization how necessary it was to press on patiently toward the goal of holiness.[48] Nevertheless, he was convinced that in harness with them lay his greatest hope of reviving the church from within.

One of the major problems that arose during this round of letters and conferences was the relationship of Wesley's preachers to these sympathetic clergy. Should the Methodist societies be handed over to them? This was apparently what Samuel Walker of Truro expected, so that he was somewhat distressed when Wesley insisted that he dare not do this even in the case of James Vowler, the curate of St. Agnes, even though he 'both preaches and lives the gospel'. For Wesley could not be fully assured either of Vowler's pastoral experience or of the Methodists' agreement to such a move, insisting: 'Before I could with a clear conscience leave a Methodist Society even to such an one all these considerations must come in.'[49] He might have added to his argument the point that there was no assurance that one evangelical ministry would be followed by another, for which reason both Grimshaw and Venn built in their parishes Methodist preaching-houses free of Anglican control.[50]

This problem came to a head in Huddersfield in 1761. The Methodist society there had been established with some difficulty shortly before Henry Venn's arrival, and although the members respected Venn they did not want to lose their Methodist identity and contacts. After an interview with Venn Wesley confessed himself 'a little embarrassed':

> Where there is a gospel ministry already we do not desire to preach; but whether we can leave off preaching because such an one comes after is another question, especially when those who were awakened and convinced by us beg and require the continuance of our assistance. I love peace, and follow it; but whether I am at liberty to purchase it at such a price I really cannot tell.

Eventually a compromise was reached, namely that Wesley's preachers should visit Huddersfield once a month, though in 1762 Wesley withdrew them altogether.[51] This kind of situation must have been discussed at the 1761 Conference. In the light of his varied problems John Wesley nevertheless wrote confidently to his brother Charles:

> I do not at all think (to tell you a secret) that the work will ever be destroyed, Church or no Church. What has been done to prevent the Methodists leaving the Church you will see in the Minutes of the Conference. I told you before, with regard to Norwich, *dixi*. I have done at the last Conference all I *can* or *dare* do. Allow me liberty of conscience, as I allow you.[52]

It can be understood that this kind of situation, and John Wesley's readiness to go only so far in sacrificing Methodism to the Church, would not endear him to those who (like his brother Charles) did not acknowledge the same scale of values. John was constantly enlarging the circle of his evangelical acquaintance, only to find his new friends growing cool. He first met Thomas Haweis in 1761. Haweis was one of

Walker's protégés, and had formed a new Holy Club in his rooms at Magdalen Hall, Oxford. In 1762 he was squeezed out of his evangelical ministry at Oxford and for two years assisted Martin Madan at the Lock Chapel, London, until in 1764 he secured the living of Aldwincle.[53] But although the Wesleys welcomed Haweis 'with particular affection' they never became close friends, and later John Wesley thought that both Haweis and Madan were antagonistic towards him.[54] In March 1761 he wrote to James Rouquet of Bristol, lamenting the 'disunion of Christian ministers':

> How many and how great are the advantages which would flow from a general union of those at least who acknowledge each other to be messengers of God! I know nothing (but sin) which I would not do or leave undone to promote it; and this has been my settled determination for at least ten years last past. But all my overtures have been constantly rejected; almost all of them stand aloof, and at length they have carried their point.

The major difficulty, he felt, was that the devout regular clergy, headed by 'poor, honest Mr. Walker' were in effect saying to those who undertook an irregular ministry: 'Stand by yourselves; we are better than you!'[55] The following month he wrote to George Downing:

> I think it great pity that the few clergymen in England who preach the three grand scriptural doctrines, Original Sin, Justification by Faith, and Holiness consequent thereon, should have any jealousies or misunderstandings between them. . . . How desirable is it that there should be the most open, avowed intercourse between them. . . . For many years I have been labouring after this—labouring to unite, not scatter, the messengers of God. Not that I want anything from them. As God has enabled me to stand almost alone for these twenty years, I doubt not but He will enable me to stand either with them or without them. But I want all to be helpful to each other— and all the world to know we are so.[56]

Even some of his own men, like Thomas Maxfield, were turning against him. One young clergyman, Benjamin Colley, was ordained in 1761 and gave himself completely to Wesley's work until his death in 1767, but for a time in 1762 he was disaffected by Maxfield, and only in 1767 did his name actually appear in the *Minutes*.[57] Wesley's only lasting success from these years was with John Richardson, the curate of Ewhurst in Sussex, who under the influence of a sermon by Thomas Rankin in March 1762 became a Methodist. In that same year he was dismissed by his rector and offered himself to Wesley, whom he served as 'a son in the gospel' throughout the remainder of Wesley's life, himself dying in 1792.[58] Wesley continued to woo the clergy, but with gradually lessening expectancy. To Samuel Furley, whom he had been nursing for eight years, and who had been ordained in 1758 and was now at Slaithwaite, he wrote in 1762:

> I still think it is not prudence, but high imprudence, for any of those who preach the essential gospel truths to stand aloof from each other. I cannot but judge there ought to be the most cordial and avowed union between them. But I rejoice that the shyness is not and never was on my side. I have done all I could; and with a single eye.[59]

Remembering especially the nearly disastrous separatist pressures of 1760, Wesley invited several evangelical clergy to his Conferences in both 1761 and 1762. At Leeds in 1762 these included Madan, Romaine, Venn, Whitefield, and the Countess of Huntingdon. Wesley was becoming more and more disillusioned, however, about the co-operation for which he hoped. On 20 March 1763 he wrote to the Countess in some distress because many of the erstwhile friendly clergy were turning against him on account of his advocacy of Christian perfection:

> I mean (for I use no ceremony or circumlocution) Mr. Madan, Mr. Haweis, Mr. Berridge, and (I am sorry to say it) Mr. Whitefield. Only Mr. Romaine has shown a truly sympathizing spirit and acted the part of a brother.[60]

Later that year he unburdened himself to Henry Venn, who had written in friendly vein. Wesley showed that he was rapidly approaching the position where he must be self-sufficient, relying only on 'those who are now connected with me, and who bless God for that connexion'. Nevertheless, he went on:

> I have laboured after union with all whom I believe to be united with Christ. I have sought it again and again, but in vain. They were resolved to stand aloof. And when one and another sincere minister of Christ has been inclined to come nearer to me, others have diligently kept them off, as though thereby they did God service.

He believed himself somewhat estranged even from Venn, perhaps partly by the agency of Venn's former curate, now vicar of Elland, 'that honest, well-meaning man, Mr. [George] Burnett, and by others, who have talked largely of my dogmaticalness, love of power, errors, and irregularities'. Even Wesley's agreement with Venn to limit the Methodist preaching in Huddersfield was not working as well as he had hoped, though he knew that both Venn and he had indeed refrained from public criticism of each other. He found it impossible to be satisfied with the typical attitude of most of the evangelical clergy: 'Be very civil to the Methodists, but have nothing to do with them.' What he wanted was 'a league offensive and defensive with every soldier of Christ'. He ended with a plea to Venn:

> We have not only one faith, one hope, one Lord, but are directly engaged in one warfare. We are carrying the war into the devil's own quarters, who therefore summons all his hosts to war. Come then, ye that love Him, to the help of the Lord, to the help of the Lord against the mighty! I am now wellnigh *miles emeritus, senex, sexagenarius* ['A worn-out old warrior of sixty years'—actually he was still a week from his sixtieth birthday]; yet I trust to fight a little longer. Come and strengthen the hands till you supply the place of
>
> Your weak but affectionate brother,
> John Wesley.[61]

The Conference met in July 1763, in the aftermath of the troubles caused by Maxfield's defection and the controversies over Christian perfection. Howell Harris was present, and his diary enables us to supplement Wesley's meagre comment, 'it was a great blessing that we had peace among ourselves while so many were making themselves ready for battle'.[62] It remains uncertain whether the Conference itself was restricted to Wesley's preachers (including Harris), but the Wesleys certainly held consultations during those days with Venn, Berridge, Madan, and Haweis. Strangely enough the last impressed Harris as being somewhat radical, for he seemed to doubt whether bishops in fact constituted a third order in the church and believed 'that each church should be independent and settle her own matters'.[63] On his return Harris called to see Richard Hart and other evangelical ministers in Bristol, who did little to ease his general forebodings about the future of Methodism:

> 30 July. Bristol. To see Mr. Camplin about using some means if possible to soften the bishops, who are going out of the spirit of moderation, which is the glory of our Church: refusing to license one and to ordain another; turning another out for believing the truth of the operation of the Holy Spirit; and turning above 20,000 souls of the best people out of the Church, who can be safe under the Toleration Act, but ruining the Church and robbing her of her best members.[64]

Harris then spent the best part of three months touring England 'striving

for universal union and for the clergy to meet each other'.[65] He echoed
Wesley's complaint that 'the awakened clergy are all separate', and his
hope that 'in coming together many clergymen would be found out
that now by fear are hid'.[66] Harris found that Venn in the north was
sympathetic, but Berridge in the south was violently opposed.[67]
Charles Wesley also was angry, charging that it was Harris and the
laymen who 'broke the Church', and apparently claiming 'that the
bishops are antichrist, that they (the Methodists) are the Church of
England'.[68] Lady Huntingdon told Harris that John Wesley was 'an
eel—no hold of him, and [one could] not come to the truth [with
him]'.[69]

Nor was Wesley himself quite ready to give up hope. He was covering similar territory to Harris with a similar purpose. In Bristol on
16 March 1764 he recorded:

> I met several serious clergymen. I have long desired that there might
> be an open, avowed union between all who preach those funda-
> mental truths, original sin and justification by faith, producing
> inward and outward holiness; but all my endeavours have been
> hitherto ineffectual. God's time is not fully come.[70]

A long-promised visit to Dr. Richard Conyers at Helmsley on 17 April
1764, following a conversation with the Countess of Huntingdon,
determined him on an all-out effort. Conyers, who had pressed him so
warmly to come—'my house and my heart are and ever shall be open
to you'—seemed quite changed, convincing Wesley that 'the Philistines
had been upon him'. Not being invited to preach, Wesley was on the
point of taking his leave when Conyers relented. As they conversed
after the evening service Conyers insisted that Wesley's dream of a
union of evangelical clergy was impracticable. When Wesley retired
for the night he prayed earnestly about this very point, and then opened
his Latin copy of the *Imitatio Christi* on the words: 'Expecta Dominum:
Viriliter age: Noli diffidere: Noli discedere; sed corpus et animam
expone constanter pro gloria Dei.' Wesley's English translation of this
passage in 1735 was: 'Wait upon the Lord, do manfully, be of good
courage, do not despair, do not fly, but with constancy expose both
body and soul for the glory of God.'[71] On the following day another
'serious clergyman' had been similarly ensnared, but had broken free.
On 19 April Wesley sat down for a time at Scarborough and wrote a
lengthy manifesto to rally such men to his side.

In this document Wesley described the beginnings of 'a great work
in England', and lamented that 'as labourers increased, disunion increased'. He then listed the most sympathetic of the Anglican clergy,

thirty-nine of them, grouped for the most part according to the part of the country in which they ministered. The last group was probably intended to link together the more irregular of them—'Mr. Berridge, Hicks, G.W[hitefield], J.W., C.W., John Richardson, Benjamin Colley'. Berridge and Hicks itinerated, though to a lesser degree than Whitefield and the Wesleys; Richardson and Colley were unbeneficed helpers of the Wesleys. The conditions which Wesley suggested for such a union were the same as those outlined in his letter to George Downing three years earlier; any clergyman would be welcomed who agreed 'in these essentials: I. Original sin. II. Justification by faith. III. Holiness of heart and life—provided their life be answerable to their doctrine'. The obvious question about the practicability of a somewhat nebulous scheme was asked and answered:

> 'But *what union* would you desire among these?' Not an union in *opinions*; they might agree or disagree touching absolute decrees on the one hand and perfection on the other. Not an union in *expressions*: these may still speak of the 'imputed righteousness' and those of 'the merits of Christ'. Not an union with regard to *outward order*; some may still remain *quite regular*, some *quite irregular*, and some *partly regular* and *partly irregular*.

There would be no attempt to alter such outward behaviour: the union would be one of spirit, of sympathy, of understanding, of hopeful love, both in thought and conduct, so that all would 'speak respectfully, honourably, kindly of each other', and 'each help other in his work and enlarge his influence by all the honest means we can'. This would not only promote their own holiness and happiness, but would be 'far better for the people, who suffer severely from the clashings and contentions of their leaders'. It would be 'better even for the poor, blind world, robbing them of their sport, "Oh, they cannot agree among themselves!"' More important still, the 'whole work of God . . . would then deepen and widen on every side'. Granted that it sounded impossible, because it was against human nature thus humbly to relinquish 'love of honour and praise, of power, of pre-eminence'. Nevertheless, ' "all things are possible to him that believeth:" and this union is proposed only to them that believe, that show their faith by their works.'[72]

Wesley wrote out two copies of this letter and sent them with covering notes to the Earl of Dartmouth and the Countess of Huntingdon, who were most closely in touch with the majority of those Calvinist clergy whose hearts he hoped to move. He appealed to Lady Selina: 'Who knows but it may please God to make your Ladyship an instrument in this glorious work? In effecting an union among the labourers in His vineyard?' Both the earl and the countess apparently approved in principle, and passed on both information and encouragement to the clergy within their orbits.[73] Wesley himself wrote a few further letters along the lines indicated, including one to Richard Hart of Bristol, who suggested that an open debate between 'the preachers of the gospel', might be of value.[74] Wesley doubted the wisdom of this particular course, for fear it 'might tear open the wounds before they are fully closed'. Nevertheless, he did invite any clergy who could be in Bristol at the time of his Conference in August to meet together on the 9th for a few hours 'either apart from or in conjunction with the other preachers'; he added the Countess also to his invitations.[75] And he continued to woo young evangelical clergy such as Cradock Glascott and John Crosse.[76]

At the Conference Martin Madan preached, and twelve clergy were present, apparently during the regular sessions. An old wound was in fact soon opened, for the main discussion seemed to centre on the removal of Methodist preaching from the parishes of evangelical clergy, such as Wesley had agreed to in the case of Henry Venn at Huddersfield. Charles Wesley sided with the clergy, maintaining that if he were a parish minister no Methodist preacher would be allowed in his parish, whereupon one of the more outspoken preachers, John Hampson, retorted: 'I would preach there, and never ask your leave; and should have as good a right to do so as you would have!' Some of the visiting clergy supported Hampson, maintaining: 'If a layman be called of God to preach the gospel, then he has as good a right to do it as any clergyman whatever'—though Madan at least was not prepared to go thus far.[77] John Wesley remained adamant. He refused to relinquish his societies, and no doubt reiterated his dissatisfaction with the Huddersfield arrangement, which he had continued for a second year, possibly a third, but which he certainly renounced in 1765.[78] Nevertheless Charles Wesley wrote on 28 August of a fruitful sequel: 'We have had a conference of the Gospel-Clergy at Lady Huntingdon's. Good, I think, will come out of it.'

John Wesley tried to remove misunderstanding by preparing a piece of irenic propaganda, *A Short History of Methodism*, of which two editions were published in 1765. He pointed out that regular and irregular clergy, Arminians and Calvinists, were alike 'included in the general name of Methodists', instancing in particular Whitefield, Venn, Romaine, Madan, and Berridge. He added:

At present those who remain with Mr. Wesley are mostly Church of England men. They love her Articles, her Homilies, her Liturgy, her discipline, and unwillingly vary from it in any instance. . . . They tenderly love many that are Calvinists, though they do not love their opinions.[79]

At least one parish clergyman proved fully co-operative. John Fletcher of Madeley wrote to Alexander Mather, the lay preacher appointed by Wesley to that area in 1765:

An occasional exhortation from you or your companion at the Bank, Dale, etc. [where Fletcher had formed his own societies] will be esteemed a favour; and I hope that my going, as Providence directs, to any of your places (leaving to you the management of the societies) will be deemed no encroachment. In short, we need not make *two parties*; I know but *one* heaven below, and that is Jesus's love.[80]

The following year he still maintained: 'The coming of Mr. Wesley's preachers into my parish gives me no uneasiness. . . . I rejoice that the work of God goes on by *any instrument* or in *any place*'.[81]

In July 1765 Whitefield returned from two years in America, weakened in body but mellowed in spirit. John Wesley spoke of him as 'an old, old man'.[82] On 6 October 1765 he opened the Countess's new chapel at Bath, and then returned to London as a healing power cementing for a time the Wesleys and the Countess and her chaplains.[83] At his Conference in August 1766 Wesley again stressed the need for his societies to cling to the Church of England. Whitefield was even more cordial, and the Countess invited Wesley to preach for her at Bath, opening both her heart and her chapels to him. Indeed all seemed set for the kind of union for which he had long prayed and laboured and suffered.[84]

So encouraging was the situation that Wesley took up the letter which he had written to the Earl of Dartmouth on the evangelical clergy in 1764 and printed it as a four-page quarto circular, mailing it to forty or fifty sympathetic ministers. First he amended the wording here and there, subtracted and added a few names in the list of clergy therein, and added a printed foreword:

Rev. Sir,
    Near two years and a half ago I wrote the following letter. You will please to observe, 1. That I propose no more therein than is the bounden duty of every Christian. 2. That *you* may comply with this proposal whether any other does or not. I myself have endeavoured so to do for many years, though I have been almost alone therein,

and although many, the more earnestly I *talk of peace*, the more zealously *make themselves ready for battle*.

I am, Rev. Sir,

Your affectionate brother,

John Wesley.

This covering note was dated 15 October 1766. It was followed by the letter of 19 April 1764, addressed to 'My Lord' and ending 'I am, my Lord, Your Lordship's affectionate and obedient Servant, J.W.' Shortly afterwards Wesley issued a revised edition of this circular letter, clothing the Earl of Dartmouth in the greater anonymity of 'Dear Sir'—which in any event seemed more suitable in a communication addressed primarily to the clergy. The date in this edition was corrected by hand to 15 December 1766.[85]

To this printed letter Wesley received three replies: one from his former Kingswood colleague Walter Sellon, one from his old friend Vincent Perronet of Shoreham, and another from the faithful Richard Hart of Bristol.[86] Hart once more offered some practical suggestions, Perronet agreed that unity of spirit was 'an indispensable duty of all Christians', but Sellon confessed himself 'an infidel' concerning Wesley's proposals, and stated that he himself was worn out through constant opposition. On 30 December Wesley replied to Sellon:

It is certain that nothing less than the mighty power of God can ever effect that union. . . . Are you tired with ploughing on the sand? Then come away to better work. It is true you would have less money, only forty pounds a year; but you would have more comfort and more fruit of your labour. Here is a wide and glorious field of action. You might exceedingly help a willing people, as well as strengthen the hand of

Your affectionate brother

John Wesley.[87]

By this time Wesley had almost given up hope of bringing the projected union to pass. Even though the Countess and Whitefield were sympathetic, their cohorts were not. In 1767 Whitefield and Howell Harris attended Wesley's Conference;[88] in 1768 Charles Wesley and in 1769 John Wesley visited the Countess's new college at Trevecka, preaching and administering communion there.[89] This promising cooperation was completely shattered by the bitter doctrinal controversy sparked by Wesley's incautious *Minutes* in 1770, the year of Whitefield's death.

Wesley turned more and more to strengthening the Methodist ranks, one of his methods being the attempted recruiting of clergy like Sellon. Symptomatic was his correspondence with Joseph Townsend, rector of Pewsey, in August 1767. From supporting Wesley's preachers and people in Edinburgh, Townsend had turned to undermining their work, claiming:

> The Methodist people are a fallen people and the preachers preach only dry morality. They are in grievous error, denying election, perseverance, and the righteousness of Christ. Therefore their work is at an end, and the work of God which is now wrought is wrought by the awakened clergy.

'Convince me of this,' replied Wesley, 'and I have done with the Methodists and with preaching.' Point by point he refuted Townsend's claims, and set up for a Calvinist model Dr. John Gillies, who in preaching for Wesley had proclaimed: 'In some opinions I do not agree with the Methodists; but I know they are a people of God: therefore I wish them good luck in the name of the Lord.'[90]

Even John Fletcher seemed to be losing some of his original spirit, so that Wesley urged him to make up his mind whether he was going to remain infected with Calvinism or come over fully to Wesley's defence.[91] In July 1768 Wesley defended himself against Thomas Adam of Wintringham, who had maintained:

> No sensible and well-meaning man could hear, and much less join, the Methodists, because they all 'acted under a lie, professing themselves members of the Church of England while they licensed themselves as Dissenters'.

Once again Wesley refuted this charge, claiming, 'We are in truth so far from being enemies to the church that we are rather bigots to it. . . . I advise all over whom I have any influence steadily to keep to the church'.[92] At the 1768 Conference he once more urged loyalty to the Establishment, in spite of unsympathetic clergy:

> 1. Let us keep to the church. Over and above all the reasons that were formerly given for this we add another now from long experience: they that leave the church leave the Methodists. The clergy cannot separate us from our brethren; the dissenting ministers can and do. Therefore, carefully avoid whatever has a tendency to separate men from the church, in particular preaching at any hour which hinders them from going to it.
>
> 2. Let all the servants in our preaching-houses go to church on Sunday morning at least.

3. Let every preacher go always on Sunday morning, and when he can in the afternoon. God will bless those who go on week-days too as often as they have opportunity.[93]

In 1769 Wesley became convinced that it was a waste of effort to plough this desert any longer, and prepared a document designed to strengthen the Methodist societies and preachers from within rather than to tie them to other Anglican ministers. After seeking his brother's emendations and additions he presented this paper to the closing session of the Conference. Its opening paragraph wrote 'finis' to a frustrating chapter in his struggle to remain within the Church of England as a working partner:

My dear brethren,

1. It has long been my desire that all those ministers of our Church who believe and preach salvation by faith might cordially agree between themselves, and not hinder but help one another. After occasionally pressing this in private conversation whenever I had opportunity, I wrote down my thoughts upon the head and sent them to each in a letter. Out of fifty or sixty to whom I wrote only three vouchsafed me an answer. So I give this up. I can do no more. They are a rope of sand: and such they will continue.[94]

TWELVE

MAINTAINING THE METHODIST WITNESS

By 1769 at the latest Wesley was convinced that he was wasting his time in trying to bring about a working partnership between the Methodist societies and the evangelical clergy, and turned his full attention to securing the future of Methodism, preferably as a movement within the Anglican Church, but if not as a denomination distinct from it. From the beginning he had taken many steps in this direction, though without acknowledging their schismatic tendency. Increasingly during the 1760's and 1770's he came to realize the direction in which he was headed. He continued to seek the company of loyal churchmen along the road which might lead to the conquest of new territory either in the name of the Established Church or of a separated Methodism, but he refused to forsake his trail-breaking ventures, Church or no Church. He became more and more determined to maintain the Methodist witness, even after his death, within a connexional organization coordinated by an itinerant ministry. New elements of connexional policy were introduced to further this end, and he continued to seek the enhancement of his preachers' status by any means short of himself laying ordaining hands on them.

One of the earliest expressions of this preparedness for Methodist independence was at the brief but momentous Bristol Conference of 1760. Although Wesley refused to ordain his preachers, he did prepare and discuss with them plans to ensure the continuance of Methodism after his death. Again we are indebted to Howell Harris for the details:

29 Aug., 1760: Bristol. . . . At 9 I went with Mr. Charles Wesley and John Jones to the New Room to meet all the preachers, I think about 40, where Mr. John Wesley, after singing and praying, laid before them what to do about settling the work if he should die. . . . He proposed that the clergy and the assistants (preachers that now superintend) should form a council then and settle matters, and call the preachers after his death and his brother's. All agreed to that.[1]

In 1763 Wesley published the fullest summary to that date of Methodist polity, in a new edition of what was familiarly known as the 'Large Minutes'. Both the general intention and the specific content showed him leaning more heavily towards denominationalism, even though this was disavowed. The assistants were instructed to attend the parish church and to exhort the people so to do, thus giving the lie to the charge that Methodism was 'unawares, by little and little, tending to a separation from the Church'. Explicitly they were warned 'against calling our Society a Church or the Church', and 'against calling our Preachers Ministers, our houses meeting-houses (call them plain preaching-houses)'. This challenge was repeated in the succeeding editions, though from 1770 onwards 'tending to a separation' became 'sliding into a separation'.[2] As we have seen, however, Wesley himself had used the word 'church' of the Foundery and possibly of West Street Chapel. He might attempt to correct his own occasional slips, might attempt to muzzle his preachers and people, but evangelical sympathizers continued to spread the phrase. In 1759 John Fletcher spoke of himself as unworthy to be a salaried minister of the Methodist Church, and in 1775 deliberately recommended the title 'the Methodist Church of England'. Vincent Perronet also wrote about 'the Methodist Church', at least in 1763 and 1765.[3]

In the same Large Minutes of 1763 Wesley furnished careful instructions for licensing Methodist premises for public worship, as well as an elaborate model deed designed to secure them for exclusively Methodist uses. Because he claimed that the Methodists were not dissenters he dodged the issue of nomenclature, merely stating that their petition should be presented to the justices in the form: 'A.B. desires to have his house in C. licensed for public worship.'[4] In the mushrooming numbers of applications for registration during the 1760's and 1770's, in fact, the term 'Methodist' seldom appeared. In Lincolnshire the Methodist registrants usually called themselves 'Independents', using the term in its generic rather than its specific denominational sense.[5] In Yorkshire they simply called themselves 'Protestants' or 'Protestant Dissenters', though frequently they avoided the issue altogether by neglecting to use any title at all, even though the Act did call for a description. In at least one instance (in Derbyshire) registration was refused by the justices on these grounds, though when the case was argued before the Court of King's Bench the justices were compelled to yield.[6] Wesley was a great believer in an appeal to the King's Bench, in spite of the expense involved, and successfully protected his followers on several occasions by such litigation. He warned one obstructive clerical magistrate in 1766: 'I have had many suits in the King's Bench, and (blessed be God) I never lost one yet.'[7] In 1760 his preacher John Morley and the tiny group of Methodists at Rolvenden, Kent, were thus vindicated even though they were not registered at all under the Act.

Wesley was enormously elated by this vindication, writing to his brother Charles:

> It is of more consequence than our people seem to apprehend. If we do not exert ourselves it may drive us to that bad dilemma—leave preaching or leave the church. We have reason to thank God it is not come to this yet. Perhaps it never may.[8]

When in 1779 one diffident Methodist complained that his application for a certificate had been turned down Wesley told him to go back and *demand* registration as a right, and to refer any further recalcitrance to Wesley himself.[9]

The model deed which Wesley published in 1763 was intended to safeguard Methodist premises for Methodist uses not only during his lifetime but after his death, thus forming another important landmark in the growing identification of Methodism as a distinct denomination. It provided that Charles Wesley should succeed his brother in appointing the preachers; Charles was to be succeeded by William Grimshaw; after Grimshaw's death the responsibility fell to 'the yearly Conference of the people called Methodists'. All the appointed trustees of each preaching-house were to be Methodists, and if any died or ceased to be members of 'the Society commonly called Methodists' the remaining trustees were empowered to make up their number to nine.[10] The 1763 Large Minutes similarly gave official countenance to the licensing of preachers, even though reluctantly and conditionally: 'Do not license yourself till you are constrained: and then not as a Dissenter, but a Methodist Preacher. It is time enough when you are prosecuted to take the oaths. Thereby you are licensed.'[11]

Licensing the preachers was an important concession, but it was far more important that Wesley should in some way encompass their ordination, for only thus might he with a good conscience secure the widespread administration of the sacraments to his people. Somewhat reluctantly he had agreed not to exercise the powers of ordination which he believed himself as a presbyter to possess, for fear that the worse evil of an avowed separation might follow. The evangelical clergy as a whole did not seem prepared to fill the gap left by the restriction preventing unordained preachers from administering. In only a few centres could Methodists take communion at the hands of their own spiritual fathers. Fletcher had been replaced in London by John Richardson; in Bristol Charles Wesley remained in charge, as did William Grimshaw in the north. John Fletcher now left his own parish little more than any other conscientious clergyman, and Wesley complained, 'I grudge his sitting still'.[12] He was ready to clutch at almost

14

any straw to secure a full church life by means of an ordained yet itinerant ministry for the Methodists, and especially for the rapidly growing London societies. The services of a Greek refugee, Bishop Erasmus, seemed to offer at least a partial solution, though Wesley soon discovered that in turning to him he had released a genie whom he was unable to control.

It is extremely difficult to secure a clear picture of Wesley's relations with Erasmus, whom he first befriended in 1763, when the Greek was 'a stranger perishing for want and expecting daily to be thrown in prison'. Wesley conversed with him in Latin and in Greek, examined the voluminous credentials supporting his claim to be the bishop of Arcadia, and finally helped secure his passage to friends in Amsterdam. Confirmation of his claims came from gentlemen who had known him in Turkey as well as from the Patriarch of Smyrna, to whom a letter was directed at Wesley's request by his trusted lay colleague John Jones, a scholarly physician turned preacher. Apparently before leaving for Amsterdam, about March 1764, at Wesley's request Erasmus ordained Jones.

Not unnaturally word of this event passed round, and shortly afterwards, while Wesley was away from London, Erasmus was prevailed upon to ordain another of his preachers, Lawrence Coughlan. On two later occasions that same year Erasmus was brought over from Amsterdam to ordain groups of Methodist preachers, on each occasion without Wesley's knowledge. On 30 May 1764 Erasmus wrote in Greek to Wesley: 'I know that I have done you wrong, but I am not to blame.'[13] The rumour was that Wesley himself was behind all this, that (via John Jones) he had even asked Erasmus to ordain him bishop, and that on being told that other bishops were necessary Wesley had 'offered a premium to fetch two foreign bishops to help Erasmus to consecrate him bishop'.[14] When at length Wesley discovered the unforeseen results of thus securing Jones's ordination he acted swiftly. He summoned a special conference, and repudiated the other men ordained, both as clergy, as preachers, and even as members of the Methodist society, because they had clandestinely purchased ordination conferred in a tongue which they did not understand. He also publicly refuted the rumour about his seeking consecration as a bishop either directly or indirectly.[15]

Meantime Charles Wesley refused to acknowledge Jones's orders, possibly because like Augustus Toplady he considered this recourse to a foreign prelate a breach of the Oath of Supremacy. In this stand he was joined by their clerical helper in London, John Richardson, who kept Charles informed about both the facts and the latest rumours; he told

Charles that he had refused to share the administration of communion with Jones, especially when aided by the renegade Maxfield, who had been responsible for engineering at least one batch of the ordinations by Erasmus.[16]

On 24 April 1764 John Newton had joined forces with the Countess of Huntingdon in commending to Wesley the 'Bishop of Arcadia' as one whose 'services would be of unestimable value in the creation of a new ministry'. Later the Countess and her advisers had second thoughts.[17] The scandal generated by the intrigues led to the complete closure of that promisingly open door. Even the worthy Jones was inevitably embarrassed, and later secured re-ordination by the bishop of London, as did Lawrence Coughlan.[18] At least two of the preachers clandestinely ordained, Thomas Bryant and James Thwaite, founded schismatic congregations.[19] In spite of Wesley's tender message to the erring preachers only one returned to the Methodist itinerancy.[20] Wesley's 'whole story of Dr. Jones's ordination' as recounted before the 1765 Conference, was received in silence, and Wesley himself was unable to live down the persistent rumours that he had been ambitiously involved in this unhappy affair.[21] Well might he have echoed Vincent Perronet's comment: 'I could wish that his Grecian Lordship had been preaching either in Lapland or Japan, instead of putting the whole Methodist Church into confusion!'[22] To crown it all, it now appears almost certain that Erasmus was indeed an impostor, as charged by Augustus Toplady.[23]

Wesley's connexional system was constantly being threatened by a drift towards congregationalism. Almost every year some small group would hive off in pursuit of an eloquent preacher, to form an independent congregation. Some of these preachers were avowedly ambitious; some, like Bryant and Thwaite, reacted adversely against discipline; others were in any case parochial in outlook, and had little use for Wesley's insistence on widespread concern for the Methodist movement as a whole, fostered by the itinerancy and a strong central control. At the 1766 Conference Wesley addressed himself at some length to these problems. He reiterated his claim that in spite of a few similarities the Methodists were 'not dissenters in the only sense which our law acknowledges: namely, persons who believe it is sinful to attend the service of the church'. He therefore urged his preachers scrupulously to avoid anything that might countenance the popular equation of Methodism with Dissent. They should so arrange their circuit duties that no preacher was 'hindered from attending the church more than two Sundays in the month'. They must 'never make light of going to church, either by word or deed'. To those who claimed, 'our own service is public worship' Wesley replied:

Yes, *in a sense*: but not such as supersedes the church service. We
never designed it should. We have a hundred times professed the
contrary. It pre-supposes public prayer, like the sermons at the
university. . . . If it were designed to be instead of church service it
would be essentially defective. For it seldom has the four grand parts
of public prayer: deprecation, petition, intercession, and thanksgiving. Neither is it, even on the Lord's Day, concluded with the
Lord's Supper.[24]

The major criticism which Wesley faced at that 1766 Conference,
however, was that in his zeal for securing a closely-knit national organization he had become an autocrat. He recounted at length the history
of the organization of the Methodist societies, from the time that a few
people in London had asked him to be their spiritual director. He made
his point firmly:

It may be observed, the desire was on *their* part, not *mine*. My desire
was to live and die in retirement. But I did not see that I could refuse
them my help and be guiltless before God.
    Here commenced my power; namely, a power to appoint when
and where and how they should meet, and to remove those whose
life showed that they had no desire to 'flee from the wrath to come'.
And this power remained the same whether the people meeting together were twelve, twelve hundred, or twelve thousand.

Each aspect of his central control arose in a similar manner. Wesley
summarized the position thus:

What is that power? It is a power of admitting into and excluding
from the societies under my care; of choosing and removing
stewards; of receiving or not receiving helpers; of appointing them
when, where, and how to help me; and of desiring any of them to
meet me when I see good. And as it was merely in obedience to the
Providence of God and for the good of the people that I at first
accepted this power, which I never sought, nay a hundred times
laboured to throw off, so it is on the same considerations—not for
profit, honour, or pleasure—that I use it at this day.

In reply to the criticism that this control was nevertheless arbitrary
Wesley agreed, in so far as the word implied that it was exercised by
one man alone. He denied any implication, however, that it was 'unjust,
unreasonable, or tyrannical', and therefore rejected the request for 'a
free conference, that is, a meeting of all the preachers wherein all things
shall be determined by most votes'. Once more he looked to the in-

definite continuance of Methodism as he added, 'it is possible after my death something of this kind may take place'.[25]

The 1768 Conference addressed itself to another question affecting the status of the preachers, many of whom had been supplementing the meagre allowances received from their circuits by following part-time trades. Sometimes this was because they needed to support a wife or aged parents, for whom the societies could hardly be held responsible. Wesley firmly set himself against this practice of divided energies, and the manner in which he did so once more enhanced the status of the preachers:

> Is it well consistent with that word, 'Give attendance to reading, to exhortation, to teaching: meditate on these things, give thyself wholly to them?' (I Tim. iv.:13,15). Can we be said to give ourselves wholly to these things if we follow another profession? Does not our Church in her Office of Ordination require every minister to do this? . . . But this plainly shows what both they and we ought to do. We indeed more particularly; because God has called us to 'provoke them to jealousy', to supply their lack of service to the sheep that are as without shepherds, and to spend and be spent therein. We above all; because every travelling preacher solemnly professes to have nothing else to do; and receives his little allowance for this very end, that he may not need to do anything else, that he may not be entangled in the things of this life, but may give himself wholly to these things.

Wesley thus challenged his preachers to be even more full-time ministers than the ordained clergy.[26]

The less anxious he was about making a suitable impression on the clergy, the easier it became for him to countenance still further irregularities. From the beginning, mindful of the spiritual influence of his own mother, he had appointed women as band and class leaders. Like his father, however, he was much more hesitant about women preachers. This matter was brought to a head by Mrs Sarah Crosby and her friend Mary Bosanquet, who later married John Fletcher. In 1761 Wesley had agreed that Sarah Crosby should not hesitate to speak in public about her Christian experience, or to read his expository *Notes* or some improving sermon. In 1769 he went further, agreeing that she might even deliver short exhortations, though not a continued discourse based upon a text. (This was the same kind of distinction that he had made a generation earlier in the case of Thomas Maxfield.) By 1771, however, he was clear that he must accept at least an occasional woman preacher by virtue of an 'extraordinary call'. His letter to Mary Bosanquet on this matter quoted Pauline precedent for this innovation in particular, but also for Methodist irregularities in general:

> My dear sister,   Londonderry, June 13, 1771.
> I think the strength of the cause rests there, on your having an *Extraordinary Call*. So, I am persuaded, has every one of our Lay Preachers: otherwise I could not countenance his preaching at all. It is plain to me that the whole Work of God termed Methodism is an extraordinary dispensation of His Providence. Therefore I do not wonder if several things occur therein which do not fall under ordinary rules of discipline. St. Paul's ordinary rule was, 'I permit not a woman to speak in the congregation'. Yet in extraordinary cases he made a few exceptions; at Corinth, in particular.
> I am, my dear sister,
>   Your affectionate brother,
>   J. Wesley.[27]

Soon Wesley was urging a more adventurous connexional outlook for Methodists in another realm—that of finance. The building of new preaching-houses had been halted in 1766 because he felt that the combined debts of those already built was too high, nor had the General Fund begun a few years earlier to aid the weaker societies attracted sufficient support. He printed a number of circular letters soliciting both wider interest and greater support, and doubtless pressed the claims of connexional as well as local advancement upon other societies besides that at Bristol:

> Give in proportion to your substance. . . . Open your eyes, your heart, your hand. If this one rule was observed throughout England we should need no other collection. It would soon form a stock sufficient to relieve all that want and to answer all other occasions. Many of these occasions are now exceeding pressing, and we are nowise able to answer them; so that the cause of God suffers, and the children of God, and that without remedy.
> This is in great measure owing to our not considering ourselves (all the Methodists) as one body. Such undoubtedly they are throughout Great Britain and Ireland; and as such they were considered at our last Conference. . . .[28]

In the interests of connexionalism and a strong central control, Wesley considered the possibilities of vesting all Methodist preaching-houses on one national trust, or at least of organizing a central depository for preaching-house deeds.[29]

At the Conference of 1769, as we have seen, Wesley publicly relinquished any hope of a union of evangelical clergy, and turned from them to the connexional unity symbolized in his preachers:

> It is otherwise with the travelling preachers in our connexion: you are at present one body. You act in concert with each other, and by united counsels. And now is the time to consider what can be done in order to continue this union. Indeed, as long as I live there will be no great difficulty: I am under God a centre of union to all our travelling as well as local preachers.

So far, so good. Increasingly, however, Wesley had his eyes on the more distant future: 'But by what means may this connexion be preserved when God removes me from you?' He believed that about a quarter of the preachers would secure church livings for themselves, while others would 'turn Independents and get separate congregations, like John Edwards and Charles Skelton'. For the remainder he suggested a procedure which followed up the 'council' idea adumbrated in 1760:

> On notice of my death, let all the preachers in England and Ireland repair to London within six weeks:
> Let them seek God by solemn fasting and prayer:
> Let them draw up articles of agreement, to be signed by those who choose to act in concert:
> Let those be dismissed who do not choose it, in the most friendly manner possible:
> Let them choose, by votes, a Committee of three, five, or seven, each of whom is to be Moderator in his turn:
> Let the Committee do what I do now: propose preachers to be tried, admitted, or excluded; fix the place of each preacher for the ensuing year, and the time of the next Conference.[30]

In order to lay a secure foundation for this future preservation of the Methodist Connexion, Wesley recommended that those who were willing should even then sign articles of agreement along the following lines:

> We whose names are underwritten, being thoroughly convinced of the necessity of a close union between those whom God is pleased to use as instruments in this glorious work, in order to preserve this union between ourselves, are resolved, God being our helper:
> 1. To devote ourselves entirely to God, denying ourselves, taking up our cross daily, steadily aiming at one thing—to save our own souls and them that hear us.

2. To preach the old Methodist doctrines and no other, contained in the *Minutes* of the Conference.

3. To observe and enforce the whole Methodist discipline laid down in the said *Minutes*.[31]

Wesley doubted, however, whether the preachers would in fact coalesce without some point of unity in an ordained and charismatic leader such as himself. A letter written to Fletcher in January 1773, as he was approaching his seventieth birthday, is eloquent of this anxiety:

I see more and more, unless there be one προεστώς [leader] the work can never be carried on. The body of the preachers are not united, nor will any part of them submit to the rest; so that either there must be *one* to preside over *all* or the work will indeed come to an end.

Wesley believed that he had discovered the happy solution:

But has God provided one so qualified? Who is he? *Thou art the man*! God has given you a measure of loving faith and a single eye to his glory. He has given you some knowledge of men and things, particularly of the whole plan of Methodism. You are blessed with some health, activity, and diligence, together with a degree of learning. And to all these He has lately added, by a way none could have foreseen, favour both with the preachers and the whole people.

Come out in the name of God! Come to the help of the Lord against the mighty! Come while I am alive and capable of labour. . . . What possible employment can you have which is of so *great importance*?[32]

To this appeal Fletcher replied that he could not leave his parish 'without a fuller persuasion that the time is quite come'.[33] In July Wesley tried to urge his claim in person, and then wrote sadly that by waiting until he was dead Fletcher was indeed missing the 'providential time'.[34]

Thus disappointed Wesley went to the 1773 Conference resolved to unite the preachers with or without a focal clergyman, no matter what his own misgivings. He reminded them of their 1769 agreement, and secured 49 signatures to a formal document drawn up in those very words. He followed the same procedure in 1774 and 1775, when 81 of the 138 British preachers signed.[35] This formal annual reminder then dropped from the printed *Minutes*, possibly in the same spirit as the answer to a question in those of 1778:

Q.22. Some Trustees may abuse their power after my death. What can be done now to prevent this?

A. It seems we need take no thought for the morrow. God will provide when need shall be.[36]

Wesley continued his search for young clergy who might both assist him maintain full sacramental worship for the London Methodists and also be 'groomed' to take over Methodist leadership after his death. Grimshaw had died, Fletcher was wedded to his parish, Richardson did not possess sufficient initiative. William Ley, an Irish itinerant who had secured episcopal ordination, and possessed the confidence of both the Wesleys, seemed a possibility, and helped in the recruiting of another likely candidate, Mark Davis. Sufficient is known about Davis to illustrate the urgency of the Wesleys' attempt to ensure that if the Methodists did not remain organically within the Church of England after their death, at least they would remain under the leadership of an ordained clergyman.

Like Ley, Mark Davis was an Irish itinerant, accepted in 1756. After being stationed in London in 1768 the 1769 *Minutes* listed him among those who 'desist from travelling'. About that time he secured episcopal ordination. While ministering in Wales, probably as curate to the rector of Coychurch, he began negotiations to return to the Methodist itinerancy as an ordained clergyman. For a time in the summer of 1772 Charles Wesley employed him in Bristol, reporting to John that he had been very frank with Davis about their differing approaches to the work:

All the difference betwixt my brother and me (I told him) was that my brother's first object was the Methodists, and then the church; mine was first the church, and then the Methodists. That our different judgment of persons was owing to our different temper: his all hope, and mine all fear.[37]

Davis knew that John Wesley was anxious about the future of Methodism after his death, and wondered what his part in this might be. Charles Wesley's letter to him of 10 December 1772 reveals both Wesley's own views and the current rumours:

You understand 'it is a matter concluded on that the people are to be directed by twelve lay preachers'. You misunderstand their misinformation. All which we would or can do for keeping them together after our departure is, to commend them to the most solid and stablished of our preachers (be they twelve, or more, or less) whom we advise to keep close together and regulate the society as near as may be according to their old rules.

So far this was in accordance with the published *Minutes* of the 1769 Conference. What followed certainly reflected John's mind as well as that of Charles, but it does not seem to have been made clear to the preachers themselves, and certainly had not been published:

> Now this is impossible without a clergyman or two at their head. Wherefore my brother has so often and so warmly invited you to come and help them, before we leave them. . . . I suppose your informer made you believe you must be under the government of lay preachers, whereas in the very nature of things both they and the society *must* be under your government. It is not in my brother's or my power to order it otherwise after our death: it is not in our will. Do what we can, the people after us will choose for themselves, and the major part of them prefer a clergyman to a lay preacher.

Charles Wesley urged Davis at least to visit London for a trial period, where he was convinced that 'the people will all look upon you as their future father and guardian, and when my brother goes, naturally cleave to you'. In response to Davis's query as to whether there was any guarantee that John Fletcher would succeed Wesley and that he himself would become Fletcher's assistant, Charles replied, somewhat impatiently:

> There is all reason to hope J.F. will succeed J.W. The Lord will give him suitable associates. I have no more to say upon the subject. You must be fully persuaded in your own mind.[38]

Somewhat to his surprise Davis did go to London, where like the other Methodist clergy he was paid a 'salary' several times that of the 'allowances' made to the lay itinerants. John Wesley became disillusioned with him, ('He is very quiet, but not very useful'), he became a centre of dispute, and after about a year's service was dismissed.[39]

Some of the trouble was undoubtedly fomented by those of Wesley's preachers who resented (perhaps unconsciously) the superior status of the Methodist clergy, and wanted to throw off this yoke. In confidence John Wesley had told Alexander Mather the salary which Davis would receive (£80 per annum), and Charles wrote to Davis:

> [Mather] and his trusty associate T[homas] O[livers] have wrote to my brother dissuading him; have tried to prejudice Mr. R[ichardso]n, the stewards and society; with very little success indeed, but their envy is restless and indefatigable. . . . In fact the salary is a mere pretence—the true and only objection is your Orders. T.O., A.M.

etc. will not be so much wanted, so much respected, so well paid, and so important (they foresee) if any clergyman succeed to the care of this flock.[40]

Nevertheless, John Wesley himself placed great reliance on his 'Assistants', upon whom he laid the responsibility for administering the various circuits. When some leading Irish laymen attempted to by-pass their Assistant by holding meetings without his presence Wesley's wrath was communicated to his printed *Minutes*:

> We have no such custom in the three kingdoms. It is overturning our discipline from the foundations. Either let them act under the direction of the Assistant, or let them meet no more. It is true they can contribute money for the poor; but we dare not sell our discipline for money.[41]

The status of the Methodist lay itinerants continued to be a source of unrest, and in 1775 a reasoned scheme was put forward to ordain them. The instigator was Joseph Benson, one of the very ablest and most scholarly of Wesley's preachers, though only twenty-six years old. He served as a master at Kingswood School, as the headmaster at Trevecka College, and also in important city circuits, the last two years at Edinburgh as 'Assistant'. In spite of having a presentation to a living and a testimonial from the bishop of St. David's he had been refused ordination by the bishop of Worcester, apparently because of his Methodist associations rather than his lack of a degree. Benson wanted to discard the preachers who were without grace or gifts, to give those who showed promise a year or more's training at Kingswood School, and to ordain the remainder. Because episcopal ordination was hardly feasible (witness his own experience) he suggested ordination by the Wesleys and Fletcher. It seems doubtful whether Benson had fully thought out the theological implications of this step, being more concerned with seeking a practicable remedy for a growing problem, a remedy surely based on his knowledge of Wesley's views on presbyterial ordination, and one which might now be accepted in a calm debate even though it had been rejected in the heated controversies of 1755–60. It was also more difficult for Benson after two years among the Presbyterians in Edinburgh clearly to visualize episcopal reactions, even if in fact these bothered him.[42]

Fletcher, whose advice Benson sought first, approved the idea of purging the preachers, doubted the practicability of improving the others sufficiently, and saw the tactical difficulties of this new ordination scheme:

The good side is obvious: it would cement our union; it would make us stand more firm to our vocation; it would give us an outward call to preach and administer the Sacraments. But at the same time it would cut us off in a great degree from the national churches of England and Scotland, which we are called to leaven. My own particular objection to it respects Messrs. Wesley, who could not with decency take the step of turning Bishops after their repeated declarations that they would stand by their mother to the last.

Nevertheless, he passed Benson's letter on to Wesley, with the added suggestion that before he ventured upon such ordinations he should publicly request the bishops to ordain his qualified preachers. Even though this would almost certainly prove a mere formality it would 'show that he would not break off without paying a proper deference to episcopacy'.[43] At the ensuing Conference Wesley was 'more exact than ever in examining the preachers both as to grace and gifts', so that 'a solemn awe was spread through the whole assembly'. At Fletcher's request Wesley gave Benson the public opportunity to explain his proposals, which were freely discussed; but no concrete step was taken towards ordaining the preachers.[44]

Perhaps this was partly because on the eve of the Conference Fletcher himself sent a greatly revised version of Benson's scheme to Wesley, one which encompassed the elevation of Methodism into a distinct denomination remaining in close association with the Church of England. This scheme was so weighty that Wesley apparently did not read it to the Conference, especially in view of the hurry of business and the fact that it was probably not delivered until the eve of the closing day. Its influence, however, remained potent. Fletcher urged Wesley to the bold step, so long considered, of presbyterial ordination:

You love the Church of England, and yet you are not blind to her freckles, nor insensible of her shackles. Your life is precarious, you have lately been shaken over the grave; you are spared, it may be, to take yet some important step which may influence generations yet unborn. What, sir, if you used your liberty as an Englishman, a Christian, a divine, and an extraordinary messenger of God? What if with bold modesty you took a farther step towards the reformation of the Church of England?

He then went on to embody Benson's ordination scheme in much fuller proposals:

1. That the growing body of the Methodists in Great Britain,

Ireland, and America be formed into a general society—a daughter church of our holy mother.

2. That this society shall recede from the Church of England in nothing but in some palpable defects about doctrine, discipline, and unevangelical hierarchy.

3. That this society shall be the Methodist church of England, ready to defend the as yet unmethodized church against all the unjust attacks of the dissenters—willing to submit to her in all things that are not unscriptural—approving of her ordination—partaking of her sacraments, and attending her service at every convenient opportunity.

4. That a pamphlet be published containing the 39 Articles of the Church of England rectified according to the purity of the gospel, together with some needful alterations in the liturgy and homilies— such as the expunging the damnatory clauses of the Athanasian Creed, &c.

5. That Messrs. Wesley, the preachers, and the most substantial Methodists in London, in the name of the societies scattered through the kingdom, would draw up a petition and present it to the Archbishop of Canterbury, informing His Grace, and by him the bench of the bishops, of this design; proposing the reformed articles of religion, asking the protection of the Church of England, begging that this step might not be considered as a schism, but only as an attempt to avail ourselves of the liberty of Englishmen and Protestants to serve God according to the purity of the gospel, the strictness of primitive discipline, and the original design of the Church of England.

6. That this petition contain a request to the bishops to ordain the Methodist preachers which can pass their examination according to what is indispensably required in the canons of the Church. That instead of the ordinary testimonials the bishops would allow of testimonials signed by Messrs. Wesley and some more clergymen, who would make it their business to inquire into the morals and principles of the candidates for orders. And that instead of a title their Lordships would accept of a bond signed by twelve stewards of the Methodist societies certifying that the candidate for Holy Orders shall have a proper maintenance. That if his Grace, &c., does not condescend to grant this request, Messrs. Wesley will be obliged to take an irregular (not unevangelical) step, and to ordain upon a Church of England-independent plan such lay preachers as appear to them qualified for Holy Orders.

Obviously this was hastily drawn up, and the implied threat in the last paragraph, as well as other infelicities in these and the succeeding seven sections, would need careful reconsideration. Fletcher only sent it to Wesley in this admittedly imperfect form after considerable hesitation. Nevertheless, it tied up with some of Wesley's earlier deliberations (including the use of the term 'Moderator'), and was almost certainly present in Wesley's mind, and possibly before his eyes, when almost ten years later he finally crossed the Rubicon of presbyterial ordination. For the time being, however, it was too radical, and lay unimplemented on Wesley's desk.[45]

As was true throughout Wesley's ministry, misunderstanding and persecution of Methodism continued, even at the highest levels. One example was furnished by a printed circular sent in 1776 to his clergy by Dr. Richard Richmond, bishop of Sodor and Man. This instructed them to repel from communion Methodist preachers, who were described as 'unordained, unauthorised, and unqualified teachers'. John Crook complained to Wesley that as a result the Methodists in the Isle of Man were 'hooted at, slutched [pelted with mud], and stoned' whenever they went to worship, and claimed that the 'Rev. Mr. Moor of Douglas' was behind it all. Wesley advised patience under persecution:

> Violent methods of redress are not to be used till all other methods fail. I know pretty well the mind of Lord Mansfield, and of one that is greater than he; but if I appealed to them it would bring much expense and inconvenience on Dr. Moor and others. I would not willingly do this; I love my neighbour as myself. Possibly they may think better, and allow that liberty of conscience which belongs to . . . every one of His Majesty's subjects in his British dominions.[46]

Nevertheless, though in most places the Methodists might be 'a poor despised people, labouring under reproach and many inconveniences', at the 1777 Conference Wesley gave the lie to the rumour spread by John Hilton that they were 'a fallen people', and issued the challenge:

> Give me one hundred preachers who fear nothing but sin and desire nothing but God, and I care not a straw whether they be clergymen or laymen—such alone will shake the gates of hell and set up the kingdom of heaven upon earth.[47]

Wesley continued to proclaim that he and his followers remained loyal to the Established Church. He used the occasion of the laying of the foundation stone for his New Chapel in City Road, London, on 21 April 1777 to emphasize this fact, and as a manifesto published this *Sermon on Numbers xxiii: 23*—'What hath God wrought!' Other re-

forming movements going under the same title of 'Methodist', he
claimed, had dissipated themselves in independency; such were those led
by Benjamin Ingham, George Whitefield, William Cudworth, and
Thomas Maxfield. An anonymous 'person of honour' (doubtless the
Countess of Huntingdon) fell into the same category, and Wesley
explicitly criticized her college at Trevecka for training more candidates
for the dissenting ministry than for the church. All such so-called
'Methodists' he repudiated:

> Now, let every impartial person judge whether we are accountable
> for any of these. None of these have any manner of connexion with
> the original Methodists. They are branches broken off from the tree:
> if they break from the church also we are not accountable for it.
> These, therefore, cannot make our glorying void, that we do not,
> will not, form any separate sect, but from principle remain what we
> always have been, true members of the Church of England.[48]

This claim, thus expressed, was vehemently and virulently challenged
by young Rowland Hill, who ranted that Whitefield had been 'black-
ened by the venomous quill of this grey-headed enemy to all righteousness' who was himself 'for ever going about raising dissenting
congregations and building dissenting meeting-houses the kingdom
over', while claiming that his was the only valid churchmanship. The
Gospel Magazine seconded Hill with equal rancour. An unedifying controversy ensued, in which the extreme Calvinists sought to avenge
themselves by violent if irrelevant invective for Wesley's and Fletcher's
stand against their teaching, while Wesley himself mildly demonstrated
that they were not uniformly speaking the truth.[49]

Yet to a certain extent Hill was right in referring to Wesley on the title
page of his *Imposture Detected* as 'laying the first stone of his new
Dissenting Meeting-House near the City Road'. Wesley's New Chapel
was not simply another preaching-house. It was seen by him as a special
symbol of connexional unity, meriting universal Methodist support.
He was even prepared to stand in the open air on his preaching tours
and collect contributions for it in his outstretched hat.[50] This new
Methodist headquarters was separatist even in its architecture, providing
a communion area in the apse behind the pulpit. For some years now
Wesley had been administering the Lord's Supper at the Foundery,
having discarded his earlier scruples about using only episcopally consecrated buildings for that rite.[51] The City Road building was from the
outset a centre for sacramental worship as well as for preaching and
fellowship and social service—as was indeed demonstrated by its name—
the New *Chapel*. These premises, in fact, functioned very much like

those of a very active Anglican parish church, though without recognizing any allegiance to diocesan or parochial authorities.

Behind the New Chapel was a burial ground, another evidence of ecclesiastical self-sufficiency, even though it was not put into use until 1782. About this feature Charles Wesley protested, and arranged that his own remains and those of his family should be interred in the churchyard of St. Marylebone. John, however, had come to regard the episcopal consecration of church buildings, furnishings, and burial-grounds as 'a thing purely indifferent, . . . a mere relic of Romish superstition'. Later he claimed:

> I never wished that any bishop should consecrate any chapel or burial-ground of mine. Indeed I should not dare to suffer it, as I am clearly persuaded the thing is wrong in itself, being not authorized either by any law of God or by any law of the land. In consequence of which I conceive that either the clerk or the sexton may as well consecrate the church or the churchyard as the bishop.[52]

Although this was in fact not penned until 1788, arising out of his brother's burial, it clearly represented convictions held for so long that they had completely erased from his memory some of his earlier ecclesiastical principles.[53]

The same kind of thing happened in Bristol.[54] Both in London and Bristol, in fact, the Methodists were becoming thoroughly spoiled, accustomed as they were to decorously conducted liturgical worship, evangelical preaching, the sacraments administered in their own buildings by their own ministers—and now their own burial-grounds! Small wonder that Methodists from other areas desired a similar independence for their own societies: small wonder that the lay itinerants stationed in London coveted the prestige of being appointed to preach at the New Chapel. Charles Wesley, however, strongly resisted any lay encroachment upon what he deemed his own ministerial prerogatives and those of his clerical assistants. He bemoaned John's partial surrender:

> I am sorry you yielded to the preachers. They do not love the Church of England. What must be the consequence when we are gone? A separation is inevitable. Do you not wish to keep as many good people in the church as you can? By what means? Something might be done to save the remainder, if you had resolution, and would stand by me as firmly as I will by you.[55]

As Charles said, separation seemed inevitable, for widespread sacramental worship was not possible without more ordained preachers, and this could not be achieved within the ordered ways of the Establishment. The question was raised once more in the Irish Conference of 1778 by Edward Smyth, a clergyman who when turned out of his curacy at Ballyculer in 1776 for Methodist practices threw in his lot with Wesley. Smyth was a sincere and eloquent firebrand, and his plea for immediate separation from the church stressed 'the wickedness both of the clergy and the people'. Wesley carried the day, however, and his Dublin journal recorded:

Tues[day, July] 7. Our little Conference began, at which about twenty preachers were present. On Wednesday we heard one of our friends at large upon the duty of leaving the church; but after a full discussion of the point we all remained firm in our judgment that it is our duty not to leave the church wherein God has blessed us, and does bless us still.[56]

Smyth was concerned in a severe test of Wesley's Anglican authoritarianism the following year. Again Wesley's journal provided a succinct summary:

Mon[day, November] 22. My brother and I set out for Bath on a very extraordinary occasion. Some time since Mr. Smyth, a clergyman whose labours God had greatly blessed in the north of Ireland, brought his wife over to Bath. . . . I desired him to preach every Sunday evening in our chapel while he remained there; but as soon as I was gone Mr. M'Nab, one of our preachers, vehemently opposed that, affirming it was the common cause of all the lay preachers— that they were appointed by the Conference, not by me, and would not suffer the clergy to ride over their heads. . . .

Tues. 23. I read to the society a paper which I wrote near twenty years ago on a like occasion. Herein I observed that 'the rules of our preachers were fixed by me before any Conference existed', particularly the twelfth: 'Above all, you are to preach when and where I appoint.'[57] By obstinately opposing which rule Mr. M'Nab has made all this uproar. In the morning, at a meeting of the preachers, I informed Mr. M'Nab that as he did not agree to our fundamental rule I could not receive him as one of our preachers till he was of another mind.

Wed. 24. I read the same paper to the society at Bristol, as I found the flame had spread thither also.

A few at Bath separated from us on this account, but the rest were thoroughly satisfied.[58]

Charles Wesley adduced strong evidence that in all this M'Nab was

15

the spokesman for a group of preachers intent on overthrowing Methodist allegiance both to the Church of England and to Wesley himself. John Pawson disagreed, protesting that it was merely a local disturbance. Charles Wesley conceded that there might as yet be no concerted scheme for a Methodist rebellion, but warned his brother against Pawson and company:

> You judge right: there is not as yet any regular plan: but there is a spirit of independency, a spirit of pride and self-seeking, which has more or less infected the body of preachers. . . . You cannot *in this matter* [trust John Pawson] or any preacher unproved.[59]

Knowing his brother's apparently exaggerated fears of the preachers' ambitions, John paid little attention to his warnings. Even though he knew that M'Nab had prayed for his death, even though he considered this rebellion 'a blow at the very root of Methodism', within two or three months M'Nab was preaching for Wesley again—though not, to be sure, at Bath.[60] Charles had applauded John's resolution in silencing M'Nab, but now chided his weakness in too speedily reinstating him without any acknowledgement of his error. As a result Charles was doubtful whether any useful purpose would be served if he responded to John's appeal that he should attend the forthcoming Conference at Bristol:

> I am not sure they will not prevail upon you to ordain them. You claim the *power*, and only say it is not probable you shall ever exercise it. Probability on one side implies probability on the other, and I want better security. So I am to stand by and see the ruin of our cause. . . . In the Bath affair you acted with vigour for the first time; but you could not hold out. . . .[61]

Charles Wesley did indeed attend the 1780 Conference, with difficulty maintaining a prudent silence even when his brother mildly gave the floor to a still unrepentant M'Nab.[62] Once more Methodist relations with the Church of England were considered with care. Once more Wesley's proclamations on the subject in the Large Minutes were confirmed without alteration for the new edition published shortly after the Conference. All this was in accordance with Wesley's prophecy made half-way through the sessions in a letter to Mary Bosanquet:

> Hitherto we have had a blessed Conference. The case of the church we shall fully consider by-and-by; and I believe we shall agree that none who leave the church shall remain with us.[63]

This official Methodist stand, indeed, was somewhat strengthened by the addition to the new edition of the Large Minutes of the resolutions passed by the 1778 Irish Conference condemning separation from the church.[64] John Wesley's grey hairs still commanded the respect of his preachers.

THIRTEEN

1784—I: THE DEED OF DECLARATION

IF EVER there was a year when Wesley could be said to have irrevocably severed himself and Methodism from the Church of England it was 1784. Dr. John Whitehead showed uncommon percipience less than a decade later in terming it 'the grand climacteric year of Methodism'.[1] As we have seen, the seeds of separation had long been sown, and re-sown. There had been earlier 'climacteric' years: 1749, when Wesley's *ad hoc* experimentation matured into a self-conscious connexionalism, 'a general union of our societies throughout England'; 1763, when the Large Minutes summarized that polity and secured a measure of legal protection and continuity; 1769, when he gave up all hopes of a union with the evangelical clergy, and looked to his itinerant lay preachers for the preservation of Methodism after his death. The separatist tendencies of Methodism had long been obvious to all but the most blind or the most prejudiced. Among the latter we must rank John Wesley, who did indeed recognize the tendencies, but was convinced that God would find a way out of the impasse. In 1784 he secured the legal incorporation of Methodism as a distinct denomination, he prepared and published a drastic revision of the *Book of Common Prayer* and the Thirty-Nine Articles, and he finally embraced presbyterial ordination in practice as well as theory—yet still he characteristically refused to admit that he had committed any irrevocable breach with the Church of England!

In a sense he was right to be surprised that other people should be surprised at his obtuseness in this matter. For these were not completely new ventures, but simply the logical culmination of other actions tending towards the same end, the final steps on a road which he had long followed. If the other actions did not constitute separation no more should these.

For nearly forty years Wesley had tried to ensure that the premises in which he preached and gathered his societies should be used in perpetuity for the same purposes. The doctrinal standards of the preaching to be permitted therein had been settled with a blend of clarity and flexibility, and his own rights and those of his brother Charles preserved. Charles, however, was more and more retiring into the background rather than interfere with his brother's somewhat radical interpretation of loyalty to the Church of England, and the two of them showed signs of outliving those promising younger clergy to whom they had been looking to guarantee the succession. In this context Charles Wesley had written to James Hutton on Christmas Day, 1773 (John was then seventy years old, Charles sixty-six): 'God will look to that matter of successors. He buries His workmen and still carries on His work. Let him send by whom He will send.'[2]

These were John's sentiments also. During his sixties and seventies, however, he had become much more anxious about supplying a helping hand to providence so as to ensure the genuine Methodist witness after his death. The clergy failing him, he turned to his preachers. In 1760 he envisaged a committee of preachers taking over the reins after both he and Charles were dead.[3] In 1763 this was crystallized in the published model deed upon which he constantly pestered his trustees to settle all the Methodist preaching-houses.[4] This document, although it named another clergyman, William Grimshaw, as a successor in his own individual right, provided that thereafter the control of the Methodist societies should pass to 'the yearly Conference of the people called Methodists'. This meant in fact the lay preachers, who alone (with a small handful of clergy and an occasional lay visitor) composed this annual gathering.[5] In 1769 Wesley authorized a detailed scheme for this eventual transfer of power, and from 1773 onwards secured the signatures of the preachers who would pledge their loyalty to it.[6]

Wesley's reluctance to delegate final authority, however, conspired with the rapid growth of the societies to raise serious difficulties at this point. The Conference, for all its key importance to Methodism, remained an ill-defined and essentially impotent body. At first Wesley had written inviting individual clergy and lay preachers to confer with him. After some years he 'gave a general permission that all who desired it might come'.[7] In 1767 he responded to a suggestion of John Whitehead, a preacher who later defected from him, by embracing a refinement of this principle:

> I have considered what you say concerning the usefulness of being present at the General Conference. And I think we may steer a middle course. I will only *require* a select number to be present. But I will *permit* any other travelling preacher who desires it to be present with them.[8]

He continued to insist that every circuit must be represented, usually by the Assistant, and at the same time tried to avoid the heavy expense and disruption of circuit activities which would result if too many preachers took advantage of their permission to attend.[9] Gradually, however, the preachers in general came to regard their Conference privileges as the inalienable rights of a democratic institution instead of the responsibilities delegated by a benevolent dictator. This came to a head with M'Nab's rebellion in 1779. In answer to one of the preachers pleading M'Nab's case, Wesley replied:

> You seem likewise to have quite a wrong idea of a Conference. . . . [In 1744 I] desired some of our preachers to meet me in order to advise, not control, me. And you may observe they had no power at all but what I exercised through them. I chose to exercise the power which God had given me in this manner both to avoid ostentation and gently to habituate the people to obey them when I should be taken from their head. But as long as I remain with them the fundamental rule of Methodism remains inviolate. As long as any preacher joins with me he is to be directed by me in his work.[10]

It should be noted that Wesley's phrase about habituating the people to obey the preachers as a preparation for his death certainly did not apply to the origins of the Conference, but it was increasingly becoming true of his present attitude. Although the preachers were unhappy because he did not delegate enough authority, and Charles scolded because he delegated too much, in fact John Wesley constantly insisted upon the authority of his Assistants over the Methodist people.[11]

As Wesley pondered the approaching 1780 Conference he was determined on two things: he would reassert his own supremacy, but he would also safeguard Methodism after his death by delegating more responsibility to his preachers. The printed revision of the large *Minutes* that year offered at least some proof of the first point, for to the sentence about giving general permission for all preachers to attend, Wesley appended the phrase: 'which I now see cause to retract'.[12] From this time he apparently reverted to his earlier practice of issuing a written invitation to those whom he wished to be present.[13] He also called Fletcher, Coke, and (probably) four lay preachers to form a kind of steering committee or 'cabinet' for the Conference.[14] Privately he announced in advance that the time devoted to the Conference would be doubled, although in his *Journal* this was tactfully described as a resolution of the Conference itself:

> Aug. 1. Tues. Our Conference began. We have been always hitherto straitened for time. It was now resolved, 'For the future we allow nine or ten days for each Conference, that everything relative to the carrying on of the work of God may be maturely considered'.[15]

At this Conference, apparently for the first time, one of the preachers,

Christopher Hopper, presided over one or more sessions during Wesley's absence, though the circumstances are not known. One point is significant: he was not delegated by Wesley to perform this function, but elected by his fellow itinerants—though surely at Wesley's instance.[16] It seems clear that Wesley was indeed easing his preachers into their future responsibilities, even though he retained the reins of authority in his own hands.

Wesley's willingness to share responsibility with the preachers in Conference during his lifetime was one thing: to ensure that they inherited it after his death was quite another. The preaching-houses were legally vested in trustees, and those who proved litigious could easily contest the claims of such an insubstantial and amorphous body as 'the yearly conference of the people called Methodists'. Even during Wesley's lifetime some threatened to do so.[17] In May 1782 one such threat came to a head. John Nelson, the eloquent stonemason turned preacher, in 1751 had erected a preaching-house in his home town of Birstall in Yorkshire. In 1782 this was rebuilt, and a new deed executed along similar lines to the earlier one. This not only vested the power of appointing preachers after Wesley's death in the trustees themselves, but even gave them power to displace preachers during Wesley's lifetime. At first John Wesley refused to sign the new deed, but then did so under protest. The 1782 Conference supported his plea that money should be solicited throughout the connexion making it possible to build another preaching-house at Birstall if the trustees would not transfer the building to the official Conference deed.[18]

Wesley saw this as a crucial test case. On 9 November he wrote to Samuel Bradburn:

> Birstall is a leading case, the first of an avowed violation of our plan. Therefore the point must be carried for the Methodist preachers now or never: and I alone can carry it; which I will, God being my helper.[19]

Later that month he drew up a lengthy account of the controversy in a letter to Joseph Benson, which he then revised, printed as a broadsheet, and apparently sent to all the preachers. He urged that he was fighting for the connexional principle and for the sovereignty of the preachers after his death:

> I am not pleading my own cause. . . . I am pleading for Mr. Hopper,[20] Mr. Bradburn, Mr. Benson, and for every other Travelling Preacher, that you may be as free after I am gone hence as you are now I am at your head; that you may never be liable to be turned out of any

or all of our houses, without any reason given but that so is *the pleasure* of twenty or thirty men.

I say 'any'; for I see no sufficient reason for giving up *any* house in England. Indeed if one were given up more would follow: it would be 'as the letting out of the water'. (cf. Prov. 17:14.)

I insist upon that point, and let everything else go: No Methodist trustees, if I can help it, shall after my death, any more than while I live, have the power of *placing* and *displacing* the preachers.[21]

In spite of negotiations undertaken by Dr. Coke as Wesley's delegate, the Birstall trustees remained stubborn. In 1783 the preachers in Conference asked Wesley himself to attempt 'bringing the trustees to reason'.[22] Eventually a compromise was reached: the Conference gave its newly-purchased land to the trustees and assumed their debts, while the trustees themselves executed a new deed safeguarding the right of the Conference to appoint preachers after Wesley's death.[23] Nevertheless, litigation over the Birstall deed occurred as late as 1853.[24]

These lengthy and trying negotiations made it abundantly clear to Wesley that he must take even greater pains to secure the status of the Methodist Conference as a corporate institution, holding and administering the preaching-houses throughout the nation. Only thus could he prevent property disputes from eventually tearing Methodism asunder. In testing the claim of the attorney for the Birstall trustees that they could not legally transfer their power to the Conference, on 24 July 1783 Coke had secured an opinion from a Welsh barrister of Lincoln's Inn, John Madocks.[25] According to Coke's own testimony he also obtained and presented to the 1783 Conference Madocks's opinion that 'the law would not recognize the Conference in the state in which it stood at that time, and consequently that there was no central point which might preserve the connexion from splitting into a thousand pieces after the death of Mr. Wesley'.[26] What seems more likely, however, is that he reported to that Conference, not a considered opinion, but the tenor of his conversation with Madocks. Clearly there was legal uncertainty and therefore just cause for anxiety. Even trustees appointed in accordance with the official Methodist deed claimed 'that the Conference was not an assembly that the law would recognize, and that therefore they would, after Mr. Wesley's death, appoint whom they should think proper'. One went so far as to say 'they might appoint a popish priest if they should think it proper'.[27]

At the Bristol Conference in 1783, therefore, the preachers asked Wesley to 'draw up a deed which should give a legal specification of the phrase "The Conference of the People called Methodists",' adding that 'the mode of doing it was entirely left to his judgment and direction'.[28] Again Wesley turned to Coke. It should be pointed out that Dr. Thomas Coke was not only an eager young clergyman who had thrown in his lot with Wesley on being turned out of his parish in 1777[29]; he was also a Doctor of Civil Law of Oxford—the 'L.L.D.' which he sometimes appended to his name was regarded as interchangeable with the D.C.L.[30] For a time he had served as the chief magistrate of Brecon. Both as a legal expert and as the most important personal influence during Wesley's closing decade he merits careful study.[31]

Wesley had sent Coke to Bath to consolidate the society torn by the M'Nab affair, and had encouraged his widespread evangelistic itinerancy. In 1781 he assisted Wesley with his publishing ventures, and took over the direction of the Tract Society, founded in 1782.[32] From that same year of 1782 onwards Wesley entrusted Coke with the major responsibility for the management of Irish Methodism, and was sympathetic (even though a little sceptical) towards his dreams of translating the phrase about a 'world parish' into reality. In the Birstall case, as we have seen, Wesley leaned heavily upon his legal experience, and increasingly looked to him for advice and assistance in the administration of the complex legal affairs of the Methodist connexion, including the settling of all the trusts on the model deed. Wesley had charged him with the task of persuading the Bristol trustees to resettle the New Room upon the official deed, but they refused, and in refusing indicated that they were fully discharging their responsibility on behalf of 'the Methodist Church in connexion with the Church of England'.[33] In many respects Coke had become Wesley's *alter ego* far more than was his brother Charles—often to the latter's discomfiture. At first Coke, like Charles Wesley, was bigoted towards the Church of England, but during the period 1783–9 he was in one of his transitional phases, and later confessed: 'I changed my sentiments, and promoted a separation from it as far as my influence reached.'[34]

On behalf of Wesley, then, Coke collaborated with a young Methodist solicitor, William Clulow, newly come to London from Macclesfield.[35] Together they prepared an official 'case' for that 'very eminent counsellor' Madocks, whose signed opinion proposing a solution for Wesley's dilemma was dated 5 December 1783:

As to the means of fixing the sense of the word 'Conference', and defining what persons are to be members of the Conference, and how the body is to be continued in succession, and to identify it, I think Mr. John Wesley should prepare and subscribe a declaration for that purpose, to be enrolled in the Court of Chancery for safe custody, naming the present members, and prescribing the mode of election to fill vacancies, and making the minutes or memorials of their proceedings, signed by their secretary, evidence of such elections, to which declaration of Mr. Wesley, so enrolled, all the trust deeds should refer.[36]

Thereupon Wesley asked Coke and Clulow to draft for his approval the main clauses of such a declaratory deed, securing the advice of Madocks on every doubtful point. Meantime he himself pondered the problem of the size and composition of the Conference thus to be legally identified.[37]

'The Revd. John Wesley's Declaration and Appointment of the Conference of the People called Methodists' was a deed poll, that is, a deed whose edges were trimmed or polled to show that it was the unique declaration of one man rather than an indenture made between two parties upon identical halves of a parchment severed by indented cutting. The Conference was Wesley's creation, his instrument, and under God he alone would determine its status and future. No difficulty seems to have arisen over the general terms of the document. Indeed, lawyers of later years have admired its concise precision.[38]

The preamble pointed out that the deed was executed in order to avoid 'doubt or litigation' about the words 'Yearly Conference of the people called Methodists' in the trust deeds of the 'chapels' conveyed to trustees upon condition that they allowed Wesley and his appointees to 'preach and expound God's holy word' therein, and that they would similarly hold these premises in trust after Wesley's death for the use of his brother Charles, and thereafter of the Conference. The term 'chapels' was used throughout, doubtless on the advice of Wesley's legal counsellors, though in his correspondence and in the *Minutes* of the Conference he continued to speak of 'preaching-houses'.

The document went on to describe the previous composition and functions of the body:

> The Conference . . . hath always heretofore consisted of the Preachers and Expounders of God's Holy Word, commonly called Methodist Preachers, in connexion with and under the care of the said John Wesley, whom he hath thought expedient year after year to summon to meet him in one or other of the said places of London, Bristol, or Leeds, to advise with them for the promotion of the Gospel of Christ, to appoint the said persons so summoned and the other preachers . . . not summoned . . . to the use and enjoyment of the said chapels, and for the expulsion of unworthy and admission of new persons under his care. . . .

There followed a list of the names and addresses of those preachers who 'have been and now are and do on the day of the date hereof constitute the members of the said Conference'. These, together with 'their successors for ever, to be chosen as hereafter mentioned, are and shall for ever be construed, taken, and be, The Conference of the People called Methodists'. (Apparently no qualms were felt about the discrepancy between the titles 'Conference' and 'yearly Conference' thus used in key positions in the document.)

Fifteen regulatory clauses defined in detail the practices to be followed by this Conference. The first specified that the assembly should meet annually in London, Bristol, or Leeds, the actual place to be designated by the preceding Conference. Even during Wesley's lifetime, however, the Conference had also met and would meet in Manchester (in 1765 and 1787), but instead of re-wording this regulation clause 12 was added for the express purpose of allowing for another venue when 'it shall seem expedient'. The reason for this somewhat clumsy expedient was undoubtedly that clause 1 was a repetition of the relevant section in the model deed on which most of the preaching-houses were held. According to clause 5 each Conference should last for not less than five nor more than twenty-one days. Clause 2 enunciated an important democratic principle which Wesley had long resisted and continued to resist as the final arbiter of Methodist action during his lifetime, though he had frequently employed it to discover the preachers' views as a guide for his own decisions:

> The act of the majority in number of the Conference assembled as aforesaid shall be had, taken, and be the act of the whole Conference, to all intents, purposes, and constructions whatsoever.

Forty was named as the necessary quorum for the transaction of business (clause 4).

The first business of the Conference, according to clause 3, was 'to fill up all the vacancies occasioned by death or absence'—which was defined in clause 7 as absence for two successive years without a dispensation. Clause 8 empowered the Conference to expel any preacher, including members of its own body, 'for any cause which to the Conference may seem fit or necessary', whereupon his place was immediately to be filled. Any preacher who had been in connexion with the Conference for a year was eligible for election—a liberal provision for rejuvenation which after Wesley's death was so interpreted that only 'the senior brethren' were so co-opted.[39] After filling vacancies the Conference was to choose from among its own members a President and a Secretary who should serve until the 'next or other subsequent Conference'—in neither case was a time limit mentioned. The President was not only to cast two votes during the sessions of the Conference, but to preserve executive continuity between sessions, on whatever terms were laid down by the assembly (clause 6).

The Conference was to appoint to the chapels (the word 'circuit' never appears) only its own members or those whom it had admitted upon trial or 'into connexion', nor might any person be appointed for more than three years successively to any one chapel 'except ordained Ministers of the Church of England'. This 'three years system' became increasingly a source of friction in succeeding generations, though in fact it embodied a liberalizing of Wesley's normal policy of 'usually one year, two years in exceptional cases'. (As a matter of fact even during Wesley's lifetime one preacher, William Hunter, was stationed for four years in succession as the Assistant of the Berwick Circuit (1783–6), and shortly after Wesley's death a special dispensation for Thomas Rutherford from the rule was noted in the *Minutes*.)[40]

By clause 13 special arrangements were made for Methodist chapels 'in Ireland or other parts out of the kingdom of Great Britain'. The Conference was empowered to appoint a delegate or delegates from among its own members who should act as its plenipotentiary, in a way similar to that in which Wesley himself and Coke were now administering the Irish Conference in alternate years. Although this provision was capable of being applied to other overseas Conferences, in fact it operated only for Ireland. Eleven Irish preachers were listed as members of the Conference, and in later years provision was made for other Irish preachers to fill the vacancies which they left.[41]

As evidence of the acts of the Conference clause 14 provided that:

All resolutions and orders touching elections, admissions, expulsions, consents, dispensations, delegations, or appointments and acts whatsoever of the Conference shall be entered and written in the Journals or Minutes of the Conference, which shall be kept for that purpose, publicly read, and then subscribed by the President and Secretary thereof for the time being during the time such Conference shall be assembled, and when so entered and subscribed shall be had, taken, received, and be the acts of the Conference. . . .

This provision was speedily carried out. A huge folio journal was purchased, into which a copy of the Deed Poll was entered, along with all the actions of the 1784 Conference. The proceedings of each subsequent Conference have been duly entered and subscribed in this or supplementary volumes to the present time. This, rather than any printed *Minutes* or *Daily Record*, was and is the legal record of Conference decisions and actions. Although Wesley's unique authority was not diminished by the deed, this immediate implementation of one of its major provisions before his death lessened the likelihood of disputes thereafter.[42]

In clause 15 provision was made for the contingency of dissolution, by whatever means or for whatever purposes. If the members failed to meet, or fell below a membership of forty, for three successive years, the Conference would be 'extinguished'. In that event the various chapels would henceforth be vested in their respective trustees, who might use them 'for such time and in such manner as to them shall seem proper'.

A closing proviso ensured that nothing in the Deed Poll should in any way alter 'the life-estate of the said John Wesley and Charles Wesley, or either of them, of and in any of the said chapels'. It was to be business as usual not only during the alterations, but until the death of the proprietors. This was the simpler because the deed for the most part described the *status quo*, almost its sole innovations being the provisions for the Conference Journal and the 'Legal Hundred'. To this latter we now turn.

In pursuance of Madocks's counsel, Wesley pondered a method of 'naming a determinate number of persons' to constitute the Conference. At first he thought it might be best 'to name a very few, suppose ten or twelve persons', remembering that 'Count Zinzendorf named only six who were to preside over the Community after his decease'.[43] Later he changed his mind:

I believed there would be more safety in a greater number of counsellors, and therefore named an hundred—as many as I judged could meet without too great an expense and without leaving any circuit naked of preachers while the Conference met.[44]

Coke strongly advised against this course. In spite of the practical difficulties he urged Wesley to avoid appearing to disfranchise anyone, suggesting:

that every preacher in full connexion should be a member of the Conference, and that admission into full connexion should be looked upon as admission into membership with the Conference.[45]

There was much to be said on both sides. It was Wesley's decision, however, and Coke could only acquiesce. Defending himself against subsequent criticism, Wesley maintained that it would have been folly to make all the preachers members, and at the same time put his finger on the major source of grievance—the omission of some of his senior preachers from the 'legal hundred'.[46]

As was to be expected, the list was headed by the clergy. Even here, however, there were omissions. The ailing John Fletcher was not included, nor was the faithful but inadequate John Richardson. To the two Wesleys and Coke was added a new recruit, James Creighton. Creighton was born in 1739 of Scotch-Irish parents settled in County Cavan, graduated from Trinity College, Dublin, in 1764, taught school for two years, and then became a Church of England curate, being ordained deacon in 1764 and priest in 1765. In 1776 he 'experienced justifying grace', largely through the influence of his Methodist brother and Wesley's *Appeals*. He maintained a devout and energetic ministry in the extensive parish of Annagh, County Cavan, into which he introduced many Methodist practices, and he also undertook occasional preaching tours among distant Methodist societies. After four months' deliberation he responded to the urging of Wesley and Coke and left his parish in September 1783, travelling to London to serve as Wesley's clerical assistant there.[47]

The lay itinerant preachers followed the clergy, their names set down in the order of their stations in the 1783 printed *Minutes*, which clearly provided Wesley with his working list of options. The *Minutes* listed 188 lay preachers. Of these, five were supernumeraries and twenty-two were 'on trial', leaving 161 preachers both in full connexion and active. In selecting his remaining 96 names, however, Wesley did not follow the obvious course of omitting either the supernumeraries or the greenhorns. One of the five supernumeraries, Thomas Rankin, was included, and no fewer than six of those on trial. In the 69 circuits the preacher first named was the Assistant (now the Superintendent Minister), but fourteen even of these were omitted, including a veteran like Joseph Pilmoor, returned from his American ministry. Only twenty of the men chosen had travelled more than twenty years, while thirty-nine had travelled fewer than ten. The main group consisted of those who had travelled from ten to nineteen years— thirty-six of them, men in their youthful prime like Joseph Benson and Samuel Bradburn. It is not quite true to say that the accent was on youth, but it most certainly avoided age, and took no account of seniority.[48] Wesley seemed to be looking for a cross-section of his preachers, incorporating the wisdom and experience of some of the 'old hands' with the solid maturity of men in the middle years and a strong dash of the vigour, imagination, and even impatience, of youth. On the other side there is evidence that Wesley by-passed those whom he suspected of being radical and iconoclastic.

Inevitably in selecting a hundred men out of 188 on principles such as these, and in doing it only on the basis of his personal knowledge, Wesley was liable to err. Among his younger recruits, for instance, he missed Adam Clarke. Doubtless if he could have foreseen the consequences of the omission of John Hampson he would have drawn the teeth of this firebrand by making room for him in the hundred, even at the expense of one of the solid, safer brethren. Wesley prepared his list in good faith, however, with an eye to a long future when even the young preachers then on trial would have become the veteran administrators of Methodism. In any selection there were dangers, and he was ready to face the consequences with a clear conscience, even though with an uneasy mind. When trouble arose he admitted:

> I am not infallible. I might mistake and think better of some of them than they deserved. However, I did my best, and if I did wrong it was not the error of my own will, but of my judgment.[49]

On 28 February 1784 Wesley visited William Clulow's chambers in Chancery Lane to sign, seal, and deliver the official copy of the deed, Clulow and his clerk serving as witnesses. Later that day the document was taken to the High Court of Chancery, where it was duly enrolled on 9 March.[50] At length Methodism was clearly identified and legally incorporated in the persons of its spiritual leaders as well as in a fragmentary way through the many trust deeds also enrolled in the High Court of Chancery.

Nowhere in the deed was any reference made to the relationships of the Methodist societies to the Church of England—in fact the only mention of the Church throughout was an incidental one, in the regulation about 'ordained Ministers of the Church of England' being exempt from the three-year rule of itinerancy. It is true that too much weight must not be placed on this argument from silence, for the deed similarly omits any mention of the doctrinal standards to be maintained by the preachers in the chapels. The chief, almost the sole, purpose of the document was to furnish a legal definition of the term 'Conference' in order to secure the preaching-houses for the preachers loyal to Wesley's ideals. Even in doing this, however, especially in doing it as if the Conference were no concern at all of the Church, Wesley was setting up Methodism as a separate institution. From 1784 his societies were fully incorporated for spiritual purposes never approved of by any ecclesiastical court, purposes to be carried out primarily by laymen not answerable to parish clergy or diocesan officials, in buildings held in trust for a private organization subject to no supervision by the Established Church. Small wonder that the claim that the Methodist societies formed an unseparated arm of that church was widely regarded as a legal fiction.

It seems likely (though not certain) that Wesley intended to keep the provisions of the deed secret until the Conference met. As a matter of course, however, printed copies were made, and apparently seen through the press by Coke. These consisted of eight folio pages, the title and endorsement reading 'An Attested Copy of the Rev. John Wesley's Declaration and Establishment of the Conference of the People called Methodists'. Though disclaiming any responsibility for the limitation of the legal Conference to a hundred preachers, or for the selection of those hundred. Coke did assume responsibility for what proved to be a tactical error:

> All things necessary being completed in the Court of Chancery, according to law, I thought it my duty to send copies of the Deed to all Assistants of Circuits throughout Great Britain, and I afterwards carried copies of it to Ireland.[51]

Among half a dozen or so copies which have survived is one actually despatched by Coke, with his covering letter:

> London, Mar. 29, 1784.
>
> My very dear Brother,
>   I take the Liberty of sending you the Inclosed: be pleased to shew it to your colleagues. I had no hand in nominating or omitting any of my brethren.
>   I am
>   Your most affectionate friend and brother
>   T. Coke.[52]

This was addressed to John Mason, one of the Assistants included in the Deed, as was also one of Mason's colleagues, though not the other, a young preacher on trial. What about the Assistants omitted? Did Coke send an official circuit copy to them or to their junior colleagues whose names were included? (There were two such cases.) In his impulsive zeal did he pause to consider the effect of an announcement made in this manner rather than by Wesley himself at Conference, probably in a few instances with some ground-preparing beforehand?

Whether because Coke had already jumped the gun or because this was also his own intention, Wesley seems to have authorized his young publishing assistant George Whitfield to distribute other copies while he toured with Wesley in April. Samuel Bradburn (not an Assistant) received his first intimation that he was among the hundred when a copy was handed to him during a preachers' gathering at Manchester.[53] Angry letters began to circulate, originating especially with those who felt that their seniority had been spurned. On 30 April Bradburn tried to console his slightly senior friend Jonathan Pritchard, pointing out that this was not the work of hypocrites or snakes in the grass, but of their honoured father in God, and that omission from the list was neither a 'fall' nor a 'lasting mark of infamy', for all the preachers would still remain on an equal footing. When Wesley met the preachers at Manchester, Bradburn stated, he had explained to Jonathan Hern (the only one of the three Manchester preachers omitted) that omission was not designed to 'give any offence', and the explanation satisfied him. (It is interesting to note that throughout Bradburn spoke of the deed as Wesley's 'Will'—as in some sense it was.)[54] John Hampson prepared an anonymous four-page leaflet entitled *An Appeal to the Reverend John and Charles Wesley*. It was addressed especially to 'the excluded 91', calling upon them in effect to come to the Conference and throw out this infamous deed and restore the 'Old Plan' for succession as put forward at the 1769 Conference. He hinted that Wesley was being used as a tool by a small group of scheming men, and declared, 'The Ministry is not so light a matter that we can take it up and lay it down at pleasure'. In July Wesley defended himself against the *Appeal* by preparing an *Answer*.[55]

At the ensuing Conference the dying Fletcher joined his pleas with those of Wesley to such effect that the whole gathering was in tears. After varying intervals, a handful of itinerants resigned, including Hampson and Pilmoor, but the remainder of the disappointed preachers either understood and forgave, or quietly licked their wounds. One vociferous opponent only, William Eells, was privately threatened with disciplinary action some weeks later. On behalf of Wesley the Assistant of his circuit, Christopher Hopper, informed Eells that he was 'no longer in the number of our itinerant preachers', and that a replacement would be found for his station in Bolton. In fact, however, Eells toed the line and was re-appointed for some years.[56] The Deed was immediately made operative by the entry of the Conference proceedings in the newly-purchased Journal, and by the substitution of two new members of the hundred for two who had 'desisted from travelling'. One vacancy was filled by the first American preacher to be named, albeit one who was never again to set foot on English soil— Francis Asbury.[57]

Wesley's *Journal* recorded: 'Our Conference concluded in much love, to the great disappointment of all.' (Surely this is not *quite* what he meant!)[58] Nevertheless, an undercurrent of unrest remained, and
16

interested laymen joined in a campaign to protect the ninety-one from any possible discrimination. Wesley's view of the deed as a whole remained unshaken, in spite of every counter-argument put forward by 'several persons of piety and ability'. On 3 March 1785 he prepared an article for his *Arminian Magazine* vindicating 'that vile wicked Deed, concerning which you have heard such an outcry'.[59] He did promise his readers, however, that 'a writing should be executed putting [all the preachers] on an equal footing'—he had apparently made a statement to this effect at the 1784 Conference.[60] This promise he fulfilled on 7 April 1785, thus anticipating the major point of a petition set on foot in June by Robert Oastler and James Oddie.[61] The document which he then wrote was consigned to the care of his trusted travelling companion Joseph Bradford (who had for a time served as the intermediary in discussions with the disgruntled John Hampson), with instructions that it should be read at the first Conference after his death:

Chester, April 7, 1785.

To the Methodist Conference.

My dear brethren,

Some of our Travelling Preachers have expressed a fear that after my decease you would exclude them either from preaching in connexion with you, or from some other privileges which they now enjoy. I know no other way to prevent any such inconvenience than to leave these my last words with you.

I beseech you by the mercies of God that you never avail yourselves of the Deed of Declaration to assume any superiority over your brethren; but let all things go on among those Itinerants who choose to remain together exactly in the same manner as when I was with you, so far as circumstances will permit.

In particular I beseech you, if you ever loved me, and if you now love God and your brethren, to have no respect of persons in stationing the Preachers, in choosing children for Kingswood School, in disposing of the Yearly Contribution and the Preachers' Fund, or any other public money. But do all things with a single eye, as I have done from the beginning. Go on thus, doing all things without prejudice or partiality, and God will be with you even to the end.

John Wesley.[62]

At the 1785 Conference the whole matter was aired still further, and almost laid to rest. The preachers who had been present signed a declaration that Wesley had in fact been unanimously requested by them in 1783 to prepare a deed to define the term 'Conference', and that 'the mode of doing it was entirely left to his judgment and discretion'. They further testified: 'We do approve of the *substance* and *design* of the Deed which Mr. Wesley has accordingly executed and enrolled'. This second testimony was signed also by the preachers present in 1785 who did not attend the Conference of 1783, sixty-nine in all, of whom seventeen were not included in the hundred.[63]

Throughout his few remaining years Wesley continued to insist on his own prerogatives in inviting preachers to the Conference and in stationing them.[64] Nevertheless, he became somewhat more flexible. Occasionally he was absent for a time from the Conference sessions, as we have noted in 1780, when Christopher Hopper took the chair, and in 1783, when Coke presided. This happened also at the 1785 Conference when some question of discipline arose. On this occasion Wesley was content to confirm the preachers' action during his absence, later writing to Hopper: 'I will not run my head against all the Conference by reversing what they determined.'[65] Along with the incorporation of Conference as a legal entity, implying the expected continuance of Methodism after his death as a body distinct from the Church of England, Wesley was also slowly loosening his grip on the reins, though this was tightened whenever he suspected some sudden spurt into an open declaration of complete independence either of him or of the Church.

FOURTEEN

1784—II: THE PRAYER BOOK REVISED

FOR John Wesley *The Book of Common Prayer* was only just less inspired than the Bible.[1] His highest tribute was:

> I believe there is no liturgy in the world, either in ancient or modern language, which breathes more of a solid, scriptural, rational piety, than the Common Prayer of the Church of England. And though the main of it was compiled considerably more than two hundred years ago, yet is the language of it not only pure, but strong and elegant in the highest degree.[2]

At the outset of the revival he embraced extempore prayer in spite of the criticism that it defied the Act of Uniformity which had made Cranmer's Prayer Book a test of Anglican churchmanship. Yet he constantly maintained that extempore prayer was no satisfactory substitute for the printed form, only a valuable supplement.[3] He even expected his lay preachers to read parts of the Order for Morning Prayer when he or his brother Charles were prevented by illness, saying:

> This both my brother and I judged would endear the church prayers to them; whereas if they were used wholly to extemporary prayer they would naturally contract a kind of contempt, if not aversion, to forms of prayer. So careful were we from the beginning to prevent their leaving the Church.[4]

For nearly half a century Wesley continued to urge this upon his preachers.[5] He knew that throwing away the printed book was no guarantee of either warmth or depth or even of spontaneity in public prayer, and claimed in 1778: 'I myself find more life in the church prayers than in the formal extemporary prayers of Dissenters'.[6]

The *Book of Common Prayer* was also for Wesley the greatest literary masterpiece after the King James Version of the Bible. So filled was his mind with its phrases that his own writings are studded with hundreds of quotations or allusions, usually woven into the texture of his own prose with no hint that they are not original. When he quoted the Psalms, indeed, it was nearly always from the version in the Prayer Book, though sometimes this was unconsciously mingled with that of the Bible.

Of course Wesley accepted the Prayer Book as a major repository of sound Anglican doctrine and practice, the standard by which true churchmanship was to be judged in 1762 as well as 1662. In his *Farther Appeal* he defended his own churchmanship by recourse to quotations from the *Book of Common Prayer*.[7] In 1755, after defining the Church of England in the terms of his favourite Article 19 Wesley furnished his own more up-to-date description:

> That body of people, nominally united, which profess to hold the doctrine contained in the Articles and Homilies, and to use Baptism, the Lord's Supper, and Public Prayer, according to the Common Prayer Book.[8]

His definition of separation from the church therefore included abandoning this volume.[9]

There is no difficulty in proving that John Wesley honoured the Church of England and revered her *Book of Common Prayer*. Neither institution nor book, however, could he regard as sacrosanct. Even before his ordination he had experienced some qualms about occasional passages in the Prayer Book, and through his decades of ecclesiastical experimentation he became increasingly prepared to criticize the minor failings of his beloved devotional companion. In 1750 he read John Jones's *Free and Candid Disquisitions relating to the Church of England*. In addition to the abridgement of the Orders for public worship and similar practical measures this influential book called for a revision of the Prayer Book along lines that would remove relics of Roman superstition such as the use of sponsors and of the sign of the cross in baptism, and also bring both content and language nearer to the Bible. Similarly, Jones called for a revision of the Thirty-Nine Articles.[10] This was a little too iconoclastic for Wesley, who maintained: 'about one objection in ten appears to have weight, and one in five has plausibility'. Even this, however, was an admission of weakness, though Wesley hastened to add:

> Even allowing all the blemishes to be real which he has so carefully and skilfully collected and recited, what ground have we to hope that if we gave up this we should profit by the exchange? Who would supply us with a Liturgy less exceptionable than that which we had before?[11]

Who indeed? This was also Jones's question. He expressed the forlorn hope that Convocation would encourage the production of revisions, failing which private persons might try their hand. As a result six revised liturgies based on the *Book of Common Prayer* were published during the following twenty years, five by churchmen, one by a dissenter. Some of the alterations in these experimental liturgies were of the kind that Wesley had seen and approved in Jones's volume, and which he eventually incorporated in his own revision. His strong prejudices would be aroused, however, by their anti-Trinitarian tendencies, deriving from Samuel Clarke and William Whiston, and finding their flowering in Theophilus Lindsey's *The Book of Common Prayer reformed* of 1774, and their full fruition in progressively Unitarian developments.[12]

Wesley's own objections to the Prayer Book were specified in the document which he read to his preachers at the 1755 Conference:

> Nay, there are some things in the *Common Prayer Book* itself which we do not undertake to defend: as, in the *Athanasian Creed* (though we firmly believe the doctrine contained therein) the *damnatory clauses*, and the speaking of *this* faith (that is, these opinions) as if it were the grand term of salvation; that expression, first used concerning King Charles the Second, 'our most religious king'; the answers in the Office of Baptism which are appointed to be made by the sponsors; the Office of Confirmation; the *absolution* in the Office for visiting the sick; the thanksgiving in the *Burial Office*; those parts of the Office for *Ordaining Bishops, Priests, and Deacons*, which assert or suppose an essential difference between bishops and presbyters; the use of those words in *Ordaining Priests*, 'whosesoever sins ye remit, they are remitted'. One might add (though these are not properly a part of the Common Prayer), Hopkins's and Sternhold's *Psalms*.[13]

All these faults Wesley was later able to put right in his own *Sunday Service*, and they form indeed the backbone of his revision.

In September 1755 Wesley told Samuel Walker that some of his followers found parts of the Prayer Book 'contrary to Scripture', and in November went further still:

> Those ministers who truly feared God near an hundred years ago had undoubtedly much the same objections to the Liturgy which some (who never read their works) have now. And I myself so far allow the force of several of those objections that I should not dare to declare my assent and consent to that book in the terms prescribed. Indeed they are so strong that I think they cannot safely be used with regard to any book but the Bible.[14]

Here Wesley showed himself both aware of and in sympathy with a movement going hand in hand with Jones's attempt to secure a reformed liturgy—the abolition of compulsory subscription to the

Prayer Book and the Thirty-Nine Articles. All beneficed clergy must publicly recite the formula: 'I *A.B.* do here declare my unfeigned assent and consent to all and everything contained and prescribed in and by the book intitled *The Book of Common Prayer.*' This and the similar subscription to the Thirty-Nine Articles had long been performed by many clergy with tongue in cheek, though also with an uneasy conscience, not completely put to rest by the generally accepted 'latitude of interpretation' by which the practice was 'no longer supposed to be a test or trial of a man's opinions at all, but merely kept up for form's sake, because it might be some trouble to amend it'.[15] Francis Blackburne's *Confessional* (published in 1766, though Wesley did not read it until 1768) led to widespread discussion of this issue and to the Feathers Tavern Association's petition to Parliament for the abolition of subscription. Wesley's increasing knowledge of and sympathy with the Puritans made him the more rebellious against liturgical tyranny, the less ready to condone any casuistical lip-service. He would agree with the *Confessional's* claim that a subscription to the Bible as the final doctrinal standard was far preferable to subscribing to any confession or creed.[16]

In 1754 Wesley had met with Edmund Calamy's *Abridgment of Mr. Baxter's History of his Life and Times,* which prejudiced him against persecuting Caroline bishops and awakened keen sympathy for the Presbyterian sufferers, as well as for the amendments of the Prayer Book which they put forward at the Savoy Conference in 1661.[17] In 1765 he read Calamy's *Continuation* of 1727, first learning of his own grandfather's share both in the testimonies and the trials of those times. He became the more convinced of the substantial rightness of the Puritans—at least of the wrongness of their persecutors.[18] His anger against the ejections brought about under the Act of Uniformity shows up in his *Thoughts upon Liberty* (1772):

> So, by this glorious Act, thousands of men guilty of no crime, nothing contrary either to justice, mercy, or truth, were stripped of all they had, of their houses, lands, revenues, and driven to seek where they could—or beg—their bread. For what? Because they did not dare to worship God according to other men's consciences![19]

A footnote in his *Concise Ecclesiastical History* (1781) emphasized his horror that ministers should thus be victimized in order to secure uniformity of worship. The text (based on Mosheim's account of the Elizabethan Act of Uniformity) claimed that 'the more moderate Puritans . . . only desired liberty of conscience, with the privilege of celebrating divine worship in their own way', to which Wesley added his own comment: 'And it was vile tyranny to refuse them this.'[20]

If in his later years Wesley had been put to the test he would surely have joined his ancestors in the Puritan wilderness rather than have violated his conscience by subscribing to everything contained in the *Book of Common Prayer* and the Thirty-Nine Articles. Certainly some of his public pronouncements would have unfailingly earned ejection a century earlier. It seems, however, that at no time during his ministry was he called upon for that 'assent and consent' which in 1755 he stated that he would not be able to give. In this matter also the facts that he was ordained as the Fellow of a College and never held a living placed him in a peculiar position. Although it is different today, in Wesley's time candidates for Holy Orders were not invariably called upon to subscribe their loyalty to the Thirty-Nine Articles and the Liturgy, and Fellows of Colleges simply declared that they would 'conform to the Liturgy'. Only incumbents of church livings and occupants of ecclesiastical office (as also Heads of Colleges) were required publicly to declare their unfeigned assent and consent to the Prayer Book—though in fact at his ordination Wesley had in good faith subscribed the Articles.[21]

Although like most of his Anglican contemporaries, clergy as well as laity, Wesley was mildly critical in his loyalty to the liturgy, he would probably have agreed with the 217 Members of the House of Commons who turned down as inexpedient the 1773 Feathers Tavern Petition to reform the Prayer Book, rather than with the 71 who supported it. There was real danger that doctrinal ambiguity would be replaced by avowed Arianism, and that licence would succeed liberty.[22]

The idea that he himself might revise the Prayer Book was seriously suggested to him in 1775 by John Fletcher, in the context of Benson's plea for ordaining the preachers. Fletcher apparently thought that an avowed evangelical might succeed where the speculative latitudinarians had failed:

What if with bold modesty you took a farther step towards the reformation of the Church of England? The admirers of *The Confessional*, and the gentlemen who have petitioned the Parliament from the Feathers' Tavern, cry aloud that our Church stands in need of being reformed; but do not they want to corrupt her in some things while they talk of reforming her in others? Now, sir, God has given you that light, that influence, and that intrepidity which many of those gentlemen have not. You can reform, so far as your influence goes, without perverting; and indeed, you have done it already. But have you done it professedly enough? Have you ever explicitly borne your testimony against all the defects of our Church? Might you not do this without departing from your professed attachment to her? Nay, might you not, by this means, do her the greatest of services?

Fletcher went on to suggest elevating the Methodist societies into a reformed 'Methodist Church of England, ready to defend the as yet unmethodized church against all the unjust attacks of the dissenters'. Two clauses of his fourteen-point plan especially interest us here:

> 4. That a pamphlet be published containing the 39 Articles of the Church of England, rectified according to the purity of the gospel, together with some needful alterations in the Liturgy and Homilies —such as the expunging the damnatory clauses of the Athanasian Creed, &c. . . .

> 10. That the most spiritual part of the Common Prayer shall be extracted and published with the 39 rectified Articles, and the Minutes of the Conferences (or the Methodist canons), which (together with such regulations as may be made at the time of this establishment) shall be, next to the Bible, the *vade mecum* of the Methodist preachers.

All this was to be offered for ratification by the archbishop of Canterbury and the bench of bishops.[23]

Wesley had read almost as much of the literature thrown up by the movement for liturgical reform and by the subscription controversy as had Fletcher. He realized that a scheme such as this would be thrown out just as speedily, for his 'enthusiasm' was equally suspect in high ecclesiastical circles with the liberalism of Blackburne and his son-in-law Theophilus Lindsey. Nevertheless, although he made no attempt at the time to carry out Fletcher's plan, both the letter and the ideas it contained were filed away for future reference.

The plight of the American Methodists, independent but spiritually deserted, made him think again about Fletcher's scheme. The revolutionary war ended with the Treaty of Paris on 3 September 1783. The letters which Wesley began to receive from his sympathizers in the new United States of America saddened yet excited him. Despite the loss of all but one of the British preachers, despite the suspicion and persecution to which their loyalist-inspired movement was subject, the American Methodist societies had continued to grow during the seven years of the war. The number of preachers, of circuits, and of members had approximately tripled, and there were now nearly 14,000 members worshipping in sixty chapels.[24] Strong pressure existed for them to form an independent church, ordaining their own preachers to administer the sacraments. One schism along these lines had been healed with difficulty, and it was mainly the powerful advocacy of Francis Asbury that persuaded them to delay action until the end of hostilities.[25]

As the war drew to its close one American preacher, Edward Dromgoole, took it upon himself to inform Wesley:

> The work in America has gone on with amazing swiftness since the war began. . . . The Lord has effectually healed our divisions, and and we are now more firmly united than ever, on the same plan that was proposed and subscribed in England in 1774.[26]

Dromgoole went on to plead that the 'great and effectual door' should not be closed by the removal of Asbury's superintendency, but he also asked for more British preachers. Wesley replied two weeks after the peace treaty had been signed:

> When the Government in America is settled, I believe some of our brethren will be ready to come over. I cannot advise them to do it yet: First let us see how Providence opens itself. And I am the less in haste because I am persuaded Brother Asbury is raised up to preserve order among you, and to do just what I should do myself if it pleased God to bring me to America.[27]

Meantime Asbury had made his first visit in nine years to British-occupied New York. Early in the last week of August he wrote to Wesley outlining the condition of American Methodism on the eve of peace. Wesley replied from Bristol on 3 October, furnishing Asbury with a document authorizing him as 'General Assistant' or plenipotentiary in place of Thomas Rankin to maintain the *status quo*. Through Asbury he charged all the preachers:

> Let all of you be determined to abide by the Methodist doctrine and discipline published in the four volumes of *Sermons* and the *Notes upon the New Testament*, together with the large *Minutes* of the Conference.[28]

Although it was almost impossible for Wesley fully to appreciate the changed situation in America, and especially to understand that the day of his own sovereignty had completely passed along with that of King George, he made an imaginative effort to read between the lines. He realized that Asbury was fighting a rearguard action, and needed reinforcement speedily if the American Methodists were not to secede and form a new denomination completely independent both of himself and of the Church of England. Indeed, it seemed almost too much to hope that rescue was even yet possible. His amazement that the war itself had not completely destroyed the work appeared in his letter to Dromgoole.[29] Political independence was a *fait accompli* about which he must be realistic. Complete ecclesiastical independence was almost sure to follow. There remained just a chance, however, that American Methodism could be kept together in a church with family ties binding it to the mother country if the matter were carefully planned and executed speedily.

Such thoughts probably ran through Wesley's mind as he travelled from Bristol through the southern counties to London early in October 1783. He recalled how in 1755 he had told his preachers:

> To form the plan of a new church would require infinite time and care, . . . with much more wisdom and greater depth and extensiveness of thought than any of us are masters of.[30]

It seemed that Providence was now forcing him to just this task. He pondered Fletcher's idea 'that the growing body of the Methodists in Great Britain, Ireland, and America be formed into a general society—a daughter church of our holy mother'. He began considering means to foster such a 'Methodist Church of England' for the U.S.A.—a church with its own doctrine, its own discipline, its own ministry, its own liturgy, all inspired by Methodist ideals within an Anglican framework, yet subject to no Anglican control, and with only the lightest of English supervision.

It seems almost certain that over the weekend of Sunday 12 October 1783 Wesley discussed this idea with Thomas Coke, for although he toyed with the idea of himself returning for a time to America, Coke was his obvious delegate.[31] Coke probably penned the summary of this event which was published shortly after Wesley's death and has been strangely neglected by historians:

> When peace was established between Great Britain and the States, the intercourse was opened betwixt the societies in both countries. Mr. Wesley then received from Mr. Asbury a full account of the progress of the work during the war; and especially of the division which had taken place, and the difficulties he met with before it was healed. He also informed Mr. Wesley of the extreme uneasiness of the people's minds for want of the sacraments: that thousands of their children were unbaptized, and the members of the societies in general had not partaken of the Lord's Supper for many years. Mr. Wesley then considered the subject, and informed Dr. Coke of his design of drawing up a plan of church government, and of establishing an ordination, for his American societies. But, cautious of entering on so new a plan, he afterwards suspended the execution of his purpose and weighed the whole for upwards of a year.[32]

As we have noted, in 1783 Coke underwent a revulsion against the

Church of England, and whatever doubts he might later have expressed about Wesley's plan of ordination (probably in February 1784), it seems unlikely that in October 1783 he raised any objections to Wesley's proposed response to Asbury's request that he should 'provide for them some mode of church government suited to their exigencies'.[33]

Wesley's famous ordinations of a year later were probably the most important climax of a carefully articulated plan to secure such a partially independent church for American Methodism, and certainly not a last minute expedient, even though cautiously delayed. The key to Wesley's scheme for America was to be found in his careful revision of the *Book of Common Prayer*. This was a deliberate attempt to make the best of both worlds by acknowledging the need for a new church on American soil, yet striving to keep it as near as possible to the best pattern which he knew—the Church of England. In his letter of 10 September 1784 Wesley stated that in response to American appeals he had 'drawn up a little sketch'. This has sometimes been mistakenly assumed to refer to the letter itself. It appears much more likely that this was a quite independent document prepared months before rather than a few days after his ordinations, and was indeed the document discussed at the Conference in July 1784. This sketch, however, has disappeared, and our best clues to its reconstruction are probably Fletcher's plan of 1775, the *Sunday Service*, and the various writings connected with the ordinations themselves. Fletcher's plan we have already discussed, and now turn more specifically to the *Sunday Service*.

We find no clue in Wesley's diary as to when he prepared this work or passed it on to Coke for seeing through the press. He may well have handed it over on 14 February 1784, although during the recorded two-hour session with Coke that day other preachers were present and the chief matter discussed was Coke's scheme to establish missions in the East and elsewhere.[34] It is likely that Wesley held a private meeting with Coke preceding or following the preachers' session, and that the plans for America were discussed. That the task of revising the Prayer Book did not stamp itself indelibly on Wesley's diary is not too surprising, for hundreds of hours are there accounted for in general terms only. It is unlikely that the oft-recurring 'prayers' ('pp' in his shorthand) had anything to do with his literary labours, which were probably accomplished at some time in the spring when his diary simply recorded 'chaise'. However challenging in its theological, liturgical, and ecclesiastical significance, this revision was a relatively simple physical task. All that Wesley did was to carry around with him a copy of the *Book of Common Prayer* (albeit a somewhat unusual edition, as we shall see), and strike out with his pen the passages which he did not wish to reproduce, at the same time inserting new words and phrases here and there. This was his normal method of abridging books for publication, and a few volumes survive which he thus prepared for the press.[35]

Nevertheless, by this simple method momentous changes were made, changes which show that Wesley was carrying out most of the reforms desired by the Puritans more than a century earlier, and by John Jones and company more recently. Wesley's recollections of the Puritans and especially of the Savoy Conference may well have influenced him, but only in a general way: he most certainly did not take the 'Reformed Liturgy' as his model. Frederick Hunter has pointed out that the commission appointed in 1689 to revise the Prayer Book in a Nonconformist direction influenced him not at all.[36] Nor, so far as we can tell, did any of the experimental liturgies prepared in response to Jones's appeal furnish a pattern, though this has never fully been investigated.[37] Wesley's *Sunday Service of the Methodists* arose from the needs of Methodism, especially of the American Methodists, and was fashioned in conformity with the personal predilections of their leader as well as the particular problems of their situation. Its overall purpose was to secure the half loaf of partial loyalty to the Church of England rather than be forced to put up with the no bread of complete independence.

In some instances Wesley abridged for abridgement's sake, with no obvious doctrinal or liturgical purpose, simply bearing in mind what he knew of the pioneering conditions in America and what he could guess about the prejudices of a newly independent nation. A few alterations were clearly dictated by the changed political scene in America. The prayers for the sovereign and the royal family in morning and evening worship were replaced by 'A Prayer for the Supreme Rulers'; the Collect and the Prayer for the Church Militant in the Communion Order similarly interceded for 'Thy servants the Supreme Rulers of these United States'. Other changes were purely stylistic. In 1789 Wesley told his poet friend Walter Churchey:

> Dr. Coke made two or three little alterations in the Prayer Book without my knowledge. I took particular care throughout to alter nothing merely for altering's sake. In religion I am for as few innovations as possible. I love the old wine best. And if it were only on this account I prefer 'which' before 'who art in heaven'.[38]

In view of this letter one suspects that some of the stylistic alterations were from the pen of Thomas Coke, and were too insignificant for Wesley to correct when he saw an advance copy. There were two such in the Lord's Prayer—'Our Father who art in heaven' (for 'which') and 'Thy will be done on earth' (for 'in'). These alterations were made

in every instance except the Order for Evening Prayer, where the
Lord's Prayer retained the traditional forms, almost certainly by an
oversight, which was corrected in later editions.

The majority of the revisions, however, were in one way or another
dictated by Wesley's churchmanship, and many had been foreshadowed
in his criticisms of 1755. In his preface (almost certainly written long
after the work of revision had been completed) Wesley summarized
some of the principles which had guided him:

> Little alteration is made in the following edition of it (which I recom-
> mend to our Societies in America) except in the following instances:
>
> 1. Most of the holy-days (so called) are omitted, as at present
> answering no valuable end.
>
> 2. The service of the Lord's Day, the length of which has been
> often complained of, is considerably shortened.
>
> 3. Some sentences in the offices of Baptism, and for the Burial of
> the Dead, are omitted—And,
>
> 4. Many Psalms [are] left out, and many parts of the others, as
> being highly improper for the mouths of a Christian congregation.

Wesley was either forgetful or disingenuous (perhaps we should say
'diplomatic') in trying to steer a middle course between the Scylla and
Charybdis of the radical and the conservative critics who would surely
challenge him. Although 'only' an abridgement the alterations were
far more numerous and substantial than he implied. The *Book of
Common Prayer*, in fact, was reduced to just over half the size of the
fullest contemporary editions, and less than six-tenths of the much
smaller original 'Sealed Books' of 1662. Of the twenty-seven contents
headings in the statutory 'Sealed Books' only fifteen are in any way
represented in Wesley's *Sunday Service*.[39] Not only did he omit most
of the prefatory matter, including the Calendar, but also the Athanasian
Creed, Private Baptism, both the Catechism and the Order for Confirmation, the Visitation of the Sick, Thanksgiving for Women after
Child-bearing, the Commination, Forms of Prayer to be used at sea,
and the four special Orders for state anniversaries. He excluded Apocryphal lessons, references to Lent, and the use of the titles 'priest' and
'bishop'. Like the Puritans he made fuller provision for extempore
prayer—in these instances *adding* to the text rather than deleting or
substituting.[40] In the offices which he did include he made hundreds of
alterations in detail, although in general the movement and texture of
the liturgy remain the same.[41]

Wesley tried to simplify the Proper Lessons for Sundays by omitting
any mention of Epiphany, Septuagesima, Sexagesima, Quinquagesima

and even Lent, leaving only the landmarks of Advent, Christmas, Easter, Ascension Day, Whitsunday, and Trinity Sunday. In this process the Fourth Sunday in Lent became the 15th Sunday after Christmas, and the Sixth in Lent 'Sunday next before Easter'. In the confusion the Fifth Sunday in Lent and the 27th after Trinity were completely omitted, both in the Proper Lessons and in the Collects—the 26th after Trinity also was omitted from the Collects.[42] Of the thirty-six holy days for which 'propers' were prescribed Wesley retained only three—the Nativity of Christ, Good Friday, and Ascension Day. He omitted even All Saints' Day, a festival which he personally continued to observe, and spoke of as 'a day that I peculiarly love'.[43] Of the six 'certain days' for which 'Proper Psalms' were prescribed he listed the three above, together with Easter Day and Whitsunday, omitting only Ash Wednesday. The four divisions of the 'Days of Fasting or Abstinence' he reduced to the last only—'All the Fridays in the Year, except Christmas Day'. This was a far cry from his Oxford and Georgia Days, though he continued sternly to insist upon fasting itself as a spiritual discipline, and appointed quarterly fast days for special Methodist observance.

In accordance with his preface, Wesley greatly shortened the orders for public worship, as the Puritans and Jones had advocated—and usually along the lines they had recommended. From Morning Prayer he removed some of the opening sentences, the Venite, Benedicite, Benedictus, the second Lord's Prayer and the following versicles, two of the closing prayers, and the Quicunque Vult. He also abridged portions which he did reproduce, including the Absolution. Here he made an important doctrinal change, not only halving its content but transforming it from a priestly declaration to a pastoral prayer. This was quite deliberate. In his *Popery Calmly Considered* (1779) he maintained: 'We believe the absolution pronounced by the priest is only declarative and conditional. For judicially to pardon sin and absolve the sinner is a power God has reserved to himself.'[44] Evening Prayer was similarly modified, with the omission of the Magnificat and the Nunc Dimittis. An interesting change was made in the titles of these orders, which were no longer set forth as for use 'daily throughout the year', but only for 'every Lord's Day'—a sign not only of Wesley's realism in not expecting daily public worship in a pioneering situation, but also of the fact that the Methodist societies were now being looked to for the whole gamut of worship, in America at least. The Litany, on the other hand, was prescribed for use only on Wednesdays and Fridays, not on Sundays.

From the title of the Order for the Administration of the Lord's Supper, Wesley omitted 'or Holy Communion', though he retained

'The Communion' for the running-head, and in the rubrics. Once more Wesley obscured the priestly role: throughout the communion rubrics 'priest' became 'elder', and the absolution was made supplicatory rather than declaratory by the alteration of 'you' and 'your' to 'us' and 'our'. Wesley's somewhat pernickety attention to the letter of the law during his Georgia ministry was forgotten, and the rubric about participants signifying their anticipated attendance was omitted, along with many others. The rubric prescribing the manual acts during the prayer of consecration was omitted in the first printing but restored by the preparation of a cancel leaf. This re-insertion was almost certainly done at Wesley's instance, because Thomas Coke (who saw the volume through the press) had omitted the manual acts on his own initiative.[45] Many of the numerous omissions were in the interest of brevity, as was possibly the case with the Nicene Creed.[46] Wesley also made several interesting additions, such as the directions 'all standing' for the Comfortable Words and 'the people all kneeling' for the Prayer of Humble Access—though he strangely omitted the direction about kneeling to receive the elements. More important was the addition to the rubric before the Benediction: 'Then the Elder, if he see it expedient, may put up an Extempore Prayer.'[47]

In The Ministration of Baptism of Infants Wesley made several significant changes. Although in 1752 he had published a tract somewhat half-heartedly defending the institution of godparents, a tract reprinted in 1758, he expunged this aspect of the baptismal order, omitting not only the answers which the sponsors were supposed to make on behalf of the child (to which he had objected in 1755), but the rubric about them and both the address and the charge to them.[48] Similarly, the minister was to ask 'the Friends of the Child' rather than 'the Godfathers and Godmothers' to announce the child's name. In this he had departed greatly from his Georgia practice. This was true also in the mode of baptism. Wesley prescribed as the norm the traditional dipping, but altered the alternative allowed for weakly children of pouring water on their heads into a simple (and different) alternative: 'he shall dip it in the water or sprinkle it therewith'. A. E. Peaston thinks that this may be 'the first reference in any baptismal rite to the use of sprinkling as a valid mode of Baptism'.[49] Making the sign of the cross upon the child's forehead was removed in the early issue (again almost certainly by Coke) and replaced by means of cancel leaves—only once more to be lost from later editions.[50] In this instance, however, there is much more doubt as to the division of responsibility, for Wesley had earlier declared himself against this usage as 'superstitious'.[51] Wesley's earlier advocacy of the doctrine of baptismal regeneration had

somewhat softened. Although he expunged some phrases which seemed
to imply that in baptism the child (or adult) was almost automatically
reborn, he retained four or five others in which that spiritual blessing
was requested, as in the Mozarabic prayer, 'sanctify this water to the
mystical washing away of sin'. In other words baptismal regeneration
was possible but not guaranteed.[52]

As has been mentioned, Wesley deleted from the Form of Solemniza-
tion of Matrimony the use of the ring and also the question 'Who
giveth this woman. . . ?' These alterations were surely deliberate.
From the Order for the Burial of the Dead he excised the Committal,
which may have been accidental; certainly his City Road colleague
John Richardson, who must have shared many funerals with him, used
the committal when burying Wesley, though he changed 'our dear
brother here departed' to 'our dear father'.[53] Wesley also omitted the
prayer of thanksgiving after the committal, to which he had objected
in 1755.

Although Wesley dearly loved the Psalter, he reduced it by one-
sixth. This was perhaps partly due to his desire for abridgement in
general, but mainly (as he stated in his preface) because he refused to
encourage the constant use (whatever might be done about occasional
Scripture readings) of the cruder aspects of Old Testament ethics. Thus
he completely omitted thirty-three Psalms and parts of fifty-six others.
The omissions led to some re-apportionment of the Psalter among the
days for which they were designed; he followed the original in making
no provision for the 31st day of the month. Some of the Psalms he
divided into two parts.

Most editions of the *Book of Common Prayer* did not contain the
Ordinal, for this was not needed by the regular worshipper. The
fact that Wesley did include this in his *Sunday Service* once more empha-
sizes the fact that he was attempting to furnish a full-orbed church life
for the American Methodists, though as like his favourite model of the
Church of England as was practicable. The original title was: 'The
Form and Manner of making, ordaining, and consecrating Bishops,
Priests, and Deacons, according to the Order of the Church of England.'
Clearly he was making a break with Anglican order, nor would the
Americans accept the last clause, which was therefore omitted. Nor did
Wesley either wish to cross swords with the bishops or pretend that he
himself was a hierarchical bishop (or that any of his followers were): he
therefore omitted the word 'consecrating' and altered 'bishops' to
'superintendants' [the modern spelling 'superintendent' also appeared
in the volume, and from 1786 became uniform]. In accordance with
his practice elsewhere 'priest' became 'elder'. Thus the new title was:

17

'The Form and Manner of Making and Ordaining of Superintendents, Elders, and Deacons.'

Each of the three Orders was characteristically abridged, though only lightly. The Oath of Supremacy was of course omitted, as were all references to the Church of England. In every instance superintendents and elders replaced bishops and priests; the elder also took the place of the archdeacon in presenting the candidates, and Wesley added a rubric about reading their names aloud. 'Ministers' replaced 'clergy'. The Deacon's office was noted as being 'to expound' as well as read the Scriptures—this was current Anglican practice, even though there was no rubric to that effect in the *Book of Common Prayer*. Similarly after the Superintendent had laid his hands on the candidate he delivered a Bible to him and said, 'Take thou authority to read the holy Scriptures in the church of God, and to preach the same'—without any condition about being 'thereto licensed by the bishop himself'.

'The Form and Manner of ordaining of Elders' also followed closely the Ordering of Priests. The examination of the candidates contained a reference to visiting the sick 'within your district' (replacing 'your cures')—the introduction of a term which later came to have important technical meaning both in American and in British Methodism. Superintendent and Elders laid their hands upon the candidate, the Superintendent saying, 'Receive the Holy Ghost for the Office and Work of an Elder in the Church of God, now committed unto thee by the imposition of our hands', but there was no commission to give absolution. In delivering a Bible the Superintendent said, 'Take thou authority to preach the Word of God and to administer the holy Sacraments in the congregation'. In the Anglican Order the Nicene Creed followed, but as Wesley had omitted this from his Communion Office it was not prescribed here; Communion followed immediately upon ordination.

'The Form of Ordaining of a Superintendent' again followed closely 'The Form of Ordaining or Consecrating of an Archbishop or Bishop', but a Superintendent replaced the Archbishop and two Elders took the place of other Bishops in presenting 'this godly man to be ordained a Superintendent'. 'District' replaced 'diocese' for the exercise of superintendency. Again Superintendent and Elders laid their hands upon 'the elected Person', and the Superintendent said, 'Receive the Holy Ghost for the office and work of a Superintendant in the Church of God, now committed unto thee by the imposition of our hands, in the Name of the Father, and of the Son, and of the Holy Ghost. Amen.' The lengthy charge in delivering the Bible was almost exactly that of the Anglican Order. Indeed, the only real difference throughout is that summarized in the variants in the rubric which followed:

| Then the Archbishop shall proceed in the Communion Service: with whom the new-consecrated Bishop (with others) shall also communicate. | Then the Superintendant shall proceed in the Communion Service: with whom the newly ordained Superintendant and other Persons present, shall communicate. |

Whatever the terminology, Bishop or Superintendent, Diocese or District, Wesley was clearly furnishing his followers with an episcopal church fashioned after the Church of England.

Perhaps even more significant as an index of Wesley's ecclesiastical intentions than the publication of the revised Ordinal was his inclusion in the *Sunday Service* of a revision of the Thirty-Nine Articles. These had been drawn up a century earlier than the statutory *Book of Common Prayer*, formed no essential part of it, and were seldom bound therewith.[54] Nevertheless, they were the acknowledged doctrinal formularies of the Church of England, and had weathered many more storms than the Liturgy itself. In 1755 Wesley had said that the Methodists could not in conscience renounce 'the doctrine of the Church, contained in the Articles and Homilies':

> For though we take knowledge that the writers of them were fallible men, though we will not undertake to defend every particular expression in them, yet we cannot but very highly esteem them as yielding to few human compositions.[55]

Although the trust deeds of Methodist premises named Wesley's *Sermons* and *Explanatory Notes upon the New Testament* as guides to the content of Methodist preaching, it seemed desirable that a truly self-contained church should have a summary of belief which was at the same time more concise and more comprehensive. As a part of his 1775 plan for such a church, Fletcher had advised Wesley to publish 'the 39 Articles of the Church of England, rectified according to the purity of the gospel'.[56] Wesley attempted just this, following (as he himself put it) only 'the Scriptures and the Primitive Church'.

It must not be thought, however, that this revision was occasioned only by the American situation. Wesley had long entertained doubts about the doctrinal soundness of some of the Articles. When in 1784 he reduced the 39 to 24 he omitted six which had been listed as scripturally suspect as early as his 1744 Conference: VIII (Of the Three Creeds), XIII (Of Works before Justification), XV (Of Christ alone without sin), XVII (Of Predestination and Election), XXI (Of the Authority of General Councils), and XXIII (Of Ministering in the Congregation).

Two more noted in 1744 as doubtful were XVI (Of Sin after Baptism) and XXVII (Of Baptism). The title of XVI was changed to 'Of Sin after Justification', but otherwise reproduced almost exactly save for a little modernizing of the language. XXVII was considerably shortened, but the doctrine of baptismal regeneration was firmly maintained:

> Baptism is not only a sign of profession and mark of difference whereby Christians are distinguished from others that are not baptized; but it is also a sign of regeneration or the new birth. The baptism of young children is to be retained in the church.

After forty years Wesley's churchmanship was even more emancipated from the traditions of his mother church, and he was prepared to discard articles of faith (or at least certain expressions of them) in a manner which in 1744 would have been almost inconceivable. Accordingly he also omitted completely a further nine: III (Of [Christ's] going down into Hell) [though the statement about this doctrine was retained in the Apostle's Creed], XVIII (Of obtaining Eternal Salvation only by the Name of Christ), XX (Of the Authority of the Church), XXVI (Of the unworthiness of the Ministers which hinders not the effect of the Sacraments), XXIX (Of the Wicked, which eat not the Body of Christ in the Use of the Lord's Supper), XXXIII (Of excommunicate persons, how they are to be avoided, XXXV (Of the Homilies), XXXVI (Of Consecration of Bishops and Ministers), and XXXVII (Of the Civil Magistrates).

In the Articles which he retained Wesley made several changes, in addition to cutting away all that to him was superfluous or distasteful. From VI he omitted the commendation and listing of the Apocryphal Books. He reduced IX (Of Original Sin) by more than half, but added three emphatic words of his own at the end: '. . . man is very far gone from original righteousness, and of his own nature inclined to evil, and that continually'. In XXXII (Of the Marriage of Priests) 'Ministers' replaced 'Priests' in the title, and 'Ministers of Christ' the opening 'Bishops, Priests, and Deacons'. 'Of the Traditions of the Church' (XXXIV) was changed to 'Of the Rites and Ceremonies of the Church'. The whole document was reduced to about half its original size, and all the Articles except two were renumbered, though the original order was retained. The American Methodists themselves added a further article—'Of the Rulers of the United States of America'—which in effect replaced the omitted XXXVII.

Some of Wesley's omissions and alterations occasion little surprise, but the total effect is somewhat unexpected, and worthy of much fuller study than can here be given. One seems to see at work not simply a

devout Arminian evangelist, but a doctrinally liberal iconoclast who
had little use for many traditional beliefs and a somewhat low view of
Church, Ministry, and Sacraments. It might be claimed that this was
due to the dominant influence of Coke during his swing away from the
church, or that Wesley was striving successfully to reflect the mood of
emancipated Americans. It is very doubtful whether he would have
gone so far, however, had he not himself responded positively to the
liberal spirit of the age—and of nonconformity—far more than might
have been expected of that prim little Tory clergyman who not long
before had proclaimed himself 'a High Churchman and the son of a
High Churchman'.[57]

For purposes of doctrinal clarity in a new situation it would doubtless
have been far more satisfactory to have prepared fresh Methodist
Articles of Religion, and this Wesley could have accomplished successfully had he been able to turn his back on the Established Church. This,
however, he was constitutionally unable to do. He therefore felt compelled to take as his starting-point Articles which had been prepared
under the shadow of specific historical problems rather than as an effort
to systemize eternal truth.[58] Nevertheless, he succeeded in retaining the
core of the Protestant Trinitarian faith, much more concisely expressed
and almost freed from its splendid but dangerous ambiguities, so that
it was nothing like so liable to antagonize critics of various colours. So
successful was he, indeed, that this document has remained the doctrinal touchstone of American Methodism, though Wesley's *Sermons*
and *Notes* have never been officially superseded, merely forgotten.[59]

To the *Book of Common Prayer* was usually appended some edition of
the metrical psalms. In spite of the crudeness of Sternhold and Hopkins,
and even of Tate and Brady's New Version, this added a new dimension of congregational song to Anglican worship, which Wesley wished
to preserve and enrich. In 1755 he had placed Sternhold and Hopkins'
Psalms on his *Index expurgatorum*, even though they were 'not properly
a part of the Common Prayer'.[60] Thirty years later, again underlining
the fact that a complete book of worship was being provided, Wesley
similarly appended to his own revision of the Prayer Book *A Collection
of Psalms and Hymns for the Lord's Day*. This comprised items selected
from two of his previous four publications with the same title (less the
last four words), beginning with his pioneer Charleston hymn-book of
1737. The basis of the 1784 collection was the 1743 work, a so-called
'Second Edition Enlarged' of the 1741 volume—though in fact it was
smaller, and while adding more of Charles Wesley's compositions
omitted those of other writers. To his selection of items from the 1743
volume, Wesley added a few rescued from the 1741 book, including

old Watts favourites such as 'Before Jehovah's awful throne' (which first appeared in his Charleston book), and 'O God our help in ages past', which made its bow in that of 1738. The 1784 book remained in two parts, and the Psalms were rearranged in correct numerical sequence in each part. Already the 1743 *Collection* had passed through fifteen editions, including three American ones, and therefore had a head start on Wesley's more famous *Collection of Hymns for the use of the People called Methodists*.[61]

Wesley asked Thomas Coke to see the *Sunday Service* through the press, and doubtless it was by Wesley's desire that it was handled by one of the best printers in London, William Strahan, who had already printed many of his works as well as Dr. Johnson's *Dictionary* and other literary classics. Strahan's ledgers show that two thousand copies of the *Sunday Service* were printed, but only just in time for their despatch to Bristol before Coke sailed for America. Strahan's was a large establishment, and the press figures in the volume show that he parcelled the job out between six of his presses. It seems likely that on his own initiative Coke not only made some stylistic alterations but omitted the sign of the cross in Baptism and the manual acts in the Lord's Supper, and that when Wesley saw an advance copy he insisted on replacing these. By this time, however, the press run had been completed, so that it was necessary to print cancel leaves.[62] Some copies were probably bound in Bristol, but most were carried over in loose sheets.[63] Nevertheless, in the confusion many copies were never corrected, and in later editions these re-insertions were overlooked.[64] The fact that Strahan's bill was not settled until after Coke's return from America the following summer raises the question whether he had offered to finance this venture in which he was so fully engaged, though this cannot take away from Wesley's responsibility—especially in view of his complaints about the 'little alterations' which Coke had made in the text.[65] Because of the importance of the *Sunday Service in North America: with other occasional services* it seems desirable to publish Strahan's record:

The Revd. Dr. Thomas Coke (at Mr. Wesley's)[66]

1784		[£. s. d.]
Septr.	Sunday Service of the Methodists in North-America, 13½ sheets, No. 2000, at £2:2:—	28. 7. –
	Extra for Calendar, and Corrections through-out	1. 9. –
	Psalms and Hymns, 4½ sheets, No. 2000	9. 9. –
	53½ R[eams] of fine Demy for the Service, at 17s. 6d.	46. 16. –

	[£. s. d.]
18 R[eam]s of Do. for the Hymns	15. 15. –
Paid Packing Do. and Porterage to Bristol	1. 9. –
Paid Aug. 22, 1785	103. 5. –

Wesley crossed the Rubicon of ordination on 2 September 1784. Exactly a week later (probably while travelling in his chaise) he wrote the preface for the *Sunday Service*. This was printed in Bristol, to be 'tipped-in' behind the title page—though in fact some copies lack the preface, and minor variants appear.[67] The following day, again probably while travelling, he composed the well-known letter 'To Dr. Coke, Mr. Asbury, and our Brethren in North America'.[68] This dealt mainly with his ordinations, set in the context of the 'very uncommon train of providences' by which most of the American provinces were 'totally disjoined from their mother country and erected into Independent States'. 'In this peculiar situation', Wesley wrote, 'some thousands of the inhabitants of these States desire my advice; and in compliance with their desire I have drawn up a little sketch.' After dealing with the need for an ordained ministry and his own attempt to fulfil that need Wesley added:

> And I have prepared a Liturgy little differing from that of the Church of England (I think, the best constituted national church in the world) which I advise all the travelling preachers to use on the Lord's Day in all their congregations, reading the Litany only on Wednesdays and Fridays, and praying extempore on all other days. I also advise the elders to administer the Supper of the Lord on every Lord's Day.

His closing paragraph not only recognized the hand of Providence in American independence, but perhaps hinted his own satisfaction at the opportunity for drawing up that 'little sketch' of a model church:

> As our American brethren are now totally disentangled both from the State and from the English Hierarchy, we dare not entangle them again either with the one or the other. They are now at full liberty simply to follow the Scriptures and the primitive church. And we judge it best that they should stand fast in that liberty wherewith God has so strangely made them free.

This document also was printed separately for insertion in copies of the *Sunday Service*, though it is found in only a handful.[69]

When Coke arrived in America Asbury was not prepared to acquiesce in all Wesley's plans without consulting his brethren, and a Conference was hastily summoned, assembling at Baltimore over Christmas 1784. In spite of attempts made by local clergy to prevent separation it was unanimously approved that the American Methodist societies 'should be erected into an independent church'.[70] The question whether the new church should be episcopalian or presbyterian in character was in effect settled by the fact that Wesley's *Sunday Service* so clearly envisaged three orders of ministry; it was therefore decided to call it 'The Methodist Episcopal Church in America'. Nevertheless, they retained Wesley's names for the three orders—superintendents, elders, and deacons. They also agreed to adopt 'the Rev. Mr. Wesley's prayer book', which thus became 'our Liturgy'.[71] As a token of its own authority the *Minutes* of that Conference were in some instances bound between liturgy and hymn-book.[72] There seems to have been little real enthusiasm for liturgical worship, however, in what for most preachers was a frontier setting, and Jesse Lee spoke for many in preferring extempore prayer. He claimed that because of this 'after a few years the prayer book was laid aside'.[73]

Nevertheless, further editions were called for every two years until 1792. Coke was certainly responsible for seeing that of 1788 through the press (once more William Strahan's), and possibly the others.[74] Further interesting variants were introduced, the most important (for our present purpose) surely with Wesley's cognizance if not at his instigation. Special editions were prepared for use in areas still officially linked with the English Crown and Church, one simply omitting 'in North America' from the title, the other entitled '*The Sunday Service of the Methodists in His Majesty's Dominions*'. Another 'British' edition appeared in 1788, and still another in 1792. These restored prayers for the King and the Royal Family, as well as a variant heading and wording for the restored Article XXIII (XXXVII)—'Of the Rulers of the British Dominions', with the occasional addition of 'in America'.[75] All this showed that Wesley had moved a step farther towards forming an independent Methodist Church in countries still loyal to the British hierarchy, a step paralleled (as we shall see) in his ordinations. Already indeed in 1784 he was deliberately planning a closer union of the various Methodist causes throughout the western world, witness his letter to Asbury on 31 October:

When you have once settled your plan with respect to the Provinces [i.e. the U.S.A.], you will easily form a regular connexion with our Society in Antigua on the one hand, and with those in Nova Scotia and Newfoundland on the other.[76]

The *Sunday Service* left little permanent mark on American life outside Methodism. Asbury presented a copy to George Washington,[77] and doubtless other copies came into the hands of the leaders of the nascent Protestant Episcopal Church. In many respects Wesley's revision anticipated both their 'Proposed Book' of 1786 and the approved one published in 1790—especially the former. This was true in major points like the omission of the Athanasian Creed and Commination, and (in the 1786 book only) of the Nicene Creed, as well as the more frequent use of 'minister' to replace 'priest'. Even stylistically there are similarities, such as the use of 'who' (1786 and 1790) and 'on' (1790 only) in the Lord's Prayer.[78] There are also parallels in the 1786 treatment of the Articles, including the complete omission of Articles 3, 13, 26, 29, 33, and 35. This general similarity, however, may well have been due to their common ancestry, and to the modernizing possibilities of the new political and ecclesiastical situation, though I would not be surprised if eventually proof were discovered of some direct borrowing.[79]

Those preachers whom Wesley ordained for Scotland from 1785 onwards were never able to persuade the Scots Methodists to adopt the *Sunday Service*, nor did they uniformly approve of it themselves.[80] In England it fared a little better, and Wesley was able to introduce it to some of his societies from 1786 onwards. Some of his followers, however, reacted strongly against his omissions, and at City Road he continued to use the *Book of Common Prayer*.[81] He instructed his preachers: 'Wherever the people make an objection, let the matter drop.'[82] The minute of the 1788 Conference giving the Assistants power 'to read the Prayer Book in the preaching-houses on Sunday mornings' probably referred to the *Book of Common Prayer*—previously they had been forbidden to 'read the church prayers'.[83] The reaction of the English bishops to the revised American Prayer Book proposed in 1786, which in most respects was nearer to the original than was the *Sunday Service*, was indicative of the censures which Wesley might have expected had he sought open conflict: the consecration of new American bishops was delayed by the hierarchy until an assurance was given that a new book along more conventional lines would be prepared.[84] For Wesley it was certainly the wiser course not to flaunt his own revision in the face of the bishops if he still wished to maintain the claim that he and his societies still formed a loyal arm of the Church of England.

FIFTEEN

1784—III: 'ORDINATION IS SEPARATION'

WESLEY'S strong churchmanship subjected him to incessant tension over the question of administering the Lord's Supper. On the one hand he urged the necessity of not only frequent but constant communion, but on the other he insisted that only a duly ordained minister was able to dispense the sacred elements. Constantly he was faced with the dilemma, both in England and America, that he must expect his sometimes unchurched members either to do without communion or receive it from lay hands. Yet if he himself ordained preachers refused by the bishops he was making an open breach with the established order of the Church of England. His churchmanship, in other words, both urged the need for sacramental worship and the impossibility of his adequately supplying it.

Throughout most of his life he remained consistently hostile to lay baptism, especially as baptism was a unique occasion for each individual, and therefore easier to supply. Early in 1783 Joseph Benson sought Wesley's advice because he had first conducted a funeral and the same evening 'with some reluctance consented to baptize a young man who appeared to be very penitent and to experience a measure of faith in the Lord Jesus'. What should he do about others who now sought baptism at his hands? Wesley replied:

> I do not, and never did, consent that any of our preachers should baptize as long as we profess ourselves to be members of the Church of England. Much more may be said for burying the dead; to this I have no objection.[1]

Lay burial caused Wesley no problem because he did not see this as 'any breach of the sacerdotal office'.[2] Baptism was quite a different matter. When other preachers similarly acted on their own initiative Wesley announced: 'I shall shortly be obliged to drop all the preachers who will not drop this. Christ has sent them not to baptize, but to preach the Gospel.'[3] Shortly afterwards he wrote peremptorily to John Hampson:

Dear Brother,
Whoever among us undertakes to baptize a child is *ipso facto* excluded
from our connexion.

I am
Your affectionate brother
J. Wesley.[4]

To one of his preachers ordained for Scotland Wesley wrote in 1787
(surely with reference to his colleagues): 'As we have not yet made a
precedent of any one that was not ordained administering baptism, it is
better to go slow and sure.'[5] During the Revolutionary War Francis
Asbury strove to safeguard the same position in America, so that in
1783 he reported that 'thousands of their children were unbaptized, and
the members of the society in general had not partaken of the Lord's
Supper for many years'.[6]

According to his own statements only the urgent need to save souls
had persuaded Wesley that he must 'appoint' or at least 'permit'
preaching by laymen upon whom God had already put His seal. He
was not convinced that any soul would similarly perish for lack of the
sacraments, and believed that although in the primitive church God
sometimes called 'extraordinary prophets' He never called 'extraordinary priests'. Believing firmly in two quite distinct orders of ministry he had appointed laymen to the indispensable task of preaching, as
deacons; without ordination he must deny them the priestly office, for
this would be 'contrary to the Word and destructive of the work of
God'. He regarded lay administration with such abhorrence that at the
1760 Conference he told the preachers that he himself would rather
commit murder than administer the Lord's Supper without ordination.[7]

It is true that he had come to regard every presbyter as a potential
bishop, whose own ordination gave him the right to pass his priestly
authority to others, at least in special circumstances.[8] Yet in 1755 he
recognized that to resolve his dilemma by exercising this right would be
'little less than a formal separation from the church', and after pondering even such a step he dismissed it as inexpedient. Over the years the
situation had steadily become more frustrating, especially as he contrasted his (in general) devout and talented lay preachers with indolent
and often incompetent clergy. After an interview in 1760 with John
Newton, who had recently been refused ordination, Wesley vented his
anger in his *Journal*:

Our church requires that clergymen should be men of learning, and
to this end have a university education. But how many have a
university education and yet no learning at all? Meantime one of

eminent learning, as well as unblameable behaviour, cannot be ordained 'because he was not at the University!' What a mere farce is this! Who would believe that any Christian bishop would stoop to so poor an evasion?[9]

Many examples could be quoted of Wesley's defence of his preachers' learning, and also of his valuation of them above many regular clergy. In 1768, for instance, he published a reply to the archidiaconal charges of Dr. Thomas Rutherforth:

> Which do you think is the safest guide—a cursing, swearing, drinking clergyman (that such there are you know), or a tradesman who has in fact 'from his childhood known the Holy Scriptures', and has for five years (to say no more) faithfully and diligently made use of all the helps which the English tongue has put into his hands, who has given attendance to reading, has meditated on these things and given himself wholly to them? Can any reasonable man doubt one moment which of these is the safest guide?[10]

Although there were more sound clergy than has often been recognized, far too many were worldly and careless. In Wesley's view such men neither constituted the church nor were they genuine members of it. 'Unless they preach the doctrines of the church contained in her Articles and Liturgy they are no true ministers of the Church, but are eating her bread and tearing out her bowels.'[11] In 1787 he stated:

> The far greater part of those ministers I have conversed with for above half a century have not been holy men, not devoted to God, not deeply acquainted either with God or themselves.[12]

Two years later he made perhaps his most scathing attack on them:

> A worldly clergyman is a fool above all fools, a madman above all madmen! Such vile, infamous wretches as these are the real 'ground for the contempt of the clergy'. Indolent clergymen, pleasure-taking clergymen, money-loving clergymen, praise-loving clergymen, preferment-seeking clergymen—these are the wretches that cause the order in general to be contemned. These are the pests of the Christian world, the grand nuisances of mankind, a stink in the nostrils of God! Such as these were they who made St. Chrysostom to say, 'Hell is paved with the souls of Christian priests'.[13]

Wesley continued to insist that the unworthiness of the administrator did not invalidate a sacrament.[14] The sad fact remained: there were not enough good ministers to go round, and the lay preachers who could admirably fill the gaps were unable to secure ordination from the bishops, nor was he willing himself to supply their lack. Not for England at any rate. Conditions in the colonies were far different, however. His preacher Francis Gilbert not only spoke for others, but struck a responsive chord in Wesley's mind when he said that although he was convinced that it was lawful for a lay preacher to administer the sacraments he would not do so—unless he were stationed 'in any distant part of the world where there was no plan of a church yet laid, and where the Sacrament was not given more than once or twice in the year in the Church after the English Establishment'.[15]

This sacramental poverty was very much the condition in America, even before the war, so that in 1773 Joseph Pilmoor wrote: 'The chief difficulty is the want of ordination, and I believe we shall be obliged to procure it in some form or other'.[16] Similarly in 1774 Pilmoor urged on Lord Dartmouth 'the desirability of having a bishop for North America'.[17] Nevertheless, the first American Conference, meeting in 1773, agreed to follow Wesley's principles by not administering.[18] The Revolutionary War worsened their plight by the departure not only of the Anglican clergy but of most of Wesley's preachers. After years of agitation, in 1779 some southern American preachers formed a presbytery, ordained each other, and began to administer the Lord's Supper. Only with great difficulty was Asbury able to halt the dissidents and prevent a schism, and that largely by pleading for delay pending an appeal to Wesley.[19] Whether Wesley received and answered the letters which Asbury certainly wrote we do not know, but either through a correspondence surviving the hazards of war or through 'natural causes' the American Methodists continued to acquiesce in 'the old plan' until the restoration of the peace, while in England Wesley persisted with his efforts to secured ordained Methodist preachers for America.[20]

The bishop of London traditionally exercised jurisdiction over the colonies, though his power had never been defined or substantiated—a constant source of irritation and frustration on both sides of the Atlantic.[21] From 1777–87 the see was occupied by Dr. Robert Lowth, with whom Wesley spent an afternoon shortly after his translation to London, finding him 'easy, affable, courteous', yet dignified.[22] Wesley admired Lowth's piety as well as his 'abilities and extensive learning', and from time to time approached him to ordain preachers, though not with the happiest results. During the 1780 Conference Wesley wrote to him ('perhaps for the last time') complaining that the bishop had previously turned down a mature person of genuine piety simply because he knew no Greek or Latin, and now had refused to ordain John

Hoskins to serve 'a little flock in America'.[23] Hoskins was a Methodist schoolmaster of sixty who had emigrated to Newfoundland and proved himself a fruitful evangelist and spiritual leader, so that the inhabitants of Old Perlican asked Wesley to secure ordination for him as their minister.

It was therefore to the plight of British North America that Wesley addressed himself in his letter to Lowth on 10 August 1780, but at the back of his mind was the similar situation south of the St. Lawrence:

> Your Lordship observes, 'There are three ministers in that country already'.[24] True, my Lord; but what are three to watch over all the souls in that extensive country? Will your Lordship permit me to speak freely? . . . Suppose there were threescore of those missionaries in the country, could I in conscience recommend these souls to their care? Do they take any care of their own souls? If they do (I speak it with concern!) I fear they are almost the only missionaries in America that do. My Lord, I do not speak rashly: I have been in America; and so have several with whom I have lately conversed. . . .
>
> Mr. Hoskins . . . asked the favour of your Lordship to ordain him that he might minister to a little flock in America. But your Lordship did see good to ordain and send into America other persons who knew something of Greek and Latin, but who knew no more of saving souls than of catching whales.
>
> In this respect also I mourn for poor America, for the sheep scattered up and down therein. Part of them have no shepherds at all, particularly in the northern colonies; and the case of the rest is little better, for their own shepherds pity them not.[25]

Whether in fact Wesley directly asked Lowth about an eventual supply of preachers for the colonists now at war with the mother country is doubtful, though the letter certainly speaks an interest in 'poor America' in general. It is almost certain that Wesley never wrote along the lines recommended by Fletcher in 1775, aiming a pistol at the bishops' heads: 'Either you ordain or I will!' But he may well have sought such co-operation as a defensive move, so that later he could say, 'But I asked the bishops, and they would not help'.[26]

Even as the 1780 Conference assembled Wesley was commiserating with Brian Bury Collins, an ordained deacon, because the bishop of Chester, Dr. Beilby Porteus, seemed unready to confer priests' orders on him. Wesley was convinced that this attitude was typical of the hierarchy, who although they might not actively persecute the Methodists were fully prepared to hamper their progress by defensive measures. To Collins Wesley wrote on 1 August:

It is not at all surprising that the bishop, though a good man, should scruple to ordain a field preacher; and I apprehend his brethren will neither endeavour [n]or desire to remove his scruple, unless it should please God to touch some of their hearts, and employ them to soften the rest.[27]

The bishop's decision came to Collins on 10 August:

I must therefore decline ordaining you . . . because you have never once expressed to me either in conversation or by letter the least degree of concern for your wandering mode of life and of preaching; nor considered it as any fault, but on the contrary spoke of it as a matter of conscience and of duty, and consequently gave no appearance of amendment for the future.

When Collins obtained a title as assistant curate to David Simpson of Macclesfield the bishop did in fact relent, by which means another Methodist itinerant was lost to the parochial ministry.[28] Porteus was in many ways the most liberal of the bishops, evangelical and anti-Calvinist, even making a sympathetic approach to the Moravian leader Benjamin LaTrobe in the 1780's.[29] He was also aide to the bishop of London in Lowth's declining years and succeeded him in that diocese. If two otherwise sympathetic bishops pleasantly but firmly closed the door on the Methodists there was little chance of an opening elsewhere.

It became quite clear to Wesley that the bishops offered him little hope. This came out vividly when he published in his *Arminian Magazine* for September 1781 the concluding instalment of 'A plain account of Kingswood School', wherein he agreed that no matter how good the education there gained it would help no one in securing honour, money, or preferment in Church or State:

'But whatever learning they have, if they acquired it there they cannot be ordained'. (You mean, *episcopally* ordained: and indeed that ordination we prefer to any other, where it can be had.) 'For the bishops have all agreed together "not to ordain any Methodists".' O that they would 'all agree together' not to ordain any drunkard, any sabbath-breaker, any common swearer! Any that makes the very name of religion stink in the nostrils of infidels! . . . But I doubt that fact. I cannot easily believe that 'all the bishops' have made such an agreement. Could I be sure they had I should think it my duty to return them my sincerest thanks. Pity they had not done it ten years ago, and I should not have lost some of my dearest friends!

Once more he pictured himself as a Luther striving against great opposition to reform the Church from within, yet determined to maintain his course in spite of persecution in high places: 'Meantime I can only say (as a much greater man said): "Hier stehe ich: Gott hilffe mich!"' [30]

When in 1782 William Black sought Wesley's help in securing ordained missionaries for Nova Scotia, Wesley must have replied that in view of his earlier experiences it was useless for him to apply to the bishop of London. Black suggested that he should write once more, in stronger terms, and Wesley replied:

> I did indeed very strongly expostulate with the bishop of London concerning his refusal to ordain a pious man although he had not learning, while he ordained others that to my knowledge had no piety and but a moderate share of learning. I incline to think the letter will appear in public some time hence. [31]

Wesley never fulfilled that threat of publishing his challenge to the bishop as an open letter, but the very fact that he pondered it underlines both his despair of receiving any help from that quarter and his readiness to pave the way by a public defence for his own ordination of his preachers. Already, in fact, he was beginning to use a formal commissioning service for his preachers in Britain, if Adam Clarke's description of his own acceptance in 1782 provides any criterion:

> He said, 'Well, brother Clarke, do you wish to devote yourself entirely to the work of God?' I answered, 'Sir, I wish to *do*, and *be*, what God pleases.' He then said, 'We want a preacher for Bradford [Wiltshire]: hold yourself in readiness to go thither. I am going into the country, and will let you know when you shall go.' He then turned to me, laid his hands upon my head, and spent a few moments in praying to God to bless and preserve me, and to give me success in the work to which I was called.
>
> I departed, having now received, in addition to my appointment from God to preach His Gospel, the only authority I could have from man in that line in which I was to exercise the ministry of the divine Word. [32]

As we have seen, the ending of the war in autumn 1783 forced the challenge and opportunity of American Methodism more urgently on Wesley. [33] As part of an articulated plan to erect a semi-independent Methodist Church there he considered once more the possibility of himself ordaining preachers. He now had before him the example of the Countess of Huntingdon's Connexion. On Sunday 9 March 1783 two of her clergy, having publicly seceded from the Church of England, ordained six candidates for her ministry, validating their power to ordain, as did Wesley, from King's *Enquiry*. After a legal dispute over her Spa Fields Chapel in 1780, the Countess had decided to register her premises as 'dissenting chapels', and this ordination completed her secession, resulting in the loss of several of her clerical sympathizers.[34] Wesley may not have heard of the ordinations for some months, being away from London for most of the year, and in any case the fact that they took place only at the cost of an acknowledged separation might well have proved a deterrent. Nevertheless, the urgent situation in America demanded bold action.

As Thomas Coke had been his confidant in the case of the Deed Poll and the Prayer Book revision, so in this matter of ordination; indeed there is little doubt that on the apparently few occasions when they met each aspect of the situation would be discussed.[35] By now Wesley had gone beyond Lord Peter King's evidence in concluding that if indeed bishops and presbyters were of the same order then they had the same right to ordain. This was not true in the Church of England, at any rate, because although bishops might not have any more spiritual grace to transmit than presbyters, they were the only persons authorized to commission Anglican clergy. Wesley was in fact once more assuming that his 'extraordinary call' would in a state of spiritual emergency validate such an action.[36] This matter was probably adumbrated when Wesley met Coke in October 1783, and discussed as part of a concerted plan in February 1784.

On this later occasion, however, Wesley went far beyond the original plan of ordaining some of the preachers, assisted by Coke and probably one other presbyter; he also broached the idea of a presbyterial ordination of bishops to supervise the work in America. Wesley claimed that for their first two hundred years the presbyters of the Alexandrian church had ordained as bishop one of themselves rather than dilute their ecclesiastical purity by seeking aid from a foreign bishop. He might well have mentioned also the primitive office of chorepiscopus, a kind of itinerant bishop exercising episcopal functions in distant areas. Wesley himself was not only a presbyter with a presbyter's inherent *right* to perform the office of the presiding presbyter or bishop; by his extraordinary call to found and rule the Methodist societies it had been demonstrated that in *function* he was the equivalent of a scriptural bishop. Clearly he was the father in God to the Methodists, their 'apostolic man', as Stillingfleet would say, and as a presbyter living in the simplicity of the primitive church he would certainly have had the power to ordain other presbyters. Both in *ordine* and *gradus* he was a scriptural *episcopos*. In an isolated area such as Alexandria (or America) during an emergency when no bishops were available (or none would act) why should he not join with other presbyters to elevate another presbyter to

18

the office of itinerant bishop, one who would superintend both the members and their ministers, whom he himself would in turn ordain? True, Wesley had received this 'extraordinary call' without any special ordination or commissioning by man, but surely this did not prevent his passing on to others his own acknowledged *episcope* or superintending authority by the normal means of an ordination? Perhaps this line of argument would not convince either the patrologists or the liturgiologists, perhaps Wesley himself was not fully convinced, but it seemed at least a viable emergency measure. [37]

Presbyters ordaining presbyters was one thing, however; presbyters ordaining a bishop was another. It was surely this added step which caused Coke to hesitate and to undertake his own patristic researches. He was quite prepared to assist in forming a college of presbyters to ordain the preachers, but it took him by surprise that Wesley suggested ordaining him a bishop, no matter under what limitations and disguising terminology. [38] Although Wesley recommended suitable reading upon the subject, and although King's *Enquiry* may have been mentioned (as Drew states), Coke would not find therein any details about the Alexandrian expedient. These Wesley derived from Stillingfleet's *Irenicum*, where he would also find a description of the chorepiscopus. [39] Two months later, after Coke had put forward the temporizing suggestion (which Wesley vetoed) that he should first visit America to spy out the land on Wesley's behalf, Coke capitulated, and said that he was ready to co-operate in whatever way Wesley desired. [40]

The following Conference in Leeds was the largest and most momentous so far. Wesley's presentation of the needs of America, and of his plan to send Dr. Coke and one or two volunteer preachers there to organize the societies, was introduced to the full Conference, where it was overshadowed by the lengthy controversy over the Deed of Declaration. [41] Only one dissentient voice was raised, apparently that of John Atlay, already disgruntled by his omission from the Deed Poll. [42] Several preachers offered themselves as Coke's companions, and Wesley chose Richard Whatcoat and Thomas Vasey. It was arranged that they should sail from Bristol about seven weeks later, meeting Wesley there for 'briefing' before departure. [43] The plan of ordination, however, was divulged only to the cabinet of senior preachers, who 'to a man opposed it', though they could see that Wesley's mind was 'quite made up'. [44] Thomas Rankin suggested shifting the responsibility for ordination to any American clergy whom Coke might be able to muster to his aid. [45] Fletcher was consulted. He agreed that it was far preferable to secure ordination from a bishop, but added that in any event Wesley himself should furnish the preachers with 'Letters Testi-

monial of the appointments he had given them'.[46] According to the
testimony of James Creighton Wesley also consulted a group of clergy
at Leeds, including both Fletcher and Walter Sellon. Creighton reported:

> They did not approve of the scheme, because it seemed inconsistent
> with Mr. Wesley's former professions respecting the church. Upon this
> the meeting was abruptly broken up by Mr. Wesley's going out.[47]

Charles Wesley, who was in Bristol at the time, was kept in the dark,
his strong prejudices against any such course being already known.
It seems likely that all those who were consulted were pledged to treat
the matter in strict confidence because John Wesley was still not quite
clear whether he himself would ordain the preachers or would leave it
to Coke and the Americans. Wesley still looked for no help from the
bishops.

A week after the Conference Coke at least was convinced about the
rightness of Wesley's original plan, and wrote to him in Wales on
9 August:

Honoured and dear sir,

> The more maturely I consider the subject, the more expedient it
> appears to me that *the power of ordaining others should be received by me
> from you*, by the imposition of your hands, and that you should lay
> hands on brother Whatcoat and brother Vasey, for the following
> reasons:
>
> 1. It seems to me the most scriptural way, and most agreeable to
> the practice of the primitive churches.
>
> 2. I *may* want all the influence in America which you can throw
> into my scale. . . . An Authority *formally* received from you will . . .
> be fully admitted by the people, and my exercising the office of
> ordination without that *formal* authority may be disputed if there be
> any opposition on any other account. I could therefore *earnestly* wish
> you would exercise that power in this instance which I have not the
> shadow of a doubt but God hath invested you with for the good o
> our connexion. . . .
>
> 3. In respect of my brethren (brother Whatcoat and Vasey) it is very
> uncertain indeed whether any of the clergy mentioned by brother
> Rankin will stir a step with me in the work, except Mr. [Devereux]
> Jarratt; and it is by no means certain that even he will choose to join
> me in ordaining: and propriety and universal practice make it expedi-
> ent that I should have two presbyters with me in this work.
>
> In short, it appears to me that everything should be prepared and
> everything proper be done that can possibly be done *this side the*

water. You can do all this in Mr. C[astleman]'s house, in your *chamber*; and afterwards (according to Mr. Fletcher's advice) give us Letters Testimonial of the different offices with which you have been pleased to invest us. For the purpose of laying hands on Brother Whatcoat and Vasey I can bring Mr. [James] C[reighton] down with me, by which you will have two presbyters with you. In respect to brother Rankin's argument that you will escape a great deal of *odium* by omitting this, it is nothing. Either it will be known, or not known; if not known then no odium will arise, but if known, you will obliged to acknowledge that I acted under your direction—or suffer me to sink under the weight of my enemies, with perhaps your brother at the head of them. I shall entreat you to ponder these things.

Your most dutiful,

T. Coke.[48]

The unsympathetic Dr. Whitehead implied that Wesley's ordinations were undertaken on the initiative of Coke, who was undoubtedly ambitious. On this occasion, however, he must be exonerated. In this instance, as in that of the Deed Poll, Coke carefully tried to shield himself from the charge of following his own devices or of exercising undue pressure upon Wesley. Nevertheless, it is clear that this letter strengthened Wesley's resolve to go ahead, whatever the consequences.

Wesley arrived in Bristol from his Welsh tour on Saturday 28 August. By the following Tuesday the stage was set, and he recorded in his *Journal*:

Tues. 31. Dr. Coke, Mr. Whatcoat, and Mr. Vasey came down from London in order to embark for America.

Sept. 1, Wed. Being now clear in my own mind, I took a step which I had long weighed in my mind, and appointed Mr. Whatcoat and Mr. Vasey to go and serve the desolate sheep in America.

The public record used the word 'appointed'. In his shorthand diary Wesley's entry reads: 'ordained Rd Whatcoat and T. Vasey'.[49] The ordinations were performed by a presbytery consisting of Wesley, Coke, and Creighton at five in the morning at Dr. John Castleman's, 6 Dighton Street, Bristol.[50] Whatcoat and Vasey were ordained deacons on Wednesday and 'elders' (presbyters) on the Thursday, almost certainly according to the Orders in Wesley's *Sunday Service*, of which at least a few copies would be available.[51]

In accordance with Fletcher's suggestion Wesley prepared for his ordained preachers parchment Letters of Orders, signed and sealed by himself alone. The deacons' certificates probably followed the same wording as that used in 1788—the earliest of those extant:

Know all men by these presents that I John Wesley, Master of Arts, late of Lincoln College in the University of Oxford, did [on 1 September 1784] by the imposition of my hands and prayer, and in the fear of God, set apart [Richard Whatcoat] for the office of a Deacon in the Church of God. Given under my hand and seal. . . .

John Wesley[52]

No matter who might assist him on any of these occasions, the Letters of Orders both for deacons and presbyters always show that Wesley assumed the full responsibility, as in fact he had done in his earlier commissioning of preachers.

The parchments prepared for the presbyters were much more elaborate. The British Museum possesses a preliminary draft of those handed to Whatcoat and Vasey on 2 September 1784. Both names are included, and the addition of their title as 'elders' seems to have been an afterthought. This unique document, the prototype of all subsequent parchments, which seem to have been written by amanuenses, and only signed by Wesley, is presented in full with its abbreviations unextended:

To all to whom these presents shall come, J° Wesley, late fellow of Lincoln College in Oxford, Presbyter of yᵉ Church of England, sendeth greeting.

Whereas many of yᵉ people in yᵉ Southern Provinces of *North-America*, wᵒ desire to continue under my care, & still adhere to yᵉ Doctrines & Discipline of yᵉ Church of *England*, are greatly distrest for want of Ministers, to administer yᵉ Sacraments of Baptism & yᵉ Lord's Supper, according to yᵉ usage of yᵉ said Church: And whereas there does not appear to be any other way of supplying yᵐ with Ministers:

Know all men, yᵗ I, John Wesley think myself to be providentially called at this time, to set apart some persons for yᵉ work of the ministry in *America*. And therefore under yᵉ protection of Almighty GOD, & wᵗʰ a single eye to his glory, I have yˢ day set apart for yᵉ said work, ['as Elders' added above the line] by yᵉ imposition of my hands & prayer (being assisted by two other ordaind Ministers) Richᵈ Whatcoat & Thomas Vasey, men whom I judge to be well qualified for yᵗ great work. And I do hereby recommend yᵐ to all whom it may concern, as fit persons to feed yᵉ flock of Xᵗ, & to administer Baptism & the Lord's supper according to the usage of yᵉ Church of England. In testimony whereof I have this day set my hand & seal, this second day of September, 1784.[53]

It seems that Wesley at first intended to use this text for the parchments themselves, but it was clearly preferable that each preacher should possess one referring to himself alone. From Wesley's draft, therefore, individual documents incorporating the necessary minor changes were prepared for his signature. Coke usually served as Wesley's amanuensis, but his own parchment was written out by James Creighton, as was that of Henry Moore five years later, and possibly others.[54] A somewhat briefer form was used in 1786, omitting the reference to the Church of England, and with Wesley's apologia amended to read:

> Whereas it hath been represented to me that many of the people called Methodists under my care in America stand in need at present of proper persons to administer the ordinances of Baptism and the Lord's Supper among them. . . .[55]

In at least one instance 'presbyter' was used instead of 'elder'.[56] In 1787 the form was still farther abridged, largely by omitting the apologia altogether.[57] The document remained the same in 1788—when Coke proved delinquent in his secretarial duty, so that two months after the ordination Wesley wrote to Joseph Cownley, whom Coke himself had nominated for ordination: 'Dr. Coke did forget, but is now writing your Letters of Orders.'[58] In 1789, with two ordinations for England, 'presbyter' once more appeared, and loyalty to the Anglican Church was once more asserted by stating that the sacraments were to be administered 'according to the usage of the Church of England'.[59]

Wesley's ordination of Whatcoat and Vasey could be defended as valid for a Presbyterian minister, though irregular in a professedly loyal Anglican priest. His ordination of Coke is quite another matter, for both were presbyters, so that if orders only were to be considered Coke had as much right to ordain Wesley as Wesley did Coke.[60] Something else entered the question, however, namely office. As an already ordained presbyter Coke was being set apart for a particular function as Wesley's deputy in the administration of Methodism and in the ordination of his preachers. Wesley himself rightly claimed that he was 'under God the father of the whole [Methodist] family', and more especially that the preachers were his 'sons in the gospel'. For over forty years he had been accepting them and dismissing them, deciding where they should go and what they should do. If a 'new plan' of an ordained ministry was to supplement the 'old plan' of a preaching itinerancy, and if this could not be secured through regular episcopal channels, then leadership and responsibility clearly rested in him as the founding father, the revered apostle of Methodism's revival of primitive Christianity. Coke was a newcomer, even though a learned and eloquent and enthusiastic and indefatigable newcomer. He himself had urged upon Wesley that he could only carry the American Methodists with him if he held tangible and dramatic evidence of Wesley's sponsorship.[61] Hence Coke also must carry some evidence that he was a special presbyter among ordinary presbyters, that he bore the staff of the Moses of Methodism.

When Coke preached at Baltimore on the occasion of Francis Asbury's ordination later that year he based Wesley's power to ordain him 'Superintendent' upon his status as the essential minister of Methodism:

> 'But what right have you to exercise the Episcopal Office?' To me the most manifest and clear. God has been pleased by Mr. Wesley to raise up in America and Europe a numerous Society, well known by the name of Methodists. The whole body have invariably esteemed *this man* as their chief pastor under Christ. He has constantly appointed all their religious officers from the highest to the lowest, by himself or his delegate. And we are fully persuaded there is no church office which he judges expedient for the welfare of the people entrusted to his charge but, as *essential* to his station, he has power to ordain. After long deliberation he saw it his duty to form his Society in America into an independent church; but he loved the most excellent Liturgy of the Church of England, he loved its rites[62] and ceremonies, and therefore adopted them in most instances for the present case.[63]

This reflected Wesley's own view, as did Coke also in a subsequent passage disavowing belief in 'the uninterrupted succession of bishops', pointing especially to the primitive churches of Alexandria, of Corinth, and Philippi, using for this purpose evidence which Wesley himself had published in his *Christian Library*.[64]

It seems doubtful that Wesley was ever able to work out a satisfying rationale of what he was doing. Yet when it meant grasping an opportunity, perhaps the only opportunity, of preserving American Methodism for a modified Anglicanism, he would not shirk the responsibility— nor the likely criticism. He knew that he was doing far more than appointing Coke as his administrative agent in America. Wesley recognized that Coke was already called of God to a special task in Methodism, and laid hands on him with the prayer and in the belief that additional grace would thus be granted him for this task; in his diary he once more used the term, 'ordained'. He signed Letters Testimonial for his deputy, prepared on the basis of his original draft for Whatcoat and Vasey, but varying the statement of ordination and the commendation:

I have this day set apart as a Superintendent, by the imposition of
my hands and prayer (being assisted by other ordained ministers)
Thomas Coke, Doctor of Civil Law, a Presbyter of the Church of
England, and a man whom I judge to be well qualified for that great
work. And I do hereby recommend him to all whom it may concern
as a fit person to preside over the Flock of Christ.[65]

According to this document Coke's office of 'Superintendent' comprised 'presiding over the Flock of Christ'—which might indeed imply
merely pastoral and administrative duties. Obviously for a presbyter
already ordained it was inappropriate to use the same terminology as
for those just entering that order, namely to feed the flock of Christ and
to administer the sacraments. Yet Coke's ordination was explicitly
within the same context of supplying more ministers to secure an adequate administration of the sacraments; his task in this area, therefore,
was clearly to lead the way in transmitting ministerial orders to others,
as he had already helped Wesley to do. In this he was to be assisted by
those whom he had assisted to ordain—and who may well, indeed,
have in turn laid hands on him. He remained their superior in office,
however, as did Francis Asbury, to whom Coke was charged by
Wesley to convey the same authority in a similar ceremony conducted
according to the Form of Ordaining a Superintendent in the *Sunday
Service*.[66]

Wesley may not have known quite how to describe what he was
doing, but he certainly knew how *not* to describe it: however much the
attendant circumstances pointed that way, he was not 'consecrating a
bishop'. This was intuitive rather than rational, like many of his relations with the Church of England. He thought of a bishop as a special
officer of the church rather than as a special transmitter of spiritual
grace through confirmation or ordination: his essential function was to
superintend, to oversee, to ensure that all was done decently and in
order. In this limited sense Wesley wished to retain the office of bishop,
but to strip it not only of its worldly trappings, which had dishonoured
it in the minds of devout episcopalians and non-episcopalians alike, but
also of the vaunted uniqueness in charismatic powers supposedly arising
from the 'uninterrupted succession' which he 'knew to be a fable'.[67] In
accordance with his father's advice, Wesley may have read Bishop
Jewel's *Apology* and his massive *Defence* thereof, and noted his marshalling of the Fathers in favour of 'superintendent' as a valued alternative
for 'bishop', giving pride of place to Augustine, who said: 'Episcopatus
nomen est operis, non honoris . . . ἐπισκοπεῖν latine superintendere
possumus dicere.'[68] Henry Moore testified: 'With respect to the title of

"Bishop" I know that Mr. Wesley enjoined the doctor and his associates, and in the most solemn manner, that it should not be taken.'[69]

Nor did they take it—at first. The Christmas Conference at Baltimore resolved:

> We will form ourselves into an Episcopal Church under the direction of Superintendents, Elders, Deacons and Helpers according to the Forms of Ordination annexed to our Liturgy, and the Form of Discipline set forth in these Minutes.[70]

When Coke ordained Asbury and others he described himself as 'Superintendent of the Methodist Episcopal Church'.[71] One of the members of the assembly set down the arguments probably used by Coke:

> With us the Superintendent answers to Bishop, who is to have the oversight of all, and we think is a better name, because *modern* Bishops being Lords are generally devourers of the flock and a curse to the the people, and the very name conveys a disagreeeable savour.[72]

In 1787, however, the *Discipline* used instead the term 'bishop'. When this came to Wesley's attention he wrote angrily to Asbury:

> How can you, how dare you suffer yourself to be called 'bishop'? I shudder, I start at the very thought! Men may call me a knave or a fool, a rascal, a scoundrel, and I am content; but they shall never by my consent call me a bishop! For my sake, for God's sake, for Christ's sake put a full end to this! Let the Presbyterians do what they please, but let the Methodists know their calling better.[73]

Why Presbyterians of all people should want to call themselves bishops is strange, but apparently some in America were in fact assuming this title by way of thumbing their noses at the Episcopalians.[74] What is quite obvious, however, is that Wesley was passionately averse to the title, though the scriptural function of overseeing or superintending he valued highly. He would therefore approve the further change which was accordingly made in the opening question of the American *Minutes*. In 1787 it appeared as 'Who are the superintendents of our Church for the United States?' which in 1788 became 'Who are the Bishops . . .?' and in 1789, after his protest, the much more subtle: 'Who are the persons that exercise the episcopal office in the Methodist Church in Europe and America?' Whether he liked it or not, his own name was added in the answer to this re-phrased question, preceding those of Coke and Asbury.[75]

In despatching his ambassadors to America Wesley armed them not

only with Letters Testimonial and a Liturgy containing forms of ordination, but with the important open letter which has been described as
the Magna Charta of American Methodism.[76] The greater part of this
document was concerned, not with presenting details of his 'little
sketch' for the proposed new church, but with defending himself and
his ordained preachers against the criticism that would surely be aroused
by his courageous unorthodoxy:

2. Lord King's account of the primitive church convinced me
many years ago that Bishops and Presbyters are the same order, and
consequently have the same right to ordain. For many years I have
been importuned from time to time to exercise this right by ordaining part of our travelling preachers. But I have still refused, not only
for peace' sake, but because I was determined as little as possible to
violate the established order of the national church to which I
belonged.

3. But the case is widely different between England and North
America. Here there are Bishops who have legal jurisdiction. In
America there are none, neither any parish ministers. So that for
some hundred miles together there is none either to baptize or to
administer the Lord's Supper. Here therefore my scruples are at an
end: and I conceive myself at full liberty, as I violate no order and
invade no man's right by appointing and sending labourers into the
harvest.

4. I have accordingly appointed Dr. Coke and Mr. Francis Asbury
to be joint *Superintendents* over our brethren in North America: As
also Richard Whatcoat and Thomas Vasey to act as *Elders* among
them by baptizing and administering the Lord's Supper. . . .

6. It has indeed been proposed to desire the English Bishops to
ordain part of our preachers for America. But to this I object, 1. I
desired the Bishop of London to ordain only one, but could not
prevail. 2. If they consented, we know the slowness of their proceedings; but the matter admits of no delay. 3. If they would ordain them
now, they would likewise expect to govern them. And how grievously would this entangle us? 4. As our American brethren are now
totally disentangled both from the State and from the English Hierarchy, we dare not entangle them again either with the one or the
other. They are now at full liberty simply to follow the scriptures
and the primitive church. And we judge it best that they should stand
fast in that liberty wherewith God has so strangely made them free.[77]

There seems no doubt that Wesley deliberately conducted the ordinations in private, deliberately kept his brother Charles and others out

of the picture in preparing his revised Prayer Book, deliberately tried to restrict the letter of 10 September to his American preachers. Although Charles had been in Bristol at the time of the ordinations, and thus was physically available as a third episcopally ordained presbyter to lay his hands on Coke, his first intimation of what had happened came nearly two months later, after he had returned to his family in Marylebone. When the letter arrived from Henry Durbin, one of the Bristol 'Old Planners', Charles Wesley was 'thunderstruck', and by turns blamed Coke's machinations and his brother's senility.[78] On 4 November Durbin followed up with a further titbit, a copy of John Wesley's 'printed declaration of ordination', which he had obtained with great difficulty, especially as the printer had been enjoined to 'the utmost secrecy'. Three weeks later Durbin wrote:

> I think somebody should let your brother know that hundreds in Bristol know of the Apology and Ordination, and are much concerned at it: your trustees in London should know it before the news comes from America; it might do him good.[79]

In his reply on 29 November Charles wrote: 'Not one word did my cautious brother drop concerning the grand arcanum.'[80] Some of Charles Wesley's verses on the occasion were also circulating in Bristol, probably including the well-known opening quatrain of his 'Epigram':

> So easily are Bishops made
>   By man's, or woman's whim?
> Wesley his hands on Coke hath laid,
>   But who laid hands on him?[81]

Like Brer Rabbit, however, Charles lay low and said nothing, deliberately honouring his brother in public, but steadily accumulating evidence with which he might be able eventually to shock John into recantation and retreat. It was almost certainly at this time that he sought out his former schoolfellow William Murray, now the first Earl of Mansfield, and from 1756–88 Lord Chief Justice of the King's Bench—one of the greatest ever to occupy that responsible position. On 28 April 1785 Charles wrote to Dr. T. B. Chandler, the American clergyman with whom he had been in touch for some months: 'Lord Mansfield told me last year that *Ordination* was *Separation*!' The same letter spoke of another American clergyman whom he had met about the time of his consecration as the first Protestant Episcopal bishop on 14 November 1784—Dr. Samuel Seabury. Seabury had been in England on an exhausting quest for bishop's orders since July 1783, passed from prelate to prelate and back again until he was led to exclaim, 'Nobody here will risk anything for the sake of the Church, or for the sake of continuing episcopal ordination in America!' After twelve frustrating months he turned to Scotland, where his patience was at length rewarded.[82] When Charles Wesley informed Henry Durbin how the Scots Non-Juring bishops had consecrated Seabury, that fellow enemy of Coke gleefully expressed the hope that this would 'disconcert the Doctor's scheme'.[83]

While collecting many documents relating to Seabury's consecration, Charles Wesley secured the copy of a letter written by an American clergyman from New York on 29 November 1784, expressing alarm at Methodist developments there:

When shall we have a Bishop? The Methodists are at this moment forming a scheme to establish a Church of their own. Wesley has just sent over three preachers, one of them a man in Orders. They have brought a Liturgy with them for the use of their people; and they mean to ordain men to perform all the duties of ministers; not only to preach and pray, but to administer the Sacraments. . . . What is become of all their professions of steadfast attachment to the Church? Are these Episcopalians? Can Wesley really suppose that he has a right to send men into this country invested with powers of ordination? We shall oppose their pretensions, and the consequence will be division and animosity. Blessed with the presence of a bishop our difficulties would vanish in an instant. . . . Are the great men in England mad? Or are they besotted?[84]

John Wesley himself continued to wrestle with the American problem, in October writing a letter to Asbury which was for Coke also, trying to help them steer such a course in this delicate situation as would preserve Methodism from the enticements both of Episcopalians and Independents:

You are aware of the danger on either hand: and I scarce know which is the greater. One or the other so far as it takes place will overturn Methodism from the foundation: either our travelling preachers turning Independents and gathering congregations each for himself: or procuring ordination in a *regular* way, and accepting parochial cures. If you can find means of guarding against both evils the work of God will prosper more than ever.[85]

Charles Wesley supported the Episcopalians by a letter to Dr. Chandler on 28 April 1785:

What will become of those poor sheep in the wilderness, the American Methodists? How have they been *betrayed* into a separation from the Church of England. . . ! Had they had patience a little longer they would have seen a *real primitive bishop* in America, duly *consecrated* by *three* Scotch bishops who had their consecration from the English bishops. . . . There is therefore not the least difference betwixt the members of Bishop Seabury's Church and the members of the Church of England.

You know that I had the happiness to converse with that truly Apostolical Man, who is esteemed by all that know him as much as you and me. He told me he looked upon the Methodists in America as sound members of the Church; and was ready to ordain any of their preachers whom he should find duly qualified. His ordinations would be indeed genuine, valid, and episcopal.

But what are your poor Methodists now? Only a new sect of Presbyterians![86]

Seabury's reaction to Wesley's ordinations was what might be expected:

The plea of the Methodists is something like impudence. Mr. Wesley is only a Presbyter, and all his Ordinations Presbyterian, and in direct opposition to the Church of England: And they can have no pretense for calling themselves Churchmen till they return to the unity of the Church, which they have unreasonably, unnecessarily, and wickedly broken by their separation and schism.[87]

He did, however, keep his promise to Charles Wesley. In a letter of 31 January 1786, Dr. Chandler reported that Charles Wesley's lengthy letter to him had proved a valuable weapon in the Episcopalians' armoury, and added that Seabury had in fact ordained two Methodist preachers. One of them was Joseph Pilmoor (ordained November 1785), whose name had been omitted from Wesley's Deed Poll, and who remained an ally of Charles rather than of John, and kept him informed of the progress of the Protestant Episcopal Church in America.[88]

How much John Wesley knew of this is uncertain, for no letters between the two brothers are extant from May 1783 to April 1785.[89] The scanty evidence suggests, however, that in this matter at any rate John simply went on his way regardless of Charles, and that the question of the ordinations was hardly ever raised between them because each knew the mind of the other, and knew also that it was fixed almost beyond the possibility of change.

John Wesley had other critics, both because of the unorthodoxy of his ordinations and because of his choice of ordinands. Against both charges he defended himself in a letter of 25 March 1785 written to a preacher of twenty years' standing, Barnabas Thomas. This contained an important statement of his principles:

> I am now as firmly attached to the Church of England as I ever was since you knew me. But meantime I know myself to be as real a Christian bishop as the archbishop of Canterbury. Yet I was always resolved, and am so still, never to act as such except in case of necessity. Such a case does not (perhaps never will) exist in England. This I made known to the bishop of London, and desired his help. But he peremptorily refused it. All the other bishops were of the same mind; the rather because (they said) they had nothing to do with America. Then I saw my way clear, and was fully convinced what it was my duty to do.
>
> As to the persons amongst those who offered themselves, I chose those whom I judged most worthy, and I positively refuse to be judged herein by any man's conscience but my own.[90]

The ordinations for America in 1784 were followed up in 1785 by the ordination of three preachers to serve in Presbyterian Scotland, where the folk did not take kindly either to lay preachers or the itinerant system. Wesley's *Journal* recorded:

> Having, with a few select friends [of whom his brother Charles was not one] weighed the matter thoroughly, I yielded to their judgment, and set apart three of our well-tried preachers, John Pawson, Thomas Hanby, and Joseph Taylor, to minister in Scotland; and I trust God will bless their ministrations, and show that He has sent them.

The public statement used 'set apart', Wesley's diary 'ordained'.[91]

Charles was in Bristol when these private ordinations took place in London as the Conference was nearing its close. Apparently he did not hear of the event for a week or two. On 14 August he wrote sadly to John:

> Dear Brother,
>
> I have been reading over again and again your *Reasons against a Separation*, . . . and entreat you in the name of God, and for Christ's sake, to read them again yourself, with previous prayer; and stop, and proceed no farther, till you receive an answer to your inquiry, 'Lord, what wouldest *thou* have me to do?' . . .
>
> But when once you began ordaining in America, I knew (and you knew), that your preachers here would never rest till you ordained them. You told me 'they would separate by and by'. The Doctor tells us the same. His 'Methodist Episcopal Church' at Baltimore was

intended to beget a 'Methodist Episcopal Church' here. You know he comes, armed with your authority, to make us all Dissenters. One of your sons assured me that not a preacher in London would refuse Orders from the Doctor. It is evident that all seek their own, and prefer their own interest to your honour, which not one of them scruples to sacrifice to his own ambition. . . .

Before you have quite broken down the bridge, *stop, and consider*! If your sons have no regard for you, have some regard for yourself. *Go to your grave in peace*; at least suffer me to go first, before this ruin is under your hand. . . . Do not push me in or embitter my last moments. Let us not leave an indelible blot on our memory, but let us leave behind us the name and character of *honest men*.

This letter is a debt to our parents, and to our brother, as well as to you, and to

Your faithful friend,
Charles Wesley.[92]

John Wesley's defence against this challenge he published in the *Arminian Magazine* for January 1786, though he did not divulge the recipient's name:

Some obedience I always paid to the bishops in obedience to the laws of the land. But I cannot see that I am under any obligation to obey them farther than those laws require.

It is in obedience to those laws that I have never exercised in England the power which I believe God has given me. I firmly believe I am a scriptural Επίσκοπος as much as any man in England or in Europe. (For the 'uninterrupted succession' I know to be a fable which no man ever did or can prove.) But this does in no wise interfere with my remaining in the Church of England: for which I have no more desire to separate than I had fifty years ago. . . .[93]

Charles answered on 8 September, agreeing with most of John's points, and laying the main burden of his wrath on Coke:

That you are a scriptural Επίσκοπος or Overseer I do not dispute. And so is every minister who has the cure of souls. Neither *need we* dispute whether the uninterrupted succession be fabulous, as you believe, or real, as I believe: or whether Lord King be right or wrong. . . . If I *could* prove your actual Separation I would not, neither wish to see it proved by any other. But do you not allow that the Doctor has separated? Do you not know and approve his avowed design and resolution to get all the Methodists of the three kingdoms into a distinct, compact body, a new Episcopal Church of his own?[94]

John's reply was in effect to end any further discussion at this point: 'I see no use of you and me disputing together, for neither of us is likely to convince the other. You say I separate from the Church: I say I do not. There let it stand.'[95]

On 30 August he had written a 'narrative' entitled 'Of Separation from the Church', which he published in the *Minutes* of the following Conference. Describing how ever since his own return from America half a century earlier he had progressively been led to 'vary' from the Church of England—variations interpreted by many critics as separation—he dealt more particularly with his ordinations for 'that vast tract of land a thousand miles long and some hundreds broad':

> Those who had been members of the Church had none either to administer the Lord's Supper or to baptize their children. They applied to England over and over, but it was to no purpose. Judging this to be a case of real necessity I took a step which for peace and quietness I had refrained from taking for many years: I exercised that power which I am fully persuaded the Great Shepherd and Bishop of the church has given me. I appointed three of our labourers to go and help them, by not only preaching the word of God, but likewise administering the Lord's Supper and baptizing their children.

In a postcript he continued:

> After Dr. Coke's return from America many of our friends begged I would consider the case of Scotland, where we had been labouring so many years and had seen so little fruit of our labours. Multitudes indeed have set out well, but they were soon turned out of the way, chiefly by their Ministers either disputing against the truth or refusing to admit them to the Lord's Supper, yea, or to baptize their children, unless they would promise to have no fellowship with the Methodists. . . . To prevent this I at length consented to take the same step with regard to Scotland which I had done with regard to America. But this is not a separation from the Church at all. Not from the Church of Scotland, for we were never connected therewith, any further than we are now: not from the Church of England, for this is not concerned in the steps which are taken in Scotland. Whatever then is done either in America or Scotland is no separation from the Church of England. I have no thought of this: I have many objections against it. It is a totally different case.[96]

This apologia implies even John Wesley's acceptance of the position that any ordination by him for the English ministry would indeed constitute separation, as does a euphemistic statement of 1786:

The alteration which has been made in America and Scotland has nothing to do with our kingdom. I believe I shall not separate from the Church of England till my soul separates from my body.[97]

Although later Wesley felt that in ordaining for Scotland he had perhaps been 'overpersuaded' he remained unrepentant.[98] When the Scots ordinations came to the attention of the London trustees he insisted that 'he never intended to ordain but for America and Scotland, and that the preachers were under the strictest promise to use none of their power in England, but to confine it to those two places'.[99] He continued to ordain—four more men for Scotland in 1786, as well as one each for service in Newfoundland, Nova Scotia, and Antigua. A strong plea that he should also ordain a preacher for 'a desolate place in Yorkshire' was debated in open Conference, and defeated after John Atlay (of all people) had taken Charles Wesley's side in proving that ordination, for England at least, was separation.[100] In 1787 he reluctantly ordained two more for Scotland, two more for Canada and the West Indies.[101]

Meantime some of Wesley's friends were trying to extricate him from the dilemma. James Creighton sought Charles Wesley's co-operation in an approach to Lord Mansfield for advice and help, with the hope that he in turn might persuade 'the higher powers' of the wisdom of accommodating Methodism within the Established Church by official enhancing of its ecclesiastical status. Creighton sent a copy of a specific scheme to bring this about, believing that there was more hope of success if it were first discussed in private rather than published as an open challenge, when as a centre of controversy its usefulness would be diminished if not ruined. The plan was incorporated in 'An Address to the Most Revd. and the Right Revd. the Archbishops and Bishops of the Church of England: upon the subject of Methodism, humbly proposing to their Lordships a Plan for preserving the people called Methodists in the Church of England'. It was signed at the end 'Episcopius', and one suspects that this was a pseudonym for none other than Dr. Thomas Coke.

After rehearsing the story of Methodism, and stressing the danger that this numerous and influential body might severely damage the Church by withdrawing after Wesley's death, the writer continued:

Supposing your Lordships should consider the Methodist Preachers as they really are, a kind of extraordinary missionaries, called to build up the church on every side by adding thousands yearly to her communion. . . . I submit to your Lordships' judgment whether it

19

might not be expedient to ordain *some* of these preachers (such as the Messrs. Wesley would recommend) for the purpose of administering the sacraments occasionally to their own societies, and that without any prejudice to the regular clergy; and allowing them in matters respecting their societies to be governed by their own rules. Thus by considering them as younger sons of the Church their labours would be secured to her interest. . . .

As a means to this end episcopacy might be introduced into the Methodist system, Wesley himself being consecrated the first bishop:

As to the mode of ordination, I submit it to the consideration of your Lordships whether it would not be best to invest Mr. Wesley with episcopal power for that purpose whilst he lives, and after his death three or four of the preachers such as he might recommend to superintend the work in Great Britain, Ireland, and the West Indies. In such case these Superintendents might lay before your Lordships from time to time such account of the missions as ye might desire, receive your counsel, and redress grievances when complained of by the regular clergy.

The closing paragraph once more emphasized the almost certain consequences unless some such desperate expedient were attempted:

If something of this kind is not done the Methodists, even though they should retain the rites and ceremonies of our Church, will unavoidably become a separate people—as appears from the mode of ordination already adopted by them for Scotland. As they were driven to that by mere necessity they would, no doubt, relinquish such a plan and adopt a more honourable if proposed to them.[102]

The remedy proved unacceptable, and the breach grew wider. 1788 proved another climactic year. Not only did Wesley ordain three more preachers for Scotland and five for overseas, but one at last for England.

That Wesley did indeed take the drastic schismatic step of ordaining Alexander Mather is quite certain. The details, however, remain tantalizingly obscure, and no Letters of Orders for him have survived. After ordaining six preachers as deacons on Sunday 3 August 1788, and as 'presbyters' on the following Tuesday, on Wednesday the 6th he recorded, 'ordained M[athe]r', and the following day, 'ordained A. M[ather]!'[103] It seems clear that Mather was ordained twice only, yet almost equally clear that Wesley intended him to be a 'Superintendent' like Coke, and to serve as such in England.

Leading preachers spoke of Mather as Wesley's right-hand man, a principal member of his inner cabinet, 'a truly apostolical man' to be compared only with Whitefield and Wesley, who at the last Conference before Wesley's death 'conducted the whole business' while Wesley remained technically (and literally) in the chair.[104] Writing in 1792, Samuel Bradburn stated specifically: 'At the Conference [of] 1788 Mr. Wesley consecrated Mr. M. a Bishop, in the manner he had done Dr. Coke.'[105] Mather himself announced at the 1791 Conference that Wesley had in fact ordained him bishop with the intention that he should ordain others.[106] Other preachers made similar statements.[107] It may be, of course, that all this evidence stems from Mather's own statement in 1791, and that none had personal knowledge of the facts. Those who probably did, Thomas Coke, James Creighton, and Peard Dickinson, do not seem to have recorded the event for a curious posterity.[108] Even though the varied evidence does not *prove* the fact of Wesley's intentions, however, it speaks strongly for Mather's credibility.

The problem remains: Why only two ordinations instead of three as in the case of Asbury? A possible earlier commissioning of Mather as a preacher would not be regarded as conferring deacon's orders, no more than it was in the case of Joseph Cownley.[109] Did Wesley omit deacon's orders, or presbyter's ('per saltum'), or superintendent's?[110] Did he simply add to Mather's ordination as elder a brief ceremony conveying authority as superintendent, or a spoken charge to the effect that as the first presbyter ordained for England he was intended to serve as 'overseer' or 'superintendent' upon Wesley's death, though not before? Perhaps we shall never know. The point is quite clear, however, that Wesley had taken steps to set up an ordained ministry for English Methodism after his death.

This step was confirmed the following year by his ordination of two more preachers who were never to leave the country. One (like Mather) was a senior preacher, Thomas Rankin, now permitted to reside in London as a supernumerary because of his wife's business and health, though he preached as frequently as ever, and attended all the Conferences.[111] This may have been partly a reward for services rendered, especially in America, but Wesley was a pragmatist, and it was therefore much more likely that he intended Rankin to aid Mather in securing stability and continuity after his death. With Rankin was associated young Henry Moore, whom Coke had tried to entice away from Wesley in order that he might become a third 'superintendent' for American Methodism.[112] It was to these two, together with his curates Creighton and Dickinson, that Wesley turned for advice in ecclesiastical problems during his later years, Mather being stationed in Yorkshire, and therefore not readily available.[113]

No preachers were ordained by the tired Wesley in 1790, though in Wesley's presence Coke publicly laid his hands on a number of men who were thus solemnly received into full connexion.[114] Altogether Wesley had ordained twenty-seven of his preachers to the order of presbyter, and had commissioned one of them to be a superintendent along with Coke.[115] Through all this, however, he continued to insist that he would remain a loyal member and minister of the Church of England till his death. Samuel Bradburn testified a year after his death: 'I am certain he never repented of the steps he had taken. . . . But he did not consider all this as making him a Dissenter.'[116] James Creighton disagreed, and it must be acknowledged that his testimony is probably of greater value in this than that of Bradburn:

> I must take the liberty positively to contradict you. He *did* repent of it [ordination], and with tears expressed his sorrow both in public and private. . . . He likewise expressed his sorrow respecting this matter at the Leeds Conference in 1789, and occasionally afterwards in London, until his death. About six weeks before that event he said to a respectable person near London, 'They (the preachers) are now too powerful for me'.[117]

There are problems here. Why should Wesley publicly express regret at the 1789 Conference, yet within a few days ordain Rankin and Moore? Perhaps at the time or upon recollection Creighton saw things differently from what Wesley had intended. Probably he later interpreted Wesley's regrets for his Scots ordinations (on Creighton's evidence, publicly expressed at the 1789 Conference) as regrets about his ordinations in general.[118] Perhaps Creighton himself has been misrepresented—for we do not have this particular piece of his testimony at first hand. By 1789 Wesley was certainly a frail old man subject to lapses of memory and bouts of trembling weakness. It seems fairly certain that at least in some of those weaker moments he confessed to some regrets in connection with his ordinations, though he knew that what had been done could not be undone, and was therefore prepared to carry full responsibility for the unorthodox behaviour into which his peculiar brand of churchmanship had led him.[119]

SIXTEEN

FROM SOCIETY TO CHURCH

MOST impartial observers would agree that long before 1784 John Wesley had effectively separated from the Church of England by founding a closely-knit 'connexion' of preachers and societies administering vast properties subject to no Anglican oversight except that of one priest with no official cure of souls and sitting very loose to episcopal authority. In 1784 he had legally incorporated this connexion to ensure its continuance under similar non-parochial, non-diocesan control, namely that of his itinerant lay preachers, some of whom he had taken it upon himself to ordain. He had also provided for the use of many of his followers an unauthorized abridgement of the *Book of Common Prayer*. All these things—and more—witnessed to a rift between Wesley and the Established Church. Yet he continued unflinchingly to proclaim his affection for it, his loyalty to it. He went on as if there had been no major departure from his previous settled policy of remaining true both to the church and to the guidance of the Holy Spirit.

He was the more easily able to do this because of his own definitions both of the church and of separation. Both words occupied his thoughts even more frequently after 1784 than before, and he felt it necessary to prepare two sermon-treatises[1] to explain his position. Both appeared in the *Arminian Magazine* for 1786 and were reprinted in 1788 in volume six of his *Sermons on Several Occasions*, where they appeared as companion pieces, though there was an interval of six months between the writing of one and the other. Easily the more important was that on Ephesians 4:1–16, which first appeared without title and in the collected *Sermons* was entitled 'Of the Church'. The general effect of this sermon-treatise was to insist that the true church was not an organized religious institution but any group of Christians who lived spiritually, whether or not they were acknowledged by an institution. In other words, his definition was such as to imply that the Society of the People called Methodists was not only a genuine spiritual part of the Church of England, but possibly the only true church in the land.

Being Wesley he turned to the Bible for his data, and insisted that he was not to be confined within narrow sectarian limits. By the church he meant 'the catholic or universal church: that is, all the Christians under heaven'. The term which best expressed this for him was 'the Church of God', as used by Paul in Acts 20:28. This phrase was used during the imposition of hands in the ordination of all three orders of the ministry, which in his *Sunday Service* Wesley faithfully copied from the *Book of Common Prayer*. Both he as a priest and his preachers as elders had been ordained to serve 'the Church of God' rather than the Church of England. Having shown that 'the Church of God' included all holy persons wherever and in whatever numbers they assembled Wesley came to his text:

> Here, then, is a clear unexceptionable answer to the question, 'What is the Church?' The Catholic or Universal Church is 'all the persons in the universe whom God hath so called out of the world . . . as to be "one body", united by "one Spirit", having "one faith, one hope, one baptism; one God and Father of all, who is above all, and through all, and in them all." '

Some parts of the Church of God were organized in national churches like the Church of England or the Church of Scotland. Other smaller units were organized in cities like those listed in Revelation. The New Testament also recognized much smaller groups: 'Two or three Christians believers united together are a church in the narrowest sense of the word. Such was the church in the house of Philemon, and that in the house of Nymphas, mentioned in Col. 4:15.' True churchhood was not a matter of numbers but of spiritual quality:

> A particular church may therefore consist of any number of members, whether two or three or two or three millions. But still, whether they be larger or smaller, the same idea is to be preserved. They are one body, and have one Spirit, one Lord, one hope, one faith, one baptism, one God and Father of all.

Wesley went on to show that this definition of the church was good Anglican doctrine:

> This account is exactly agreeable to the nineteenth Article of our Church, the Church of England (only the Article includes a little more than the apostle has expressed):
> 'Of the Church.
>   The visible Church of Christ is a congregation of faithful men, in which the pure word of God is preached, and the sacraments be duly administered.'
>   It may be observed that at the same time our Thirty-Nine Articles

were compiled and published a Latin translation of them was published by the same authority. In this the words were *coetus credentium*, 'a congregation of believers', plainly showing that by 'faithful men' the compilers meant men endued with *living faith*. This brings the Article to a still nearer agreement to the account given by the Apostle.

In view of this many of those who considered themselves loyal sons of the Church of England were in fact not so:

> According to this definition those congregations in which the pure word of God (a strong expression!) is not preached are no parts either of the Church of England or the Church catholic: as neither are those in which the sacraments are not duly administered.

The same was true of individuals:

> If the Church, as to the very essence of it, is a body of believers, no man that is not a Christian believer can be a member of it. . . . It follows that not only no common swearer, no Sabbath breaker, no drunkard, no whoremonger, no thief, no liar, none that lives in any outward sin, but none that is under the power of anger or pride, no lover of the world, in a word none that is dead to God, can be a member of His church.

Wesley closed with an appeal to his own Methodist followers, whom he clearly considered the Christian remnant, the true Church of England and undoubtedly a part of the Church of God: 'Let all those who are real members of the Church see that they walk holy and unblameable in all things.'[2]

It is noteworthy that during the following years the phrase 'Church of God' frequently occurred in Wesley's writings in the context of the Methodist societies. It was clearly a non-sectarian term. Rather it seemed to imply an extension of his calling from that of bringing new life to the Church of England by spreading scriptural holiness through the land to that of being a spiritual witness of the Church Universal. Thus the Methodist Societies (occasionally the title 'the Methodist Church' creeps in) constituted a rallying point rather than a rival for the spiritually-minded members of the Church of England, and were equally ambassadors of the Church of God throughout the world. In 1789 Wesley referred to 'any of the Churches of God that are under my care', and in 1790 wrote to Richard Whatcoat in the United States: 'There seems to be a general expectation of great things in the Church of God throughout our Connexion in these kingdoms.'[3]

With the church thus defined, Wesley was able to turn to another misused term. Writing from I Corinthians 12:25, 'On Schism', he opened: 'If there be any word in the English tongue as ambiguous and indeterminate in its meaning as the word "Church" it is one that is nearly allied to it—the word "Schism".' Once more he turned to scripture to correct common errors:

> The whole body of Roman Catholics define schism 'a separation from the Church of Rome'; and almost all our own writers define it 'a separation from the Church of England'. Thus both the one and the other set out wrong, and stumble at the very threshold. This will easily appear to any that calmly consider the several texts wherein the word 'schism' occurs, from the whole tenor of which it is manifest that it is not a separation *from* any church (whether general or particular, whether the Catholic or any national church), but a separation *in* a church.[4]

Nevertheless, even such a separation should carefully be avoided as 'a grievous breach of the law of love'. Sometimes, however, it was necessary to undertake it boldly at the call of conscience. A member of the Church of Rome might blamelessly separate rather than commit idolatry, or a member of the Church of England might find it impossible to remain within that church without 'doing something which the word of God forbids, or omitting something which the word of God positively commands'. Wesley then turned to the specific situation of the Methodists:

> I will make the case my own: I am now, and have been from my youth, a member and a minister of the Church of England: and I have no desire to separate from it till my soul separates from my body. Yet if I was not permitted to remain therein without omitting what God requires me to do it would then become meet and right, and my bounden duty, to separate from it without delay. . . .

He then became 'more particular':

> I know God has committed to me a dispensation of the gospel. . . . If then I could not remain in the church . . . without desisting from preaching the gospel I should be under a necessity of separating from it, or losing my own soul. In like manner, if I could not continue united to any smaller society, church, or body of Christians without committing sin, without lying and hypocrisy, without preaching to others doctrines which I did not myself believe, I should be under an absolute necessity of separating from that society.

Whatever blame might be attached to such 'schism' lay squarely at the door of those who imposed unscriptural conditions:

> In all these cases the sin of separation, with all the evils consequent upon it, would not lie upon me, but upon those who constrained me to make that separation by requiring of me such terms of communion as I could not in conscience comply with.

Nevertheless, loyalty to one's spiritual family was so important that it was also a sin to separate lightly, like the people who 'leave a Christian society with as much unconcern as they go out of one room into another'. They knew no better; but he (and now the Methodists) did:

> Suppose the church or society to which I am now united does not require me to do anything which the Scripture forbids, or to omit anything which the Scripture enjoins, it is then my indispensable duty to continue therein. And if I separate from it without any such necessity I am justly chargeable (whether I foresaw them or no) with all the evils consequent upon that separation.[5]

The sermon left untouched a problem of casuistry to which Wesley addressed himself elsewhere: 'What is specifically involved in the act of separation?' His answer was that it implied separating oneself physically from the church by not attending her worship.[6] Although many theologians and ecclesiastics might view other things as constituting separation, and though the highest contemporary legal expert might pronounce that ordination by a presbyter entailed separation from an episcopal church, there was much point in what Samuel Bradburn maintained, that in the common law of England (apart from the rare cases of excommunication) only absence from public worship cut a person off from membership in the national church. Bradburn was one of the more radical of Wesley's preachers, eager for the recognition of the Methodist societies as an independent church, and in his private annotations on Wesley's *Journal* he sometimes scoffed at the old gentleman's credulous conservatism. A pamphlet which he wrote in the year following Wesley's death throws much light on Wesley's churchmanship, and is far from deserving of the oblivion into which it has fallen. He entitled it, *The Question, Are the Methodists Dissenters? fairly examined.*

In Bradburn's view the Methodists became Dissenters when they began to allow services to be held at the same time as public worship in the local parish churches. In effect they thus said to their people: 'Choose where you will go, for you cannot worship at both Church and Methodist preaching-house.'[7] They had thus destroyed the double loyalty which Wesley himself had maintained and had made available to his followers—had, indeed, constantly urged upon them. Wesley had said that they could be both Methodists *and* Churchmen; now they must be either Methodists *or* Churchmen. The nub of the challenge was neither acceptance of any doctrinal formulary nor observance of sacramental rites in a special way at a special time by a special person, no more than it was obedience to ecclesiastical authority—it was assembling for public worship in the parish church. Wesley's definition of the church was pared down to the core of Article XIX—'a company of faithful or believing people'.[8] Separation from a church therefore meant separating oneself from their worship. Any 'variation' of customary church order could be permitted without entailing separation, but regular absence from Anglican worship in order to attend the worship of some other Christian body clearly constituted separation from the Church of England.

This was in fact how Wesley himself had viewed the matter in 1755, when he spoke thus about 'frequenting any Dissenting meeting':

> Now this is actually separating from the Church. If therefore it is (at least) not expedient to separate, neither is this expedient. Indeed we may attend our assemblies and the church too, because they are at different hours. But we cannot attend both the meeting and the church, because they are at the same hours.[9]

This was the burden of the charges made by a writer in *Lloyd's Evening Post* in December 1760. They were apparently addressed to Charles Wesley, because he had recently published his brother's *Reasons against a Separation* as a distinct pamphlet:

> 1. Are you not a sworn member and minister of the Church of England?
> 2. Are you not bound, as such, to discountenance and prevent . . . every schism and division in the Church, or separation from it?
> 3. Do not you countenance and support this by administering the sacrament at Kingswood, near Bristol, and other places in London, not licensed by the bishop, in time of divine service at the parish churches?
> 4. Is not the attending such meetings at such time an actual separation from the Church of England, according to the doctrine laid down in a small tract lately published by you? . . .
> 9. Is not your late incapacity to preach, and the distractions among you, a judicial stroke for your gross disingenuity and sin against God?[10]

To those who at the 1766 Conference objected ,'Our own service is public worship', Wesley replied:

Yes, *in a sense*: but not such as supersedes the church service. . . . It pre-supposes public prayer. . . . The hour for it on that day (Sunday), unless where there is some peculiar reason for a variation, should be five in the morning, as well as five in the evening. Why should we make God's day the shortest of the seven?

But if the people put ours in the place of the church service, we hurt them that stay with us, and ruin them that leave us. For then they will go nowhere, but lounge the Sabbath away without any public worship at all. I advise, therefore, all the Methodists in England and Ireland who have been brought up in the Church constantly to attend the service of the Church, at least every Lord's Day.[11]

This whole section was written into the 1770 and 1772 Large Minutes, together with a section insisting that the preachers should set the people a good example by so arranging their services that they themselves could attend the parish church on at least two Sundays out of four.[12] By 1780 the situation had so altered that this regulation was dropped from the *Minutes*, and other abridgements made. The reference to the early morning service was omitted, because by that time in most places this had become a quaint relic or a nostalgic memory; so also was the statement that Methodist worship did not normally include Holy Communion. Lest these relaxations might be interpreted too liberally, however, a section was added disavowing any thought of separating from the church.[13]

Attendance at Anglican worship, even though only occasional, remained Wesley's test of whether or not Methodism had separated from the Church of England. Samuel Bradburn pointed out, however, that Wesley had himself created a dangerous precedent when he agreed to allow services during 'church hours' in London:

He changed the *time* of service in the Foundry from being early in the morning only, on Sundays as well as other days, to Church Hours on Sundays in the forenoon. And notwithstanding the insignificance of this change, it was the real source of every alteration that followed. For, as Mr. Wesley could not always be in London, and at that time his brother also travelled, he hired clergymen to supply his place when absent. They had the full, regular service of the Church, and the Lord's Supper, every Sunday; and being performed by episcopal[ly] ordained ministers the generality of the people did not consider it as dissenting from the Church, though they had no more to do with the Church, as to real connection or subordination, than with the Jews. This practice has continued in London ever since.[14]

Eventually the privileges of sacramental worship and services in church hours were extended to a handful of other cities where special circumstances could similarly be pleaded. This demand gained momentum during the early 1780s. In this matter Wesley seems to have allowed a good deal of local option, though he recorded his own gratification when Methodists suffered no obstacle in the way of frequent attendance at their parish church. To his Assistant at Birstall he wrote in March 1782: 'You have done well in changing the hours of preaching at Morley. I would encourage all persons to go to church as much as they possibly can.'[15] At the Leeds Conference in 1781 strong opposition against growing Methodist freedom in such matters was voiced by a prominent physician, William Hey, whom Wesley allowed to address the preachers. When their resentment made itself audible Wesley interposed, asking Hey to 'defer reading the remainder of his paper to another time'.[16]

At this same 1781 Leeds Conference Wesley aired a letter he had received from some Yorkshire Methodists, who had asked whether in fact he would insist on their attending the parish church if only Calvinist sermons were preached there. After a lengthy debate the preachers passed a unanimous resolution:

> 1. That it was highly expedient all the Methodists (so called) who had been bred therein should attend the service of the Church as often as possible, but that, secondly, if the Minister began either to preach the absolute decrees, or to rail at and ridicule Christian perfection, they should quietly and silently go out of the church: yet attend it again the next opportunity.

Wesley's correspondents had requested that he should publish his reply in the *Arminian Magazine*. This he did, confessing that the letter had caused him to review his ideas, and closing:

> It is a delicate as well as important point, on which I hardly know how to answer. I cannot lay down any general rule. All I can say at present is, 'If it does not hurt you, hear them; if it does, refrain. Be determined by your own conscience.'

In the magazine for February 1782 this reply was entitled 'Some Thoughts upon an Important Question'. He followed it in March with an article under the title 'On hearing Ministers who oppose the Truth', in which he printed the Conference resolution and signified his own approval. In the issue for July, under the heading 'Of attending the Church', Wesley answered queries put by another reader who was disturbed by his liberal position. He made it clear that he still advised Methodists to attend church services, though not necessarily those at their own parish church, and that although they were 'at liberty to absent themselves' they were not at liberty to censure the clergy whose ministrations they thus forsook.[17]

Doubtless this public airing of an under-current of dissatisfaction increased the desire of Methodists in general to enjoy full public worship in their own preaching-houses, whether or not the local clergyman was obnoxious to them. Nor did Wesley's sitting on the fence and merely offering advice—so different from the directness of his early rules—serve to discourage them. This published correspondence, indeed, caused Samuel Bradburn to date from 1782 'a manifest relaxation in some things relating to the Church upon which great stress had been laid'.[18]

This readiness on the part of Wesley to give his members and preachers a fairly free hand in organizing their times of worship rested partly on his conviction that the work of God in Methodism was not merely increasing steadily, but that a new revival was in progress, especially in the rapidly growing areas most affected by the Industrial Revolution. This came out frequently in his letters during the early 1780s. One example may be given:

> Whom does [God] now own like them [the Methodists] in Yorkshire, in Cheshire, in Lancashire, in Cornwall? Truly these are the tokens of our mission, the proof that God hath sent us. Three score thousand persons setting their faces heavenward, and many of them rejoicing in God their Saviour.[19]

No union restrictions must be put on labourers in these fruitful fields. To John Baxendale, in Wigan, he wrote: 'You do well to lose no opportunity of enlarging your borders. It is an acceptable time. We are now more especially called to preach the gospel to every creature; and many of the last shall be first.'[20] Against this reviving work, however, Calvinism was seen as the arch-enemy—a fact which influenced Wesley's permissiveness about services in church hours, especially in Scotland.[21]

A study of Wesley's own attendance at public worship, as revealed by his diary, is illuminating. The Sunday services which he shared or attended in parish churches throughout the country during 1783 usually began at 10.0 or 10.15, but varied up to 11.0 a.m. The main services at the London Foundery and the Bristol New Room began at 9.30, and

(with communion) went on until noon, quite prohibiting morning
attendance at the parish church. At most other places Methodist preaching services began at 8.0 or 8.30 on Sunday mornings, thus leaving the
members free to attend their parish churches also. In a few cities, however, Wesley himself attended Methodist services in church hours.
This was the case at King Street, Bath, and Oldham Street, Manchester,
both 'proprietary chapels' founded and to some extent governed by
wealthy shareholders.[22] Oldham Street, Manchester, was rapidly
becoming a 'Church-Methodist' centre similar to the New Room at
Bristol, and for a time had its own resident clergyman.[23]

Along with service in church hours went an attempt wherever possible to secure the administration of the Lord's Supper to Methodist
congregations, at least occasionally, as well as the reading of the Order
for Morning Prayer from the *Book of Common Prayer*. When Wesley
opened the new King Street Chapel in Bath on Thursday 11 March
1779 he read prayers, preached, and administered communion, and this
remained the normal Sunday pattern also when he visited Bath on
subsequent occasions.[24] He followed a similar pattern in opening Oldham Street Chapel, Manchester, on Sunday 1 April 1781:

> I began reading prayers at ten o'clock. Our country friends flocked
> in from all sides. At the communion was such a sight as I am per-
> suaded was never seen at Manchester before: eleven or twelve
> hundred communicants at once, and all of them fearing God.[25]

There was no communion service when he and Dr. Coke opened
Hockley Chapel at Nottingham on Friday 4 April 1783, but the following Sunday morning was the occasion of prayers, sermon, and communion, beginning at 10.0 a.m.[26]

Although Wesley was thus giving freedom with one hand, he took
it away with the other. He insisted that all these were special concessions, and he would not condone any deliberate general loosening of
Methodist ties with the Church. In public and private utterances he
continued to emphasize that deserting the Church meant forsaking
Methodism, if for no other reason than that he would no longer
acknowledge seceders as his followers. To his preacher Joseph Taylor
he wrote in January 1783:

> In my *Journals*, in the *Magazine*, in every possible way, I have advised
> the Methodists to keep to the Church. They that do this most prosper
> best in their souls; I have observed it long. If ever the Methodists in
> general were to leave the Church, I must leave them.[27]

The breaking away of his connexion as a whole which he thus envisaged was an almost impossible contingency, which by means of the Deed Poll and zealous propaganda for the model deed he had tried to forestall. The secession of local groups of trustees, however, was an ever-present possibility, as was seen at Birstall in 1783 and later at Dewsbury. Even though not laying claim to Methodist premises, a large dissenting group might split a flourishing cause.

Wesley tried to tighten the reins lest his steed run away with him. One example was a letter of 4 March 1784, designed to curb local preachers in Manchester who sought higher status for themselves as well as greater independence for their congregations:

> I desire Mr. Murlin, if any of our lay preachers [i.e. in this instance apparently the local as opposed to the itinerant lay preachers] talk either in public or private against the Church or the clergy, or read the Church Prayers, or baptize children, to require a promise from them to do it no more. If they will not promise, let them preach no more. And if they break their promise, let them be expelled the society.[28]

Three weeks later he wrote to Zechariah Yewdall in Liverpool (where also a new chapel was being built): 'You must mend or end that local preacher. Make an example of him for the good of all.'[29]

New preaching-houses were proliferating rapidly, frequently with insufficient financial support. The 1783 Conference agreed that 'the needless multiplying of preaching-houses [had] been a great evil', and resolved not only to offer no grants and to prohibit trustees from begging money outside their own circuit, but even to refuse building permission for any not yet begun. After a year's enforced inactivity a flood of applications swamped the Conference—25 in 1785, 17 in 1786, 22 in 1787, 21 in 1788.[30] Clearly these were conditions of mushrooming progress in which it would be extremely difficult to secure acceptance of conservative standards of churchly behaviour.

The whole problem of permitting services during the normal hours of worship in the Established Church, and thus in effect declaring Methodism itself a church rather than a society, came to a head at the Conference of 1786. It was in fact linked with a demand for a formal separation. On 16 April 1786 John Wesley began to soften up his brother Charles for yet another battle over this question:

> Eight or ten preachers, it is probable (but I have not met with one yet), will say something about leaving the Church before the Conference ends. It is not unlikely many will be driven out of it where there are Calvinist ministers. The last time I was at

Scarborough I earnestly exhorted our people to go to church; and I went myself. But the wretched minister preached such a sermon that I could not in conscience advise them to hear him any more.[31]

Charles agreed to come and lend his assistance at the Conference, and John eagerly grasped at a concession in his letter:

As you observe, one may leave *a* church (which I could advise in some cases) without leaving *the* Church. Here we may remain in spite of all wicked or Calvinistical ministers.[32]

At the Conference Charles was happy that what seemed the major question of further ordinations, for England this time, was quashed, and reported to his wife Sally, 'I am in high favour with the preachers'. This may well have been because on the matter of service in church hours, if not on ordination, he was ready to give ground. Nevertheless, the one contribution which he made throughout the debates on the subject was when Coke was pleading for services during church hours at least in the large towns; Charles cried out 'No!' and subsided once more into silence.[33] A few days before the Conference, John Wesley had summoned his cabinet to meet with him and Coke. The following resolutions were drawn up, debated in the full Conference, and inserted in the published *Minutes*:

Bristol, July 22, 1786.

Perhaps there is one part of what I wrote some time since which requires a little further explanation. In what cases do we allow of service in Church Hours? I answer:

1. When the Minister is a notoriously wicked man.

2. When he preaches Arian or any equally pernicious doctrine.

3. When there are not churches in the town sufficient to contain half the people: And

4. When there is no church at all within two or three miles.

And we advise every one who preaches in the Church Hours to read the Psalms and Lessons with part of the Church Prayers: Because we apprehend this will endear the Church Service to our brethren, who probably would be prejudiced against it if they heard none but extemporary prayer.[34]

In October 1787 Wesley prepared a sermon on this very theme, from I Samuel 2:17, later published in the *Arminian Magazine*.[35] His main purpose was to show that although 'many, if not most' clergymen were not 'eminent either for knowledge or piety', this was not a sufficient reason for forsaking their ministry. This anti-clerical prejudice had been imported into his societies, he believed, by the many ex-Dissenters who had been welcomed into membership. He demolished the argument 'that wicked ministers do no good, that the ordinances administered by them do not convey saving grace to those that attend them', and summarized his case:

> The reason is plain, because the efficacy is derived, not from him that administers but from Him that ordains it. He does not, will not suffer His grace to be intercepted, though the messenger will not receive it himself. . . . We know by our own happy experience, and by the experience of thousands, that the word of the Lord is not bound, though uttered by an unholy minister, and the sacraments are not dry breasts, whether he that administers be holy or unholy.[36]

Although the 1786 regulations seemed to open the door for many societies in the country as well as in the cities to become almost independent of their parish churches, Wesley was not prepared to let liberty deteriorate into free licence. He told Henry Moore that he had 'made just allowance enough for leaving the church'.[37] Speedily he made an example of one of the oldest London societies, determined to stamp out the possible abuses of this permissive ruling before they multiplied beyond control. The large preaching-house built by the soldier-preacher Sampson Staniforth for the Deptford Methodists had been opened in 1757 by Charles Wesley. It housed an active and progressive society. One of the London preachers apparently relayed the news of the Conference decisions to the Deptford leaders, who immediately petitioned Wesley for permission to change the hours of their services. Wesley claimed that in their particular case there was no special justification, but suspected that they might not accept 'No!' for an answer. On the eve of embarking for a month's tour in Holland, therefore, he asked Samuel Bradburn to keep an eye on the situation for him, writing:

> I beg there may be no preaching at Deptford in church hours before my return. What need of any innovation there? The case does not fall under any of those four that were allowed at the Conference.
>
> And pray give an hint to Benj. Rhodes. . . . I fear he has underhand abetted the malcontents there.[38]

When Wesley visited the society some weeks later he had to defend his earlier ruling, and in his *Journal* recorded publicly the principles which had directed his decision:

> Tues. 24 [October]. I met the classes at Deptford, and was vehemently importuned to order the Sunday service in our room at the

20

same time with that of the church. It is easy to see that this would
be a formal separation from the Church. We fixed both our morning
and evening service, all over England, at such hours as not to interfere with the Church; with this very design—that those of the
Church, if they chose it, might attend both the one and the other.
But to fix it at the same hours is obliging them to separate either from
the Church or us; and this I judge to be not only inexpedient, but
totally unlawful for me to do.[39]

The ambiguity of the last sentence was thus explained by Samuel
Bradburn in the manuscript annotation on his own copy: 'Just then
and there.' Under certain circumstances Wesley had now come to
believe that it was in fact both expedient and lawful to allow Methodist
groups to separate from their local church, but he dare only offer that
alternative in extraordinary circumstances.[40]

Their request seemed the less reasonable to Wesley because the
rector of St. Paul's, Deptford, was none other than that good evangelical Dr. Richard Conyers, and his curate was Wesley's own great-
nephew the Rev. Peter Lievre, to whom Wesley wrote an account of
the contretemps the following day:

Last night I had a long conversation with a few sensible men concerning going to church. I asked them what objection they had to
the hearing of Mr. L[ievre]. They answered, '*They could not hear him.*
He generally spoke so low that they lost a good part of what he said;
and that what they *could* hear was spoken in a dead, cold, languid
manner, as if he did not *feel* anything which he spoke.' This would
naturally disgust them the more because Dr. C[onyers] leaned to the
other extreme. But I should think you might easily remove it.

I asked again, 'Have you any objection to anything in his behaviour?' They answered, 'One thing we cannot approve of—his being
ashamed of the Methodists. His never recommending or defending
them at all, we think, is a full proof of this; for everyone knows his
near relation and his many obligations to *you*.'

Wesley followed this up with a spiritual exhortation to the young man,
who had earlier offered such rich promise.[41]

Two months later the situation was little improved, and Wesley was
constrained to resort to threats:

I went over to Deptford, but it seemed I was got into a den of lions.
Most of the leading men of the society were mad for separating from
the Church. I endeavoured to reason with them, but in vain; they
had neither sense nor even good manners left. At length, after meeting

the whole society, I told them: 'If you are resolved, you may have your service in church hours; but remember, from that time you will see my face no more.' This struck deep; and from that hour I have heard no more of separating from the Church.[42]

A few weeks afterwards he visited Dorking, and noted somewhat gleefully in his *Journal* that this society furnished added proof that forsaking church worship was no panacea for all spiritual ills, as some had claimed:

> The congregation was, as usual, large and serious. But there is no increase in the society. So that we have profited nothing by having our service in the church hours, which some imagined would have done wonders. I do not know that it has done more good anywhere in England: in Scotland I believe it has.[43]

Already before the 1786 Conference had passed its resolutions there were signs that a major controversy upon the issue of services in church hours was blowing up in Dublin. This proved to be the occasion for some of Wesley's most important pronouncements on his relations with the Church, and merits fairly full treatment. Wesley's old friend Henry Brooke sent a remonstrance from the conservative leaders there deprecating the attempts being made to turn them into 'mere Dissenters or arrant seceders', which would 'fritter the little flock to pieces in endless independencies, divisions, and subdivisions'. Wesley responded with a lengthy summary of the history of Methodist relations with the Church of England from 1729, showing how they had 'constantly attended the Church', but had never objected to any Dissenter who wished to join them in fellowship 'attending that worship to which he had been accustomed'. The 1743 *Rules* required that all members (again except Dissenters) must 'attend the Church and Sacrament'. He closed:

> We are members of the Church of England, we are no particular sect or party; we are friends to all, we quarrel with none for their opinions or mode of worship; we love those of the Church wherein we were brought up, but we impose them upon none; in some unessential circumstances we vary a little from the usual modes of worship, and we have several little prudential helps peculiar to ourselves; but still we do not, will not, dare not separate from the Church till we see other reasons than we have seen yet.[44]

In February 1787 he wrote, with special reference to Dublin:

We have at present such peace with . . . the clergy that if possible we should avoid taking any step which would be likely to anger them. . . . Now it is certain nothing would anger them more than the appointing *our* preaching in church hours, as this would imply a formal separation from the Church, which I believe to be both inexpedient and unlawful.[45]

Nevertheless, whenever the spiritual work of the Methodist societies was threatened, Wesley had no hesitation in putting his loyalty to that work above his loyalty to the Anglican institution. The dissident tendencies in Dublin were strongly reinforced by reaction against the growth of Calvinism in the city, so that some Methodists, repelled by the somewhat drowsy worship in their parish churches, were in danger of being won over by the 'gospel ministers' imported by the Dissenters. Wesley wrote to Henry Moore, the native Dublin preacher who was now in charge of the work there:

In such a case as you have mentioned you are justified before God and man for preaching at eleven o'clock on Sunday morning, only earnestly advising them that have heretofore received the sacrament at church to do so still.[46]

He added a statement of his conviction that there would remain at least one evangelical clergyman whose ministry they could attend without boredom or qualms, Edward Smyth: 'I do not imagine any barefaced Calvinism will be soon preached at Bethesda.' This church had been opened by Smyth a year earlier. In fact Smyth joined with some of the conservative Methodists in vehement objections against Methodist worship in church hours, so that in May 1788 Wesley instructed Moore to discontinue this practice on prudential grounds.[47] In answer to the pleading of both Moore and Coke, however, he relented so far as to agree that while Coke was in Dublin he could hold services at 11.0 a.m. as before. He also agreed that if the Methodists attended Holy Communion at St. Patrick's Cathedral (or their own parish church) on the first Sunday in the month, then on the other Sundays Moore might read prayers for them at 11.0 in the 'New Room' in Whitefriar Street.[48]

Wesley had sent his hand to the plough, but he continued to look back wistfully. On 13 June 1788 he wrote to Mrs. Jane Freeman:

If all the members of our society could be persuaded to attend St. Patrick's Church we should not need the Sunday service at the New Room. I wish you would always attend the church, except when I

am in Dublin; . . . unless you choose to make another [exception]—
namely, when Dr. Coke is in Dublin.[49]

And to Henry Brooke on 21 June:

> Of the Methodists and the Church I think as you do: they *must* not
> leave the Church—at least, while I live; if they leave it *then*, I expect
> they will gradually sink into a formal, honourable sect.[50]

The 1788 Conference approved a general statement similar to and
probably based upon the Dublin ruling. In spite of its somewhat involved wording this made it clear that Wesley was prepared to give
advice about services in church hours, but felt unable to lay down strict
and inexorable rules:

> Q. 21. What further directions may be given concerning the
> Prayers of the Church of England?
> A. The Assistants shall have a discretionary power to read the
> Prayer Book in the preaching-houses on Sunday mornings where
> they think it expedient, if the generality of the Society acquiesce with
> it; on condition that Divine service never be performed in the
> Church hours on the Sundays when the sacrament is administered in
> the parish church where the preaching-house is situated, and the
> people be strenuously exhorted to attend the sacrament in the parish
> church on those Sundays.[51]

This had apparently been the kind of compromise favoured by Charles
Wesley, whose obituary was recorded in the same minutes. Later John
Wesley wrote:

> I concur in the judgement of my brother, that the using of the form
> of prayer will tend to unite our people to the Church rather than
> to separate them from it, especially if you earnestly insist on their
> going to church every fourth Sunday.[52]

In general, however, Charles was not given to compromise on any
issue related to separation from the Church. Adam Clarke summed it
up thus: 'Mr. J. Wesley *mildly* recommended the people to go to
Church and Sacrament. Mr. C. Wesley threatened them with damnation if they did not.'[53]

Wherever it could be proved that attendance at the parish church
was impracticable or detrimental to the Methodist witness, John Wesley
had little hesitation about allowing service in church hours, even
though society after society might thus separate piecemeal from the
Establishment. He could still claim that this did not constitute separation

in the narrowly constricted sense in which he explained it in a letter
inserted in the *Arminian Magazine* under the title of 'Thoughts on
Separation from the Church':

> The question properly refers (when we speak of a separation from
> the Church) to a *total* and *immediate* separation, such as[54] that of Mr.
> Ingham's people first, and afterwards that of Lady Huntingdon's,
> who all agreed to form themselves into a separate body *without delay*:
> to go to Church no more, and to have no more connexion with the
> Church of England than with the Church of Rome.
>
> Such a separation I have always declared against, and certainly it
> will not take place (if ever it does) while I live. But a kind of separa-
> tion has already taken place, and will inevitably spread, though by
> slow degrees. Those Ministers, so called, who neither live nor preach
> the Gospel, I dare not say are sent of God. Where one of these is
> settled many of the Methodists dare not attend his ministry, so if
> there be no other church in that neighbourhood they go to church
> no more. This is the case in a few places already, and it will be the
> case in more, and no one can justly blame *me* for this, neither is it
> contrary to any of my professions.[55]

In Dublin opposition grew, however, coming to a head the following
spring. On Sunday 29 March 1789 Wesley himself arrived just in time
to preach at noon and to administer the Lord's Supper in the New
Room at Dublin. He was so ill that he asked his preacher William Myles
not only to read Morning Prayer for him but to serve the cup at
Communion. This seemed to emphasize the separatist tendencies
already implicit in the noon service. Later Wesley summarized in his
Journal one aspect of the many complaints which this occasioned:

> I had letter upon letter concerning the Sunday service, but I could
> not give any answer till I had made a full inquiry both into the
> occasion and the effects of it.
>
> The occasion was this: About two years ago it was complained
> that few of our society attended the Church on Sunday, most of
> them either sitting at home or going on Sunday morning to some
> dissenting meeting. Hereby many of them were hurt, and inclined
> to separate from the Church. To prevent this it was proposed to have
> service at the room, which I consented to on condition that they
> would attend St. Patrick's every first Sunday in the month.
>
> The effect was (1) That they went no more to the meetings.
> (2) That three times more went to St. Patrick's (perhaps six times)
> in six or twelve months than had done for ten or twenty years before.

Observe! This is done not to *prepare for*, but to *prevent*, a separation from the Church.[56]

To the local Methodists, headed by Arthur Keen, who charged him with fostering a separation by thus allowing service in church hours, Wesley replied on 31 March:

I do not separate from the Church, nor have any intention so to do. Neither do they that meet on Sunday noon separate from the Church any more than they did before: Nay, less, for they attend the Church and Sacrament oftener now than they did two years ago.

He went on to challenge them about the separation which they themselves had made both by attending dissenting services in preference to the Church, and by causing strife; closing with a plea for their continued loyalty.[57] Some of the more influential did in fact leave the Methodist cause. Wesley was distressed that 'an artful busy man' had thus 'thrown wildfire among them that were quiet in the land', and claimed that 'when we began the service on Sunday mornings in London, and afterwards in Bristol, no living creature ever said it was "leaving the Church".' Nevertheless, he promised to hold a referendum of the Dublin Methodists to determine who wished to continue with the 'new plan'.[58]

This still left untouched the charge of employing a layman at communion. A writer in the *Dublin Evening Post* expounded this issue the following week, charging that 'the Church was in danger', and calling upon the archbishop and clergy to use their authority against 'the greatest innovation that had occurred for the last fifty years'.[59] The *Dublin Chronicle* took up the controversy by publishing an article by 'Observer'. The Rev. Edward Smyth, though denying the rumour that he was this anonymous writer, made similar complaints against Wesley.[60] Eventually Wesley was constrained to public reply, writing on 2 June from Londonderry to the *Dublin Chronicle*. He defended himself against the charge of being 'a double-tongued knave, an old crafty hypocrite . . . saying one thing and meaning another', and again protested his loyalty to the Church of England. He claimed that holding services during church hours in Dublin was no more separation from the Church than it was in London, where he had been doing it 'for between forty and fifty years'. He admitted that he did ask William Myles to help him in delivering the cup at communion, but maintained that this broke no law either of the primitive or the modern church. He closed on a familiar note: 'I will not leave the Church of England as by law established while the breath of God is in my nostrils'.[61]

When Wesley returned to Dublin later that summer—it was to be his last visit—he continued to hold service in church hours and to administer the Lord's Supper, except on 5 July when he attended prayers and communion at St. Patrick's. That weekend was the occasion of his Irish Conference, and Wesley recorded in his *Journal*:

> I never saw such a number of preachers before, so unanimous in all points, particularly as to leaving the Church, which none of them had the least thought of. It is no wonder that there has been this year so large an increase of the society.[62]

The following appeared in the printed *Minutes*:

> Q. 24. A common report has run through Ireland that the Methodists were resolved to separate from the Church. Is that report true?
> A. Nothing can be more false. Although Mr. Wesley believes it right to continue the Sunday morning service in Dublin, yet he never had any design of having it in any other part of the kingdom; not that he could be justly complained of if he did, seeing he is a regularly ordained minister. He thinks it needful to observe further, that the Methodists will never separate from the Church till God calls him hence.[63]

One of the good Dublin friends whom Wesley lost through this controversy was Arthur Keen, to whom he sadly wrote a farewell message: 'Dublin, 6 July 1789. . . . You have made away from me, and I from you. I stand where I have stood these fifty years. I no more leave the church than I leave the body.'[64] Only a few weeks before his death Wesley wrote to Adam Clarke: 'Be firm, and duly attend St. Patrick's once a month.'[65]

The English Conference of 1789 was again held in Leeds, beginning 28 July. To the assembled preachers, in the light of his Dublin difficulties, Wesley tried to explain more fully the rulings on holding services in church hours which had been approved at the preceding English Conference. The four permissible reasons for not attending church services were reduced to two: '1. If the parish minister be a notoriously wicked man. 2. If he preach Socinianism, Arianism, or any other esentially false doctrine.'[66] On the opening day he had written to curb the eagerness for innovation of one of his East coast laymen:

> For many years there were no meetings of the Methodists anywhere in the church hours. There never were any either at Yarmouth or Norwich by my advice or approbation. I like the old way best, because I abhor the thought of separation from the Church.[67]

It was true that Wesley still preferred the old way of the Methodist society, but the abhorrent concept of separation was rapidly becoming an actuality as more and more of his societies were being transformed, sometimes with and sometimes without his permission, into Methodist churches.

SEVENTEEN

AN ANGLICAN TILL DEATH

MANY Methodists undoubtedly regarded their society as a true church, and would have echoed a letter written in 1780 by James Chubb, who in his many wanderings always headed for a sure welcome among his fellow Methodists: 'Give my kind love to all the Methodists. Tell them it is a great favour to be a true member of that church.'[1] Adam Clarke was convinced that during the last decade of Wesley's life the bulk of the Methodist people desired a formal separation from the Church of England, but respected their founder's wishes too much to rebel against him.[2] At almost every Conference during these closing years the question of Methodist relations with the Church of England arose in one form or another, and the last six were occasions either for a strong undercurrent or a specific resolution calling for a deliberate breaking of the tenuous ties holding Methodism to the Church. Always, however, Wesley managed to postpone the issue at least until after his death.

At the 1781 Conference it was agreed that in exceptional circumstances Methodists might desert their parish church. In 1782 and 1783 the domestic problems of the societies largely held the stage, and the recalcitrant Birstall trustees provided trouble enough, thereby underlining the necessity for the legal incorporation of the Methodist Conference achieved by Wesley's Deed Poll. The 1784 Conference was agitated by preachers dissatisfied by this Deed of Declaration, but also gave itself to furthering the cause of American Methodism, though only a handful of the preachers realized how drastically Wesley was preparing to break with orthodox Anglicanism in order to supply American needs. Once the storm broke over the issue of ordination no peace was possible at any future Conference. The great increase in membership, in preachers, in preaching-houses, meant also great increases in evangelistic opportunity, but also in the ferment of new ideas among those who recognized no long-standing ties to Anglican order.

Charles Wesley was far more distressed by this than was John, and began to look elsewhere for assistance in the losing battle against Methodist independence. He turned to the Moravians in the hope that they, as an episcopal church whose orders had been recognized as valid by the Church of England, and yet who maintained an evangelical witness, might be persuaded to legitimize the Methodists. He approached their leader Benjamin La Trobe, who reported to the Brethren's senior agent at Herrnhut, Johannes Loretz:

> Charles . . . wishes that the Brethren might be of the use they were originally intended for, to nurse these souls who are truly awakened and who adhere to the Church of England. John says that he does not intend to establish his church in England, but, says Charles, Dr. Coke etc. will, and this seems indeed probable.

La Trobe accurately reflected Charles Wesley's view that Coke, 'a young clergyman who is very fiery', had 'got an ascendancy over' John Wesley:

> This young man has at length persuaded him that he is as truly an apostolic bishop as any now living, and he should use his authority. There was now a fair opening. America was separated from England, and it would not be acting against either the law of God or man to establish a new Episcopal Church among the Methodists. . . . Dr. Coke went to America to establish this church. Before his departure Mr. Wesley ordained or consecrated him superintendent of the American Church, with a commission to him to consecrate a Mr. Asbury. . . . Dr. Coke is returned and will not rest until he has formed a Methodist Episcopal Church in England.[3]

On 27 November 1785 La Trobe reported that he had held 'several solid conversations with Charles Wesley', who was frank about the serious difficulties that faced the proposed union: 'He told me his brother would be pope, and was already envious of my entrance among the Methodists.'[4] The following month Coke joined in the negotiations on behalf of John. Charles Wesley warned La Trobe to be on his guard, but his interview with Coke on 4 January 1786 went off happily. Coke confessed to La Trobe that Wesley had reproved him personally for administering the Lord's Supper 'in the Presbyterian way' in Scotland, and added that Wesley had 'not yet made up his mind about forming the Methodist Episcopal Church in England'.[5] Loretz in Herrnhut was not enthusiastic about the amalgamation, especially as it appeared that the Methodists were merely seeking to legitimize their own ordinations and general constitution.[6] La Trobe, nevertheless, kept hoping and trying, and held several interviews with Coke and others, as well as planning carefully for one with John Wesley. He turned down one scheme presented by Coke in April 1786 until he could be assured that in fact Wesley had not 'resolved to form a new church in England'.[7] Charles informed him that 'he had reason to hope that

[John] was coming round and would not begin a new church-system in England', and he reported that his brother had declared publicly in Manchester 'that no such new Church should be established in England during his life'.⁸ Loretz was unconvinced, and wrote in July: 'As long as John Wesley lives and rules we have little hope,' because he would never accept the Moravians on their own terms, for fear he might 'lose his influence and authority in his party'.⁹ Charles continued to press the issue, writing to La Trobe on 30 July 1786:

> My brother is very well inclined to such a correspondence. . . . If our Lord is pleased to use us as peacemakers under Him, we may yet do something towards preventing any separation at all.
>
> The Doctor is returning to his Diocese; another good circumstance for my brother, whom that poor tool can do what he will with.
>
> The great evil which I have dreaded for near fifty years is a schism. If I live to see that prevented, and also to see the two sticks, the Moravian and the English Church, become one in our Saviour's hand, I shall then say, 'Lord, now lettest Thou thy servant depart in peace'.¹⁰

It is doubtful whether the long-planned and long-deferred interview between John Wesley and Benjamin La Trobe ever took place. La Trobe's death in November 1786 ended whatever hopes there might have been for a rapprochement which would add the bond of a Methodist-Moravian union to Methodism's fraying ties with the Anglican Church. It must be admitted that in this whole enterprise, however, it was Charles Wesley and Coke who maintained the initiative, each from a slightly different angle. John, while acquiescing, remained somewhat lukewarm, perhaps because he doubted whether the union was practicable, perhaps because he believed much more in the present reality of a vigorous though semi-independent Methodist church than in vague hopes of possible legitimization and rejuvenation that might flow from union with a sister episcopalian church.

Scotland had confronted Wesley with peculiar problems, yet also with a peculiar opportunity. Here he saw himself challenged by some of the greatest spiritual need embodied in a narrow and militant Calvinist formalism which had as little use for Methodist itinerancy as for Anglican bishops. Surely this misdirected enthusiasm might be diverted to better ends! Methodism got off to a very slow start in Scotland, and Wesley was reluctant to adapt his evangelistic methods to these very different conditions. The important concession of providing an ordained and comparatively settled ministry, however, had clearly proved fruitful, though it was perhaps still too early to prophesy about the permanence of the results. The cost of progress was the formation of a Methodist Church in Scotland, complete with its own ministry, its own sacraments (here administered by elders to seated communicants in typical Scots tradition), its own public worship,[11] its own discipline, its own complete separation from the national churches of both England and Scotland.[12]

To at least one of the preachers whom Wesley ordained for Scotland in 1785, John Pawson, this daring experiment was an outstanding success. He developed a Scots accent and became enthusiastic for still further doses of separation. Charles Atmore told him of Wesley's reply to Charles Wesley's attacks, which had been published in the *Arminian Magazine* for January 1786. Pawson replied from Glasgow on 13 February:

> I have not seen any Magazine for the present year, but am unkah well pleased at the hint you gave respecting our leaving the old Kirk. It appears to me high time to come out from among Heathenish Priests and Mitred Infidels.[13] What may we call that Church where such blessed wretches preside but an old withered harlot who has lost all that is truly excellent in the religion of Jesus Christ? I hope that Mr. Wesley is now paving the way for our complete deliverance from all that yoke of bondage by which we have been held down too long. . . . I never thought so much of the loss you sustain in England for want of the service at the proper hours on Sunday as I have since I tasted the sweetness of those happy seasons. Our Sunday forenoons are precious times indeed. The minds of the people at that time are best prepared to receive divine impressions. . . . I hope to go to the Conference if the Lord spares me so long, were it only to give my vote against the old Kirk, if any such good thing should come upon the carpet.[14]

Though Pawson was thus enthusiastic about complete separation, he realized that there were immense practical difficulties standing in its way. For one thing:

> Every circuit would want more preachers than they have at present in order that we might have the church service at the proper time in all the large places.

Therefore it could come about only by degrees, so that he expressed his own hopes for a course similar to that which in fact Wesley followed, whether with Pawson's advice or (more likely) without it:

I could wish that Mr. Wesley would ordain preachers this next Conference for those places where the bulk of the people greatly desire it, and so go on from time to time as providence may open the way, and let those places remain upon the old plan who wish to be as they are.[15]

Although Pawson left behind him increased congregations in Scotland, he also left problems. He gladly received not only presbyterial ordination but Scots Presbyterian polity, and himself ordained a session of elders to administer Methodist discipline in Glasgow. Of this Wesley remained strangely ignorant until it was brought to his attention in 1788 by Jonathan Crowther. Wesley ordered its immediate extermination at whatever cost:

'Sessions!' 'Elders!' We Methodists have no such customs, neither any of the Churches of God that are under my care. I require *you*, Jonathan Crowther, immediately to dissolve that session (so called) in Glasgow. Discharge them from meeting any more. And if they will leave the Society, let them leave it. We acknowledge only Preachers, Stewards, and Leaders, among us, over whom the Assistant in each circuit presides.[16]

Nevertheless, Wesley continued sensitive to the special position of Methodism in Scotland. Of all his twenty-seven ordinations of lay preachers, twelve were specifically for service in Scotland. Constantly he undergirded their local status, dignifying them with the titles 'minister' and 'Reverend'—and dropping those terms once the preacher in question returned to England.[17] Even more interesting was his acceptance of the title 'church' or 'chapel' for his Scots buildings, witness letters addressed thus: 'Rev. Mr. Cownley, Minister of the Methodist Church, Leith-Wind, Edinburgh', and 'To the Revd. Mr. Cownly at the Methodist Chapel in Glasgow'.[18]

The prospect in England also was greatly encouraging. The revival had far from spent its course. Methodism continued to make converts. New preachers, new societies, new preaching-houses, multiplied at a phenomenal rate, especially in the rapidly-growing areas most affected by the Industrial Revolution. During these years we note Wesley's increasing pride in the Methodist people. He wrote reproachfully to his great-nephew the Rev. Peter Lievre at Deptford in October 1786:

Not one of your genteel friends can be depended on: they are mere summer flies. Whereas had you condescended to make the *Methodists* your friends they would have clave to you, one and all. And they are already no inconsiderable body of people; besides that they are increasing more and more.[19]

In November that year he wrote to William Black in Nova Scotia:

It is indeed matter of joy that our Lord is still carrying on His work throughout Great Britain and Ireland. In the time of Dr. Jonathan Edwards there were several gracious showers in New England, but there were large intermissions between one and another; whereas with us there has been no intermission at all for seven-and-forty years, but the work of God has been continually increasing.[20]

In 1787 Wesley wrote a sermon on Methodism as 'God's Vineyard', designed by Him to 'put forth great branches and spread over the earth'. Once more he stressed, however, that God's purposes for Methodism were national yet not separatist:

If it be said, 'He could have made them a separate people, like the Moravian Brethren,' I answer, this would have been a direct contradiction to His whole design in raising them up, namely to spread scriptural religion throughout the land, among people of every denomination, leaving everyone to hold his own opinions and to follow his own mode of worship. This could only be done effectually by leaving these things as they were, and endeavouring to leaven the whole nation with that 'faith that worketh by love.'[21]

He remained convinced that this spiritual prosperity continued and increased because of rather than in spite of maintaining their links with the Church of England, however tenuous:

I still think, when the Methodists leave the Church of England God will leave them. Every year more and more of the clergy are convinced of the truth and grow well-affected toward us. It would be contrary to all common sense, as well as to good conscience, to make a separation now.[22]

Not everyone agreed with him, of course. Nor was he himself fully convinced. Yet as he countered his critics he tried to reassure himself. Some of them cavilled that if indeed more clergy were sympathetic to Methodism—and certainly they honoured John Wesley personally— why did they not make fuller use of Methodist preachers? Wesley replied that the less worthy clergy resented those who put them to shame, and many even of the pious ministers merely wanted help in improving the morals of their parishioners, not in transforming them into warm-hearted Bible Christians.[23] His grief that his nephew

Samuel had turned Roman Catholic arose mainly, not from prejudice against that communion, but because he was thus cut off from 'that preaching which is more calculated than any other in England to make you a *real Scriptural* Christian'.[24]

During his later years, and especially after the death of his younger brother Charles had emphasized his own mortality, Wesley never ceased to marvel at what God had accomplished in and through Methodism. In the summer of 1788 he wrote an article for his *Arminian Magazine* entitled 'Thoughts upon a late Phenomenon'. He recalled how through the Christian centuries revivals of religion had speedily died out, 'seldom lasting (as Martin Luther observed) longer than a generation, that is, thirty years'. Usually the leaders separated from the body which they were attempting to reform, and themselves degenerated into 'a dry, cold sect'. With the Oxford Methodists, however, sixty years earlier, a 'new phenomenon' had appeared, to be continued in the Methodist societies, still increasing in number both in Europe and America. This was largely because they had resisted many solicitations to become a body completely independent of their mother church:

> This is a new thing in the world: this is the peculiar glory of the people called Methodists. In spite of all manner of temptations, they will not separate from the Church. What many so earnestly covet, they abhor: they will not be a distinct body. . . . The Methodists will not separate from the Church, although continually reproached for doing it. Although it would free them from abundance of inconveniences, and make their path much smoother and easier: although many of their friends earnestly advise and their enemies provoke them to it—the clergy in particular, most of whom, far from thanking them for continuing in the Church, use all the means in their power, fair and unfair, to drive them out of it.[25]

Although he blocked some of Coke's attempts to cream off his outstanding young preachers for overseas missions, Wesley also admired the progress of Methodism in other lands, which added still another dimension to his thankful rejoicings, as well as to his problems.[26] He tried unsuccessfully to assert his authority over the Methodist Episcopal Church in America, and spoke somewhat unrealistically of the Methodists across the Atlantic as 'no otherwise divided than as the Methodists on one side of the Thames are divided from the other'.[27] He rejoiced with William Black over the success of Methodism in Nova Scotia, and sought to prevent services in church hours there as elsewhere.[28] In 1790 he wrote to Thomas Morrell in the U.S.A.: 'It is expedient that the

Methodists in every part of the globe should be united together as closely as possible.'[29] Only a few weeks before his death he wrote to the American preacher Ezekiel Cooper: 'Lose no opportunity of declaring to all men that the Methodists are one people in all the world; and that it is their full determination so to continue.'[30]

With the death of Charles Wesley in 1788 the separatists thought that the major obstacle preventing the formation of a Methodist Church in England had been removed. Dr. Coke was quite convinced, and believed that John Wesley was at least three-quarters convinced, that the wearying and frustrating series of attempts to prevent Methodists from straying too far from the Established Church had created more problems than it had solved. At the 1788 Conference, therefore, he boldly proposed 'that the whole Methodist body should make a formal separation from the Church'. In this plea, reported Adam Clarke, he was 'not only earnest, but vehement'. When he sat down Wesley rose, and quietly stated his own point of view:

> Dr. Coke puts me in mind of the German proverb, which I may apply to himself and to myself. 'He skips like a flea; I creep like a louse.' He would *tear* all from top to bottom. I will not *tear*, but *unstitch*.'[31]

He foresaw the inevitable end of this process of severing the Methodist bonds to mother Church a stitch at a time, but he was not prepared to forsake the principles which had so far guided him, and which he enunciated to the Conference in the course of an historical summary of Methodist relations with the Church:

> (1) That in a course of fifty years we had neither premeditatedly nor willingly varied from it in one article either of doctrine or discipline.
> (2) That we are not yet conscious of varying from it in any point of doctrine.
> (3) That we have in a course of years, out of necessity, not choice, slowly and warily varied in some points of discipline, by preaching in the fields, by extemporary prayer, by employing lay preachers, by forming and regulating societies, and by holding yearly Conferences. But we did none of these things till we were convinced we could no longer omit them but at the peril of our souls.[32]

Whether he was prepared to face up to this fact or not, he had also been undoing further important stitches in his handful of ordinations, gradually extending in purpose from America to Scotland, and in a few

21

days after this statement from Scotland to England itself. This was also what he had been doing in the matter of permitting services in church hours, allowing occasional exceptions to a general prohibition until eventually the exceptions would become the rule.

In order to remain true to his declared purpose of not tearing apart too rapidly his ties with the Church of England, Wesley was prepared to make great sacrifices, relinquishing whole societies as well as preachers rather than be betrayed into what he considered a formal separation. He did not flinch in 1785 when one of his preachers carried away a hundred members in an attempt to force Wesley's hand into allowing him to administer the Lord's Supper to the society in Plymouth Dock.[33] In 1788 he wrote to Jasper Winscomb:

> If all our society at Portsmouth or elsewhere separate from the Church I cannot help it. But I will not. Therefore I can in no wise consent to the having service in church hours. *You* used to love the church; then keep to it, and exhort all our people to do the same.[34]

In complaining that 'modern laziness has jumbled together the two distinct offices of preaching and administering the sacraments' he added: 'But be that as it may, I will rather lose twenty societies than separate from the church.'[35] Writing to Henry Moore he went farther:

> The more I reflect the more I am convinced that the Methodists ought not to leave the Church. I judge that to lose a thousand, yet ten thousand, of our people would be a less evil than this. . . . Our glorying has hitherto been not to be a separate body.[36]

His relations with one of the lost preachers show that Wesley was not quite as reckless as the last statement implies, was indeed cautious and long-suffering in enforcing discipline. After William Green's resignation he wrote:

> His bitter enmity against the Church made him utterly unfit to be a Methodist preacher, and his elaborate discourse against going to church was enough to confound anyone that was not used to controversy. Yet I did not dare to *put him away*—but I am not at all sorry that he is gone away.[37]

In the early summer of 1789, while Wesley was embroiled in Ireland over the question of separation, he penned one of his most remarkable sermons. Surrounded by preachers who apparently had no ambition to set up as independent ministers, and after having employed one of them to assist him in administering the Lord's Supper, he prepared an appeal to preachers intent on usurping priestly authority! In spite of

Whitehead's statement, frequently copied, that this sermon was 'some-times preached at the Conference before the preachers then assembled', this was strictly a literary sermon, and his diary records no preaching of it either in Ireland or elsewhere.[38] It was dated at the end, 'Cork, May 4, 1789', and was first published in the *Arminian Magazine* for May and June 1790.[39] Clearly this so-called sermon was an attempt to secure the continuance after his death of an itinerant preaching ministry within the Methodist connexion, a piece of pious propaganda rather than a sermon. Wesley gave it no title, simply describing it as 'On Hebrews v.4.' In later years it was known variously as 'the Korah sermon' and 'The Ministerial Office'.

Nor is this one of Wesley's best essays, for its two main themes of 'no separation' and 'no priesthood' are not always juxtaposed or inter-woven convincingly, and a paragraph defending services in church hours in Dublin was apparently thrown in as a make-weight simply because it was on his mind at the moment. Tracing the story of the ministry from Old Testament times to those of the New Testament and the primitive church, Wesley showed that the offices of prophet and priest were always kept distinct, and usually filled by separate men, until the time of Constantine. 'In that evil hour' it became common for a man to secure financial support by serving both 'as priest and prophet, as pastor and evangelist'. Nevertheless, it continued normal that although a layman might occasionally preach he was not allowed to administer the sacraments without ordination. This was true of the young men whom the Wesleys had accepted to serve them as 'sons in the gospel': they were appointed 'wholly and solely to preach', not 'to exercise the priestly office'. Any preacher who ventured to administer the sacraments, as in Norwich in 1760, 'was informed it must not be, unless he designed to leave our connexion'. This made clear, Wesley rhapsodized:

> Now as long as the Methodists keep to this plan they cannot separate from the Church. And this is our peculiar glory. It is new upon the earth. . . . The Methodists . . . are not a sect or party; they do not separate from the religious community to which they at first be-longed; they are still members of the Church; such they desire to live and to die. And I believe one reason why God is pleased to continue my life so long is to confirm them in their present purpose not to separate from the Church.

This was followed by another list of the 'few instances' in which he judged that there had been an 'absolute necessity' to 'vary' from the Church, as in 'preaching abroad', 'praying extempore', forming 'little companies', meeting his preachers in Conference and stationing them.

All this, however, he maintained, was not 'separating from the Church', for whenever he had opportunity he attended church services and advised his people so to do. To those who criticized his inconsistency he explained his two-fold approach:

> The one, that I dare not separate from the Church, that I believe it would be a sin so to do; the other, that I believe it would be a sin not to vary from it in the points above mentioned.

Turning once more to the preachers, he reminded them of their first call to preach, in a paragraph which, though not the last, formed the climax of the sermon:

> Ye did not then, like Korah, Dathan, and Abiram, 'seek the priesthood also'. Ye knew 'no man taketh this honour unto himself but he that is called of God, as was Aaron'. O contain yourselves within your own bounds! Be content with preaching the gospel. 'Do the work of evangelists'. . . . I earnestly advise you, abide in your place: keep your own station. . . . Ye yourselves were at first called in the Church of England: and though ye have and will have a thousand temptations to leave it and set up for yourselves, regard them not. Be Church of England men still. Do not cast away the peculiar glory which God hath put upon you and frustrate the design of Providence, the very end for which God raised you up.[40]

At the English Conference of 1789 the preachers once more debated the question of separation from the Church. Once again Wesley recorded that after it had been 'largely considered . . . we were all unanimous against it'.[41] It would perhaps have been more accurate to say that no one remained vociferously in its favour. In a closing sermon on I Peter 4:11 Wesley charged the preachers with their high responsibility: 'If any man speak, let him speak as the oracles of God'.[42] This positive approach was far removed from the negative (though necessary) cautions of the unpreached 'Korah' sermon.

One of the major preoccupations of the 1789 Conference was with a further revision of Methodist discipline in preparation for what was to be Wesley's final edition of his Large Minutes. The lengthy section on securing Methodism after his death, added from the 1769 annual *Minutes* to the Large Minutes of 1770, 1772, and 1780, was dropped, because this matter had now been cared for by the 1784 Deed Poll.[43] Among the passages added was a comment appended to the 1763 statement about the Assistant's duty of 'loving the Church of England, and resolving not to separate from it'; 'Let this be well observed. I fear, when the Methodists leave the Church, God will leave them. But if they are thrust out of it they will be guiltless.'[44] Wesley also added a wry comment about Methodist criticism of the Established Church: 'What they do in America, or what their *Minutes* say on this subject, is nothing to us. We will keep in the good old way.'[45]

In some respects 1789 was a watershed in Wesley's life. On 20 February he had executed what turned out to be his last will, leaving his vast literary property in trust 'for the General Fund of the Methodist Conference in carrying on the work of God by Itinerant Preachers', his possessions in Kingswood in trust to teach and maintain the children of poor travelling preachers, his library for the benefit of the preachers themselves, his clerical robes for the use of the clergymen officiating at City Road Chapel, London. For City Road and for the new chapel in Bath, both of which were on special trust deeds, he nominated committees to secure preachers. As a last little token of love—and a hostage to sound doctrine—he left a set of the eight volumes of his *Sermons* 'to each of those Travelling Preachers who shall remain in the Connexion six months after my decease'.[46] On 25 February, when a codicil was added to his will bequeathing his printing presses and type to the Conference, he strove to ensure the supply of dedicated and (probably) ordained preachers for the Connexion by himself ordaining Thomas Rankin and Henry Moore for the English work. Now at the Conference he had made his last major appeal for loyalty to the Church, and prepared his last major revision of the *Minutes* which supplied the marching orders for the Methodist preachers and people. Symbolically his *Journal* recorded that immediately after the Conference he returned to London and settled all his temporal business before setting out on what might well be his last preaching tour.[47]

Until August 1789 old age had touched John Wesley only lightly, though he was then 86. In that month came a sudden change which he later recorded in his *Journal* during the last of his annual birthday reflections:

> My eyes were so dim that no glasses would help me. My strength likewise now quite forsook me, and probably will not return in this world. But I feel no pain from head to foot; only it seems nature is exhausted and, humanly speaking, will sink more and more, till
> 'The weary springs of life stand still at last.'[48]

Habit and will-power kept him moving, however, and his preaching itinerary became a royal progress through curious crowds for whom he had become a living legend—awed thousands who wanted to see him even if they could not hear. Wherever he went he 'explained at large the rise and nature of Methodism', maintaining:

> I have never read or heard of, either in ancient or modern history, any other church which builds on so broad a foundation as the Methodists do: which requires of its members no conformity either in opinions or modes of worship, but barely this one thing, to fear God and work righteousness.[49]

He continued to practise and to inculcate most of those activities which during half a century had gradually driven a wedge between him and the Church of England—even field-preaching. In 1739 he had first 'consented to be more vile' and accepted the standard from White-field's hand, in Bristol. Fifty-one years later, during his last Conference in Bristol, he preached from his favourite open-air stand in Carolina Court for forty minutes to about fourteen hundred people.[50] His last sermon in the open air was preached under a tree at Winchelsea on 7 October 1790, and the text showed that his message was unaltered: 'The kingdom of heaven is at hand; repent and believe the gospel.'[51]

He continued his attempts to preserve Methodism, with its societies, its discipline, its itinerant system, its connexionalism, as a living entity, regardless of whether this were practicable within the framework of the national church: 'I have only one thing in view—to keep all the Methodists in Great Britain one connected people.'[52] Although he came to see more clearly each year that such continuance must almost inevitably entail separation after his death, this seemed a lesser evil than neglecting the present God-given task: 'The Methodists are to spread life among all denominations—which they will do till they form a separate sect.'[53]

He continued to defend his societies and his preachers from the persecution which still occasionally rewarded their evangelism. There remained indeed one important last battle for him if they were to be secured in their anomalous position as declared churchmen seeking legal protection under a law designed only for dissenters from the church.[54]

In the summer of 1787 Wesley had heard that one of his preachers in Northamptonshire (apparently William Hoskins) had been refused a licence to preach by a justice because he was a Methodist. Wesley was prepared to press the issue and 'open a scene which the good justice little expects!' In fact it turned out that the young man had invited trouble 'by preaching in church time, and so near the church as to disturb both the minister and the congregation'.[55] It was clear, however, that the innocent might suffer from such victimization as well as the guilty. Wesley took counsel with his trusted solicitor William Clulow, and they agreed that in order to secure the fullest legal protection it was desirable to register all Methodist 'chapels' and travelling preachers. At the same time they insisted that the term 'Dissenter' should not be used, claiming that 'no justice or bench of justices has any authority to refuse licensing either the house or the preachers'.[56] That very summer Robert Gamble, whom Wesley was to ordain the following year, had secured a licence from the Norfolk justices on these lines, in which he was described as 'a public preacher and teacher of the gospel'.[57] Not that Wesley henceforth *required* his preachers 'to license either themselves or the places where they preached'. In fact he still maintained that they were just as safe unlicensed as licensed.[58]

It seems possible, however, that a concerted move was being undertaken by Church authorities in different parts of the country to deny Methodists any legal rights unless they frankly declared themselves 'Protestants dissenting from the Church of England'.[59] In 1788 Methodists were prosecuted for holding open-air services in Northamptonshire, though one-third of the money collected in fines was distributed to the poor.[60] Even preachers who held licences were occasionally victimized because they claimed to be both Protestants and churchmen but not dissenters, whereupon a clergyman justice might say: 'As a churchman you can have no claim on the privileges afforded by that Act.' This was true of Andrew Inglis, who preached on his way to the Bristol Conference in 1790. To pay his fine Adam Clarke went from house to house begging subscriptions.[61] The lawyer heading the case against Inglis 'boasted that he would drive Methodism out of Somersetshire'. To which Wesley replied, 'Yes, when he drives God out of it'.[62] It may well have been to the bishop of Bristol on this occasion that Wesley wrote:

> My Lord, I am a dying man, having already one foot in the grave. . . . But I cannot die in peace before I have discharged this office of Christian love to your Lordship. . . . Why do you trouble those that are quiet in the land? Those that fear God and work righteousness? Does your Lordship know what the Methodists are? That many thousands of them are zealous members of the Church of England? . . . Why should your Lordship (setting religion out of the question) throw away such a body of respectable friends? Is it for their religious sentiments? Alas, my Lord, is this a time to persecute any man for conscience' sake? I beseech you, my Lord, do as you would be done to. You are a man of sense: you are a man of learning: nay, I verily believe (what is of infinitely more value) you are a man of piety. Then think, and let think.[63]

Wesley was caught up in other incidents during this campaign, and

regarded them as constituting a kind of complex test case for proving
the legitimacy of the Methodist societies vis-à-vis the Church of England. On 26 June 1790 he wrote in similar vein to the bishop of Lincoln
about the persecution of a family of poor Methodists in his diocese, whose
furniture had been seized for allowing a Methodist meeting in their
home:

My Lord,
    It may seem strange that one who is not acquainted with your
Lordship should trouble you with a letter. But I am constrained to
do it; I believe it is my duty both to God and your Lordship. And
I must speak plain; having nothing to hope or fear in this world,
which I am on the point of leaving.
    The Methodists in general, my Lord, are members of the Church
of England. They hold all her doctrines, attend her service, and
partake of her sacraments. They do not willingly do harm to anyone,
but do what good they can to all. To encourage each other herein
they frequently spend an hour together in prayer and mutual exhortation. Permit me then to ask *Cui bono?*—'For what reasonable end'—
would you drive these people out of the Church? . . .
    Do you ask, 'Who drives them out of the Church?' Your Lordship
does, and that in the most cruel manner, yea, and the most disingenuous manner. They desire a licence to worship God after their own
conscience. Your Lordship refuses it—and then punishes them for
not having a licence! So your Lordship leaves them only this alternative, 'Leave the Church or starve'. And is it a Christian, yea, a
Protestant bishop, that so persecutes his own flock? I say 'persecutes',
for it is persecution to all intents and purposes. You do not burn
them indeed, but you starve them. . . . And your Lordship does this
under colour of a vile, execrable law not a whit better than that *de
Haeretico comburendo*![64] So persecution, which is banished out of
France, is again countenanced in England.
    O my Lord, for God's sake, for Christ's sake, for pity's sake, suffer
the poor people to enjoy their religious as well as civil liberty![65]

On this same incident, as well as another, Wesley wrote a month
later to William Wilberforce, and through him sought the support of
William Pitt:

Dear Sir,
    When I had the pleasure of conversing with you some time since,
you was deeply engaged for the liberty of poor Africans.[66] I cannot
but think you are full as much concerned for the liberty of your own
countrymen. By this persuasion I am induced to mention to you a

peculiar species of oppression which if it continues will soon reduce both me and many of my friends either to violate our consciences or to want a piece of bread.

Last month a few poor people met together in Lincolnshire to pray and praise God in a friend's house. (There was no preaching at all.) Two neighbouring Justices fined the man of the house twenty pounds. (I suppose he had not twenty shillings.) Upon this his household goods were distrained and sold to pay the fine. He appealed to the Quarter Sessions: But all the Justices averred, 'The Methodists could have no relief from the Act of Toleration, because they went to Church, and that as long as they did so the Conventicle [Act] should be executed upon them.'

Last Sunday, when one of our preachers was beginning to speak to a quiet congregation, a neighbouring Justice sent a Constable to seize him, though he was licensed, and would not release him till he had paid twenty pounds, telling him his licence was good for nothing 'because he was a Churchman'.

Now, sir, what can the Methodists do? They are liable to be ruined by the Conventicle Act, and 'they can have no relief from the Act of Toleration!' If this is not oppression, what is? Where then is English liberty? The liberty of Christians? Yea, of every rational creature? Who, as such, has a right to worship God according to his own conscience. But waiving the question of right and wrong, what prudence is there in oppressing such a body of loyal subjects? If those good magistrates could 'drive them not only out of Somersetshire' but out of England, who would be gainers by it? Not His Majesty, whom we honour and love: Not his Ministers, whom we love and serve for his sake. Do they wish to throw away so many thousand friends, who are now bound to them by [ties] stronger than that of interest?

If you will speak a word to Mr. Pitt upon this head you will much oblige,

Dear Sir,
Your affectionate servant
John Wesley.[67]

John Wesley also continued to proclaim his own loyalty to the Established Church. To Henry Moore he wrote in 1788: 'I am a Church of England man, and, as I said fifty years ago, so I say still, in the Church I will live and die, unless I am thrust out.'[68] He would try both to preserve the continuity of Methodism and to protect the Methodists against persecution while he lived, and to delay any formal break with the Church until after he was dead. Constantly he urged his more impetuous followers: 'Stay till I am in a better place. It will hardly be while I live.'[69] His passing from the scene would remove both the centre of unity for the Methodists themselves and their strongest link to the Church. For some years, therefore, he had carefully been taking steps to prevent this inevitable separation from entailing the complete dispersion of the Methodist Connexion into several sects or a thousand independent causes. In July 1788 he wrote:

> For upwards of fifty years my language respecting the Church has been just the same as it is now. Yet, whenever I am removed, there can be no doubt but some of the Methodists [i.e. the Methodist preachers] will separate from it and set up independent meetings; some will accept of [Church] livings; the rest (who will, I trust, be the largest third) will continue together on the itinerant plan; and if they abide by their old rules, God will give them His blessing.[70]

It is clear that he saw the system of itinerant preaching as the key to Methodism's spiritual prosperity. This he hoped might never fully disappear. To Lady Maxwell he wrote in August 1788: 'For fifty years God has been pleased to bless the itinerant plan. . . . It must not be altered till I am removed; and I hope will remain till our Lord comes to reign upon earth.'[71]

Wesley himself provided the best summary of his church-founding actions over half a century, in an article written in December 1789 when he was eighty-six years old, and published the following April in his *Arminian Magazine*. His perspective was obviously different from ours, and he completely ignored the crucial events of 1784. A few of his statements betray a faulty memory. Nevertheless, this document offers strong testimony both to the continuing clarity of his mind and the constant singleness of his purpose. We therefore present it in full:

FARTHER THOUGHTS on Separation from the Church.
    1. From a child I was taught to love and reverence the Scripture, the Oracles of God: and next to these to esteem the primitive Fathers, the writers of the three first centuries. Next after the primitive church I esteemed our own, the Church of England, as the most scriptural national church in the world. I therefore not only assented to all the doctrines but observed all the rubric[s] in the liturgy, and that with all possible exactness, even at the peril of my life.
    2. In this judgment and with this spirit I went to America, strongly attached to the Bible, the primitive church, and the Church of England, from which I would not vary in one jot or tittle on any

account whatever. In this spirit I returned, as regular a clergyman as any in the three kingdoms, till after not being permitted to preach in the churches I was constrained to *preach in the open air*.

3. Here was my first *irregularity*. And it was not voluntary but constrained. The second was *extemporary* prayer. This likewise I believed to be my bounden duty, for the sake of those who desired me to watch over their souls. I could not in conscience refrain from it, neither from accepting those who desired to serve me *as sons in the gospel*.

4. When the people joined together (simply to help each other to heaven) increased by hundreds and thousands, still they had no more thought of leaving the church than of leaving the kingdom. Nay, I continually and earnestly cautioned them against it, reminding them that we were a part of the Church of England, whom God had raised up not only to save our own souls but to enliven our neighbours, those of the church in particular. And at the first meeting of all our preachers in Conference, in June 1744, I exhorted them to keep to the church, observing that this was our peculiar glory, not to form any new sect, but abiding in our own church to do to all men all the good we possibly could.

5. But as more Dissenters joined with us, many of whom were much prejudiced against the church, these, with or without design, were continually infusing their own prejudices into their brethren. I saw this, and gave warning of it from time to time, both in private and in public. And in the year 1758 [this should be 1755][72] I resolved to bring the matter to a fair issue. So I desired the point might be considered at large, whether it was expedient for the Methodists to leave the church? The arguments on both sides were discussed for several days, and at length we agreed without a dissenting voice, 'It is by no means expedient that the Methodists should leave the Church of England'.

6. Nevertheless the same leaven continued to work in various parts of the kingdom. The grand argument (which in some particular cases must be acknowledged to have weight) was this: 'The minister of the parish wherein we dwell neither lives nor preaches the gospel. He walks in the way to hell himself and teaches his flock to do the same. Can you advise them to attend his preaching?' I cannot advise them to it. 'What then can they do on the Lord's Day, suppose no other church be near? Do you advise them to go to a dissenting meeting? Or to meet in their own preaching-house?' Where this is really the case I cannot blame them if they do. Although therefore I earnestly oppose the *general* separation of the Methodists from the

church, yet I cannot condemn such a *partial* separation in this particular case. I believe to separate thus far from these miserable wretches who are the scandal of our church and nation would be for the honour of our church as well as to the glory of God.

7. And this is no way contrary to the profession which I have made above these fifty years. I never had any design of separating from the church. I have no such design now. I do not believe the Methodists in general design it when I am no more seen. I do and will do all that is in my power to prevent such an event. Nevertheless in spite of all that I can do many of them will separate from it—though I am apt to think not one half, perhaps not a third of them. These will be so bold and injudicious as to form a separate party, which consequently will dwindle away into a dry, dull, separate party. In flat opposition to these I declare once more that I live and die a member of the Church of England, and that none who regard my judgment or advice will ever separate from it.

JOHN WESLEY.

London, Dec. 11, 1789.[73]

Largely because of his careful preparations for the future and his gradual relaxing of control over the preachers, at Wesley's death Methodism survived the tremendous strain with remarkable resilience. Inevitably difficulties arose. A few bickerings occurred among the preachers, but the letter appealing for their unity which he had written in 1785 and entrusted to Joseph Bradford was read in the 1791 Conference and cemented their union.[74] Controversies about the measure of allegiance to the Church and churchly worship developed in some places, such as Bristol,[75] Manchester,[76] and Liverpool.[77] Yet few preachers or societies left; Methodism remained a strong and united body. Perhaps the representative response was that of William Thompson, whom the preachers elected as their first President at the Conference immediately following Wesley's death on 2 March 1791. On 28 June Thompson wrote to Joseph Benson:

I would have the preachers to follow the Methodist plan just as Wesley left it, without attempting the smallest alteration in it one way or other. That is, where they then read prayers, continue to do so; where they prayed without book, do so still; where they preached in church hours, and where they did not, still continue to preach at the same time; and where they baptized and buried the dead, do so still, and where they did not these things let them not begin till the people force them to do otherwise.

But at the same time make no public or private declarations of what they will do in future; but follow the footsteps of Providence, as He shall see proper to open their way.[78]

Long and sometimes heated correspondence and debates took place before a working compromise in Methodist-Anglican relationships was reached by the Plan of Pacification in 1795, and the first major secession took place two years later. Throughout this trying decade, however, for the most part dirty Methodist linen was not washed in public, and Methodism remained a strong evangelical force. This was true both of Methodism itself as a society gradually feeling its way to churchhood, and also in so far as it served as a catalyst arousing and reinforcing evangelical zeal in both Church and Dissent. If the Church of England was not obviously the stronger for Wesley's ministry, at least his connexion of societies and preachers had enlarged and strengthened the Church of God.

EPILOGUE

In September 1784, when John Wesley laid ordaining hands on Dr. Thomas Coke, he was eighty-one. His seventy-six-year-old brother Charles charged, ' 'Twas age that made the breach, not he!'[1] Nor can this be completely dismissed as poetic licence or blind anger. John Wesley was indeed old—but he was far from senile. Increasingly during his last eighteen months his eyes became dim, his hands shaky, his voice shrill. Yet not only did he remain physically active far beyond the expectancy for his years; he was mentally alert and adventurous, and usually calm and controlled withal.[2] Occasionally he embarrassed his inner circle of preachers by lapses of memory about past events, about announced plans, and even about declared principles, yet it was abundantly clear that he fully knew what he was doing.[3]

Granted the peculiar situation of his day, the separatist actions of his last seven years were neither crazy whims nor the result of scheming pressure upon senile malleability; they were the logical culmination of all that had gone before. Frequently he had claimed that in his relations with the Church of England he followed two principles: to stay as close as possible to her doctrines and discipline and worship, but to make variations in these whenever and wherever this was demanded by the peculiar work of God to which he was called.[4] This really amounted to one master principle, of course: he would follow the dictates of his own conscience, his own reading of the will of God for the opportunities and challenges of each changing situation. Looking back in 1786 on earlier narrow escapes from separation he wrote to one of his preachers:

> I believe if we had *then* left the Church we should not have done a tenth part of the good we have done: but I do not trouble myself on this head. I go calmly and quietly on my way, doing what I conceive to be the will of God. I do not, will not concern myself with what will be when I am dead. I take no thought about that. If I did I should probably hide myself either at Kingswood or Newcastle, and leave you all to yourselves.[5]

The phrase that came most readily to Wesley's lips when he tried to describe this attitude to his life and work was 'following the leadings of providence'. This he had announced as his guiding principle when first he called his preachers together in Conference as a virile young evangelist: 'We desire barely to follow Providence as it gradually opens.'[6] Commenting on Freeborn Garrettson's move from Nova Scotia to the United States in 1789, Wesley remarked: 'You are following the order of His Providence wherever it appear[s], as an holy man strongly expressed it, in a kind of holy disordered order'—words which might well be applied to Wesley's own ecclesiastical statesmanship.[7] He closed one of his last letters to William Black: 'It is our part to wait the openings of divine Providence, and follow the leadings of it.'[8] As he bade his last good-bye to Peard Dickinson a few days before his death he spoke of 'following the leadings of providence'.[9] His preachers echoed his language and sought a similar spirit. In describing the gradual development of Methodist polity, John Pawson wrote: 'Our Old Plan has been to following the openings of Providence, and to alter and amend the plan as we saw needful, in order to be more useful in the hand of God.'[10] The preacher elected to fill Wesley's shoes as the first President of the Conference after his death approached his heavy responsibilities for the Methodists with the same purpose, to 'follow the footsteps of Providence, as He shall see proper to open their way'.[11]

Mistakes of judgement Wesley certainly made. Though never boorish, he was occasionally tactless and peremptory with people. Impatient of incompetence and wilful obstruction, he was admittedly a dictator—but a benevolent dictator. No one could show that John Wesley lived for his own pleasure or profit or prestige: he lived unshakeably and unstintingly for the glory of God. He claimed that he lived and died a member and minister of the Church of England. Although many of his words and actions during eighty years of supposed loyalty to his beloved church appear somewhat bizarre in a churchman; although he frequently shifted ground in his constant protestations of never separating from the church; although he certainly founded a great daughter church in spite of those protestations—and towards the end knew that he was doing it; although he was (in a word) inconsistent in his relationships with the Church of England, yet throughout his life was revealed a higher consistency: it was indelibly stamped with the hallmark of 'following providence as it slowly opened out'.

APPENDIX

'OUGHT WE TO SEPARATE FROM
THE CHURCH OF ENGLAND?'

The origin of this document is described on pp. 164–6 above, and a brief summary of its contents given on pp. 166–7. Shortly after the crucial Conference of 1755, for presentation at which John Wesley prepared this paper, Charles Wesley seems to have borrowed his brother's manuscript in order to make his own copy. This was entered on pp. 1–45 of a duodecimo notebook which he used also to preserve transcripts of related documents arising during the years 1755 and 1756, including correspondence between himself and his brother and between Samuel Walker and John Wesley. The copying was done in part by Charles Wesley himself, in part by John Nelson as his amanuensis. This opening document is wholly in the hand-writing of Nelson.

It is clear that Nelson introduced his own spelling errors, and possibly some of the abbreviations and capitalizations and underlinings. In the circumstances it seems desirable not only to correct the spelling and as far as possible modernize the punctuation, but to extend all abbreviations. All underlined words have been retained in italics, however, except where these clearly represented merely the contemporary convention for italicizing either quotations or proper names. For ease of reference Nelson's own pagination has been inserted within square brackets in the text.

This notebook is numbered 'MS 170' in the Methodist archives, London, and grateful acknowledgement is here made to the Archivist, Rev. Dr. John C. Bowmer, M.A., B.D., and to the Book Steward, the Rev. Dr. Frank H. Cumbers, B.A., B.D., for their invaluable help in making available both this and the many other documents used throughout this volume.

[1] OUGHT WE TO SEPARATE FROM THE CHURCH OF ENGLAND?
I. This is a question which has been proposed to us many times, and

indeed many years since. It has been moved by very serious and pious men zealous for God and the salvation of men, to whose minds it has frequently been brought at the times of their nearest approach to God, in private and in public prayer, at the Lord's Supper, and at seasons of solemn humiliation. I in particular have had many thoughts concerning it, which were chiefly occasioned by a serious man who, when I was in Dublin, pressed me upon the head, and urged several reasons for it.[1]

It is evidently a question of vast importance, as affecting so great a number of people called Methodists who[2] (whether they joined in it or not) would be deeply concerned in such a separation, but likewise the whole [2] body of people commonly termed the Church of England. It concerns all these in a very tender point. With many it is touching the apple of their eye. It appears to them to be like removing ancient landmarks and throwing all things into disorder and confusion.

It is therefore highly necessary to be considered, and that with the utmost care and exactness—the rather because it has been so much canvassed already both by our friends and our enemies. But with how little effect! And that for a plain reason: scarce any of the disputants on either side understood in any tolerable degree the question of which they disputed. Nor is this any wonder, seeing the terms of it are extremely complex and ambiguous.

II. Wherefore before any reasonable answer can be given it is necessary to fix the meaning of these terms. What then do we here mean by the 'Church of England', [3] and what by 'separating from it?' As to the former, 'A Church' (according to our Nineteenth Article) 'is a congregation or company of faithful (believing) people, in which the pure Word of God is preached and the Sacraments duly administered, in all that essentially pertains thereto'.[3]

It has been questioned whether according to this definition the Church of England, so called, be any church at all. But waiving this let us take that term in the usual sense, meaning thereby, 'that body of people, nominally united, which profess to hold the doctrine contained in the Articles and *Homilies*, and to use Baptism, the Lord's Supper, and Public Prayer, according to the Common Prayer Book'. Perhaps some would add, 'And to submit to the governors of the church, and obey the laws of it'.

By the *laws* of the church I mean the *rubrics*. Whether the *Canons* are laws of the Church of England is doubtful, [4] seeing it is a question whether they were ever confirmed by any competent authority.

Many affirm that we have separated from the church already, to whom we answer plainly:

We do not *separate* from the *people* of the church as such. We were

22

bred up with them, and we remain with them. We are now as much united with them as ever we were, and as the rest of them are with one another.

We do not *separate* from the *doctrine* of the church. We receive both the Articles and *Homilies* as excellent compendiums of Christian doctrine, and can make it appear that we keep closer thereto than any other body of people in England.

We do not *separate* from the *Sacraments* or *Prayers* of the church, but willingly attend them at all opportunities.

We submit to the *governors* and *laws* of the church in all things not contrary to Scripture.

But we dare not so submit to those [5] governors or those laws as to omit (1) preaching the gospel in all places, (2) using sometimes extemporary prayer, (3) assisting those which desire to forward each others' salvation, (4) encouraging others to do the same, though they are not episcopally ordained. If any *will* call this 'separating from the church' they are at liberty so to do.

[1.] Ought we to *separate* from the church any farther? Should we renounce all religious intercourse with the *people* of the church? It is not clear to us that this is lawful. Certainly it is not expedient.

2. Ought we to renounce the *doctrine* of the church, contained in the Articles and *Homilies*? We cannot in conscience. For though we take knowledge that the writers of them were fallible men, though we will not undertake to defend every particular expression in them, [6] yet we cannot but very highly esteem them as yielding to few human compositions.

3. Ought we to refrain from the *public service* of the church? The Prayers, sermons, and Lord's Supper? This would amount to a formal separation from the church. This properly constitutes a Dissenter.

And it may be pleaded for it, 'That the ministers are wicked men. They not only know not, but flatly deny the truth. They rail at those who either teach it or hold it. Therefore no blessing can attend their ministrations. Nay, we should receive more harm than good therefrom. Therefore we scruple to attend them. Yea, we sometimes doubt, after hearing a railing sermon, whether we should not openly protest against it!'

Suppose they are wicked men (though this is not true of all, nor should you think it of any without full proof), had you this [7] scruple when you received the love of God first? Perhaps some had; but many had not. In some doubtless it may have proceeded from tenderness of conscience; but I fear not in all. Let each of you, then, consider when and how came this scruple into your mind. Perhaps you heard a railing sermon, and instead of the tenderest pity toward him you felt your heart rise against the preacher. Was it not then first that thought arose, 'Hear these blind guides no more?' And who, think you, suggested it? I fear, not the God of love. Had you been full of his spirit it could have found no place. It did find none while you simply waited on God in lowliness and meekness of wisdom. But 'can no blessing attend the ministration[s] of a wicked minister?'[4] You yourself can witness the contrary. You attended them many years, and you [8] know you not only received no harm but received many blessings thereby. So have I myself, even under a very bad sermon, and much more in the Prayers and at the Lord's Table. So have hundreds, yea, thousands of the people. And so they do to this very day, God hereby witnessing that the virtue of the ordinance does not depend on him that ministers but Him that ordains it, and calling us to continue in the church for our own sake as well as for [an] example to others. Although therefore it is highly to be desired that all who[2] either preach or administer the Sacraments were holy men (nay, and all who[2] receive it—for it is a grievous thing to see servants of the devil at the Table of the Lord) yet that the ministers are not so is no reason for your scrupling to attend the church, much less for openly protesting against them, even when they rail against the truth. Neither our [9] blessed Lord himself nor any of his apostles ever gave us a precedent of this. This would indeed do infinitely more harm than good, and bring numberless difficulties both on ourselves and our brethren.

But how is it that you are grown so impatient? This is not the temper which you had once. What spirit are you of? If you cannot bear this, how would you bear the spoiling of your goods? How, when smitten on the cheek, turn the other also? How resist unto blood? Be not overcome of evil, but overcome evil with good.[5]

Indeed while you have a scruple, which may sometimes be very innocent, you must act accordingly. But beware that your scruple be not your sin—as it certainly is if it springs from anger, impatience, resentment, or any wrong temper, or if you have not used and do not still use all possible means to remove it.

4. Ought we, lastly, to renounce all submission to the governors and laws of the church? [10] It is not plain to us that it is either expedient or lawful, seeing the rubrics are laws confirmed by Parliament, and the bishops are constituted (in some measure) governors by the same authority. Therefore we hold ourselves obliged in things indifferent to submit to both, and that by virtue of God's command: 'Submit yourself to every ordinance of man for the Lord's sake.'[6]

Indeed some affirm, 'We may not submit to any ordinance of man relating to the worship of God: (1) Because Christ is the only lawgiver in his church. (2) Because the Bible is the only rule of Christian worship, (3) Because Christ himself has said, "Call no man Rabbi, Master, Father",[7] on earth and again, "In vain do they worship me, teaching for doctrines the commandments of men".[8]

We answer, first, The Jewish church was Christ's as really as the Christian. And he [11] was the only lawgiver in the Jewish as well as in the Christian church. Yet King Jehoshaphat proclaimed a fast without any derogation to Christ's authority.[9] Yet King Josiah commanded the law to be read, and gave many other directions to that church.[10] Yet Nehemiah ordained the whole form of divine worship, and Christ was honoured, not injured, thereby. Yea, himself honoured with his presence the yearly Feast of the Dedication, instituted long before by Judas Maccabeus.[11]

It plainly follows that magistrates may regulate divine worship without any infringement of his supreme authority, and that although Christ is the only *supreme* lawgiver therein, yet magistrates are *subordinate* lawgivers, even to the church.

2. 'But is not the Bible the only rule of Christian worship?' Yes, the only *supreme* rule. But there may be a thousand rules *subordinate* to this, without any violation of it at all. [12] For instance the supreme rule says, 'Let all things be done decently and in order'.[12] Not repugnant to, but plainly flowing from this, are the subordinate rules concerning the time and place of divine service. And so are many others observed in Scotland, Geneva, and in all other Protestant churches.

3. Therefore that text, 'Call no man Rabbi, Father, Master', is absolutely wide of the point. This has no relation at all to modes of worship, but means this and nothing else: do not pay any such *implicit* faith or obedience to any mere man as the Jews pay to their Rabbis, whom they generally call 'Father' or 'Master'.

As wide of the point is that other, 'In vain do they worship me, teaching for doctrines the commandments of men'—that is, *such* commandments of men as 'make void the commandments of God'.[13] Our Lord immediately instances in that commandment of men which made void the Fifth Commandment. [13]

It remains, it is not a sin but our bounden duty, in all things indifferent, of whatever kind, to 'submit to every ordinance of man for the Lord's sake'.[14]

[4.] But is it not our duty to separate from it, because (4) 'the church is only a creature of the state?' If you mean only that King Edward the Sixth required several priests in the then Church of England, to 'search into the law of God and teach it the people';[15] that afterwards he restored the scriptural worship of God to the utmost of his knowledge and power, and (like Josiah and Nehemiah) gave several rules for the more decent and orderly performance of it—if you mean this only by saying 'the church is a creature of the state'—we allow it is, and praise God for it. But this is no reason at all why we should separate from it.

5. Neither is this, that 'the king is the supreme governor of the Church of England'. We think the king ought to [14] be the supreme governor of his subjects. And all of the Church of England are his subjects. Therefore (unless he should command anything contrary to the law[16] of God) we willingly obey him as our supreme (visible) governor.

6. 'But can you defend the *spiritual courts,* so called?' No. They call aloud for a reformation. But we cannot reform them. Neither need we on this account separate from our brethren, many thousands of whom, as well as we, esteem them the scandal of our nation.

7. No more can we defend several of the *Canons.* Yet neither for this need we separate from our brethren, many of whom groan under the same burden, and patiently wait for deliverance from it.

8. Nay, there are some things in the *Common Prayer Book* itself which we do not undertake to defend: as, in the *Athanasian Creed* (though we firmly believe the doctrine contained therein), the [15] *damnatory clauses,* and the speaking of *this faith* (that is, these opinions) as if it were the ground term of salvation; that expression, first used concerning King Charles the Second, 'our most religious king'; the answers in the *Office of Baptism* which are appointed to be made by the sponsors; the Office of *Confirmation;* the *absolution* in the Office for visiting the Sick; the thanksgiving in the *Burial Office;* those parts of the Office for *Ordaining Bishops, Priests and Deacons,* which assert or suppose an essential difference between bishops and presbyters; the use of those words in *Ordaining Priests,* 'Whose soever sins ye remit, they are remitted'; one might add (though these are not properly a part of the Common Prayer) Hopkins' and Sternhold's *Psalms.*

But supposing these are blemishes in that book, which is the general rule of public [16] worship to that body of men which are termed the Church of England, still we do not see that this is a sufficient cause to separate from them. We can leave the evil and keep the good. And so may every private member of this body. We could not indeed 'declare our unfeigned assent and consent to *all and everything* prescribed and contained in that book'. But this is not required of us, nor of any ministers but those who[2] are inducted to a benefice.

Therefore it does not yet appear to be either lawful or expedient (much less necessary) to separate from the church.

'But ought you not to do this one thing: to appoint persons to baptize and administer the Lord's Supper?'

III. It must be acknowledged this would answer many good ends. It would save our time and strength, and probably prolong our lives.[17] It would prevent abundance of trouble and much expense to several of our preachers, as well as the hazard of losing either in part or in whole the assistance of our most useful fellow-labourers, [17] who after they are ordained seldom give themselves to the work so entirely as they did before.

But notwithstanding these great advantages which might result from it, we doubt whether it be either lawful or expedient. And indeed were the thing in itself lawful, yet if it is not expedient it is not now lawful to us.

If it be said, 'The doubt comes too late. You have done it already in appointing to preach,' we answer: we have not (in the sense in question) *appointed* any man to preach. There is not one of you who[2] did not preach more or less antecedent to any appointment of ours. The utmost we have ever done is this: after we were convinced that God had *appointed* any of you an extraordinary preacher of repentance, we *permitted* you to act in connexion with us. But from our *permitting* you to preach with us it does not follow that we either did or can *appoint* you to administer the Sacraments. We always acknowledged that nothing but absolute necessity could justify your [18] preaching without being ordained in the scriptural manner by the 'laying on of the hands of the presbytery'.[18] Without your preaching numberless souls must have perished. But there is no such necessity for your administering the Sacraments. It does not appear that one soul will perish for want of your doing this.

'But you *have allowed* [them] to administer the Sacraments in permitting them to preach. For everyone who[2] has authority to preach has authority to administer them.'

We cannot believe that all who have authority to preach have authority to administer the Sacraments.

1. Because from the beginning of the Jewish church it was not so. Quite from the giving of the Law by Moses, to the destruction of Jerusalem, the preachers (anciently called 'prophets', afterwards 'scribes') were one order, the *priests* another. Nor during all that time did the highest prophet as [19] such, no, not Moses himself, meddle with the priestly office.

It is true *extraordinary prophets* were frequently raised up, who had not been educated in the 'schools of the prophets', neither had the outward, ordinary call. But we read of no *extraordinary priests*. As none

took it to himself, so none exercised this office but he that was outwardly 'called of God, as was Aaron'.[19]

2. Because from the beginning of the Christian church it was not so.
Both the evangelists and deacons preached. Yea, and women when
under extraordinary inspiration. Then both their sons and their
daughters prophesied, although in ordinary cases it was not permitted
to 'a woman to speak in the church'.[20] But we do not read in the New
Testament that any evangelist or deacon administered the Lord's
Supper; much less that any woman administered [20] it, even when
speaking by extraordinary inspiration, that inspiration which authorized them for the one not authorizing them for the other. Meantime
we do read in all the earliest accounts (whatever were the case with
baptism, which deacons it seems did frequently administer by the
appointment of superior ministers) that none but the president or
ruling presbyter ever administered the Lord's Supper. Nor is there now
any one Christian church under heaven, Greek, Latin, Lutheran,
Calvinist, or any other, that affirms or allows every preacher as such
to have a right of administering it.

3. Because this supposition absolutely destroys the different orders
of Christian ministers, and reduces them to one, contrary both to the
New Testament and to all antiquity. It is evident these always describe,
if not more, at least two orders distinct from each other, the one having
power only to preach and (sometimes) baptize, the other to ordain also
and administer the Lord's Supper.

'But is there any priest or any sacrifice under the New Testament?'
As sure as there [21] was under the Old. The 'unbloody sacrifice' of
wine and oil and fine flour was one of the most solemn which was then
offered, in the place of which and [of] all the other Jewish sacrifices is
the one *Christian sacrifice* of bread and wine. This also the ancients
termed 'the unbloody sacrifice', which is as proper a sacrifice as was the
minchah or 'meal offering' (not the 'meat offering', as it is stupidly false-
printed).[21] And he that offers this as a memorial of the death of Christ
is as proper a priest as ever Melchisedec was.

If it be asked, 'But is this a propitiatory sacrifice?' I answer, 'No'.
Nor were there every any such among the Jews. There never was or
can be more than one such sacrifice, that offered by 'Jesus Christ the
righteous'.[22]

But to proceed. It has been said, 'If you do not ordain ministers, who
can? Not wicked bishops, for they are no ministers themselves.' We
answer:

1. Are you assured, have you full proof, that all the bishops in
England [22] are wicked men? Dare you make the supposition without

full proof? Who art thou that thus judgest of another's servants? Is it a little breach either of wisdom, justice or love, to pass so harsh a sentence on a considerable number of persons without any proof at all against a great part, perhaps against any one of them?

2. If a wicked bishop, and consequently a wicked priest (the reason being the same) is no minister, then there were no priests in the whole Jewish church for many hundred years together. And if they had no priests, then (their administrations being null and void) they had no sacraments for so many ages. But is it possible any should believe this who reads over the Epistle to the Hebrews? Did St. Paul ever dream while he was writing it that those priests were no priests and their sacrifices no sacrifices? Does he ever charge the inefficacy of those ministrations upon the wickedness of the ministers?

3. If a wicked bishop is no bishop, and his ordination by consequence is no ordination, then the sacraments administered by him whom such a bishop ordains are no sacraments. It follows, if we suppose [23] two or three bishops of London successively are wicked men (by whom the ministers of London in general are ordained) that there are no ministers and so no sacraments there, that there is neither baptism nor the Lord's Supper administered in any church in London. Come closer yet. Are *you* baptized? Are you sure of it? Are you sure the minister who baptized you was an holy man? If you are, that is not enough. Was the bishop likewise who ordained him a real Christian? If not your baptism is no baptism. You are unbaptized to this day.

4. The Papists maintain that 'a pure intention in him that administers is necessary to the very being of a sacrament,'[23] and consequently that wherever this is wanting that which is administered is no sacrament. You have therefore these on your side. But you flatly contradict every other church in the world. All these maintain that the unworthiness of the minister does not destroy the effect, much less the nature, of the sacrament, seeing this depends not on the character of the administrator but the truth, love, and power of the Ordainer. [24]

We cannot therefore allow that sacraments administered by unholy men are no sacraments, or that wicked ministers are no ministers at all, or that every preacher has a right to administer the sacraments. Nor yet that it is expedient for us (suppose it were lawful) to ordain ministers, seeing it would be little less than a formal separation from the church, which we cannot judge to be expedient:

1. Because it would at least be a seeming contradiction to the solemn and repeated declarations which we have made in all manner of ways, in preaching, in print, and in private conversation.[24]

2. Because (on this as well as many other accounts) it would give

huge occasion of offence to those who seek and desire occasion, to all the enemies of God and his truth.

3. Because it would exceedingly prejudice against us many who fear, yea who love, God, and thereby hinder their receiving so much, perhaps any farther, benefit from [25] our preaching.

4. Because it would hinder multitudes of those who neither love nor fear God from hearing us at all, and thereby leave them in the hands of the devil.

5. Because it would occasion many hundreds if not some thousands of those who are now united with us to separate from us, yea and some of those who have a work of grace in their souls.

6. Because it would be throwing balls of wild fire among them that are now quiet in the land. We are now sweetly united together in love. We mostly think and speak the same thing. But this would occasion inconceivable strife and contention between those who left and those who remained in the church, as well as between those very persons who remained, as they were variously inclined one way or the other.

7. Because, whereas controversy is now asleep and we in great measure live peaceably [26] with all men, so that we are strangely at leisure to spend our whole time and strength in enforcing plain, practical, vital religion (O what would many of our forefathers have given to have enjoyed so blessed a calm!), this would utterly banish peace from among us, and that without any hope of its return. It would engage me for one in a thousand controversies both in public and private (for I should be in conscience obliged to give the reasons of my conduct, and to defend those reasons against all opposers) and so take me off from those more useful labours which might otherwise employ the short remainder of my life.

8. Because to form the plan of a new church would require infinite time and care which might be far more profitably bestowed, with much more wisdom and greater depth and extensiveness of thought than any of us are [27] masters of.

9. Because from the bare entertaining a distant thought of this evil fruits have already followed, such as prejudice against the clergy in general, an aptness to believe ill of them, contempt (and not without a degree of bitterness) of clergymen as such, and a sharpness of language toward the whole order, utterly unbecoming either gentlemen or Christians.

10. Because the experiment has been so frequently tried already, and the success never answered the expectation. God has since the Reformation raised up from time to time many witnesses of pure religion. If these lived and died (like John Arndt, Robert Bolton, and many others)

in the churches to which they belonged, notwithstanding the wickedness which overflowed both the teachers and people therein, they
spread the leaven of true religion far and wide, and were more and [28]
[more] useful, till they went to Paradise. But if upon any provocation
or consideration whatever they separated and founded distinct parties,
their influence was more and more confined; they grew less and less
useful to others, and generally lost the spirit of religion themselves in
the spirit of controversy.

11. Because we have melancholy instances of this even now before
our eyes. Many have in our memory left the church and formed themselves into distinct bodies. And certainly some of them from a real
persuasion that they should do God more service. But have any separated themselves and prospered? Have they been either more holy or
more useful than they were before?

12. Because by such a separation we should only throw away the
peculiar glorying which God has given us, that we do and will [29]
suffer all things for our brethren's sake, though the more we love them
the less we be loved, but should act in direct contradiction to that very
end for which we believe God hath raised us up. The chief design of his
Providence in sending us out is undoubtedly to quicken our brethren,
and the first message of all our preachers is to the lost sheep of the
Church of England. Now would it not be a flat contradiction to this
design to separate from the church? These things being considered, we
cannot apprehend (whether it be lawful in itself or no) that it is lawful
for us—were it only on this ground, that it is by no means expedient.

IV. It has indeed been *objected*, that till we do separate, at least so far
as to *ordain*, that our helpers may administer the sacraments, [30] we
cannot be a compact, united body. It is true we cannot till then be a
'compact united body' if you mean by that expression a body of people
distinct from and independent on all others. And we do not desire so
to be. Nay, we earnestly desire not to be so, but to remain united as far
as is possible with the rest of the Church of England till either a little
leaven leaven the whole or they violently cast us out.

It has been objected, secondly, 'it is mere cowardice and fear of persecution which makes you desire to remain united with them'. This
cannot be proved. Let everyone examine his own heart, and not judge
his brother.

It is not probable. We never yet for any persecution, when we were
in the midst of it, either turned back from the work or even slackened
our pace. [31]

But this is certain, that although persecution many times proves an
unspeakable blessing to them that suffer it, yet we ought not wilfully

to bring it upon ourselves; nay, we ought to do whatever can lawfully be done in order to prevent it. We ought to avoid it so far as we lawfully can; when persecuted in one city to flee into another. If God should suffer a general persecution, who would be able to abide it we know not. Perhaps those who talk loudest might flee first. Remember the case of Dr. Pendleton.[25]

V. Upon the whole one cannot but observe how desirable it is that all of us who are engaged in the same work should think and speak the same thing, be united in one judgement and use one and the same language.

To this it may contribute not a little, by the blessing of God, that we have now thoroughly considered [32] this great point: and the far greater part of us more nearly agree than ever we did before.

Do we not all now see *ourselves*, the *Methodists* in general, the *church*, and the *clergy* in a clear light?

We look upon *ourselves*, not as the authors or ringleaders of a particular sect or party (it is the farthest thing from our thoughts!) but as messengers of God to those who are Christians in name but heathens in heart and life, to call them back to that from which they are fallen, to real, genuine Christianity. We are therefore debtors to all these, of whatever opinion or denomination, and are consequently to do all that in us lies to please all, for their good, to edification.

We look upon the *Methodists* in general, not [33] as any particular party (this would exceedingly obstruct the Grand Design for which we conceive God has raised them up) but as living witnesses in and to every party of that Christianity which we preach, which is hereby demonstrated to be a real thing, and visibly held out to all the world.

We look upon *England* as that part of the world, and the *Church* as that part of England, to which all we who were born and have been brought up therein owe our first and chief regard. We feel in ourselves a strong Στοργή, a kind of natural affection for our country, which we apprehend Christianity was never designed either to root out or to impair. We have a more peculiar concern for our brethren, for that part of our countrymen to whom we have been joined from our youth up by ties of a religious as well as a civil [34] nature. True it is that they are in general 'without God in the world'.[26] So much the more do our bowels yearn over them. They do lie 'in darkness and the shadow of death'.[27] The more tender is our compassion for them. And when we have the fullest conviction of that complicated wickedness which covers them as a flood, then do we feel the most (and we desire to feel yet more) of that inexpressible emotion with which our blessed Lord beheld Jerusalem, and wept and lamented over it. Then are we the most willing 'to spend and to be spent' for them, yea, to 'lay down our lives for our brethren'.[28]

We look on the *clergy*, not only as a part of these our brethren, but as that part whom God by his adorable Providence has called to be watchmen over the rest, for whom therefore they are to give [35] a strict account. If these then neglect their important charge, if they do not watch over them with all their power, they will be of all men most miserable, and so are entitled to our deepest compassion. So that to feel, and much more to express, either contempt or bitterness toward them betrays an utter ignorance of ourselves and of the spirit which we especially should be of.

Because this is a point of uncommon concern, let us consider it in another view. The clergy wherever we are are either friends to the truth, or neuters, or enemies to it.

If they are friends to it, certainly we should do everything and omit everything we can with a safe conscience in order to continue and, if it be possible, increase their goodwill to it. [36]

If they neither further nor hinder it, we should do all that in us lies, both for their sakes and for the sake of their several flocks, to give their neutrality the right turn, that it may change into love rather than hatred.

If they are enemies, still we should not despair of lessening if not removing their prejudice. We should try every means again and again. We should employ all our care, labour, prudence, joined with frequent prayer, to overcome evil with good, to melt their hardness into love.

It is true that when any of these openly wrest the Scriptures and deny the grand truths of the gospel, we cannot but declare and defend at convenient opportunities the important truths which they deny. But in this case especially [37] we have need of all gentleness and meekness of wisdom.

Contempt, sharpness, bitterness, can do no good. 'The wrath of man worketh not the righteousness of God.'[29] Harsh methods have been tried again and again: at Wednesbury, St. Ives, Cork, Canterbury.[30] And how did they succeed? They always occasioned numberless evils, often wholly stopped the course of the gospel. Therefore were it only on a prudential account, were conscience unconcerned therein, it should be a sacred rule to all our preachers—'No contempt, no bitterness to the clergy'.

2. Might it not be another (at least prudential) rule for every Methodist preacher, 'Not to frequent any Dissenting meeting?' (Though we blame none who have been always [38] accustomed to it.) But if *we* do this certainly our people will. Now this is actually separat-

ing from the church. If therefore it is (at least) not expedient to separate, neither is this expedient. Indeed we may attend our assemblies and the church too, because they are at different hours: but we cannot attend both the meeting and the church, because they are at the same hours.

If it be said, 'But at the church we are fed with chaff, whereas at the meeting we have wholesome food', we answer, (1) The Prayers of the church are not chaff: they are substantial food for any who are alive to God. (2) The Lord's Supper is not chaff, but pure and wholesome food for [39] all who receive it with upright hearts. Yea, (3) in almost all the sermons we hear there we hear many great and important truths, and whoever has a spiritual discernment may easily separate the chaff from the wheat therein. (4) How little is the case mended at the meeting? Either the teachers are 'new light men', denying the Lord that bought them and overturning his gospel from the very foundations, or they are predestinarians and so preach predestination and final perseverance more or less. Now whatever this may be to them who are educated therein, yet to those of our brethren who have lately embraced it, repeated experience shows it is not wholesome food: rather to them it has the effect of deadly poison. In a [40] short time it destroys all their zeal for God. They grow fond of opinions and strife of words. They despise self-denial and the daily cross, and to complete all, wholly separate from their brethren.

Which then is the safer way, to attend that place where you have good food though it is often mixed with chaff, or that where it is generally mixed with poison? Indeed there may be poison at church too, but it is gross, fulsome poison, such as *we* can in no wise swallow, whereas that at the meeting is sweet to your taste, though to you it proves death to your soul.

3. Nor is it expedient for any Methodist preacher to imitate the Dissenters in their manner of praying: either in his [41] *tone*—all particular tones both in prayer and preaching should be avoided with the utmost care; nor in his *language*—all his words should be plain and simple, such as the lowest of his hearers both use and understand; or in the *length* of his prayer, which should not usually exceed four or five minutes, either before or after sermon. One might add: neither should we sing like them, in a slow drawling manner—we sing swift, both because it saves time and because it tends to awaken and enliven the soul.

4. Fourthly, if we continue in the church not by chance or for want of thought, but upon solid and well-weighed reasons, then we should never speak contemptuously of the church or anything pertaining to it. In [42] some sense it is the mother of us all, who have been brought up

therein. We ought never to make her blemishes matter of diversion, but rather of solemn sorrow before God. We ought never to talk ludicrously of them; no, not at all, without clear necessity. Rather we should conceal them as far as ever we can without bringing guilt upon our own conscience. And we should all use every rational and scriptural means to bring others to the same temper and behaviour. I say 'all', for if some of us are thus minded and others of an opposite spirit and behaviour, this will breed a real schism among ourselves. It will of course divide us into two parties, each of which will [43] be liable to perpetual jealousies, suspicions, and animosities against the other. Therefore on this account likewise it is expedient in the highest degree that we should be tender of the church to which we belong.

5. In order to secure this end, to cut off all jealousy and suspicion from our friends, and hope from our enemies, of our having any design to separate from the church, it would be well for every Methodist preacher who has no scruple concerning it to attend the service of the church as often as conveniently he can. And the more we attend it, as constant experience shows, the more we desire to attend it. On the contrary, the longer we abstain from it, the less desire we have to attend it at all.

6. Lastly, whereas we are surrounded on every side by those who are equally enemies to us and to the Church of England, and whereas these [44] are long practised in this war and skilled in all the objections against it, while our brethren on the other hand are quite strangers to them all, and so on a sudden know not how to answer them, it is highly expedient for every preacher to be provided with sound answers to those objections, and then to instruct the societies where he labours how to defend themselves against those assaults. It would therefore be well for you carefully to read over the controversial tracts which we have published, in particular, *A Word to a Protestant*, with *The Advantage of the [members of the] Church of England over [those of] the Church of Rome*, *A Letter to a Quaker*,[31] *Thoughts concerning Infant Baptism*,[32] *[Serious] Thoughts concerning Godfathers and Godmothers, Serious thoughts concerning* [45] *perseverance*,[33] and *Predestination calmly considered*. And when you are masters of them yourselves it will be easy for you to recommend and explain them to our societies, that they may 'no more be tossed to and fro by every wind of doctrine', but being settled in one mind and one judgement by solid scriptural and rational arguments 'may grow up in all things into Him who is our head, even Jesus Christ'.[34]

NOTES

NOTES TO INTRODUCTION, pp. 1-6

1. Benjamin Gregory, *Sidelights on the Conflicts of Methodism*, London, 1898, p. 161
2. Sermon on 'The Ministerial Office' in John Wesley, *Works*, London, Wesleyan-Methodist Book-Room, n.d., 14 volumes (henceforth *Works*) VII. 279.
3. George Eayrs, *John Wesley, Christian Philosopher and Church Founder*, London, 1926, pp. 201-26, especially pp. 224, 226.
4. *Works* VIII. 253-4, 258-9.
5. Ibid., XIII. 272.

NOTES TO CHAPTER ONE, pp. 7-21

1. *Proceedings of the Wesley Historical Society* (henceforth *WHS*), XXXV. 88.
2. See Frank Baker, 'Wesley's Puritan Ancestry', *London Quarterly Review* (henceforth *LQR*), CLXXXVII. 180-6, especially pp. 184-5 (July, 1962).
3. Susanna was not quite thirteen when she transferred her allegiance; the MS account outlining her reasons was destroyed in the rectory fire of 1709. See her letter of 11 October 1709 to her son Samuel, in Methodist archives, London.
4. *The Letters of the Rev. John Wesley. A.M.*, Standard Edition, Ed. John Telford, 8 vols, London, 1931 (henceforth *Letters*) VI. 156.
5. Martin Schmidt, *John Wesley; a theological biography. Volume One*, trans. Norman P. Goldhawk, London, 1962, p. 138; see below, p. 42. Even though it is clear that some of these notions were more recent developments, Spangenberg's contention was in general true, and was surely derived from Wesley's own testimony.
6. Cf. John A. Newton, *Methodism and the Puritans*, London, Dr. William's Trust, 1964, pp. 6-7.
7. *The Journal of the Rev. John Wesley, A.M.*, Standard Edition, Ed. Nehemiah Curnock, 8 vols, Bicentenary Issue, London, 1938 (henceforth *Journal*), I. 465; cf. III. 38-9.
8. *Journal* III. 36.
9. *Works* VII. 92; cf. VII. 103, 'Break their wills, that you may save their souls'.
10. *Journal* III. 36-7.

11. Ibid., p. 38.
12. Cf. *Journal* I. 280*n*.
13. *Journal* I. 465.
14. *WHS* XXIX. 50-7.
15. Henry Moore, *The Life of the Rev. John Wesley, A.M.*, 2 vols, London, 1824, I. 112.
16. Ziegenbalg, Bartholomew, *Propagation of the Gospel to the East, Being an Account of the success of two Danish missionaries lately sent to the East Indies for the conversion of the heathens in Malabar*; the English translation by A. W. Boehm was first published in 1709; cf. *Journal* III. 33. Wesley published extracts from this in the *Arminian Magazine* for 1789 and 1790.
17. *Journal* III. 32-4.
18. Ibid., p. 33; cf. *Letters* I. 119-20.
19. Moore, *Wesley*, I. 116-17.
20. Joseph Benson, *An Apology for the People called Methodists*, London, 1801, p. 1, claims that he 'partook of the Lord's Supper when only eight years old'; cf. John Whitehead, *The Life of the Rev. John Wesley, M.A.*, 2 vols, London, 1793, 1796, I. 381. For Wake's confirmations see Norman Sykes, *William Wake*, 2 vols, Cambridge, 1957, I. 173-4; cf. *Confirmation: By various writers*, 2 vols, London, S.P.C.K., 1934, I. 186.
21. *Journal* I. 466; cf. Moore, *Wesley*, II. 117. Although from his later viewpoint Wesley criticized his youthful religion he maintained that he still 'had a kindness for religion', and Tyerman grossly exaggerated the situation in stating that 'John Wesley entered the Charterhouse a saint and left it a sinner'. See Luke Tyerman, *The Life and Times of the Rev. John Wesley, M.A.*, 3 vols, London, 1870-1, I. 22.
22. *Letters* I. 120.
23. G. J. Stevenson, *Memorials of the Wesley Family*, London 1876, p. 183; cf. pp. 175-93, 236-8.
24. Cf. *Journal* I. 465.
25. See Whitehead, *Wesley*, I. 80-96, Stevenson; *Wesley Family*, pp. 231-57; *WHS* XI. 25-31, etc.
26. *Letters* I. 26-7.
27. Whitehead, *Wesley*, I. 381.
28. Stevenson, *Wesley Family*, pp. 243, 245; for Wesley's 1722 timetable see *Journal* I. 42-6, especially p. 43.
29. *Letters* I. 16.
30. *Letters* I. 5; but cf. V. H. H. Green, *The Young Mr. Wesley*, London, 1961, p. 61.
31. Green, op. cit., pp. 61-2.
32. Francis Paget, *An Introduction to the Fifth Book of Hooker's Treatise of the Laws of Ecclesiastical Polity*, Oxford, 1899, p. 266; H. R. McAdoo, *The Spirit of Anglicanism*, London, 1965, p. vi.

33. [Wesley, Samuel, ed. John Wesley], *Advice to a Young Clergyman*, London, 1735, p. 43.
34. *Letters* I. 119.
35. Adam Clarke, *Memoirs of the Wesley Family*, 4th edn, revised, corrected; and considerably enlarged, 2 vols, London, 1860, I. 294; cf. I Samuel 2. 36. Not for 150 years were college fellowships made generally available for married laymen; see C. E. Mallet, *A History of the University of Oxford*, 3 vols, Oxford, 1924–8, III. 315–16, 348.
36. Luke Tyerman, *The Life and Times of the Rev. Samuel Wesley, M.A.*, London, 1866, p. 393. Tyerman omits, however, the following (among other passages), which is found in the original preserved at Wesley's Chapel, City Road, London: 'As for your standing at Lincoln, I waited on Dr. Morley (and found him civiller than ever) in a day or two after I had yours. He says the election is talked of to be about or on St. Thomas's Day; that you are welcome to stand, and that he knows but one that will stand against you, and that him you have no great reason to apprehend. (But for all that, study hard, lest the tortoise should beat you: for which you'll have near quarter of a year after you're in Orders.) The doctor says he keeps up his correspondence with Mr. Nichols, and I doubt not but Sam will ply him for you, as I'll set Sir N. Hickman, Mr. Downs, and Mr. Kirkby, upon the doctor. I'll write to the Bishop of Lincoln again. You shan't want a black coat, as soon as I've any *white* &c.' [i.e. 'weight'; spelling and punctuation modernized.] An earlier letter, of 26 January 1724–5, refers to Samuel Wesley's sounding Dr. Morley, who was the Rector of Lincoln College (see Clarke, *Wesley Family*, I. 294).
37. In spite of John Wesley's own statement in 1738 it seems fairly certain that the initiative in his seeking Holy Orders came from John himself, not from his father; see Tyerman, *Samuel Wesley*, pp. 391–2; cf. *Journal* I. 466.
38. Tyerman, *Samuel Wesley*, pp. 392–4. The *Advice* is now exceedingly rare, but a reprint may be found in Thomas Jackson, *The Life of the Rev. Charles Wesley*, 2 vols, London, 1841, II. 500–4.
39. Wesley, *Advice*, pp. 43–7.
40. *Journal* I. 466–7; *Letters* I. 10–22; cf. *WHS* XXXVI.105–7.
41. John Wesley, *Christian Library*, 50 vols, Bristol, 1749–1755, XVI. 96 (1752).
42. Ibid., p. 20.
43. Cf. H. Trevor Hughes, 'Jeremy Taylor and John Wesley', in *LQR* CLXXIV. 298–9 (October 1949).
44. Jeremy Taylor, *Works*, Ed. R. Heber and C. P. Eden, 10 vols, London, 1862, IX. xiv. Both Wesley's copy of *Ductor Dubitantium* (1671) and *The Great Exemplar* (1653) are at Kingswood School, Bath. For his reading of *The Golden Grove*, see Green, *The Young Mr. Wesley*, p. 316; for his reading of *The Liberty of Prophesying*, see p. 150 below.

23

45. Whitehead, *Wesley*, I. 397; cf. Susanna Wesley's letter to John, 21 July 1725, a copy of which is preserved in his MS letter book in the Methodist archives, London: 'Since I find you've some scruples concerning our Article of Predestination, I'll tell you my thoughts on the matter, and if they satisfy not, you may desire your father's direction, who is surely better qualified for a casuist than me.'

46. *Letters* I. 22–3. For Samuel Wesley's letter cf. the one possibly misdated 'Oct. 19' in *Arminian Magazine*, 1778, p. 31; Tyerman, *Samuel Wesley*, pp. 396–7, implies that this letter is in fact correctly dated.

47. *Wesley's First Sermon*, London, 1903, p. 23, a photograph of the original dated 1 September 1725; cf. Tyerman, *Samuel Wesley*, p. 395, which is, however, incorrect in several details.

48. *Letters* I. 25.

49. A long-planned sermon on universal charity (allied to his later discourse on a catholic spirit) was taken by his father as a pointed criticism of his somewhat harsh treatment of Hetty Wesley; see *Letters* I. 33–9.

50. *Letters* I. 41–2 (1727).

51. In 1731 he defended the damnatory clauses as 'not rashly adopted' in the Liturgy, even though he wished to modify their application; see *Letters* I. 91. He remained firmly opposed to any view of predestination which regarded damnation as both predetermined and irrevocable.

52. Green, *The Young Mr. Wesley*, pp. 76–80. In December 1725 his parents had given up hope of his success; see Susanna's letter to John dated 7 December, a copy of which is preserved in his MS letter book in the Methodist archives, London.

53. See below, pp. 71, 95.

54. Green, op. cit., p. 100. On 14 February 1726/7 he began a brief experiment with an hour-by-hour diary, one of the records for that day being: '11. Took my M[aste]r's Degree'.

55. *Letters* I. 39, 43; cf. *Journal* I. 52, showing how as early as 29 January 1726 he had unsuccessfully resolved to rise at 5.0 a.m.

56. *Journal* I. 467.

57. *Journal* I. 467; cf. Green, op. cit., pp. 102, 107, 113–5. But see my forthcoming article, 'John Wesley's introduction to William Law,' in *WHS* XXXVII.

58. A letter written to his mother on 19 March 1727 claimed that he was 'rising an hour sooner in the morning', but this apparently meant 7.0 a.m. instead of 8.0 a.m. His diary for 30 April 1729 shows that by that time he was usually rising at 6.0, but sometimes earlier, sometimes later. In June that year 5.0 became the normal hour, but again with many variants. On 17 August he reverted to a normal 7.0, which lasted until 11 September, when for some weeks he varied between 5.0 and 6.0, but for six days in November rose at 8.0 a.m. In 1730 once more 5.0 became frequent, and from 9 August onwards he regularly rose between 4.0 and 5.0 a.m. with hardly a break. Cf. *Works* VII. 69.

59. MS in Wesley's hand, Methodist archives, London, endorsed by him, 'Tr. Sat. Octob.6. 1727'; cf. *Works* VII. 473.
60. Cf. *Works* VII. 470.
61. *Works* XIII. 268–9.
62. *Letters* I. 113.

NOTES TO CHAPTER TWO, pp. 22–38

1. V. H. H. Green, *The Young Mr. Wesley*, pp. 145–58. Close study of Wesley's diaries by my graduate student and colleague Richard P. Heitzenrater shows that Francis Gore (named by Dr. Green as the other member of the group instead of Kirkham) did not appear in the diary until 28 November 1729. 'M' occurs in earlier references, and that this is a somewhat unusual cipher indication of Kirkham is confirmed by other evidence.
2. *Works* XIII. 268–9; cf. *Letters* IV. 27–8.
3. Green, op. cit., pp. 131–5.
4. *Letters* I. 79, 167, 173–5.
5. *Methodist Magazine*, 1798, pp. 118–9.
6. *Letters* I. 128.
7. *Journal* I. 90–4; cf. pp. 98–100 and *WHS* XVIII. 170.
8. *Letters* I. 92–3.
9. Ibid., p. 93; cf. p. 114.
10. Ibid., pp. 128–9, 138.
11. *Methodist Magazine*, 1798, p. 117.
12. *Letters* I. 92–6; cf. pp. 113–14.
13. Ibid., p. 113; cf. Frank Baker, *Charles Wesley as revealed by his letters*, London, 1948, pp. 11–12.
14. *Letters* I. 175–6, especially p. 176; cf. *The Oxford Methodists*, London, 1733, p. 9, describing the anonymous author's interview with Wesley: 'I threw in his way two or three objections ... to the *Singularity* of the thing, and wish'd their Zeal were not too warm and active, &c. But I found he was very well prepared to give solid answers to what I said, and such as shewed that their notions and principles were better considered and digested than their ill-willers generally imagine them to be.'
15. *Journal* I. 94, 98–101, VIII. 281; *Oxford Methodists*, pp. 9–10, 19, 27.
16. *Works* VII. 203.
17. *Journal* I. 89.
18. Rupert Davies and Gordon Rupp (editors), *A History of the Methodist Church in Great Britain*, Vol. I, London, 1965, p. 216; cf. *Journal* I. 94.
19. Robert Nelson's *Companion for the Festivals and Fasts*, for instance, which Wesley set several of his pupils to read in 1730, strongly commended

in the preface 'the pious and devout practices of the Religious Societies, who . . . distinguish themselves by their regular conformity and obedience to the laws of the Church' in spite of criticism raised against them. The rules of these societies, from Josiah Woodward's *Account* of them, are given in John S. Simon, *John Wesley and the Religious Societies*, London, 1921, pp. 10–15. The *Country Parson's Advice* also commended the societies, but Wesley did not discover this work until 1733 (see below, p. 34.)

20. *Works* XIII. 307.
21. Simon, op. cit., pp. 17–27. See also John Walsh, 'Origins of the Evangelical Revival', pp. 132–62 of G. V. Bennett, and J. D. Walsh (editors). *Essays in Modern Church History*, Oxford, 1966, especially pp. 141–8.
22. H. Trevor Hughes, *The Piety of Jeremy Taylor*, London, 1960, pp. 176–7, which reprints the article from *LQR* CLXXIV. 303–4 (October 1949); cf. *Journal* I. 96–7. It was probably from Taylor more than from anyone else that Wesley also copied the methodical habit of dividing his various writings into numbered sections and sub-sections. For Wesley's pursuit of holiness at Oxford under the influence of John Norris, see Charles A. Rogers, 'The Concept of Prevenient Grace in the Theology of John Wesley' (Ph.D. dissertation, Duke University, Durham, North Carolina, 1967), pp. 136–43.
23. Cf. Simon, op. cit., pp. 11, 13–14.
24. Wesley seems first to have read Cave in 1732; see Green, *The Young Mr. Wesley*, p. 314; cf. John S. Simon, *John Wesley and the Methodist Societies*, London, 1923, pp. 105–23.
25. Green, op. cit., pp. 148, 151, 154; John C. Bowmer, *The Sacrament of the Lord's Supper in Early Methodism*, London, 1951, pp. 18–22; Baker, *Charles Wesley*, pp. 14–17 'From the outset Wesley and his colleagues took communion at the cathedral, Christ Church, in preference to the university church of St. Mary's. His allegiance to Christ Church was reinforced after he came under the influence of John Clayton and the Non-Jurors in 1732, for here the mixed chalice was offered. See Green, op. cit., pp. 154, 171–3, and Frederick Hunter, *John Wesley and the coming Comprehensive Church*, London, Epworth Press, 1968, pp. 16–17. Through the kindness of the Rev. Gordon S. Wakefield I was able to read a page-proof copy of Mr. Hunter's volume while my own work was in the press. Although this confirmed and illustrated several points it did not bring about any major change in my views. In this present instance I believe that Mr. Hunter places undue emphasis upon Wesley's attendance at Christ Church communion, as if this were at Christ Church *qua* college chapel, and as if it began only after he came to favour the mixed chalice.
26. *Journal* I. 466–7; cf. pp. 95, 98–9.
27. Bowmer, op. cit., pp. 48–55.
28. *Methodist Magazine*, 1794, pp. 120, 169; *Journal* I. 95, 98n; Wesley's

sermon 'The Duty of Constant Communion', *Works* VII. 147–57. The MS of this sermon (Methodist archives, London) is dated 'Oxon. Feb. 19, 1732', and Clayton's reference to 'your sermon' in September 1732 surely implies that the 'Sacramentarians' used copies of the sermon to win others to sacramental observance; see *Journal* VIII. 280–1.

29. *Methodist Magazine*, 1798, p. 120.

30. *Journal* I. 90–4; cf. *Oxford Methodists*, pp. 3–8, and Matt. 25: 35–6.

31. Ibid. I. 94; cf. *Oxford Methodists*, p. 4, which states that the chaplain 'soon after signified his Lordship's permission and great satisfaction in the undertaking, and hearty wishes for the good success of it'.

32. Ibid. I. 468; cf. Luke 6: 22.

33. Ibid. I. 95.

34. Ibid. I. 51; cf. Green, op. cit., pp. 82–3. The influence of John Norris's *Practical Treatise on Humility*, which he read in 1730, should not be overlooked; cf. Rogers, 'Prevenient Grace', p. 139.

35. See p. 11 above and *Journal* I. 465; *Letters* II. 135.

36. *Journal* I. 466–7; *Works* II. 366.

37. Ibid. I. 467, 469.

38. Wesley, *Works*, Vol. VIII (Bristol, Pine, 1772), pp. 142–3, 253, 256–7; Green, op. cit., pp. 154, 155, 274–5n; cf. pp. 305–16; see Leslie Stephens's article on Norris in the *Dictionary of National Biography* (henceforth *DNB*).

39. John Locke, *An Essay concerning Human Understanding*, IV. xix. 8. Cf. Wesley's description of himself after reading William Law: 'The light flowed in so mightily upon me that everything appeared in a new view', see *Journal* I. 467.

40. William Morgan died in Ireland 26 August 1732 after an illness both physical and mental lasting over a year. On 15 October the Wesleys were accused of having hastened his death by encouraging him to fast, though in fact this had been his own idea, and his illness had compelled him to forsake it for over a year. See Luke Tyerman, *The Oxford Methodists*, London, 1873, pp. 9–14; cf. *Journal* I. 87–8.

41. Sermon 'On Grieving the Holy Spirit', see *Works* VII. 491–2; cf. *Methodist Magazine*, 1798, pp. 612–13 and the MS sermon in Methodist archives, London. For Tilly's authorship see Charles Roger's article in *WHS* XXXV. 137–41, June, 1966.

42. Wesley, *Sermons on Several Occasions*, Vol. II, London, 1748, pp. 9–10; Wesley's footnote stating that part of the preceding paragraph was 'now added to the sermon formerly preached' surely implies that the remainder followed the 1733 original, which has disappeared.

43. *Letters* I. 138.

44. Ibid. I. 139.

45. *Journal* I. 416, 420, 469–70.

46. *Works* XIV. 321, the preface to *Hymns and Sacred Poems*, 1739.

47. See p. 20 above.

48. Sermon 'On God's Vineyard', *Works* VII. 203; cf. *Arminian Magazine*, 1789, p. 68, where it is dated 'Witney, October 17, 1787'. Wesley's diary shows that he wrote this important sermon between 9.0 and 11.0 a.m. that day, preaching it on Sunday morning 9 December 1787 at the New Chapel, City Road, London; see *Journal* VII. 334d, 346d.

49. See his *Short History of Methodism* in *Works* VIII, 348; cf. *Answer to . . . Hervey*, November, 1765, in *Works* X. 316, and *A Plain Account of Christian Perfection*, 1766, in *Works* XI. 367, 373. He corrected this error in his *Concise Ecclesiastical History*, 1781; see *Works* XIII. 303.

50. *Oxford Methodists*, p. 3; cf. *Journal* I. 90, and the MS account of his pupils' studies in 'Colman VII' (Methodist archives, London.)

51. *Methodist Magazine*, 1798, p. 170; the MS records divide the notes into 'Lectiones Grammaticae, Analyticae, and Exegeticae'; see Methodist archives, London.

52. In Methodist archives, London. The use of sortilege was also adopted by the Holy Club missionaries *en route* to Georgia on 3 November 1735, probably through the influence of their new-found Moravian friends, but Wesley always preferred to open his Bible, and especially his Greek New Testament, for divine guidance in emergency. See Tyerman, *Oxford Methodists*, p. 70; cf. *Letters* II. 245–6, and *Journal* I. 472.

53. *Oxford Methodists*, 1733, p. 9; cf. *Journal* I. 101, VIII. 281.

54. *Journal* I. 468.

55. Ibid., I. 52.

56. Robert Nelson, *A Companion for the Festivals and Fasts of the Church of England*, 7th edn, London, 1712, pp. 436–7.

57. Tyerman, *Oxford Methodists*, pp. 24–34; cf. *Works* VII. 288–9.

58. Thomas Deacon, *A Complete Collection of Devotions*, London, 1734, Appendix, pp. 72–4. The essay itself appears no longer to be extant, though other fragments are contained in the MS notebook 'Colman XIII' in the Methodist archives, London. Cf. *Letters* I. 183, Henry Broxap, *A Biography of Thomas Deacon*, Manchester, 1911, pp. 176–7, Tyerman, *Oxford Methodists*, pp. 35–6, Green, *The Young Mr. Wesley*, pp. 185–6 and Hunter, *Wesley*, pp. 30–44.

59. Green, op. cit., p. 79.

60. Daniel Benham, *Memoirs of James Hutton*, London, 1856, p. 8.

61. Green, op. cit., p. 159.

62. Whitehead, *Wesley*, I. 368. This signature by Wesley appears in Jeremy Taylor's *Ductor Dubitantium*, dated 29 June 1732, and in Charles Daubuz, *Revelation*, dated 14 November 1733, both volumes preserved at Kingswood School, Bath. Examples of the convention used as a book-inscription by Samuel Wesley occur in the library of Emory University, Atlanta, Georgia (dated 1723, 1726, and 1738), and

by Charles at Richmond College, Surrey (dated 1756 and 1785). Dr. Norman Sykes told me shortly before his death that he had not met this usage elsewhere.

63. *Journal* I. 37, 89n.
64. Ibid. I. 419, where Wesley mentions in particular Beveridge and Jeremy Taylor.
65. 'The consensus of the ancients: what has been believed by everyone, everywhere, always.' See the notes on this on Albert C. Outler, *John Wesley*, New York, 1964, p. 46 and in Hunter, *Wesley*, pp. 12–13.
66. Deacon, *Devotions*, Appendix, p. 73.
67. Ibid., pp. 73–4.
68. Mr. Hunter believes that the Non-Jurors drew Wesley's attention not only to the ideal unity of the church universal but also to the possibilities of church union, specifically with 'German Lutheranism, Gallican Catholicism, and the Eastern Orthodox Church.' (*Wesley*, pp. 17–24, espec. p. 24.)
69. *Journal* I. 419.
70. Deacon, *Devotions*, pp. iii–iv.
71. *Works* XIV, 223–6.
72. *Letters* IV. 119.
73. Wesley, *Christian Library*, XLV. 273–91.
74. Tyerman, *Wesley*, I. 94, implying that the letter was written about 1733; but cf. Stevenson, *Wesley Family*, pp. 270–2, which includes part of Tyerman's quotation in a letter of 13 August 1735.
75. *Works* VIII. 259, IX. 55–6, X. 123–4, 135–7.
76. Cf. Wesley's extract from A. H. Francke's *Nicodemus: or a treatise on the fear of man*, in Richard Green, *The Works of John and Charles Wesley: a bibliography*, 2nd edn, London, 1906, No. 12; cf. Frank Baker, *A Union Catalogue of the Publications of John and Charles Wesley*, Durham, North Carolina, Duke University, 1963, No. 12. This extract Wesley inserted in his own collected *Works*, Vol. VIII, Bristol, 1772, pp. 188–240; see especially p. 208.
77. *Letters* I. 152, 155, 158, 160.
78. In MS 'Colman VII' in Methodist archives, London. This covenant was repeated on 12 October 1733 with a variant ending: 'By Translating Affectionate Divinity for All. Amen!'
79. *WHS* XIII. 25.
80. MS notebook 'Colman X', Methodist archives, London.
81. No copies of the editions of 1733 and 1736 have so far been discovered; the opening paragraph in two editions of 1738 contains this passage, which is omitted from those of 1740 onwards, in which other important changes were also made. These latter included the addition of one passage from 'the ancient liturgy commonly called St. Mark's'—a clear proof that the omission from the preface was not motivated by a declining love of the early church, as also a proof of the importance

for Wesley of the Alexandrian Church, for whom this was the traditional eucharistic liturgy.

82. The manuscript copy of the catalogue of John Byrom's personal library, preserved in the Chetham Library, Manchester, notes under Clayton: 'Prayers by him & J. Westley 8vo. L[ondon]. 1733' Cf. *WHS* III. 202–4.

83. It is advertised in the *Gentleman's Magazine*, the *Craftsman*, the *Daily Journal*, and the *London Evening Post*.

84. Joseph Priestley (ed.), *Original Letters by the Rev. John Wesley and his friends, illustrative of his early history*, Birmingham, 1791, pp. 18, 43.

85. MS letter, 10 November 1725, in Methodist archives, London.

86. *Letters* VIII. 268–9, corrected from the original in Methodist archives, London.

87. *Letters* I. 182; cf. *Wesley Banner*, 1851, p. 70 for the full text of Potter's letter, of which the original is at Wesley College, Bristol.

NOTES TO CHAPTER THREE, pp. 39–57

1. *The Diary of Viscount Perceval afterwards First Earl of Egmont*, 3 vols, London, 1920, 1923, II. 481.

2. *WHS* VII. 100–1.

3. Tyerman, *Oxford Methodists*, pp. 67–8.

4. Ibid., p. 70. John Wesley's diary records 'Agreed with Charles and company.'

5. Ibid., p. 69.

6. *Journal*, I. 110, 123.

7. Ibid., I. 146.

8. Tyerman, *Oxford Methodists*, p. 75.

9. Journal I. 111, 146. Actually Wesley's diary for 5 February 1736 makes no note of this; he turned back to the opening blank page of the diary volume in order to add this resolution in Latin. It seems that Ingham decided to throw in his lot on this optional matter at the last minute, for 'tres' is squeezed in above the line after 'Nos' (MS Diary, Methodist Archives, London.)

10. This document is discussed and reproduced in Bowmer, *Lord's Supper*, pp. 233–6, and described in Hunter, *Wesley*, pp. 52–3. Page 1 consists of notes not reproduced by Bowmer, but which Hunter states are from Beveridge's *Synodikon*, pp. 9–55. (N.B. I:1–57 of Beveridge's work reprints the Apostolic Canons, with commentaries by Theodore Balsamon, Johannes Zonar, and Alexius Aristenus.) Page 2 contains other notes from some pages numbered between 58 and 99, but contrary to Mr. Hunter's statement these are not from any part of Beveridge's two volumes but from some other work which I have

not been able to trace. They tend to support the antiquity and authenticity of the Apostolic Canons. Page 3 gives Wesley's resolutions here reproduced, presumably linked in some way with the accompanying documentation, though not necessarily so; they may well have been written earlier, though not (I think) later. Page 4 has been used to list some of the members of Wesley's English Methodist societies. I am quite certain that Dr. Bowmer is correct in suggesting that this page was written after, not before, the resolutions. (There exist plenty of examples of Wesley's using blank or partly-filled pages in old documents for completely new purposes, as for example the resolution described in Note 9 above, and in fact most of the Colman notebooks in the Methodist Archives, London.)

The external evidence for dating these resolutions is unsatisfactory, and has led several scholars astray. Just as it is not safe to deduce that they must be later than 1739 because of the Methodist names on page 4, no more must it be assumed that they belong to 1736 because we know that in that year Wesley read Beveridge, for he had at least dipped into it earlier.

Internal evidence seems more reliable. The following guiding principles may be stated:

(a) The resolutions could hardly have been written until after Wesley came under the influence of the Non-Jurors, i.e. 1733, and more especially would they fit the period after the publication of Deacon's *Complete Devotions* in 1734.

(b) They envisage a situation in which Wesley was the priest of an Anglican parish rather than a private Christian only or the leader of Methodist societies. After 1733 only his Georgia ministry is appropriate.

(c) Because of the strong dependence of the resolutions upon the authority of antiquity, and especially the authority of the Apostolic Canons, they were almost certainly penned before Wesley became somewhat disillusioned about this criterion, as noted in his *Journal* for 24 January 1738 (I. 418–20), and probably before he was convinced of the late origin of the Canons in September 1736 (ibid., I. 276–7.)

Thus the document in all probability originated in the period 1735–6, either while he was in Oxford directing the Holy Club or preparing for his Georgia ministry, on board the *Simmonds*, or in Georgia itself.

Wesley's observance of the resolutions is not susceptible of proof or even of illustration except by chance, but in fact clues do exist to show that from the outset of their ministry in Georgia all three of the clerical colleagues did follow at least some of these rules, particularly baptism by trine immersion, the stationary fasts (by that time a long-established observance with them), Lent, and Holy Week.

Until Wesley's early diaries have been fully deciphered, transcribed, and annotated, no statement about their contents can be categorical, but I believe that the only possible reference during the period especially under review is an entry at 8.0 a.m. on 29 January: 'r[ead] r[esolutions?] to Charles and company'. I do not feel at all confident about this, however, and look forward to a definitive solution of this curious problem by someone with greater resources available.

11. N.B. In this and the other notes illustrating this document I shall list in abbreviated form the liturgical documents appropriate for our purpose which support Wesley's usage (ignoring those which do not) of the following: Apostolic Constitutions ('Constit.') and separately the Apostolic Canons ('Canons') even though they form chapter 47 of Book VIII of the Constitutions: the First Prayer Book of Edward VI ('1549'), the Book of Common Prayer ('1662') and *A Compleat Collection of Devotions*, published 1734 ('Deacon'). For the Constitutions and Canons I have used the American reprint of the *Ante-Nicene Fathers*, ed. A. Cleaveland Coxe, Grand Rapids, Eerdmans, 1951, Vol. VII, pp. 385–508. For both '1549' and '1662' I have in most instances used *The Book of Common Prayer Illustrated*, by William Keatinge Clay, London, Parker, 1841, supported by the massive annotated edition by Archibald John Stephens, London, Ecclesiastical History Society, 1849, and the 3 vols. of *Hierurgia Anglicana*, new edn, ed. Vernon Staley, London, Moring, 1902.

'To baptize by immersion.' Both brothers did in fact baptize by *trine* immersion, which here and elsewhere Wesley intends by the term. See *Journal* I. 166–7, 210–1, 303, and Charles Wesley, *Journal* ed. Thomas Jackson, 2 vols, London, nd, I. 2, 4. This practice was laid down in Canon 50, and found in 1549 and Deacon.

12. 'To use water . . . in the Eucharist;' mingling wine and water in the chalice is assumed in Constit. VIII. 12 (p. 489), and is found in 1549 and Deacon. Tailfer's *True Narrative* spoke of Wesley's 'mixing wine with water in the Sacrament' (Cf. *Journal* VIII. 305); in 1749 Wesley defended the practice, in his *Letter to the Rev. Dr. Conyers Middleton* (*Works* X. 8–9, 48).

13. 'oblation of elements'; Constit. VIII. 11,12: 1549, 1662, Deacon. It is difficult to be sure whether here Wesley intended only the taking up of the paten and chalice in his hands or the lifting of them over his head ('elevation'), though one might assume the latter, because only this implied a deviation from orthodox Anglican practice. (For a discussion of the different usages see Stephens, pp. 1200–1.) Deacon does not prescribe elevation of the elements, but only that the priest should take the paten and cup into his hands. His rubric following their replacement on the altar, however, may well have influenced Wesley's practice:

'Therefore in commemoration of his passion, . . . *Here the Priest is to lift up his hands and eyes to heaven, . . .* we Offer to thee . . . *And here to point with his right hand to all the bread* . . . this Bread and . . . *And here to point with his left hand to the cup and every vessel on the Altar, in which there is any wine and water* . . . this Cup; . . .' (p. 92).

14. 'Alms'; Constit. VIII. 12, 1549, 1662, Deacon. The rubric for the offertory actually speaks of 'alms' only in 1662, when the intention was to include other purposes in addition to the care of the poor. For the practice in Methodism see Bowmer, op. cit., pp. 98–9.

15. 'invocation' of the Holy Ghost in consecrating the elements, Constit. VIII. 12 (p. 489), 1559, Deacon. This, the 'epiclesis', must be meant, rather than the simple invocation of God the Father only as in the 1662 prayer of consecration. (See Stephens 1196–8, and Bowmer, *Lord's Supper*, pp. 86–7.) Mr. Hunter points out (*Wesley*, p. 34) that the sequence 'Oblation . . . Invocation' reverses the order of these two usages in the 1549 book in accordance with the order in the Apostolic Constitutions, followed by the 1718 Usagers' Liturgy and Deacon's *Devotions*.

16. 'A prothesis' or sidetable for preparation of the elements to be placed on the altar, introduced from the Eastern Church by the Non-Jurors, and present in Deacon's *Devotions*; cf. Hunter, op. cit., p. 36.

17. 'in the Eucharist'; Wesley's usual term was 'Holy Communion', but 'Eucharist' was an occasional variant, cf. *Journal* I. 209, 376; this title is implied in 'the Sacrifice of Thanksgiving', ibid., I. 311. For Wesley's use of 'Holy Communion' in his diary see 8.0 a.m. on 29 March 1737 (*Journal* I. 34), where this is what the shorthand outline *must* mean, whereas his cipher use of 'D' might imply 'C' for 'Communion' or 'E' for 'Eucharist' (ibid., I. 77). Cf. Hunter, *Wesley*, p. 65. Wesley continued to use the term Eucharist occasionally, as in his *Letter* to Middleton in 1749 (*Works* X. 9).

18. 'To pray for the faithful departed'; Constit. VIII. 41, 42; 1549, 1662 (see below), Deacon. The 1662 Prayer Book is much more indirect and ambiguous than the others in its prayer 'that we, with all those that are departed in the true faith of Thy holy name, may have our perfect consummation and bliss . . . in Thy eternal and everlasting glory', (Burial Office) but it was undoubtedly a prayer for the dead, which in later years Wesley defended as a Prayer Book usage having no 'Papist' implications (*Letters* III. 326, *Works* X. 9–10; cf. Hunter, op. cit., p. 35.)

19. 'To pray standing on Sunday and in Pentecost'; one of Deacon's 'General Rubricks' (p. ix) ran thus: 'The posture for the Faithful in prayer, and at the reception of the Eucharist, is Kneeling, on all days but the Lord's days and all the days between Easter and Pentecost, on which it is Standing, in respect to and remembrance of our Saviour's resurrection: and therefore where-ever in the book the Faithful are ordered to kneel, those times are supposed to be excepted.' Wesley's own rule has been observed by the omission of 'and' ('—' in his cipher) from earlier transcriptions Cf. Hunter, op. cit., p. 40.

20. 'To observe Saturday, Sunday and Pentecost as festival'; Deacon listed

among the 'Lesser Festivals': 'All the days between Easter and Pente-cost, except Sundays', and 'All Sabbath-days or Saturdays, except the Saturday next before Easter'. (p. xxx; cf. also p. ix, quoted in Note 19.)

21. 'To abstain from blood and things strangled'; based on Acts 15.29—'abstain from meats offered to idols, and from blood, and from things strangled'; cf. v. 20. Constit. VII. 21 mentions 'things offered to idols',and Canon 63 adds 'flesh with the blood of its life'. Cf. note 9 above on the Wesleys' vegetable diet. In July 1737 Wesley sought the Moravians' point of view on this subject (*Journal* I .373).

22. 'Prudent', 'prudence', 'prudential' were important words in Wesley's religious vocabulary; on the influence of Norris's *Christian Prudence* see previous chapter, p.25; cf. Hunter, op. cit., pp. 49–50.

23. 'To observe the stations'; Constit. V. 15, VII. 23. For Wesley's essay on the stationary fasts, from which Deacon published excerpts in his *Devotions*, see above, pp. 30–1.

24. 'Lent, especially the Holy Week'; Canon 69, 1549, 1662, Deacon. The emphasis upon Holy Week was to Wesley the more ancient and im-portant observance; throughout his first Holy Week in Georgia he ate only bread, and Ingham wrote in his journal: 'This being the great and holy week, I dedicated it to devotion, observing the discip-line of the Primitive Church.' (*Journal* I. 198, Tyerman, *Oxford Methodists*, p. 79.) During Wesley's second Easter both his diary (in Greek) and his *Journal* (in English) used the same phrase—'The Great and Holy Week.' (*Journal* I. 345.)

Mr. Hunter (op. cit., p. 50) argues that neither Stations nor Lent were quite so essential to Wesley as the preceding 'duties' because by the time he penned this document he had discovered the late origin of the Apostolic Constitutions. Certainly on the associated document (see Note 75 below) he spoke of them as not extant in Tertullian's time, but even so they could still be ante-Nicene observances. I believe that this second document was prepared at a later date, and that these practices were regarded as no more than prudential because they affected only his personal spiritual health, not that of the people to whom he ministered, like most of the preceding duties. I admit, how-ever, that duty 6 does not fall into the same category.

25. 'To turn to the east at the Creed'; Constit. VII. 44. This custom was assumed in the practice of facing the altar in churches oriented to-wards Jerusalem. Similarly Deacon does not specifically prescribe this, but incorporates it into his general rubric: 'The People during the time of Divine Service are always to have their faces turned towards the Altar: the same is supposed of the Priest and Deacon whenever they kneel, and likewise when they stand, except where it is otherwise ordered' (pp. ix–x); see Stephens, op. cit., pp. 447–9.

26. See Frederick Hunter, 'The Manchester Non-Jurors and Wesley's High Churchism', *LQR* CLXXII. 57–9 (January 1947) and cf. his *Wesley*, p. 33.

27. *Journal* I. 371. Charles Wesley in his report to the Trustees some months earlier had estimated 'about 200 houses . . . and 700 souls' (Egmont, *Diary*, II. 313).

28. Egmont, *Diary*, II. 314.

29. *Journal* I.393; cf. pp. 176, 179; there is an error in the date, which was in fact Sunday 7 March 1735–6.

30. Ibid., I. 385–395: cf. Sunday 1 May 1737, when at 9.0 a.m. Wesley 'subscribed the Prayers' (ibid., I. 353), which indeed seems to be the correct transcription of the shorthand, though 'circumscribed [in] prayers' is possible. In any case the interpretation is uncertain, and the minority had no knowledge of any official public subscription.

31. David Nitschmann was the Moravian bishop when Wesley arrived in Savannah; in view of his return to Germany Seifert was elected and consecrated his successor; see *Journal* I. 170–1.

32. Schmidt, *Wesley*, p. 138; for a different translation of the complete document by Douglas L. Rights, see *South Atlantic Quarterly* XLIII. 407–9 (October, 1944).

33. *Journal* I. 370, III. 434, *Works* VII. 422; cf. Schmidt, *Wesley*, p. 179; Hunter, *Wesley*, pp. 41–2.

34. Schmidt, op. cit., pp. 179–80.

35. *Journal* I. 212–3; cf. pp. 272, 390, 393.

36. Egmont, *Diary*, II. 313–4.

37. *Works* VII. 422.

38. Sophy Williamson's affidavit claimed that Wesley 'always prescribed . . . the same way of life he then led as the only means of obtaining salvation; to corroborate which he always added that he endeavoured to imitate the primitive fathers, who were strict imitators of the life of Christ.' (*Journal* I. 384.)

39. Cf. *Journal* I. 233, 244, 296.

40. This is true; see *Letters* I. 229.

41. Provision was made for deaconesses in the Apostolic Constitutions (II. 57, III. 15, 16, VIII. 19, 20). Deacon's *Devotions* also allowed for them, stating that they must be women of forty years of age and over, and that their duties were 'to assist at the baptism of women, to instruct (in private) children, and women who are preparing for baptism; to visit and attend women that are sick and in distress; to overlook the women in the church, and to correct and rebuke those who behave themselves irregularly there; and to introduce any women who want to make application to a Deacon, Presbyter, or Bishop.' (Pp. 240–6, espec. p. 244.) It seems clear that Wesley did make use of women as pastoral assistants, calling them deaconesses, though without any formal ordination, just as later in his English societies he was to use women extensively as sick visitors, class leaders and (in a few instances, after much cogitation) in the superior office of deacon, i.e. as preachers. See *Journal* I. 272, 276, 314, 320 and below, Notes 81–3.

42. P. Tailfer and others. *A True and Historical Narrative of the Colony of Georgia*, Charleston, S.C., [1741], pp. 41-4, espec. pp. 42-3: cf. *Journal* VIII. 304-7.

43. *Journal* I. 386, 390, 395; cf. pp. 234, 270, 398, where one man claimed that Wesley called himself 'Bishop and Ordinary'. See also *WHS* XXXII. 190-2, where Mr. Victor Vine points out that the Georgia Trustees were Wesley's ecclesiastical superiors, not the bishop of London, and that therefore in effect he needed no episcopal authorization. This may well have been of some partial influence as the background for his later acceptance of Lord Peter King's teaching on the status of bishops.

44. *Journal* I. 165d, 231, 235, 240, 350-1.

45. Cf. ibid., I. 362.

46. Cf. ibid., I. 196-7, 280-3n, 324, *Letters* I. 220.

47. *Journal* I. 118-9, 127; cf. pp. 305, 324, 331.

48. Ibid., I. 236-40, 299, 345-6, 354-5, 371, 396-8, 435.

49. Ibid., pp. 223, 357, 371.

50. Ibid., pp. 213-4; cf. pp. 272-3.

51. *Works* XIII. 305-6; cf. *Journal* I. 193, 235, 302. See also the testimony of Mrs. Stanley, Savannah's public midwife, before the Georgia Trustees, 'greatly commending Mr. John Wesley, our minister at Savannah, who goes from house to house exhorting the inhabitants to virtue and religion.' (Egmont, *Diary*, II. 370.)

52. *Journal* I. 322, 358-9; laymen and laywomen assisted him in conducting communion classes; see Notes 80-3.

53. Ibid., I. 182, 222, 361, 363; Cf. Bowmer, *Lord's Supper*, pp. 31-2, 56-7.

54. *Journal* I. 371.

55. *Letters* I. 229.

56. *Journal* I. 298, 317-8, etc.

57. *Letters* I. 225, 229.

58. *Journal* I. 316-7.

59. *Letters* I. 218.

60. *Journal* I. 358-9, 361; *Letters* I. 220, 222.

61. *Letters* I. 204-6, 211-2.

62. *Journal* I. 282, 400.

63. Ibid., I. 337-9.

64. Ibid., I. 381-3, 385-95.

65. Ibid., I. 385.

66. MS Diary: cf. *Journal* I. 175.

67. See *John Wesley's First Hymn-Book*, a facsimile edited with notes by Frank Baker and George W. Williams, London and Charleston, S.C., 1964, pp. xxvii-xxviii.

68. Egmont, *Diary*, II. 451; cf. *Journal* I. 379, 394.

69. *Journal* I. 169-70.

70. Ibid., I. 185, 187.

71. Schmidt, *Wesley*, p. 162; there is some confusion about the date, nor do the letters and journals of either Ingham or the Wesley brothers resolve the difficulty.

72. *Journal* I. 270, 280, 282.

73. Ibid., I. 274–5; cf. MS Diary for 25 February 1734–5 (Methodist Archives, London); Hunter, *Wesley*, p. 48, points out that Wesley was quoting Article XXI.

74. *Journal* I. 276–8.

75. Ibid., I. 419–20. To about this time probably belongs a four-page document in Wesley's hand similar to that described in Note 10 above, with which it has been associated since their first publication in the *Guardian* for November 1867. (See R. Denny Urlin, *John Wesley's Place in Church History*, London, Rivingtons, 1870, pp. 68–84.) They were probably also associated among Wesley's own personal papers. Both arose from the patristic researches allied to his Georgia ministry, and when that ministry was over, its lessons learned, in strange symbolism both were used as scrap paper for furthering the new Methodist societies which replaced the old.

    Page 1, headed 'Apost. Const.' contains some notes on the Stations from Book V, chapter 15 of that work. Page 2, similarly headed, has notes on passages from VI. 24 to VIII. 32. Page 3, with the same heading continues with notes from VIII. 33, 42, and 47—the latter with its own sub-heading "Canones Apost." Page 4 again contains a fragmentary class list of some of Wesley's English members. (See Bowmer, *Lord's Supper*, pp. 236–7, Hunter, *Wesley*, p. 52.)

    This document is much more clearly a unity (apart from the membership list) than the other. Internal evidence again suggests its origin during Wesley's Georgia ministry, but after he had become somewhat disillusioned with the Apostolic Constitutions, possible in September 1736 or the following winter. On VII. 46 he notes "therefore S. Hilary [c. 315–67] knew not these Constitutions; for he calls Philemon a layman'; he queries whether Canon 27 was extant before the Council of Nicaea, notes that others were of the third century, and that Canon 85 was 'quite novel'. The general tenor of the two documents seems to have been: in the one case 'Apostolic Canons early', in the other 'Apostolic Constitutions late'. Their date and full significance, however, is by no means settled.

76. *Journal* I. 170–1, 278–9.

77. Ibid., I. 308–10; cf. p. 52 below.

78. Ibid., I. 372–4; in most instances Wesley also added 'the substance of their answer'.

79. Schmidt, *Wesley*, p. 185; cf. *Journal* I. 374–6, and see above, p. 43.

80. *Journal* I. 322, 353, 413, VIII. 308–10.

81. *Journal* I. 320, 326, 340, 343, 355, 357, 359, 363, 364, 387; cf. VIII. 309, 312, 313, and Coulter, *Settlers*, p. 24.

82. *Journal* I. 240-6, 272, 276, 314, 329, 337, and Coulter, *Settlers*, pp. 65, 66, which omits the younger sister Rebecca.

83. *Journal* I. 274, 279, 319, 320, 355, 370, and Coulter, op. cit., p. 75.

84. *Journal* I. 243, 343, 387; Coulter, op. cit., p. 65.

85. *Journal* I. 125, 131, 193, 195, 232, 268, Charles Wesley, *Journal*, I. 14, 17, Coulter, op. cit., p. 93, Will 'Reid', Dr. Patrick Tailfer's servant, seems to be the only one in the Earl of Egmont's admittedly imperfect list to fit the Wesleys' references.

86. *Journal* I. 116, 232, 233, 264, Charles Wesley, *Journal* I. 13, 17; Coulter, op. cit., p. 12.

87. *Journal* I. 114-7, 229, 231, 264, 267, 272, 320, 354, 358. Mark's father Thomas was one of the constables in Frederica, not Mark himself, see Coulter, op. cit., p. 23.

88. *Journal* I. 273-4; cf. *Letters* I. 205, 211.

89. *Journal* I. 377.

90. *Works* XIII. 305-6; cf. *Journal* I. 197-205, 226-233, and Tyerman, *Oxford Methodists*, p. 79; for a society founded at Savannah by Wesley's predecessor Samuel Quincey, see Leslie F. Church, *Oglethorpe*, London, 1932, p. 193.

91. *Journal* I. 201-2.

92. Ibid., I. 142-3, 168-71, 371-6.

93. Ibid., I. 171.

94. Ibid., I. 429.

95. Ibid., I. 309 and diary; the Journal passage added by Curnock is corrected from the manuscript in the Methodist Archives (p. 8); it does not appear in Wesley's own printed extract, doubtless because he had long changed his mind about the subject when he came to publish this extract.

96. Ibid., I. 351.

97. Ibid., I. 374.

98. Ibid., I. 449.

99. Charles Wesley, *Journal*, I. 103, 131, 143, etc.; these instances, however, all occur within private groups.

100. 16 April 1739; see Priestley, *Original Letters*, p. 96.

101. Ibid., p. 114.

102. *Journal* VI. 96.

103. Tyerman, *Oxford Methodists*, p. 68; Wesley's *Journal* (I. 111) reads 'first preached extempore', implying that this was the first of a deliberate series of such events.

104. Egmont, *Diary*, II. 313.

105. Charles Wesley, *Journal* I. 132-3.

106. John Byrom, *Private Journal and Literary Remains*, Chetham Society, 2 vols, 1854-7, II. 232.

107. *Journal* II. 404. Wesley demolished Mr Allen's false logic in trying to prove that no one can think and pray at the same time, but his hesitancy remained.

108. *Works* VIII. 437.

109. *Letters* II. 77.

110. Ibid., VI. 326.

111. *Journal* I. 386.

112. *Works* VIII. 227.

113. Phil. 1. 10, 'approve things that are excellent'.

114. *Journal* II. 3–63, espec. pp. 15, 28, and *Letters* I. 252; cf. Schmidt, *Wesley*, pp. 298–302.

115. *Journal* II. 53.

116. William Bowyer, MS Ledgers, Vol. I., p. 98, Grolier Club Library, New York.

117. *Wesley's Standard Sermons*, ed. Edward H. Sugden, 2 vols, London, Epworth Press, 1921, I. 35–52.

118. Baker, *Union Catalogue*, No. 8; see advertisements in the *London Evening Post*, 24 and 31 October, 7 November, 1738.

119. Ibid., No. 9; this went through nineteen or twenty editions during Wesley's lifetime, and has recently been made available in Outler, *John Wesley*, pp. 120–133.

120. Priestley, *Original Letters*, pp. 105–8.

121. 27 October 1739 (*WHS* XXXIII. 101).

NOTES TO CHAPTER FOUR, pp. 58–73

1. Priestley, *Original Letters*, pp. 110–11.

2. Of the eight archbishops of Canterbury enthroned during the seventeenth century seven had been translated from London (two from the deanship of St. Paul's) and one from Lincoln. Of the seven enthroned during the eighteenth century two were from York, two from Oxford, and the other three from Lincoln, Lichfield and Coventry, and Bangor.

3. Norman Sykes, *Church and State in England in the XVIIIth Century*, Cambridge, 1934, p. 157; Frank Baker, *William Grimshaw, 1708–1763*, London, 1963, pp. 130–2.

4. Not when he was archbishop of Canterbury, as Daniel Benham's *James Hutton* states, pp. 24–7; he did not become archbishop until 28 February 1737. For Potter and Wesley at Oxford see V. H. H. Green, *The Young Mr. Wesley*, pp. 143, 159, 161, 182.

5. *Journal* I. 270; *The Journal of the Rev. Charles Wesley*, ed. Thomas Jackson, 2 vols, London, (1849), I. 148.

6. *Works* VII. 185. On its original publication in the *Arminian Magazine* for 1788 the sermon was dated 'Bristol, Oct. 7, 1787'.

7. Letter of Charles Wesley to Benjamin La Trobe, 20 July, 1786—not to James Hutton, as John Telford states in Wesley's *Letters* VIII. 267. The

original is in the Moravian archives, London, and a contemporary copy in the Methodist archives, London.

8. Charles Wesley, *Journal* I. 81.

9. Ibid., I. 133.

10. Ibid., I. 133. The question of rebaptism had been hotly debated in 1712, when the bishops resisted Non-Juring pressures and continued to maintain that lay-baptism was valid though irregular. Bishop Wake's visitation sermon at Epworth in 1712 (on the occasion when in all probability John Wesley was confirmed) was on this vexed question, Wake taking the traditional position espoused by Gibson. See Sykes, *Wake*, I. 180-1.

11. *Certain Sermons or Homilies . . . To which are added the Constitutions and Canons Ecclesiastical set forth in the year MDCIII*, Oxford, 1844, pp. 566-7.

12. Charles Wesley, *Journal* I. 133, with the date corrected from John Wesley's diary, *Journal* I. 93-4. For Wesley's fear of legal problems arising from the old Conventicle Act see *WHS* XI. 56-8.

13. Charles Wesley, *Journal* I. 135-6.

14. Ibid., I. 143-4; cf. p. 136. It should be noted that in his earlier interview with Charles Wesley, the bishop said that he had detected a tendency towards antinomianism in John Wesley's recently published *Sermon on Salvation by Faith*.

15. Ibid., 151, 163.

16. Cf. I Cor. 9: 16, 17, and Acts 5: 29.

17. *Journal* II. 217-18. The italics are introduced from Wesley's original edition of 1742, pp. 55-6; the actual letter was almost certainly written 20 March 1739, though introduced into the *Journal* under the date 11 June. Echoes and even quotations from this important letter appear in John's letter to his brother Charles on 23 June 1739, and in November George Whitefield was able to apply it more literally, writing on board a vessel bound for America, 'the whole world is now my parish.' (*The Works of the Reverend George Whitefield*, London, 6 vols, 1771-2, I. 105.)

18. *Letters* I. 323.

19. *The Works of . . . Mr. Richard Hooker*, arranged by Rev. John Keble, 7th edn, revised by R. W. Church and F. Paget, 3 vols, Oxford, 1881, III. 154-5, 168-9.

20. Ibid., III. 203-35, especially 213, 231-2.

21. Ibid., III. 231-2.

22. Ibid., III. 232.

23. *Letters* III. 150, V. 257.

24. Ibid., I. 323; cf. III. 130-1, where he says that *antistes* here simply means 'the minister of a parish'.

25. Charles Wesley, *Journal* I. 137, 156.

26. Cf. Richard Green, *Anti-Methodist Publications*, London, 1902, Nos. 6-92.

27. Charles Wesley, *Journal* I. 126.
28. Whitefield, *Works* IV. 5–16, especially p. 10.
29. *WHS* XI. 57–62; cf. C. W. Towlson, *Moravian and Methodist*, London, 1957, p. 224, and Bennet and Walsh, *Essays*, pp. 134–5.
30. *Journal* I. 111, 169, II. 101–2, 168; cf. Charles Wesley, *Journal* I. 122–3, *Works* VIII. 112.
31. *Journal* II. 172–3; cf. *Cambridge History of England*, Cambridge, 1909, VIII. 83, which affirms that the date marked 'a new era in the religious history of England'.
32. *Journal* V. 484; cf. Mark 16: 15.
33. Charles Wesley, *Journal* I. 135–6 may contain a hint that Gibson himself was advising the rebellious parishioners, who may well have complained to him direct. Adult re-baptism was conducted by Charles Wesley in St. Mary's, Islington, in the teeth of the bishop's opposition, Stonehouse being one of the witnesses. Perhaps it is too un-Christian, however, to imagine the bishop murmuring angrily, 'I'll fix him!' It is also possible that the idea for circumventing the Methodists came from someone who had heard of the attempt two months earlier to exclude Whitefield from the Bristol churches by a similar method, though again Gibson was the most likely 'someone'. A great friend of Gibson's, Dr. Richard Venn, had already let it be known in December 1738 that no Methodist would be allowed to preach in his pulpit at St. Antholin's. (Charles Wesley, *Journal* I. 138–9; see *DNB* under Venn; cf. Luke Tyerman, *Life of the Rev. George Whitefield*, 2 vols, London, 1890, I. 181–2.)
34. *Certain Sermons . . . To which are added the . . . Canons*, pp. 557–8.
35. Charles Wesley, *Journal* I. 146.
36. *George Whitefield's Journals: a new edition*, London, 1960, p. 259.
37. *WHS* V. 238.
38. Charles Wesley, *Journal* I. 149, 154; *WHS* V. 238. For a few months Stonehouse continued at least a measure of his Methodist witness, and on 2 June accepted a Quaker for re-baptism on Whitefield's recommendation, but within a year he was frozen out of his parish for such practices; see Whitefield's *Journal*, p. 277 and *WHS* V. 239.
39. Acts V: 38–9.
40. Charles Wesley, *Journal* I. 154.
41. Whitefield, *Journals*, pp. 213–224, 233–4, 276; when he waited on Butler in London in May, however, he was treated 'with the utmost civility' and received a substantial benefaction for his Georgia orphanage.
42. Ibid., p. 299.
43. Ibid., p. 303.
44. Moore, *Wesley* I. 465. For a discussion of Wesley's supposed right to preach anywhere because he was ordained while a Fellow of Lincoln College see *WHS* XX. 64–7, 193–4, and XXI. 31–2; cf. Outler, *Wesley*, p. 21*n*.

45. Charles Wesley, *Journal* I. 192–3; cf. John Wesley's *Letters* I. 358, which may come from a variant copy of Charles's letter with incorrect dates supplied, or possibly even from a form letter for such occasions. Telford's source is not known.

46. *Letters* VII. 332 dates this incident as 1740, but *Letters* VIII. 141 states that it was before Wesley had met the bishop.

47. *Works* X. 376.

48. *Works* XI. 12; cf. *Letters* III. 157, 167, 172; the reference in Wesley's diary on 7 November 1739, 'writ Christian Perfection,' does not fit this sermon, and his diary is missing from 8 August 1741 onwards. The interview almost certainly took place shortly thereafter, and Strahan's ledgers record the printing of 2,000 copies of the sermon on 26 September 1741.

49. *Journal* III. 9.

50. Cf. Tyerman, *Whitefield*, I. 554–8.

51. Moore, *Wesley* I. 543–5. It seems just possible that Wesley's unnamed inquirer was John de Koker, the Amsterdam physician whom he had met in 1738. See *Journal* II. 4, 63; III. 445–8, and *Letters* I. 261–2.

52. Cf. Priestley, *Original Letters*, pp. 110, 113.

53. *Journal* II. 533.

54. *Works* XIII. 269; cf. *Letters* VIII. 141.

NOTES TO CHAPTER FIVE, pp. 74–87

1. *Works* XIII. 307.

2. See Simon, *John Wesley and the Religious Societies*, pp. 10–27.

3. Charles Wesley, *Journal* I. 150, 153, 216; John Wesley, *Journal* II. 223; cf. Whitefield, *Journal*, p. 272.

4. Davies and Rupp, *Methodist Church*, I: 189–91, 218–25.

5. *Journal* II. 194–230.

6. The term remains in the Large Minutes of 1772, disappearing from the edition of 1780 (*Minutes*, 1862 edn, I. 493). It remained in the title of the *General Rules* until after Wesley's death.

7. Charles Wesley, *Journal* I. 241.

8. *Works* VIII. 250; cf. p. 269.

9. Ibid., VIII. 251–2, 354, 356.

10. Ibid., XIII. 310.

11. *Journal* II. 535; cf. *Works*, Vol. 28 (1774), p. 49.

12. Cf. *Letters* VII. 332. For the later acceptance of services in 'church hours' see Chapter Sixteen below, pp. 283–303.

13. Griffith T. Roberts, *Howell Harris*, London, 1951, p. 48.

14. *Works* VIII. 269–71; cf. V. 268.

15. *Letters* I. 272–3.

16. Charles Wesley, *Journal* I. 147; cf. *WHS* XVI. 144-6.
17. Ibid., I. 149-51.
18. Ibid., I. 152-3. In one case Shaw's colleague is named Fish, in the other Wolf.
19. Ibid., I. 159.
20. Roberts, *Harris*, pp. 19-40, especially p. 34; cf. Charles Wesley, *Journal* I. 243; Charles prudently omitted any entry from his diary on this day, but his entries for adjoining days confirm Harris's records.
21. Tyerman, *Whitefield*, I. 163-7.
22. *Journal* VIII. 93.
23. See his MS 'Experiences', dated 3 December 1741, in Methodist archives, London, *Wesleyan Methodist Magazine*, 1884, and *The Christian's Amusement*, Nos. 14, 15. Many of Humphreys' letters appear in the successor to this latter periodical, *The Weekly History*, from 1741 onwards. Whatever we make of his preaching for Wesley in 1738, the 1740 date fits in neatly with John Wesley's leaving London to join his brother Charles in Bristol, and with his diary note immediately upon his return just over a week later—'Conversed to Bro. Humphreys, etc' (*Journal* II. 380, 383).
24. *WHS* VI. 106-7; cf. his autobiographical preface to *Sacred Hymns for the Children of God*, 1741; *Journal* II. 426-34.
25. *Journal* II. 434.
26. *Journal of the Historical Society of the Presbyterian Church of Wales* XLVIII. 30 (June 1963).
27. *Minutes of some late conversations* (1766), p. 10. This was incorporated into the Large Minutes from 1780—see *Minutes* I. 501. Cf. *Works* VII. 277. Wesley strangely omits the matter from his 'Short History of the People called Methodists' (1781). For Maxfield's separation from Wesley see *Journal* V. 4-7.
28. *WHS* XXVII. 7-15.
29. Bowmer, *Lord's Supper*, pp. 62-4.
30. Moore, *Wesley* I. 464.
31. Wesley's 'Dr. Deleznot' must surely be identified with the Rev. J. L. Delezenot who ministered at a Huguenot chapel in Swanfields in 1734 and 1735; see *Proceedings* of the Huguenot Society of London VIII. 53 (1905-8). The name does not appear in the *Gentleman's Magazine* throughout the century.
32. *Journal* II. 484, 504. It seems more likely that a different 200 attended each Sunday than that 1,000 members communicated each Sunday in groups of 200, though this remains uncertain. The system of 200 communicants per Sunday had already been established for St. Luke's parish church. Cf. *Minutes* I. 192, and *Wesleyan Methodist Magazine*, 1855, p. 224.
33. *Journal* II. 535.
34. *Works* XIII. 269.

35. See J. E. Rattenbury, *The Eucharistic Hymns of John and Charles Wesley*, London, 1948.
36. Bowmer, *Lord's Supper*, pp. 82–102.
37. Tom Beynon, *Howell Harris, Reformer and Soldier (1714–1773)* Caernarvon, 1958, p. 139.
38. *Minutes* I. 59.
39. See pp. 213–4 below.
40. Davies and Rupp, *Methodist Church*, I. 272–3.

NOTES TO CHAPTER SIX, pp. 88–105

1. *Works* VIII. 1–45. The *Earnest Appeal* was advertised in the *Newcastle Journal* in April 1743.
2. *Earnest Appeal*, Newcastle, 1743, p. 46; cf. *Works* VIII. 32–3, which omits the original italicizing.
3. Ibid., pp. 47–8; cf. *Works* VIII. 34.
4. Ibid., p. 48; cf. *Works* VIII. 34–5. The Ordering of Priests (during the bishop's examination) reads 'contrary to God's word'.
5. Ibid., pp. 48–9; cf. *Works* VIII. 35.
6. The clause in parentheses was added in the second edition, published the same year in Bristol.
7. *Earnest Appeal*, Newcastle, 1743, pp. 49–50; cf. *Works* VIII. 35–6.
8. Acts 5: 38–9.
9. *Earnest Appeal*, Newcastle, 1743, p. 49; cf. *Works* VIII. 42.
10. *Journal* III. 226.
11. *Works*, Bristol, 1772, Vol. XIV, p. 198; cf. *Works* VIII. 58.
12. For almost certain proof of Gibson's authorship see Tyerman, *Whitefield* II. 89–91. Cf. *Works* VIII. 59, 482, 486, and Richard Viney's MS Journal for 1 April 1744: 'Read a pamphlet lately published & call'd *Observations upon the . . . Methodists. . . .* Mr. Bailey ye Minister of Pudsey [in the diocese of York] invited several of his hearers to his House after morning service and distributed 10 or 12 of ye abovemention'd Pamphlets, saying they were sent him by ye Bishop to dispose of as he thought fitt. . . . 'Tis ye same which was publish'd only a few Copys of just before I went to London, suppos'd to be by, or at least with ye approbation of ye Bishop of London.' (Moravian archives, London; transcript by Marmaduke Riggall.)
13. See above, p. 61.
14. [Gibson], *Observations*, p. 4.
15. Ibid., p. 8. cf. J. S. Simon, *John Wesley and the Methodist Societies* p. 319, for Gibson's criticism of Wesley's sermon, *Scriptunal Christianity*, (Oct. 1744)
16. William Strahan's ledgers list the cost of 3,000 copies of each on 20 December 1744 and 15 December 1745, respectively, and they were

advertised in the *Gentleman's Magazine* for January 1745 and January 1746. Part III was dated at the end 18 December 1745. Both publications were dated '1745' on the title page.

17. *Farther Appeal*, Part I, London, 1745, pp. 12–13; cf. *Works* VIII. 55–6.
18. *Works* VIII. 59, 482.
19. On his way out to America Whitefield also prepared a reply to Smalbroke's *Charge*, but Wesley probably did not know of this until later. See Richard Green, *Anti-Methodist Publications*, No. 19.
20. *Works* VIII. 78–110.
21. In Wesley's *Works* (1772) XIV. 291 'doctrine' is altered to 'doctrines'.
22. *Farther Appeal*, Part I, London, 1745, pp. 78–9; cf. *Works* VIII. 112–13. In Wesley's *Works* (1772) 'long' is omitted from 'till long after' in section 2 of the summary.
23. *Farther Appeal*, 1745, p. 81; cf. *Works* VIII. 115.
24. Ibid., p. 80; cf. *Works* (1772) XIV. 294, and *Works* VIII. 113–14.
25. Ibid., pp. 83–4; cf. *Works* VIII. 116–17.
26. *WHS* XXI. 31–2. On the occasion in question Charles cited his Master's degree as giving him the right 'to preach throughout England and Ireland', but acquiesced when his interrogator spoke of him as a 'Fellow of a College'. This was in July 1744.
27. *Farther Appeal*, 1745, Part I, pp. 85–6; cf. *Works* VIII. 118–19.
28. Ibid., pp. 86–7; cf. *Works* VIII. 119.
29. *Works* VIII. 136–200; see especially pp. 171, 174–200.
30. Ibid., pp. 205–8.
31. *Letters* I. 176–7; cf. pp. 181, 183, and p. 25 above.
32. *Works* XIII. 227.
33. Wesley's own account was dated at the end 22 October 1743, but he included other narratives dated as late as 5 March 1743/4; the pamphlet was first advertised in the *Newcastle Journal* of 9 November 1745. See *Works* XIII. 169–233.
34. *Works* VIII. 210–14.
35. Cf. Cuthbert Atchley, *The Parish Clerk and his right to read the Liturgical Epistle*, London, 1903.
36. *Works* VIII. 217–28.
37. Ibid., pp. 229–32.
38. *Farther Appeal*, Part III, London, 1745, pp. 125–6; cf. *Works* VIII. 235–6.
39. Ibid., pp. 134–5; cf. *Works* VIII. 243–4.
40. *Journal* II. 327.
41. Ibid., pp. 361–2. This he had believed even in Georgia; see Spangenberg's testimony in 1737: 'Wesley has long been accustomed to hold that the Holy Communion is a means of grace, and has thought that a man can be converted thereby.' (*South Atlantic Quarterly* XLIII. 408).
42. See below, p. 103.
43. *Journal*, London, 1744, p. 26; cf. *Journal* II. 335–6.

44. *Works* VIII. 247; cf. Ezekiel 14: 13–23.
45. Edmund Gibson, *The Charge of the Right Reverend Father in God, Edmund Lord Bishop of London. At the Visitation of his Diocese in the years 1746 and 1747*, np, np, nd, p. 4.
46. *Works* VIII. 481–95, especially pp. 482–3, 493.
47. Ibid., VIII. 375; cf. X. 450.
48. Ibid., VIII. 414–481. Advertised in the *Bristol Journal* for 19 July 1746. The title referred back to *The Principles of a Methodist*, published in 1742 as an antidote to the misconceptions in Josiah Tucker's *Brief History of the Principles of Methodism* (see *Works* VIII. 359–74), but there was no organic link between the two apologiae.
49. *Works* VIII. 444.
50. *WHS* XXVIII. 47–9; cf. *Journal* of the Calvinistic Methodist Historical Society, XXVII. 108–9 (1942), for the silencing of Howell Harris in 1743 by this method.
51. *Works* IX. 1–64, especially pp. 2–3, 40, 49; cf. *WHS* XXXIV. 37–42.
52. Ibid., VIII. 248.
53. Ibid., pp. 251–3.
54. *An Answer to a late pamphlet entitled 'A Plain Account of the People called Methodists'*, London, for E. Withers, 1749, pp. 9–10.

NOTES TO CHAPTER SEVEN, pp. 106–119

1. *Journal* III. 123–4; Charles Wesley, *Journal* I. 354–5; cf. Frank Baker, 'Methodism and the '45 Rebellion', *LQR*, CLXXII. 325–33 (October 1947).
2. *Journal* of the Historical Society of the Presbyterian Church of Wales XLVIII. 29 (1963).
3. For the first Conference, see Simon, *John Wesley and the Methodist Societies*, pp. 202–21; cf. *Minutes*, I. 1–6, 21–5.
4. *Works* XIII. 248; cf. Chapter 13 below, especially pp. 220–1, 225, 232–3.
5. These documents were reprinted in *Minutes* (1862 edn) I. 1–21, 21–43. The manuscript minutes of the individual conferences for 1745–1748 were printed as Publication No. 1 of the Wesley Historical Society, London, 1896. They are mostly in the handwriting of John Bennet, but those for 1746 are in that of John Wesley. A supplement to this, containing the manuscript minutes for 1749, 1755, and 1758, was published in the *Proceedings* of the Wesley Historical Society, Vol. IV, Part 5 (1904), paged continuously with the earlier publication, (61)–73.
6. MS Minutes, p. 12 (1744). The question about the Articles does not appear in the printed version.
7. *Minutes*, I. 8–11, 64, 618.
8. MS Minutes, pp. 40, 42, 46.
9. *Journal* II. 197; cf. *Letters* VII. 149.

10. Baker, *Grimshaw*, pp. 160–1; for the 1784 Deed Poll see Chapter 13 below.
11. See Davies and Rupp, *Methodist Church*, pp. 228–9; cf. *Works* XIII. 274–8.
12. W. W. Stamp, *The Orphan-House of Wesley*, London, 1863, p. 269.
13. Wesley, *Sermons*, Vol. I, London, 1746, pp. (iii)–iv, viii–ix; cf. *Works* V. 1, 4.
14. Ibid., p. iv; cf. *Works* V. 2.
15. *Journal* VIII. 171–252.
16. MS Minutes, p. 13.
17. Acts 5; 29; cf. pp. 63, 65, 71, 89–90 above.
18. *Minutes* I. 26–7; cf. John Kent, *The Age of Disunity*, London, 1966, pp. 171–2.
19. Ibid., I. 27, 30–2.
20. Ibid., I. 30.
21. Ibid., I. 31.
22. Ibid., I. 34–5. Wesley's acid comment on I Cor. 11:18 in his *Explanatory Notes* emphasizes the same point: 'Both *Heresy* and *Schism*, in their modern sense of the words, are sins that the Scripture knows nothing of; but were invented merely to deprive mankind of the benefit of private judgments and a liberty of conscience.'
23. *Minutes* I. 35–6.
24. Ibid., p. 36.
25. Ibid., p. 39.
26. Ibid., p. 48.
27. Frank Baker and Frederick Hunter, 'The Origins of the Methodist Quarterly Meeting', *LQR* CLXXIV. 28–37 (January 1949).
28. Many puzzling circumstances surround this conference. Neither the *Journal* of John nor of Charles Wesley mentions it. John seems to have been in London, Charles in Bristol, at the time. Our only information about it comes from John Wesley's MS Minutes and from a summary of some extracts which were incorporated in the 1753 edition of the 'Large Minutes'. A small conference was held in Bristol at the more normal time that year—the beginning of August—but this also seems to have been a special *ad hoc* meeting between the two Wesleys, Whitefield, and Harris, called to discuss a closer union between them, though possibly others were present. See Charles Wesley, *Journal* II. 63; cf. Baker, *Grimshaw*, pp. 158–9. The summer and autumn months of this year witnessed some personal turmoil both for Charles Wesley (who had been married in April) and John, whose espoused Grace Murray was married off to John Bennet by Charles Wesley in September.
29. *Minutes* I. 44; cf. MS Minutes, p. 63.
30. *Minutes* I. 44, 594.
31. MS Minutes, pp. 63–4—omitted from the printed record. In 1755 Wesley's *Reasons against a Separation* disavowed any desire to be 'a

compact united body'—cf. *Works* XIII. 227. This was merely wishful thinking.

32. See Brian Frost, 'Orthodoxy and Methodism', *LQR* CLXXXIX. 13–22 (January 1964).

33. Cf. John Kent, *The Age of Disunity*, 'Anglican Episcopacy and Anglican-Methodist Relations', especially Section Two: (c), pp. 182–90; this essay is for the most part a reprint from the author's 'Episcopacy in Church and Society' in *Anglican-Methodist Relations* (ed. W. S. F. Pickering), London, 1961; see especially pp. 105–10.

34. *Minutes* I. 446.

35. *Letters* III. 192–6.

NOTES TO CHAPTER EIGHT, pp. 120–136

1. *Bathafarn: the Journal of the Historical Society of the Methodist Church in Wales* (henceforth *Bathafarn*) II. 50 (1957).

2. *Journal* III. 334–5.

3. *Letters* II. 129.

4. F. E. Stoeffler, *The Rise of Evangelical Pietism*, Leiden, 1965, p. 7. See II Kings 10:15.

5. See Richard Green, *Wesley Bibliography*, and Baker, *Union Catalogue*, No. 109. I am grateful for the generous co-operation of Miss K. Monica Davies of the National Library of Wales, Aberystwyth (which owns the first edition of 1748) for preparing the basic translation. The adjusting I have attempted myself, with the aid of Spurrell's Welsh dictionaries. I have also collated the first edition with the copy of the second at the British Museum.

6. G. Nesta Evans, *Religion and Politics in Mid-Eighteenth Century Anglesey*, Cardiff, 1953, pp. 102–16, especially pp. 103, 107; cf. *WHS* XXIV. 121–5, XXV. 4–8, 23–9, especially pp. 25–6.

7. *Sermons*, Vol. III, London, 1750, pp. 187–8; the 'as' in the penultimate sentence of section 10 is Wesley's replacement for 'that' in the original, a correction made in the errata to Vol. III of his *Works* (1771); cf. *Works* V. 496–7.

8. *Works* X. 71–2, 75, 79.

9. *Sermons*, Vol. III, London, 1750, pp. 171–2; cf. *Works* V. 487.

10. Ibid., pp. 177–8; cf. *Works* V. 491–2. Cf. also Charles Wesley's use of the same quotation from Calvin (in Latin) in a letter to Whitefield dated 1 September 1740 (Charles Wesley, *Journal* II. 169).

11. *Works* X. 83.

12. Ibid., pp. 85–6.

13. *WHS* XV. 120–1; cf. Tom Beynon, *Howell Harris' visits to London*,

Aberystwyth, 1960, pp. 118–19, and *Journal* of the Historical Society of the Presbyterian Church of Wales L. 41, 59 (July 1965).

14. MS at Methodist Historical Library, Lake Junaluska, North Carolina; cf. *WHS* V. 108–10.

15. *Journal* of the Calvinistic Methodist Historical Society VII. 33–4, which gives a fuller and seemingly better transcript than that in Beynon, op. cit., pp. 229–39.

16. Ibid., p. 34.

17. Charles Wesley, *Journal* II. 63.

18. Beynon, op. cit., pp. 249–65; cf. Tyerman, *Whitefield*, II. 246–8, *Journal* III. 452.

19. *Minutes* I. 717–18.

20. Tyerman, *Whitefield* II. 406; cf. *Journal* V. 182n.

21. *Journal* V. 182n.

22. M. H. Jones, *Trevecka Letters*, Caernarvon, 1932, pp. 186–206; *WHS* XVI. 114–17.

23. Roberts, *Harris*, p. 79; cf. Tyerman, *Whitefield* II. 496–7.

24. *Journal* V. 228.

25. Ibid., V. 74. On Harris as mediator, see Roberts, *Harris*, pp. 76–8.

26. *Journal* IV. 303.

27. Ibid., p. 302.

28. Ibid., IV. 351, V. 36.

29. Ibid., IV. 100; cf. below, pp. 175–8.

30. Ibid., V. 36–7.

31. Baker, *Grimshaw*, p. 235.

32. *Minutes* I. 717.

33. Baker, *Grimshaw*, pp. 236–8, 250; Tyerman, *Oxford Methodists*, pp. 137–9.

34. Baker, *Charles Wesley*, pp. 40–1.

35. *Selected Trevecka Letters (1747–1794)*, ed. Gomer M. Roberts, Caernarvon, 1962, pp. 77–8; cf. C. W. Towlson, *Moravian and Methodist*, London, 1957, pp. 131–3.

36. William G. Addison, *The Renewed Church of the United Brethren, 1722–1930*, London, 1932, pp. 96–103.

37. A. J. Lewis, *Zinzendorf*, Philadelphia, 1962, pp. 139–41, 150–9.

38. Beynon, *Harris's visits to London*, pp. 258, 261–3.

39. Beynon, *Harris the Reformer*, p. 79.

40. Ibid., pp. 81–2.

41. Ibid., p. 82; cf. Harris's letter to Watteville in *Selected Trevecka Letters (1747–94)*, pp. 79–80.

42. Ibid., p. 84.

43. Ibid., pp. 168–9, 213; meantime Charles Wesley had kept in touch with Nyberg (ibid., p. 154).

44. *Journal* IV. 93; cf. *Works* XI. 39.

45. *Works* VII. 182–3; cf. *Letters* IV. 151–2; but see also the *Farther Appeal*

(1745), where Wesley spoke of Luther and Calvin as leading a separation (*Works* VIII. 242).

46. *Letters* IV. 136–8 (1761).
47. *Works* X. 133–40, 86–128.
48. Moore, *Wesley*, II. 340–1; cf. *WHS* XXVI. 38–45.
49. *Works* VII. 182–3; cf. *Letters* VI. 326.
50. *Works* VIII. 242–3.
51. 27 March 1760, in Methodist archives, London; cf. Jackson, *Charles Wesley* II. 184–5.
52. *Works* VIII. 180–91.
53. This is also the reverse order of his condemnations in Part III of the *Farther Appeal* noted earlier; see *Works* VIII. 242–3 and p. 99 above.
54. *Journal* III. 206, 244–5; *Letters* VIII. 189; *Arminian Magazine*, 1778, pp. 419–25.
55. *Journal* IV. 62–3, 117, VII. 389d, etc.
56. Ibid., IV. 326–6; cf. *WHS* VIII. 25–9. For some notes on Wesley's preaching in dissenting meeting-houses see A. Skevington Wood, *The Burning Heart: John Wesley, Evangelist*, Grand Rapids, Michigan, Eerdmans, 1967, p. 135.
57. E.g. Edwards and Skelton in 1769; cf. Baker, *Grimshaw*, pp. 242–4.
58. *Journal* V. 180; cf. *Letters* V. 143–5, 260, VI. 326; Baker, *Grimshaw*, pp. 242–4; Davies and Rupp, *Methodist Church*, I. 293–5.
59. *Letters* III. 222.
60. *The Centenary of Methodism*, Dublin, 1839, p. 232.
61. Wesley, *Explanatory Notes upon the New Testament*, London, Bowyer, 1755, p.v.
62. 'Thoughts upon a late phenomenon', dated 13 July 1788, in *Arminian Magazine*, 1789, p. 49; cf. *Works* XIII. 266.

NOTES TO CHAPTER NINE, pp. 137–159

1. *Arminian Magazine*, 1790, p. 214; cf. *Works* XIII. 272.
2. *Journal* II. 150.
3. Ibid., I. 346.
4. Richard Baxter, *Practical Works*, 23 vols, London, 1830, XXII. 8; V. H. H. Green, *The Young Mr. Wesley*, p. 315; on 25 October 1732 Susanna Wesley commended Baxter, obviously in answer to John's inquiry (*WHS* XVIII. 171).
5. *Standard Sermons* II. 130, 133; see above, pp. 111–13.
6. *Letters* I. 272–3; cf. Benham, *Hutton*, pp. 11, 29.
7. *Letters* I. 274, collated with the original in Moravian archives, London.
8. Ibid., I. 276.
9. Hooker, *Works* III. 232.

10. MS Minutes, p. 47.

11. *Letters* I. 350.

12. *Extract* IV from Journal, London, 1744, pp. 102-9; cf. *Journal* II. 490-5, *Letters* I. 344-51.

13. [Erskine, Ralph], *Fraud and Fals[e]hood Discovered*, Edinburgh, 1743, p. 32.

14. Ibid., pp. 34-5.

15. MS Minutes, p. 25; this was confirmed by the 1746 Conference.

16. *Letters* III. 223.

17. Edward Stillingfleet, *Irenicum*, 2nd edn, London, 1662, preface, p. xiv.

18. *Arminian Magazine*, 1779, pp. 598-601; cf. *Letters* III. 181-3, 201, and James Clark, *Montanus Redivivus*, Dublin, 1760, the reading of which may well have prompted Wesley's inscription in the Kingswood copy of Stillingfleet's work.

19. See pp. 63, 71; cf. *Letters* I. 322-3.

20. MS Minutes, p. 13.

21. *Extract* VI from Journal, London, 1753, p. 118; this passage is asterisked in *Works* XXVIII. 347 (1774); cf. *Journal* III. 229-31.

22. *Works* VIII. 497.

23. Cf. Norman Sykes, *Old Priest and New Presbyter*, Cambridge, 1956, p. 81.

24. *Letters* IV. 150, VII. 21.

25. *Journal* III. 232; see 'An Impartial Hand' [Peter King, later first Lord King], *An Enquiry . . .*, London, nd [1691], Part I, chapter IV, pp. 54-78, especially pp. 64, 68-9.

26. Edgar W. Thompson, *Wesley, Apostolic Man*, London, 1957, pp. 23-9. In later years Wesley drew the additional conclusion, unwarranted by King's evidence alone, that bishops and presbyters, being of the same order, 'consequently have the same right to ordain'. (*Letters* VII. 238; see Chapter 15 below.)

27. King, *Enquiry*, Part I, Chapters II and VIII, pp. 14-42, 136-52, especially pp. 14-17, 136-40.

28. MS Minutes, pp. 47-8.

29. *Letters* II. 76-8.

30. Ibid., II. 96.

31. Beynon, *Howell Harris, Reformer and Soldier*, p. 81.

32. E.g. 16.5 (p. 536), and 18.19 (p. 578) of Taylor's *Works*, 1862, Vol. V.

33. *Works* X. 28. It may well have been his reading of Stillingfleet's *Irenicum* that made Wesley realize that the Apostolic Constitutions were not what they purported to be. Stillingfleet (p. 275) referred to Daillé's *De Pseudepigraphis Apostolicis* of 1653 as having 'everlastingly blasted' the credit of the work; Wesley himself certainly read Daillé's *De usu Patrorum* in English translation, and turned it against Conyers Middleton in the same *Letter* in which he noted the spuriousness of the Apostolic Constitutions (*Works* X. 12).

34. *Journal* III. 434.

35. See Chapter 8 above, especially pp. 123-5.

36. See Chapter 7 above, especially pp. 115–18.
37. *Journal* III. 229–30; cf. *Letters* I. 274, quoted pp. 141–2 above.
38. *Irenicum* II. vi. 18, especially p. 322.
39. MS Minutes, p. 48.
40. *Works* X. 47–9; cf. *Journal* II. 263.
41. *Journal* IV. 438; cf. *Letters* IV. 139–40, VII. 284–5.
42. *Works* VIII. 220; cf. *WHS* XXXIV. 141–7, where Albert B. Lawson quotes William Law's *Second Letter to the Bishop of Bangor*: 'if there be no *Uninterrupted Succession*, then there are no Authorised Ministers from Christ; if no such Ministers, then no Christian sacraments. . . .'
43. *Works* XI. 187–91; cf. *Journal* II. 263–4.
44. *Works* X. 136.
45. John Wesley, 'Ought we to separate from the Church of England?' (see Appendix below), p. 15; in his revision of 1784 he did in fact omit absolution from the *Book of Common Prayer*; see pp. 236, 245–6, 331 below.
46. Cf. Rattenbury, *Eucharistic Hymns*, pp. 81–100. Clearly it is folly to claim that in 1738 Wesley forsook his sacerdotal views; on the other hand I think that Rattenbury goes too far in insisting that he never modified those views, but simply abandoned the theory of apostolic succession.
47. Wesley, 'Ought we to separate?', pp. 20–1; cf. *Letters* III. 132. Charles Wesley continued to be even more fully convinced of this; in 1772 he wrote to Joseph Benson: 'I cannot help believing that you will be called to the sacerdotal as well as the prophetic office' (Baker, *Charles Wesley*, p. 129).
48. Wesley, 'Ought we to separate?', p. 20.
49. As in the case of the essential identity of presbyters and bishops, for which see the note on I Tim. 3:8.
50. 'Ought we to separate?' see Appendix.
51. *Works* VI. 261–2 (1783), VII. 26–7 (1787), 164 (1787), 276 (1789).
52. 'Ought we to separate?', pp. 13–14.
53. *Letters* IV. 146–52.
54. 'Ought we to separate?', p. 15; cf. *Works* V. 496.
55. *Works* X. 136.
56. Ibid., X. 126–7, cf. p. 154.
57. This is in fact genuine Wesley, owing nothing to his major source, Bengel's *Gnomon*; cf. *Letters* III. 200, where in effect Wesley quotes his own note.
58. Wesley, *Explanatory Notes upon the New Testament*, London, 1755, p. 353 of Wesley's proof copy, by courtesy of Mrs. Prothro, the owner, and the dean and librarian of Perkins Theological Seminary, Dallas, Texas, Dr Joseph D. Quillian and Mr Decherd Turner.
59. *The Lives of Early Methodist Preachers*, ed. Thomas Jackson, 4th edn, 6 vols, London, 1871, II. 7; cf. *LQR*, CLXXVI. 157 (April 1951).
60. Outler, *Wesley*, p. 17; cf. *LQR* CLXXXV. 214–51 (July 1960).

61. *Works* VII. 151–6.
62. *Standard Sermons* II. 226–43.
63. MS in Methodist archives, London; for this collated with the text as published in *Works* X. 188–201 see Outler, *Wesley*, pp. 317–32.
64. *WHS* XXXII. 154–5; cf. XXIX. 19; King, *Enquiry*, Part II, pp. 73–8, proved that this was valid in the early church.
65. *Works* X. 8–9; cf. pp. 246, 252 below.
66. For Wesley's views on baptism see John R. Parris, *John Wesley's Doctrine of the Sacraments*, London, 1963, pp. 35–61; B. J. Galliers, 'Baptism in the Writings of John Wesley', in *WHS* XXXII. 121–4, 153–7; Robert E. Cushman, 'Baptism and the Family of God', pp. 70–102 of *The Doctrine of the Church*, ed. Dow Kirkpatrick, Nashville, 1964; John C. English, 'The Heart Renewed: John Wesley's Doctrine of Christian Initiation', pp. 112–92 of *The Wesleyan Quarterly Review*, Vol. IV (May 1967).
67. Norman Sykes, *Church and State in England in the XVIII Century*, Cambridge, 1934, pp. 115–37; *Confirmation. By Various Writers*, 2 vols, London, 1934, I. 176–245; for Wesley's own confirmation, see above, p. 10. Wesley omitted from his revision of the *Book of Common Prayer* the Order for Confirmation.
68. See Outler, *Wesley*, pp. 332–44; cf. *Works* VII. 147–57.
69. *Works* VI. 420, VII. 154; cf. 'Ought we to separate?' (see Appendix), p. 8: 'the virtue of the ordinance does not depend on him that ministers but Him that ordains it'.
70. See John C. Bowmer, 'A Converting Ordinance and the Open Table', in *WHS* XXXIV. 109–13; cf. Bowmer, *Lord's Supper*, pp. 166–86; see also p. 144 above.
71. *Works* X. 8–9; cf. Bowmer, *Lord's Supper*, pp. 92, 137–46, 175–6, and pp. 40–1 above.
72. See Parris, op. cit., pp. 62–96, and A. Raymond George, 'The Lord's Supper', pp. 140–60 of Kirkpatrick, *Doctrine of the Church*.
73. Ernst Troeltsch, *The Social Teaching of the Christian Churches* (trans. Olive Wyon), 2 vols, Harper Torchbook edn, New York, 1960, especially I. 328–43; cf. H. R. Niebuhr, *Christ and Culture*, New York, 1951; Bryan R. Wilson, *Sects and Society*, London, 1961; *LQR*, April 1963, including a symposium on 'The Church as an Institution'.
74. Troeltsch, op. cit., II. 721–4.
75. *LQR* CLXXXVIII. 117 (April 1963).

NOTES TO CHAPTER TEN, pp. 160–179

1. *Journal* III. 351–3.
2. Charles Wesley, MS. 'The Preachers 1751' (Methodist archives, London).

3. Ibid.

4. Baker, *Charles Wesley*, pp. 79–87.

5. *Journal* IV. 8–11.

6. Copy of letter, endorsed by Charles Wesley, in Methodist archives, London.

7. Document of 8 May 1754 (Methodist archives, London); *Journal* IV. 186*n*; Thomas Marriott in *Wesleyan Methodist Magazine*, 1847, p. 869, assumes that a similar agreement was signed in 1755; in any case the Conference endorsed the same principle; cf. Edwin Sidney, *Life and Ministry of the Rev. Samuel Walker*, 2nd edn, London, 1838, pp. 201–3.

8. *Works* VIII. 444.

9. Wesley's memory was at fault on this occasion, nor did he consult his concordance. There are other examples of σχίσματα translated 'divisions', including I Cor. 11:18, on which he gave an important note to the same effect: 'it is plain that by *Schisms* is not meant any separation from the church but uncharitable divisions in it. . . .'

10. MS Minutes, pp. 46–7.

11. *Letters* III. 146; cf. III. 201–2 and Wesley's notes on I Cor. 11:18.

12. Cf. Wesley's admission to Thomas Adam in 1755: 'It is not clear to us that presbyters so circumstanced as we are may *appoint* or *ordain* others, but it is that we may *direct* as well as *suffer* them to do what we conceive they are *moved to by the Holy Ghost*' (*Letters* III. 150).

13. Tyerman, *Wesley*, II. 202.

14. This passage Wesley asterisked in his collected *Works*; cf. *Works* VIII. 113–14.

15. MS letter, Charles Wesley to Walter Sellon [29 November 1754], Drew University, Madison, New Jersey; cf. Tyerman, *Wesley*, II. 201–2.

16. Cf. Hebrews, Chapters 5, 6, 7, especially 7:15, 'another priest is raised up after the likeness of Melchisedec' (John Wesley's translation). Charles Wesley frequently used this term of the ambitious preachers, claiming that they sought to become priests of a different order and by a different method from that which was normal.

17. MS letter, Drew University; cf. Tyerman, *Wesley* II. 202.

18. 'But I do not give much credence to *them*.'

19. MS letter, Drew University; cf. Tyerman, *Wesley* II. 203.

20. Baker, *Grimshaw*, pp. 249–50.

21. *Journal* IV. 114.

22. MS letter, 30 April 1755 (imperfect) at Methodist archives, London; cf. *Journal* IV. 114, 247.

23. Methodist archives, London; see Appendix.

24. 'Ought we to separate,' p. 6.

25. Ibid., p. 14.

26. Ibid., pp. 14–16; cf. Chapter 14, especially p. 236 below.

27. Ibid., pp. 24–9; cf. *Letters* III. 186, and *Works* XIII. 225–7.

28. *Letters* III.144.

29. Frank Baker, *Representative Verse of Charles Wesley*, London, 1962, pp. 287–94.

30. MS letters, 26 and 30 May 1755, at Drew University.

31. MS Letter, Drew University.

32. Ibid., Drew University.

33. Wesley quoted some words from Virgil, 'I am proximus ardet Ucalegon!'; see *Letters* III. 131.

34. This man has not been identified, but the *Gentleman's Magazine* notes that on 7 June 1755 a Mr. Smith lost an appeal against the London consistory court for preaching without a licence. The bishop involved was Dr. Thomas Sherlock. Excommunication for such a misdemeanour would have been an extreme penalty, and no such case is mentioned in Edward Carpenter, *Thomas Sherlock*, London, 1936.

35. Cf. Wesley's Latin, 'actum est', *Letters* III. 131.

36. MS letter, 28 June 1755, Drew University.

37. *Letters* III. 133.

38. Ibid., III. 132.

39. Ibid., III. 135.

40. Ibid., III. 136.

41. Sidney, *Walker*, pp. 161–7, especially p. 165; cf. G. C. B. Davies, *The Early Cornish Evangelicals, 1753–1760*, London, 1951, p. 89.

42. Sidney, *Walker*, pp. 164–70.

43. *Letters* III. 146.

44. *Arminian Magazine*, 1779, pp. 371–6; cf. *Letters* III. 149–52.

45. *Letters* III. 183.

46. Baker, *Charles Wesley*, p. 95; cf. Sidney, *Walker*, pp. 201–3, collated with the original in the Historical Society of Pennsylvania, Philadelphia.

47. Sidney, *Walker*, pp. 207–12, 216–20.

48. Baker, *Grimshaw*, pp. 157, 251.

49. Quoted in Charles Wesley's letter to Walker, 6 September 1756, at Emory University, Georgia; cf. Sidney, *Walker*, p. 228.

50. *Journal* IV. 186; cf. Sidney, *Walker*, p. 229.

51. *Letters* III. 195.

52. Ibid, III. 243.

53. Ibid., III. 192–6.

54. Baker, *Charles Wesley*, pp. 95–7.

55. Ibid., p. 97; cf. letter of 19 October 1756, at Methodist archives, London.

56. *Journal* IV. 212, 232.

57. Ibid., IV. 108.

58. *Arminian Magazine*, 1780, pp. 100–3; cf. *Letters* III. 226–8.

59. *Letters* III. 182.

60. *WHS* XXIV. 91–2.

61. Cf. Jackson, *Charles Wesley* II. 180; for the certificate, made out to Rowell as 'a preacher to the people commonly called Methodists', see *WHS* XX. 180–1.

25

62. *WHS* XX. 180–1.
63. Diocesan Registry, York.
64. Diocesan Registry, Lincoln.
65. Green, *Wesley Bibliography*, and Baker, *Union Catalogue*, No. 191.
66. MS Minutes, p. 71; cf. *Journal* IV. 281. The title 'Preservative' was mentioned in a letter of 16 November 1756 from Charles to John Wesley; cf. Tyerman, *Wesley*, II. 253.
67. *Journal* IV. 348.
68. See above, pp. 128–9.
69. See John Murlin, printed letter dated 23 December 1794 to Joseph Benson; copy at Duke University, Durham, North Carolina.
70. Baker, *Charles Wesley*, p. 99.
71. Ibid., p. 99.
72. MS letter, 7 March 1760, Charles Wesley to John Johnson, in Methodist archives, London.
73. MS letters, 17 and 26 March 1760 to his wife, in Methodist archives, London. For John Wesley's reply see *Letters* V. 97–8.
74. William Strahan, Ledgers, British Museum Add. MSS. 48802A, p. 37.
75. 27 March 1760, copy by Charles Wesley in Methodist archives, London; cf. Baker, *Grimshaw*, pp. 254–5.
76. Baker, *Grimshaw*, pp. 255–7.
77. MS letter, 13 April 1760, Methodist archives, London; cf. Baker, *Charles Wesley*, pp. 102–3.
78. MS letter, Dublin, 17 April 1760, Methodist archives, London.
79. *Letters* IV. 100.
80. Tom Beynon, *Howell Harris, Reformer*, pp. 79–80, 82–3.
81. *Letters* IV. 197.

NOTES TO CHAPTER ELEVEN, pp. 180–196

1. Beynon, *Howell Harris, Reformer*, p. 139; Onslow was Speaker 1728–61 and died in 1768.
2. *Works* VII. 210. Wesley also felt assured in later years of the sympathy of George III, who succeeded his grandfather in 1760, witness his hint in 1776 about knowing the mind of one greater than Lord Mansfield on the subject of freedom of conscience (*Letters* VI. 228).
3. Green, *Anti-Methodist Publications*, No. 282; cf. *Works* IX. 96–109.
4. Green, op. cit., Nos. 273, 275, 276, 277, 278, 279; cf. *Works* VIII. 500–12.
5. Green, op. cit., No. 272; cf. *Works* IX. 89–96.
6. Green, op. cit., No. 330; cf. *Works* IX. 110–17.
7. Green, op. cit., No. 342; cf. *Works* IX. 117–173.
8. Green, op. cit., No. 343; cf. *Works* XIV. 347–59. (The title page of Wesley's answer is incorrectly dated 1767.)

9. In the paper which he read before the 1755 Conference he defined the church along these lines, concluding 'Perhaps some would add, "And to submit to the Governors of the Church, and obey the laws of it".' See 'Ought we to separate?', p. 3, in Appendix.

10. *Arminian Magazine*, 1781, pp. 220–1; cf. *Letters* IV. 147–8.

11. *Arminian Magazine*, 1781, pp. 219–26; cf. *Letters* IV. 146–52.

12. Cf. 'Ought we to separate?', pp. 34–6.

13. *Letters* III. 151.

14. Davies, *Cornish Evangelicals*, pp. 74–87.

15. John Gillies, *Appendix to the Historical Collections*, Glasgow, 1761, pp. 98–100.

16. *WHS* XXII. 52–7; cf. XXI. 194–5.

17. *Letters* III. 224.

18. Ibid.

19. *Arminian Magazine*, 1779, pp. 537–8; cf. *Journal* VII. 68d.

20. *Letters* III. 117; cf. *WHS* XVII. 174–81.

21. *Arminian Magazine*, 1779, p. 536; cf. 1797, pp. 611–3.

22. Ibid., 1780, 106–7, 168–9, 332–5, 560–1; 1797, 407–8, 459–60.

23. G. R. Balleine, *A History of the Evangelical Party in the Church of England*, London, 1933, pp. 55–6; *Letters* IV. 23; *Journal* IV. 300.

24. *Arminian Magazine*, 1779, pp. 540–1.

25. Luke Tyerman, *Wesley's Designated Successor: the life . . . of the Rev. John William Fletcher*, London, 1882, pp. 23–59.

26. Ibid., pp. 58–9.

27. Davies, *Cornish Evangelicals*, passim.

28. Ibid., pp. 102–5, etc.

29. *Journal* III. 363, IV. 110; *Letters* III. 151; *Arminian Magazine*, 1779, pp. 320–1.

30. *WHS* IX. 11–14, 123–5; XIX. 88–9.

31. *WHS* II. 116–17; cf. XXI 205–6.

32. *Journal* IV. 120.

33. See J. S. Reynolds, *The Evangelicals at Oxford, 1735–1871*, Oxford, 1953, especially pp. 24–42.

34. *Letters* III. 243.

35. *Journal* IV. 291, 300, 317–22, 335, 338–43, 359–60.

36. *Arminian Magazine*, 1797, pp. 353–4; cf. Tyerman, *Wesley*, II. 335–7.

37. *Letters* IV. 23, 136–52; *Journal* IV. 300; *Arminian Magazine*, 1780, pp. 672–3.

38. *Arminian Magazine*, 1780, 165–8; cf. *Journal* IV. 461, 463, V. 16.

39. *Arminian Magazine*, 1780, pp. 164–5; cf. *Journal* IV. 300, 361.

40. *Arminian Magazine*, 1797, pp. 355–7; cf. pp. 457–8; *Journal* IV. 256, 327, 372–3.

41. *Journal* IV. 254; Tyerman, *Wesley* II. 301–2; *Minutes* I. 69.

42. *Arminian Magazine*, 1780, pp. 54–5; *Letters* IV. 48; cf. Tyerman, *Wesley*, II. 315–17.

43. J. C. Ryle, *The Christian Leaders of the last century*, London, 1873, pp. 159–61; *Letters* IV. 58; *Journal* IV. 300, 361; Wesley knew *about* Romaine before 1758, and may have met him; Charles Wesley dined with him and Madan on 21 September 1757.

44. MS letter, 4 March 1759, at Methodist archives, London.

45. [A. C. H. Seymour], *The Life and Times of Selina Countess of Huntingdon*, London, 1840, 2 vols, II. 4*n*, 218; Tyerman, *Whitefield*, II. 414–16; *Journal* IV. 300.

46. *Journal* V. 11.

47. Ibid., IV. 300; cf. MS letter of Charles Wesley, 27 February 1759, who adds the definite information that Dartmouth was present (Methodist archives, London).

48. *Journal* IV. 57–8.

49. Ibid., IV. 234; *Letters* III. 223–4.

50. Baker, *Grimshaw*, pp. 223, 252–3.

51. *Letters* IV. 160–1, 216–17; Jackson, *Early Methodist Preachers*, IV. 34.

52. *Letters* IV. 162.

53. *WHS* XXVIII. 106–8, XXIX. 73–5; cf. A. Skevington Wood, *Thomas Haweis, 1734–1820*, London, 1957, pp. 75–6.

54. *Letters* IV. 206.

55. Ibid., IV. 143.

56. *Arminian Magazine*, 1780, p. 672; cf. *Letters* IV. 146.

57. Charles Atmore, *The Methodist Memorial*, Bristol, 1801, pp. 78–80; *Letters* IV. 290*n*.

58. *WHS* XXI. 97–101; Atmore, *Memorial*, pp. 356–65; Thomas Coke, *Sermon preached . . . on the death of the Rev. John Richardson*, London, 1792, pp. 14–23.

59. *Letters* IV. 182.

60. Ibid., IV. 206.

61. *Arminian Magazine*, 1782, pp. 495–9; cf. *Letters* IV. 215–18.

62. *Journal* V. 24.

63. Beynon, *Howell Harris, Reformer*, pp. 183–6.

64. Ibid., p. 187. Harris spoke on a later occasion about Wesley and 'the vast work [God] has done by him—above 20,000 souls under his care' (ibid., p. 189); for the Bristol visitation sermon see ibid., p. 294; cf. p. 200, where he spoke to the Earl of Dartmouth about the bishops and their persecution of the Methodists.

65. Ibid., p. 213.

66. Ibid., pp. 202–3.

67. Ibid., p. 204.

68. Ibid., p. 205; frequently, as here, Harris's peculiar English leaves his meaning uncertain.

69. Ibid., p. 205.

70. *Journal* V. 47. James Rouquet and Richard Hart would be present, and probably also John Camplin, vicar of St. Nicholas's, Bristol.

71. *Letters* IV. 239; the quotation is from III. xxxv. 3 of the *Imitatio*, and is not included in Wesley's briefer *Extract of the Christian's Pattern*. For Conyer's invitation see *Arminian Magazine*, 1782, pp. 216–17.

72. See copies of each edition at Duke University; cf. *Journal* V. 60–2. *Letters* IV. 236–9, and *WHS* XII. 29–32.

73. *Letters* IV. 244, 259.

74. *Letters* IV. 244.

75. Ibid., IV. 243–4.

76. Ibid., IV. 242–3.

77. *Journal* V. 91; Tyerman, *Wesley* III. 471; Jackson, *Early Methodist Preachers* IV. 28–9.

78. Jackson, op. cit., IV. 34.

79. *Works* VIII. 350–1.

80. Tyerman, *Fletcher*, pp. 99–100.

81. Ibid., p. 107.

82. *Journal* V. 150; cf. pp. 153–4.

83. Tyerman, *Wesley* II. 556.

84. *Journal* V. 182–3, 188–9; Tyerman, *Wesley* II. 556–9.

85. The Duke copy of the first edition ('My Lord') is addressed by Wesley 'To the Revd Mr Spencer'; the other edition ('Dear Sir') has several initials of the clergy extended to complete names, as well as other revisions, and the Duke copy is addressed by another hand to the Rev. John Newton at Olney. Cf. *Letters* IV. 236, *WHS* XXI. 205.

86. *Journal* V. 63–6; the letters from Sellon and Perronet are surely in reply to the 1766 'printed letter', 'yours of the 15th', and that of Richard Hart seems to be different from the one noted in *Letters* IV. 244; Wesley did not publish this *Journal* extract until 1768, and inserted the 1766 replies under the date of the original letter, rather than leave them for the next extract containing the 1766 entries, which in fact did not appear until 1771.

87. *Letters* V. 34.

88. *Journal* V. 228.

89. *WHS* XVI. 116–17; *Journal* V. 228, 335.

90. *Letters* V. 57–9.

91. Ibid., V. 83–5.

92. Ibid., V. 97–9.

93. *Minutes* I. 82.

94. Ibid., I. 87–8; cf. *Letters* V. 143–5.

NOTES TO CHAPTER TWELVE, pp. 197–217

1. Beynon, *Howell Harris, Reformer*, p. 79.

2. *Minutes* I. 540–1, 602. From 1766 onwards one of the questions asked of

itinerants before admission into full connexion with Wesley was: 'Do you constantly attend the church and sacraments?' (Ibid., p. 54).

3. Ibid., pp. 135, 174; *Journal* VIII. 332; John Fletcher, *Posthumous Pieces*, ed. Melville Horne, Madeley, 1791, p. 90; Jackson, *Charles Wesley* II. 219: cf. below, p. 201.

4. *Minutes* I. 602; cf. pp. 540–1.

5. The Methodists in Maldon, Essex, similarly described themselves as 'Independents' in applying for a licence in 1785 (*WHS* XVIII. 17).

6. *WHS* VII. 148–51.

7. *Letters* V. 22; cf. VII. 269–70, 337.

8. *WHS* XVIII. 113–20; cf. *Letters* IV. 99–100.

9. *Letters* VI. 336–7; cf. *Journal* VIII. 339. Wesley put to rest the fears of some Cheshire Methodists in 1780 thus: 'It is my opinion that house is sufficiently licensed according to the Act of Toleration, and that (however they may *talk*) no one will be in haste to contest it with you.' (*WHS* XIX. 1.)

10. *Minutes* I. 602–10; cf. E. B. Perkins, *Methodist Preaching-Houses and the Law*, London, 1952, pp. 32–8.

11. *Minutes* I. 604; cf. pp. 540–1, and *Journal* V. 278–9; for Methodists and the Conventicle Act see *WHS* XI. 82–93, 103–8, 130–7.

12. *Letters* VII. 272.

13. Ibid., IV. 289–91; contemporary translation of Erasmus's letter, by 'an Oxford Scholar', in Methodist archives, London.

14. MS letter from John Richardson to Charles Wesley, 20 January 1765, in Methodist archives, London.

15. *Letters* IV. 290–1.

16. MS letter, Richardson to Charles Wesley, as in Note 14; cf. *Letters* IV. 230; cf. MS letter of Charles Wesley to his wife, 29 May (1764): 'Dined today at M. Heritage's, after a conference with Dr. J[one]s and J. D[ownes]. One more cloud is blown over.' (Methodist archives, London.)

17. Newton's MS letter in possession of Dr. F. E. Maser, Old St. George's Church, Philadelphia; cf. Seymour, *Huntingdon* II. 331, and *Letters* IV. 291.

18. Atmore, *Memorial*, pp. 81, 224.

19. Richardson to Charles Wesley, 20 January 1765 (as Note 14); MS account of James Thwaite, in Methodist archives, London; *Letters* IV. 288–91; James Everett, *Historical Sketches of Wesleyan Methodism in Sheffield*, Sheffield, 1823, Vol. I (all published), pp. 185–9.

20. *Letters* IV. 290–1. The solitary exception, as revealed by the annual *Minutes*, was John Oliver. Charles Wesley added a sarcastic endorsement to his brother's account of his disciplinary action: 'Jan. 11. 1765. B[rother] expelling his Witnesses because ordained by J. Jones's Ordainer' (Original of *Letters* IV. 287–8 at Emory University, Atlanta, Georgia.)

21. MS letter, Mark Davis to Charles Wesley, 25 August 1765, in Methodist archives, London; cf. Tyerman, *Wesley* II. 486-9, and *Works* X. 450. Especially interesting is *Diotrephes and Stentor: a New Farce, acted near Moorfields*, London, 1765, a verse satire on the ordinations written with some inside knowledge. Accusing Wesley both of ambition and chicanery, it depicts him as singing:

> O what pleasures will abound,
> When I am a bishop found;
> O what Flattery
> At the Foundery
> When I am a bishop found.

22. MS letter to Charles Wesley, 30 August 1765, Methodist archives, London.

23. See George Tsoumas, 'Methodism and Bishop Erasmus', pp. 61-73, *The Greek Orthodox Theological Review*, Vol. II (Christmas, 1956); in spite of many inaccuracies in detail Mr. Tsoumas proves that Erasmus did not follow the canonical procedure of the Greek Orthodox Church, and that his name is not to be found in the episcopal catalogues in Crete.

24. *Minutes* I. 58-9; cf. pp. 540-7.

25. Ibid., pp. 60-2. This whole section was reprinted in his Large Minutes and remained almost word for word the same until his death; see ibid., pp. 497-507, 638-48.

26. Ibid., p. 78. The whole section was reprinted in the Large Minutes for 1770 and 1772 with no material change except for the addition of a paragraph enforcing the principle in 1770. The principle once secured the supporting arguments were dropped from later issues (ibid., pp. 510-17).

27. *Letters* IV. 257, corrected from the original in the Methodist archives, London; it was apparently written on the same sheet as one of the same date to Sarah Crosby, who lived with her. Cf. *WHS* XXVII. 76-82; for the document giving Sarah Mallet official authorization to preach in 1787 see John S. Simon, *John Wesley: The Last Phase*, London, 1934, pp. 181-2.

28. *Letters* IV. 273; this letter surely belongs to March 1768, not October 1764; cf. Davies and Rupp, *Methodist Church*, I. 252-3.

29. *Minutes* I. 77, 93. A letter of John Horton to Charles Wesley shows that in 1773 John Wesley was again 'drawing up a plan for settling all the preaching houses in one general trust', but supposedly with the purpose 'of keeping the preachers in some tolerable order'. (6 August, 1773, in Methodist archives, London.)

30. Ibid., I. 87-9; cf. *Letters* V. 143-5.

31. Ibid., I. 88-9. This whole lengthy section was reprinted in the Large Minutes of 1770 and 1772. Colin Williams, in his *John Wesley's Theology Today*, London, 1960, p. 215, speaks of Wesley thus envisaging 'a type of Church of England Franciscan order, [though]

without ecclesiastical portfolio'. It seems to have been even more than this, though this comparison of Wesley's preachers with the preaching friars has real cogency, as pointed out by H. B. Workman sixty years ago. (*A New History of Methodism*, ed. W. J. Townsend, H. B. Workman, and George Eayrs, 2 vols, London, 1909, I. 44–50.)

32. *Letters* VI. 10–12.
33. Moore, *Wesley* II. 260.
34. *Journal* V. 517, *Letters* VI. 33–4; cf. *Works* XI. 302, and Tyerman, *Wesley* III. 213.
35. *Minutes* I. 88, 110, 116, 121, 648–54.
36. Ibid., I. 136; cf. pp. 585–9.
37. *WHS* XXIII. 7–14, especially p. 11.
38. MS letter, 1 January 1773, Methodist archives, London.
39. *WHS* XXIII. 7–14; cf. MS letters from John Horton to Charles Wesley, with shorthand endorsements by the latter, 11 December 1773, and 28 February 1774, in Methodist archives, London.
40. *WHS* XXIII. 9–10; cf. Charles Wesley's shorthand copy in Methodist archives, London.
41. *Minutes* I. 125.
42. James Macdonald, *Memoirs of the Rev. Joseph Benson*, London, 1822, pp. 12–49; *Journal* VIII. 328–9.
43. *Journal* VIII. 330.
44. *Letters* VI. 174; cf. *Journal* VI. 72–3.
45. *Journal* VIII. 331–4; the original is in the Methodist archives, London.
46. Tyerman, *Wesley* III. 229–30; cf. Crook's letter to Wesley, 24 July, 1776, in Methodist archives, London.
47. *Journal* VI. 167–8; *Letters* VI. 272.
48. *Works* VII. 428–9.
49. Ibid., X. 446–54; Tyerman, *Wesley* III. 255–60.
50. G. J. Stevenson, *City Road Chapel, London*, London, (1872), p. 72.
51. Charles Wesley's letters combine with other evidence to indicate that in London during the 1760s the Lord's Supper was still administered only in Wesley's Huguenot chapels in West Street and Spitalfields. The Foundery accounts show that at least from 1774 onwards expenses were incurred for 'Sacrament at Foundry' (Stevenson, *City Road*, pp. 58–9). Cf. Prof. Liden's detailed account of the services which he attended in 1769, *WHS* XVII, 2–4. The Lord's Supper was not administered elsewhere in 1766; see *Minutes* I. 218. The first clear evidence for the use of the New Room, Bristol, for communion is similarly in 1770; cf. Bowmer, *Lord's Supper* pp. 65–6.
52. *Arminian Magazine*, 1788, pp. 541–3, dated 14 May 1788; cf. *Works* X. 509–11.
53. *Letters* VIII. 52, 57. Wesley certainly repudiated consecration from 1764 onwards; see *Journal* V. 92, 447.

54. Samuel Bradburn, *The Question, Are the Methodists Dissenters? Fairly Examined*, London, 1792, p. 11.

55. Whitehead, *Wesley* II. 372; cf. Tyerman, *Wesley* III. 221–2, 296–302, 309–13. The regular appointment of lay preachers to the New Chapel pulpit remained a bone of contention until long after the deaths of both Wesley brothers; see *WHS* XXIX. 178–84.

56. *Journal* VI. 203; cf. William Myles, *A Chronological History of the People called Methodists*, 4th edn, London, 1813, p. 141, and C. H. Crookshank, *History of Methodism in Ireland*, 3 vols, Belfast, 1885, I. 306–7, 324, and *Letters* VII. 284.

57. This first quotation is not from Wesley's 1766 manifesto, for which see *Minutes* I. 60–2, but from some document which has disappeared, probably prepared by him for use against the Norwich preachers in 1760. The second is a paraphrase from the twelve 'Rules of a Helper', for which see *Minutes* I. 496–7; cf. p. 54 (1766), where the 12th is specially stressed.

58. *Journal* VI. 262–3. Much fuller accounts are to be found in Charles Wesley's letters of 28 November, 1 and 6 December 1779; see Mrs. Richard Smith, *Raithby Hall*, London, 1859, pp. 8–12, *WHS* VII. 132–5, XVIII. 166–7 (=XXIX. 22), and Tyerman, *Wesley* III. 303–13.

59. MS letter 6 December 1779 in Methodist archives, London; the bracketed words are in shorthand; in his letter of 1 December Charles had complained 'Surely you cannot still allow J[ohn] P[awson] or any other to open your letters in your absence!' Had Tyerman known the full correspondence he might have been less hard on both the Wesleys.

60. *Letters* VI. 375–6.

61. Whitehead, *Wesley* II. 379.

62. Ibid., pp. 380–1.

63. *Letters* VII. 29.

64. *Minutes* I. 547; cf. Green, *Wesley Bibliography*, pp. 195–6.

NOTES TO CHAPTER THIRTEEN, pp. 218–233

1. Whitehead, *Wesley* II. 404.

2. MS letter, Moravian archives, London.

3. Beynon, *Howell Harris, Reformer*, p. 79.

4. *Minutes* I. 50 (1765), 57 (1766), 73–4 (1767), 157 (1782), 165 (1784); cf. pp. 604–11 for the Model Deed of 1763.

5. See Davies and Rupp, *Methodist Church*, p. 244.

6. See p. 206 above.

7. *Minutes* I. 61, (1766), repeated in the Large Minutes of 1770 and 1772 (ibid., pp. 642–3).

8. *Letters* V. 60; cf. *Arminian Magazine*, 1785, p. 267, speaking of his earlier

position: 'Though I *invited* only a part of the travelling Preachers, yet
I *permitted* any that desired it to be present.'

9. *Works* XIII. 248; cf. *Minutes* I. 74–5 (1767), 105–6 (1772), 115 (1774),
126 (1776), 150 (1781).

10. *Letters* VI. 376; cf. pp. 215–6 above.

11. See above, p. 209.

12. *Minutes* I. 503.

13. *Journal* VI. 330.

14. Davies and Rupp, *Methodist Church*, p. 254; cf. his meeting with Coke
only in 1783, *Journal* VI. 437d.

15. *Journal* VI. 290; cf. his letter of 31 July, in which he stated that it would
last two days longer still (*Letters* VII. 26).

16. Jackson, *Early Methodist Preachers*, I. 219.

17. Moore, *Wesley* II. 295.

18. *Minutes* I. 157; *Letters* VII. 124–5, 148–51; Perkins, *Methodist Preaching
Houses*, pp. 25–30; Tyerman, *Wesley* III. 373–83.

19. *Letters* VII. 147.

20. The broadsheet, dated 3 January 1783, read 'Hopper'; when it was
reprinted in the *Arminian Magazine* for 1788, p. 207, the date was
altered to 12 January 1788, and this name to 'Taylor'.

21. *The Case of Birstall House*, 1783; cf. *Works* XIII. 274–8, *Letters* VII. 148–51,
and *Journal* VI. 383d.

22. *Journal* VI. 438; cf. *Letters* VII. 184.

23. *Journal* VI. 437–8; Tyerman, *Wesley* III. 381–3; cf. *WHS* VIII. 23, 34, 67.

24. Simon, *John Wesley, the Last Phase*, p. 195.

25. Tyerman, *Wesley* III. 381; cf. *The Records of the Honourable Society of
Lincoln's Inn, 1420–1893*, ed. W. P. Baildon, London, 1896, especially
I. 445. Coke spells the name 'Maddox'.

26. Thomas Coke, *An Address to the Methodist Society . . . on the settlement of
the Preaching Houses*, Liverpool, 1795, p. 6.

27. Moore, *Wesley* II. 295.

28. *Minutes* I. 181; cf. *Works* XIII. 249.

29. *Journal* VI. 169.

30. *WHS* XXXV. 42.

31. Ibid., XXXIV. 129–34.

32. MS letter of Coke to the bookseller Robert Dodsley, 24 February 1781,
in the Methodist archives, London; *WHS* XII. 136–8.

33. *Minutes* I. 165; Simon, *Wesley, the Last Phase*, p. 203.

34. Letter of 14 May 1791 to Bishop Samuel Seabury, New York Historical
Society, *Facsimiles of Church Documents*, 1874–9

35. *WHS* XX. 74.

36. Samuel Warren, *A Digest of the Laws and Regulations of the Wesleyan
Methodists*, 2nd edn, London, 1835, p. 2n.

It is more than usually difficult to be sure of the actual course of
events and of the roles played by the main participants. Wesley's

accounts of the negotiations tend to omit any reference to Coke, e.g.: 'I consulted a skilful and honest attorney, and he consulted an eminent counsellor'. Coke implied that the initiative was always with him (see *Address*, pp. 6–7). The truth is surely somewhere between the two, though Wesley's diary shows that he did indeed visit Clulow on 1 December 1783. Coke says that he prepared and presented Madocks's opinion to the Conference of 1783, but it is dated 5 December 1783. The source for this document appears to be Warren's *Digest*, 2nd edn, 1835, p. 2—it does not appear in the first edition of 1827. There is a discrepancy between the case prepared by Clulow and the quoted answer: the case asks (a) whether the usual description of the Conference is legally satisfactory, and (b) what steps should be taken if it is not; Madocks's answer, as quoted by Warren, applies only to (b). Perhaps there were two successive cases and two opinions, one of which was presented to the 1783 Conference in addition to that on the Birstall controversy, but it seems more likely that a section has been omitted from Madocks's 'Answer'. The three editions of William Peirce's standard *Ecclesiastical Principles and Polity of the Wesleyan Methodists* (1854, 1868, and 1873) apparently copy the passage from Warren, though without acknowledgement.

37. *Works* XII. 13; Coke, *Address*, p. 7.

38. Cf. John Fletcher Hurst, *History of Methodism*, 8 vols, London, 1901, II. 975–6. Nevertheless, it is far from flawless, either in content or arrangement, witness the somewhat unhappy sequence of the fifteen regulatory clauses, the first being marred by a minor administrative detail and subsequently amended by the twelfth. For the text see *Journal* VIII. 335–41.

39. *WHS* XII. 90, XIII. 17–21.

40. *WHS* I. 41.

41. Ibid., XIII. 16–17.

42. Cf. *WHS* I. 38; XIII. 15–16.

43. *Works* XIII. 249. Probably Wesley's information came from James Hutton, with whom his friendship was renewed in 1771. Hutton had been appointed secretary of a 'commissariat committee' of six, first formed by Zinzendorf in 1752, which seems to have been replaced in 1754 by a 'board of administrators'; in 1756 this was given its more familiar title of 'Directory'—still with six members. See *Journal* V. 441, Benham, *Hutton*, pp. 258–9, Addison, *Renewed Brethren*, pp. 105–24, and J. Taylor Hamilton, *A history of the church known as the Moravian Church*, Bethlehem, Pennsylvania, 1900, pp. 152–3, 157, 200, 203.

44. *Works* XIII. 249.

45. Coke, *Address*, p. 7.

46. *Works* XIII. 249–50.

47. *Arminian Magazine*, 1785, pp. 241–4, 297–302, 354–9, 398–403; 'Extracts from the Revd. James Creighton's letters to his sister', MS in World

Methodist Building, Lake Junaluska, North Carolina; Tyerman, *Wesley* III. 276–7.

48. Cf. *WHS* XII. 86–7, and Tyerman, *Wesley* III. 422–3.
49. *Works* XIII. 249.
50. *Journal* VI. 479, 481; VIII. 34.
51. Samuel Drew, *The Life of the Rev. Thomas Coke*, London, 1817, p. 39.
52. Copy in Bridwell Library, Perkins School of Theology, Dallas, Texas.
53. *WHS* X. 111; the date was probably 13 April (see *Journal* VI. 495d).
54. *WHS* X. 111–12.
55. The copy of the *Appeal* in the Methodist archives, London, was posted to John King, one of the younger preachers not included in the legal hundred. For Wesley's *Answer* see *Journal* VI. 526; VII. 4.
56. Simon, *John Wesley, The Last Phase*, pp. 217–18; cf. Macdonald, *Benson*, p. 160; the Irish Conference had also rejected the *Appeal* (see *Letters* VII. 226.) For Eells see *Letters* VII. 234 and *Minutes* I. 163, 173; cf. Atmore, *Memorial*, pp. 116–17.
57. *WHS* XIII. 15–16.
58. *Journal* VII. 7; cf. *WHS* VIII. 35.
59. *Works* XIII. 248–50; it appeared in the issue for May, pp. 267–9, entitled 'Thoughts upon some late occurrences'; cf. *WHS* II. 21–2.
60. See John Hampson's letter to Wesley, 25 January 1785, in *WHS* II. 21–22.
61. See J. W. Laycock, *Heroes of the Great Haworth Round*, Keighley, 1909, pp. 365–9; the letters are in the Methodist archives, London. Tyerman, *Wesley* III. 424, is incorrect in suggesting that Oddie's petition was the cause of Wesley's letters.
62. *Minutes* I. 242–3.
63. Ibid., pp. 181–2.
64. E.g. *Letters* VII. 279, 282.
65. Ibid., VII. 286.

NOTES TO CHAPTER FOURTEEN, pp. 234–255

1. *Letters* IV. 115, 125.
2. Preface to the *Sunday Service*, 1784.
3. See pp. 52–4 above.
4. *Works* XIII. 269–70.
5. Cf. *Letters* VII. 370.
6. Ibid., VI. 326.
7. *Works* VIII. 51–2, 102–3, 171.
8. 'Ought we to separate?', p. 3; see Appendix.
9. *Letters* IV. 121.
10. *Journal* III. 490–1; A. E. Peaston, *The Prayer Book Reform Movement in the XVIIIth Century*, Oxford, 1940, pp. 6, 39–53; cf. C. J. Abbey and

J. H. Overton, *The English Church in the Eighteenth Century*, 2 vols, London, 1878, I. 434-5.

11. *Journal* III. 490-1.
12. Peaston, op. cit., pp. 6-21, 39-53, 59-83.
13. 'Ought we to separate?', pp. 14-15; see Appendix.
14. *Letters* III. 145, 152; cf. 'Ought we to separate?', p. 37.
15. See [Wollaston, Francis] *The State of Subscription to the Articles and Liturgy of the Church of England, towards the close of the Year 1773*, London, 1774, especially pp. 40-8. Gibbon's sneer was justified: 'The forms of orthodoxy, the articles of faith, are subscribed with a sigh, or a smile, by the modern clergy.' Quoted by G. R. Cragg, *Reason and Authority in the Eighteenth Century*, Cambridge, 1964, pp. 251-2. Cf. Abbey and Overton, op. cit., I. 435-42, 515-16; John Hunt, *Religious Thought in England*, 3 vols, London, 1870, III. 300-3, 361-2; Sykes, *Church and State*, pp. 381-4.
16. Cf. *Journal* V. 295 and Peaston, op. cit., pp. 7-24.
17. *Journal* IV. 93; cf. *WHS* XXIII. 123-33, 173-5; a full account of the Savoy Conference was added to the 2nd edn, 1713, Vol. I, pp. 153-70, and to that same volume was appended Baxter's *Reformed Liturgy*, with 82 separately numbered pages.
18. *Journal* V. 119-24.
19. *Works* XI. 39.
20. *Concise Ecclesiastical History* III. 246-7; cf. *LQR* CLXXXVII. 184-6.
21. *Works* IX. 49, *Letters* IV. 150; for the general situation see *WHS*. XXXI. 147-8, and E. H. Carter, *The Norwich Subscription Books*, London, 1937, pp. 9-15, 50, and the illustrations after pp. 8, 10; cf. 'Ought we to separate?', p. 37.
22. Sykes, *Church and State*, pp. 381-90; Peaston, *Prayer Book Reform Movement*, pp. 7-12.
23. *Journal* VIII. 331-4.
24. Norman W. Spellman, 'The Formation of the Methodist Episcopal Church', pp. 185-232 of Emory Stevens Bucke (ed.), *The History of American Methodism*, 3 vols, Nashville, 1964 (henceforth *HAM*), I. 186-8.
25. Ibid., I. 176-80, 186-95.
26. *Arminian Magazine*, 1791, pp. 219-20; for the 1774 plan (i.e. that of 1769 confirmed in 1774), see *Minutes* I. 115-16 and above, pp. 255-7.
27. W. W. Sweet, *Religion on the American Frontier, 1783-1840: Vol. IV. The Methodists*, Chicago, 1946, pp. 12-15.
28. Jesse Lee, *A Short History of the Methodists in the U.S.A.*, Baltimore, 1810, pp. 85-6, where Lee states that the document (as given in *Letters* VII. 191) is an extract only; *The Journal and Letters of Francis Asbury*, ed. Elmer T. Clark, 3 vols, London and Nashville, 1958, I. 450. There was *just* sufficient time for Wesley to have received and answered Asbury's letter as noted. Sometimes the west-east voyage occupied only a

month, though five or six weeks was more common. Asbury had the advantage of writing from a port to a port, and of knowing in advance by which vessel his letter would be carried. He had already written from Pennsylvania to George Shadford about the situation, and the letter to Wesley could be written the more speedily, though at greater length.

29. Sweet, op. cit., pp. 13–14.

30. 'Ought we to separate?', pp. 26–7 (see Appendix); cf. *Works* XIII. 226.

31. It is difficult to follow Coke's itineraries, but a letter of Charles Wesley to John Fletcher dated 11 October 1783 (in the Methodist archives, London) shows that Coke was in London the previous evening, and he would almost certainly stay over the week-end at least. During this period John Wesley also was in London, and they would probably meet at West Street Chapel. Their known rendezvous in February 1784 has tended to draw attention away from this and possibly other meetings late in 1783 when the American situation was surely discussed.

32. T. Coke and H. Moore, *The Life of the Rev. John Wesley*, London, 1792, p. 458; repeated in Moore, *Wesley* II. 326.

33. Drew, *Coke*, p. 63, probably quoting Coke's own records (ibid., p. 69n), though Drew may well have pieced things together from documents insufficiently dated; but cf. also Moore's statement that in some respects Drew was misled by being misinformed (Moore, *Wesley* II. 308).

34. *Journal* VI. 476. A copy of Coke's *Plan of the Society for the Establishment of Missions among the Heathens* was sent to Fletcher with a covering letter dated 6 January 1784 (Hurst, *Methodism* III. 1063–4).

35. In his *The Rites and Ritual of Episcopal Methodism*, Nashville, 1926, p. 43, Nolan B. Harmon (now Bishop Harmon) came to the same conclusion from a careful collation of the *Sunday Service* and the *Book of Common Prayer*, and pointed out that Wesley's work throughout consisted basically of deletion, not of addition or substitution.

36. *WHS* XXIII. 124–33. Hunter's claim that Wesley worked with the physical aid of Baxter's 'Reformed Liturgy' is just possible, but unlikely. Although this work followed the general order of the *Book of Common Prayer* he completely rewrote the offices which he selected, so that it was a new work rather than a revision. Wesley was much more faithful to the order and contents than Baxter, but even so he omitted some offices and sections included by Baxter, while inserting others which Baxter had omitted. Baxter included the Commination, though in disguise; Wesley omitted it entirely. In Matrimony it is true that Wesley like Baxter dropped the use of the ring, but unlike Baxter he also omitted all reference to the 'giving away' of the bride. Wesley's language throughout was that of the Prayer Book, and only in occasional single words can parallels be traced to Baxter, where they are probably coincidence rather than deliberate borrowing, as in the use of 'minister' for 'priest' and 'curate'.

37. A. E. Peaston, *The Prayer Book Tradition in the Free Churches*, London, 1964, pp. 35–56, follows earlier Methodist scholars in linking the *Sunday Service* only with the Puritan tradition.

38. *Letters* VIII. 144–5.

39. For the many variations even in 'official' editions see A. J. Stephens, *The Book of Common Prayer: with notes, legal and historical*, 3 Vols, London, 1849, pp. clxxii–clxxv, ccx(a). The word 'fullest' is used because most contemporary editions omitted the Act of Uniformity, the Articles, and the Ordinal, though the edition abridged by Wesley almost certainly included them.

40. As in the rubric before the Benediction after the Lord's Supper; see below p. 246.

41. For fuller details on some points see Frederick Hunter's article, *WHS* XXIII. 125–31, Peaston, *Prayer Book Tradition in the Free Churches*, pp. 41–51, and Harmon, *Rites and Ritual*, where some of the major orders are arranged in parallel columns with the *Book of Common Prayer* and other liturgies. The statements made, however, are all based on personal research with the first and subsequent editions of the *Sunday Service*.

42. For a much fuller discussion of this particular problem and its peculiar results see W. F. Swift, 'John Wesley's Lectionary', *LQR* CLXXXIII. 298–304 (October 1958).

43. *Journal* VIII. 21; cf. Swift, op. cit., p. 301.

44. *Works* X. 153; cf. ibid., pp. 124 (*Roman Catechism*, 1756) and 136 (*Advantage of Members of the Church of England*, 1753); cf. also *Letters* VII.5 and *WHS* XXVI. 41–2.

45. The cancel leaf is signed 'F8' and contains pp. 135–6; cf. *WHS* XXXII. 97–101.

46. It is also quite possible, however, that Wesley deliberately omitted the Nicene Creed. He did not include it in his version of the Ordinal, and omitted from the Thirty-Nine Articles No. VIII on the Three Creeds. Quite certainly he objected to the Athanasian Creed, and his objections may well have stretched to the Nicene also, not so much for its doctrinal content as because of its origin during the suspect era of Constantine or (worse still) later. In 1782 he told Joseph Benson, 'I regard no authorities but those of the Ante-Nicene Fathers; nor any of them in opposition to Scripture' (*Letters* VII. 106).

47. *Sunday Service of the Methodists in North America: with other occasional services*, London, 1784, p. 138; cf. Harmon, *Rites and Ritual*, pp. 77–155; Bowmer, *Lord's Supper*, pp. 206–15; Peaston, *Prayer Book Tradition in the Free Churches*, pp. 44–6; *WHS* XXXI. 133–4.

48. *Works* X. 056–9.

49. Peaston, op. cit., p. 47, strengthening W. F. Swift's 'probably' in *WHS* XXIX. 19. N.B. Pouring as an additional mode was added to the 1786 and later editions. In 'Baptism of such as are of riper years' the

1784 edition (p. 148) called for dipping or pouring, to which was added sprinkling in 1786.

50. The cancel leaves are signed 'F11' and 'F12' and numbered 141–4. The signation is missing from 1786 onwards, nor did it appear in 'Baptism of such as are of riper years' in any edition.

51. *Works* X. 8–9; cf. pp. 156–7 above.

52. *Sunday Service*, 1784, pp. 141, 148; this phrase and its parallel in the opening prayer were omitted from the editions of 1786 and later, probably not by any deliberate action of Wesley, but simply by default in giving Coke his head. Cf. John C. English, 'The Sacrament of Baptism according to the Sunday Service of 1784' in *Methodist History* V. 10–16 (January 1967).

53. Coke and Moore, *Wesley*, p. 511.

54. Cf. W. K. L. Clarke (ed.), *Liturgy and Worship*, London, 1932 (edn of 1936, misprints corrected), pp. 857–8; it is not quite true, however, that the Articles were not even 'sometimes printed' with the Prayer Book during the eighteenth century, witness no fewer than three copies at Duke University which include them—all printed at Oxford, in 1701, 1752, and 1777. It was surely a similar edition that Wesley used for his revision.

55. 'Ought we to separate?', pp. 5–6 (see Appendix).

56. *Journal* VIII. 332; see p. 239 above.

57. *Letters* VI. 161. For the Articles see *Sunday Service*, 1784, pp. 306–14; they are arranged in parallel columns with the Thirty-Nine Articles in Nolan B. Harmon and John W. Bardsley, 'John Wesley and the Articles of Religion', *Religion in Life* XXII. 280–91 (Spring 1953). Cf. Paul F. Blankenship, 'The Significance of John Wesley's Abridgement of the Thirty-Nine Articles', *Methodist History* XII. 35–47 (April 1964). Mr. Blankenship discusses articles altered for the following causes: the new situation in America, doctrinal differences (particularly absolute predestination and christian perfection, but also Christology, prevenient grace, and the sacraments), and the need for clarity and preciseness. Cf. also *HAM* I. 332–3.

58. The same is true of the documents prepared by Coke, Clarke and Benson in response to the request of the 1806 Conference for Methodist Articles of Religion. See *WHS* Publication No. 2, 1897.

59. See Frank Baker, 'The Doctrines in the *Discipline*', pp. 39–55, *Duke Divinity School Review*, Winter 1966; cf. *HAM* I. 223–5, 332–3.

60. 'Ought we to separate?', p. 15 (see Appendix).

61. Green, *Wesley Bibliography*, Nos. 6, 7, 30, 378, and Baker, *Union Catalogue*, No. 30.

62. See above, p. 246.

63. See John Emory, *A Defence of 'Our Fathers'*, 5th edn, New York, 1838, p. 68—a valid deduction from the fact that all the copies he had seen contained the 1785 American *Minutes* inserted between the Liturgy

and the *Collection*; of the thirty-one copies now known this is true of ten only (see Baker, *Union Catalogue*, p. 173, to which some additions should now be made). Confirmation comes in the letter of an American clergyman to Dr. Samuel Seabury dated 29 November 1784: 'they hurried away from England and brought their Prayer Books with them unbound—they are getting them bound in this City' (i.e. New York; copy in Methodist archives, London).

64. Of the thirty-one known copies fifteen have cancels, thirteen do not. That in the Pierpoint Morgan Library, New York, contains both cancellands as well as both cancels; that at the Pittsburgh-Xenia Theological Seminary, Pittsburgh, has both the cancellands and the Baptism cancel; that in the New York Public Library has the cancelland for Communion but the cancel for Baptism.

65. *Letters* VIII. 145; see above, p. 243.

66. British Museum, Add. MSS. 48809, folio 5v. The mention of 'Extra for Calendar' is puzzling. The brief Table of Lessons occupying three pages at the beginning can hardly be intended, especially as these formed a part of the original gathering and comprise only material associated with the Calendar. Possibly this was an addition to Strahan's original estimate or had been composed twice at an early stage of the work; perhaps a few broadsheet copies of a Calendar had in fact been included in the order, though none have so far been identified.

67. See Baker, *Union Catalogue*, p. 173.

68. *Letters* VII. 238–9.

69. The more 'official' copy of the letter was printed on quarto pages in a larger type, and doubtless circulated by Coke, though of this still fewer copies survive. See Baker, *Union Catalogue*, No. 376A. It is possible, however, that these are copies made by the printer William Pine of Bristol at Henry Durbin's request (MS letter, Durbin to Charles Wesley, 25 November 1784, in Methodist archives, London).

70. *HAM* I. 214.

71. Ibid., I. 213–32.

72. See note 63 above.

73. Lee, *History*, p. 107; cf. *HAM* I. 313.

74. British Museum, Add. MSS. 48809, folio 62.

75. *WHS* XXIX. 16–20; Baker, *Union Catalogue*, pp. 174–5.

76. Ibid., XXXIII. 11.

77. *Journal and Letters*, III. 47.

78. See p. 243 above.

79. See William McGarvey, *Liturgiae Americanae*, Philadelphia, 1895, especially pp. ix–xxx; cf. F. Procter and W. H. Frere, *New History of the Book of Common Prayer*, London, 1925, pp. 234–47; W. J. Seabury, *Memoir of Bishop Seabury*, New York, 1908, pp. 325–48; *Facsimiles of Church Documents*, New York, 1874–9, items 24–33.

80. *Letters* VIII. 137 refers to Alexander Suter's 'refusing to read the Prayers

26

and speaking contemptuously of them'; John Pawson had pointed out in 1785 that the 'new plan' of ordaining preachers for Scotland would hinder rather than help the work there if Wesley insisted on the Anglican Communion order, because the Prayer Book was regarded as 'a limb of Antichrist' (*WHS* XI. 50-1; cf. p. 114); cf. *WHS* XVIII. 1, 5.

81. Bradburn, *The Question*, pp. 13-14, 17-18; when Bradburn came to London in 1786 he found the *Sunday Service* in use at Snowsfields and Wapping.

82. MS letter to an unknown correspondent, dated 10 March 1787, referring to 'reading Prayers' at Exeter and Cullompton (Methodist archives, London).

83. *Minutes* I. 213; *Letters* VII. 213. Certainly some Methodist societies used Wesley's revision before his death, and this was secured by the Plan of Pacification in 1795 (*Minutes* I. 340). Editions varying little from his continued to be published even into the present century for British use, though the undiluted *Book of Common Prayer* still maintained a firm hold. See *WHS* XXVII. 36-41, XXXI. 112-18, 133-43.

84. Procter and Frere, *History of BCP*, p. 241.

NOTES TO CHAPTER FIFTEEN, pp. 256-282

1. *Letters* VII. 179.
2. Ibid., III. 133.
3. Ibid., VII. 203; cf. VII. 213.
4. Undated MS letter in Methodist archives, London.
5. *Letters* VIII. 23.
6. Coke and Moore, *Wesley*, p. 458.
7. 'Ought we to separate?' (see Appendix), pp. 37-9; *Letters* III. 186-7; Beynon, *Howell Harris, Reformer*, p. 82.
8. See above, pp. 146-8.
9. *Journal* IV. 373.
10. *Works* XIV. 351-2; cf. VIII. 174-80, 496-9.
11. *Letters* IV. 303.
12. *Works* VII. 179.
13. Ibid., VII. 303.
14. Article XXVI, which stated this, was omitted from his *Sunday Service*, but in 1787 he still proclaimed this doctrine: 'We know by our own happy experience and by the experience of thousands, that the word of the Lord is not bound, though uttered by an unholy minister, and the sacraments are not dry breasts, whether he that administers be holy or unholy.' (*Works* VII. 185; cf. *Letters* VI. 327; see pp. 295 below.)

15. *WHS* XXVII. 147.

16. John P. Lockwood, *The Western Pioneers* (Boardman and Pilmoor). London, 1881, p. 177.

17. *Historical Manuscripts Commission, Fourteenth Report, Appendix*, Part X., 'The Manuscripts of the Earl of Dartmouth', Vol. II, American Papers, London, 1895, p. 244.

18. *HAM* I. 176–7.

19. Lee, *History*, pp. 69–74; cf. W. W. Sweet, *Virginia Methodism: A History*, Richmond, 1955, pp. 79–86, and *HAM* I. 177–80.

20. Asbury, *Journal* I. 359, 378; III. 24.

21. See *The Fulham Papers in the Lambeth Palace Library. American Colonia Section: Calendar and Indexes*, compiled by W. W. Manross, Oxford Clarendon Press, 1965, pp. xvii–xviii; cf. *WHS* XXXII. 190–2.

22. *Journal* VI. 175–6; the *DNB* adds that the bishop refused to sit above Wesley at dinner.

23. *Letters* VII. 30–1. The earlier person turned down by Lowth may have been a preacher who wanted to go to America as a chaplain in Lord Cornwallis's army; see H. M. Smith, *Life and Correspondence of the Rev. William Smith*, Philadelphia, 1880, II. 245.

24. In St. John's, Trinity Bay, and Harbour Grace; for the latter area Lowth's predecessor Richard Terrick had ordained Wesley's preaches Lawrence Coughlan in 1767. See G. G. Findlay and W. W. Holdsworth, *The History of the Wesleyan Methodist Missionary Society*, London, 1921, 5 vols, I. 259–63.

25. *Letters* VII. 30–1.

26. *Journal* VIII. 333. It is just possible that this explains an enigmatic sentence in his letter to Charles on 8 June 1780: 'I am fully persuaded the Bishop will never meddle with us. He is a wiser man.' On the face of it this refers to some possible victimization of the Methodists, but it might imply that the bishop would not take the risk of ordaining Wesley's preachers. Certainly at this time Charles Wesley was afraid that at the forthcoming Conference the preachers would prevail upon John to ordain them (*Letters* VII. 21–2; Whitehead, *Wesley* II. 379).

27. *Letters* VII. 29.

28. *WHS* IX. 49–53.

29. Addison, *United Brethren*, pp. 207–8. Addison quotes a 1786 letter of La Trobe, who says 'The Bishop of Exeter is a friend of John Wesley', Wesley had indeed been on friendly terms with Dr. John Ross, bishop of Exeter, for several years, and had not only dined with him but assisted at Holy Communion in his cathedral (*Journal* VI. 365).

30. *Arminian Magazine*, 1781, pp. 492–3; cf. *Works* XIII. 300–1.

31. Matthew Richey, *Memoir of the late Rev. William Black*, Halifax, Nova Scotia, 1839, p. 98; cf. *Letters* VII. 169. It seems clear that there was earlier correspondence, which has disappeared.

32. J. B. B. Clarke. *An Account of . . . Adam Clarke*, London, 1833, p. 165.

33. See pp. 239–40 above.

34. Seymour, *Countess of Huntingdon*, II. 309–11, 434–50; cf. Wood, *Haweis*, pp. 149–53, 157–8, 168–9.

35. See pp. 241–2 above.

36. See pp. 62–3 above.

37. Cf. Thompson, *Wesley, Apostolic Man*, pp. 28–30, 72–4. A. R. George in *WHS* XXXI. 27–31, and V. E. Vine, ibid., pp. 65–70, 102–3.

38. Drew, *Coke*, pp. 63–4, apparently quoting Coke's own memoranda of the occasion.

39. Stillingfleet, *Irenicum*, II. vi. 13: 'For at Alexandria, from Mark the evangelist to bishops Heracles and Dionysius, the presbyters always elected one from amongst themselves, and having placed him in a higher rank named him bishop' (translated from Jerome's Latin, which only is given on p. 299 of the 1662 edn); cf. II. vii. 4, pp. 368–9 for the *chorepiscopoi*.

40. Drew, *Coke*, p. 64; cf. his letter of 17 April, in J. W. Etheridge, *Life of the Rev. Thomas Coke*, London, 1860, pp. 101–2, and Tyerman, *Wesley* III. 428.

41. Cf. *Letters* VII. 224–5.

42. Moore, *Wesley*, II. 329.

43. Coke and Moore, *Wesley*, p. 458; *Letters* VII. 262.

44. Tyerman, *Wesley* III. 428, from John Pawson's MS life of Whitehead.

45. Whitehead, *Wesley* II. 417.

46. Ibid., II. 415; cf. p. 417 (where Coke speaks of the Letters Testimonial as certifying the offices with which Wesley had 'invested' them) and *Journal* VIII. 332–3.

47. Alexander M'Caine, *Letters on the Organization and early history of the Methodist Episcopal Church*, Boston, 1850, p. 64, quoting a letter from Creighton to Samuel Bradburn, printed London, 1793, which seems to have disappeared. (Cf. note 117.) Whitehead, *Wesley* II. 415, states that 'a plan was proposed in private to a few clergymen who attended the Conference this year at Leeds, that Mr. Wesley should ordain one or two preachers for the societies in America; but the clergymen opposed it'.

48. Whitehead, *Wesley* II. 415–17; cf. Moore, *Wesley* II. 330–2.

49. *Journal* VII. 14–16. The first edition of this Journal *Extract*, published in 1789, noted under Thursday 2 September: 'I added to them three more; which I verily believe will be much to the glory of God.' This entry was dropped from a revised edition published the same year, possibly because it implied three more people instead of three more acts of ordination.

50. *WHS* II. 101–9.

51. Cf. Henry Durbin's MS letter to Charles Wesley on 28 October 1784, in which he speaks of Coke at least as being ordained 'by a new form' (Methodist archives, London).

52. The original deacons' parchments for Robert Gamble and Thomas Owens are in the Methodist archives, London, and facsimiles are given in John Telford, *The Life of John Wesley*, 3rd edn, revised and enlarged, London, 1910. See table in *WHS* XXXIII. 118–21. Coke ordained Robert Johnson as deacon in 1785, and his parchment also is in the Methodist archives; this is somewhat more elaborate, and he is described as 'a man whom I esteem duly qualified to preach the Word of God, baptize, perform the office of marriage, and all the other duties pertaining to the office of a Deacon'.

53. British Museum, Add. MSS. 41295E.

54. 'Elders', 'men', 'them', and 'fit persons' in the draft were altered in the individual parchments to 'as an elder', 'a man', 'him', and 'a fit person'. Cf. *WHS* X. 66; XXXII. 63.

55. See *WHS* X. 158; XVIII. 112.

56. That of Robert Johnson; see *WHS* XXXIII. 119.

57. Ibid., XV. 34; XXV 47.

58. Ibid., XVII. 121; *Letters* VIII. 59, 98.

59. *Journal* VII. 505; cf. *WHS* IX. 153. Although in accordance with long ecclesiastical tradition the ordaining presbytery remained three, after 1784 the known documents speak of Wesley's being assisted by 'other ordained ministers', omitting the word 'two'.

60. Whitehead, *Wesley* II. 423.

61. Ibid., II. 416; see p. 265 above.

62. The original reads 'rights'.

63. Thomas Coke, *The Substance of a Sermon, preached . . . at the Ordination of the Rev. Francis Asbury to the office of a Superintendent*, London, 1785, pp. 7–8.

64. Ibid., pp. 8–9. Coke quotes some material not included in Vol. I of the *Christian Library*, however, so like Wesley he probably used William Wake's *Genuine Epistles of the Apostolical Fathers*; the pagination does not correspond to that of the 3rd edn, 1719. Some of the material is in fact not very relevant. The early American Methodists undoubtedly thought highly of Wesley and his spiritual authority in spite of occasional criticism of him; Coke and Asbury referred to him as the greatest divine since the apostles, and a member of the 1784 Christmas Conference claimed: 'Wesley ordained Coke his apostle or messenger to us. . . . We . . . received Thomas Coke, L.L.D., with his testimonials from the greatest man to us in the world.' (John J. Tigert, *A Constitutional History of American Episcopal Methodism*, 6th edn, Nashville, Tenn., 1916, p. 204; *WHS* XXXIV. 104.)

65. *Journal* VII, facsimile facing p. 16; but cf. Thompson, *Wesley, Apostolic Man*, pp. 9–10.

66. Creighton was apparently the only other clergyman present with Wesley and Coke, but Coke's parchment speaks of Wesley's being assisted by 'other ministers'. Who was the other? Vasey or Whatcoat

after their ordination? Or even both of them, making an unusual college of four? Or Mr. X?

67. *Letters* VII. 284; cf. pp. 151–2 above.

68. Augustine, *Civitas Dei,* XIX. 19: 'The episcopate is the title of a duty, not an honour. . . . the Latin translation of the Greek "to exercise the episcopal office" means "to superintend".' See John Jewel, *Works,* ed. John Ayre, 4 vols, Cambridge, 1845–50, IV. 906; cf. Norman Sykes, *Old Priest and New Presbyter,* pp. 14–16, 246–7, and E. W. Thompson, 'John Wesley, Superintendent', *LQR* CLXXXIV. 325–30 (October 1959). For Samuel Wesley's recommendation of Jewel see above, p. 16.

69. Moore, *Wesley* II. 334; when Wesley reprinted his manifesto of 10 September 1784 in the *Minutes* and in the *Arminian Magazine* a year later he introduced it with the words: 'If anyone is minded to dispute concerning Diocesan Episcopacy, he may dispute. But I have better work.' (*Minutes* I. 179; *Arminian Magazine,* 1785, p. 602.)

70. *Minutes . . . composing a Form of Discipline,* Philadelphia, 1785, reproduced in parallel columns with Wesley's Large Minutes of 1780 in Tigert, *Constitutional History,* p. 535; cf. pp. 196–7, where Tigert points out that only in later reprints was the term 'bishop' introduced.

71. Tigert, op. cit., p. 196; cf. Coke's parchment for Robert Johnson, 24 October 1785, where he describes himself as 'Thomas Coke, Doctor of Civil Law, Superintendent of the Methodist Episcopal Church' (Methodist archives, London).

72. *HAM* I. 214, quoting a MS letter of Adam Fonerden, 30 December 1784.

73. *Letters* VIII. 91.

74. *WHS* IV. 22.

75. *Minutes of the Methodist Conferences annually held in America, from 1773 to 1794, inclusive,* Philadelphia, 1795, pp. 95, 107, 119 (pp. 12, 69, 77 of the 1813 edition). In fact the Methodists, even in England, did come to use this title of Wesley. Writing on 29 May 1789 Joseph Cownley spoke of his ordination by 'our venerable bishop', though he also used the title 'our dear old Father'. On 5 July 1791 Cownley wrote of him as 'our late bishop' (MS letters in Methodist archives, London).

76. *Letters* VII. 238–9; cf. Tigert, op. cit., pp. 174–5.

77. Italicization as in the copy inserted in the 1784 *Sunday Service.*

78. Baker, *Charles Wesley,* pp. 134–7.

79. MS letter, 25 November, Durbin to Charles Wesley, in Methodist archives, London.

80. Transcribed from Wesley's shorthand endorsement on Durbin's letter of 25 November.

81. See Baker, *Representative Verse of Charles Wesley,* pp. 367–70.

82. W. J. Seabury, *Memoir of Bishop Seabury,* New York, 1908, pp. 201–19, 266.

83. Durbin to Charles Wesley, 25 November 1784, as Note 79.

84. Copy in Methodist archives, London.

85. *WHS* XXXIII. 11–12.

86. The original letter eventually came into the hands of Bishop Seabury and was published in his life by W. J. Seabury, pp. 377–81; it is also reproduced in *Facsimiles of Church Documents*, item 49. See also Wesley's draft, and also a copy inserted in his letter book, both at the Methodist archives, London—the latter being reproduced in Jackson's *Charles Wesley* II. 389–92. Minor variants occur; the draft reads 'duly consecrated', and the letter book copy underlines 'His' in 'His ordinations would be . . . valid. . . .'

87. 15 August 1785 to Dr. Smith: see E. E. Beardsley, *Life and Correspondence of the Right Reverend Samuel Seabury*, Boston, 1881, p. 230.

88. MS letter, Chandler to Charles Wesley, in Methodist archives, London; cf. Seabury, *Seabury*, p. 375. See letters of Pilmoor to Charles Wesley, 17 December 1785, and 10 April, 27 September 1786, in Methodist archives, London.

89. One supposedly from John Wesley on 17 March 1785 in fact belongs to 1788; see *Letters* VII. 261; VIII. 45.

90. *Letters* VII. 262.

91. *Journal* VII. 101; once more they were ordained deacon and elder on successive days at 5.0 a.m. James Creighton maintained that it was Coke who persuaded Wesley to this step, and that he himself advised him 'to do nothing hastily', claiming that there was not 'the same necessity of ordination for Scotland that there had been for America'. See 'Extracts from the Revd. Jas. Creighton's letters to his sister', 22 August, 1789 (World Methodist Building, Lake Junaluska, N.C.).

92. Charles Wesley's MS Letter Book, Methodist archives, London; cf. Jackson, *Charles Wesley* II. 393–4. Charles may not have heard of the ordinations for Scotland at this time, though he certainly knew within two weeks, witness his letter to his wife which mentions the '3 scotch Presbyters'; this was dated simply 'Thur. Morn.', which might have been 18 or 25 August, or (far less likely) 1 September. On 8 September he was back in London.

93. *Arminian Magazine*, 1786, pp. 50–1, entitled 'On the Church: in a Letter to the Rev. — —.' cf. Charles Wesley's MS Letter Book, Methodist archives, London, and *Letters* VII. 285.

94. Charles Wesley's MS Letter Book; cf. Jackson, *Charles Wesley* II. 396–8.

95. *Letters* VII. 288–9.

96. *Minutes*, 1786, pp. 20–1; cf. *Minutes* I. 191–3.

97. *Letters* VII. 321 (4 March 1786).

98. Tyerman, *Wesley* III. 443. Creighton, however, claimed that Wesley came to believe that the Scots ordinations at least were a mistake, writing on 22 August 1789: 'Mr. W. at the late Conference declared

he was sorry he had ordained any for Scotland, for he saw no good arisen from it, but much evil.' ('Extracts', as in note 91.)

99. MS letter of Mr. E. Johnson, a Dublin Methodist, to Charles Wesley, 27 September (1785), in Methodist archives, London. Charles Wesley replied: '*His* charity believeth all things, even the preachers' promises "not to use their power in England".'

100. MS letter of Charles Wesley to Benjamin La Trobe, 30 July 1786, in Moravian archives, London; cf. Jackson, *Charles Wesley* II. 402–3.

101. Cf. Tyerman, *Wesley* III. 497.

102. MS letter, James Creighton to Charles Wesley, 6 October 1787, in Methodist archives, London.

103. *Journal* VII. 422–3, compared with Wesley's MS diary in Methodist archives, London.

104. Atmore, *Memorial*, p. 259; Jackson, *Early Methodist Preachers* II. 218–19; *WHS* XV. 58.

105. Bradburn, *The Question*, p. 14.

106. George Smith, *History of Wesleyan Methodism*, 3 vols, 5th edn, London, 1872, I. 97–8; cf. Tyerman, *Wesley* III. 443.

107. John Murlin in 1794 (Open letter to Joseph Benson, 14 February 1794), Alexander Kilham in 1795 (*Earnest Address to the preachers assembled in Conference, by . . . Paul and Silas*, p. 4), Coke in 1798 (in the annotated *Discipline*; see Tigert, *Constitutional History*, 204), and Jonathan Crowther in 1815 (Crowther, *Coke*, p. 55, where he somewhat vaguely stated: 'Mr. Wesley, I believe, consecrated some other persons Bishops besides Dr. Coke. But I believe not more than one of these is now living'; in this he probably had Henry Moore in mind.)

108. All three were available at the time. Myles, *History*, p. 175, implies that Wesley was assisted by Creighton and Dickinson in the case of Mather as well as those of Rankin and Moore, but he places the event incorrectly between November 1787 and March 1788. In 1789 Wesley was certainly attempting to by-pass Coke a little, accusing him of enticing away his younger preachers, so that it would be natural for him to place more responsibility instead upon his British clergy and preachers; see *Letters* VIII. 129.

109. Jackson, *Early Methodist Preachers*, II. 7; *Journal* VII. 395.

110. Cf. A. Raymond George, 'Ordination in Methodism', *LQR* CLXXVI. 156–69, especially p. 163 (April 1951).

111. MS Journal of Thomas Rankin, Garrett Theological Seminary, Evanston, Illinois, p. 7.

112. Mrs. Richard Smith, *Life of Rev. Henry Moore*, New York, 1845, p. 95.

113. *Letters* VIII. 129.

114. *WHS* XV. 60; cf. George, op. cit., p. 161.

115. *WHS* XXX. 118–21.

116. Bradburn, *The Question*, p. 14.
117. Alexander M'Caine, *Letters on the Organization and early history of the Methodist Episcopal Church*, Boston, 1850, p. 85, referring to p. 13, apparently of a published letter which he uses elsewhere, and which is also used in the *Centenary of Methodism*, Dublin, 1839, quite independently. No trace of this printed letter has been found, however. Creighton wrote to his sister in November 1794: 'B[radbur]n (who is one of the high fliers for Sacra[men]ts) wrote a book two years ago, to prove that we were all Dissenters already, and Mr. Wesley too. I wrote a few short remarks at that time for my own use: but of late I am enlarging them to make a pamphlet. I am not sure whether I will print it; but I think fit to leave some of my thoughts behind me for posterity. There is a good deal of his book to which I agree: in other things I differ in judgment.' ('Extracts' as in note 91; this reference was pointed out to me by the Rev. Richard P. Heitzenrater.)
118. See note 98 above.
119. For further discussion of the motives and validity of Wesley's ordinations, see E. H. Nygren, 'John Wesley's Changing Concept of the Ministry' in *Religion and Life* XXXI. 264-74 (Spring 1962); G. S. M. Walker, 'The Historic Episcopate Locally Adapted', *LQR* CXCI. 289-96; A. B. Lawson, *John Wesley and the Christian Ministry*, London, 1963; John C. English, 'John Wesley and the principle of ministerial succession', *Methodist History* XII. 31-6 (January 1964).

NOTES TO CHAPTER SIXTEEN, pp. 283-303

1. There is no contemporary evidence of either sermon having been preached, and whereas most of Wesley's preached sermons have three or four major 'points' with subdivisions, these two (in common with most of his treatises) comprise consecutively numbered sections, though 'On Schism' does reveal a half-hearted attempt at subdivision.
2. *Arminian Magazine*, 1786, pp. 8-15, 71-5, dated at the end 'Bristol, Sept. 28, 1785'; *Sermons*, Vol. VI, 1788, pp. 171-90; cf. *Works* VI. 392-401.
3. *Letters* VIII. 135-6 (10 May 1789), and 249 (undated, but November 1790).
4. Cf. 1747 *Minutes* (*Minutes* I. 35) and Wesley's comments on 1 Cor. 1:10 and 11:18 in his *Explanatory Notes upon The New Testament*; see also above p. 99.
5. *Arminian Magazine*, 1786, pp. 238-44, 293-8, dated at the end 'Newcastle-under-Lyne [i.e. Lyme], March 30 1786'; *Sermons*, Vol. VI, 1788, pp. 191-210; cf. *Works* VI. 401-10.
6. *Minutes* I. 5-6; cf. *Works* VIII. 35-6, 236, and see below, pp. 287-9.
7. Bradburn, *The Question*, pp. 17-18, 22-4.
8. *Works* VIII. 30 cf. *LQR* CLXXXV. 214-15 (July 1960).

9. 'Ought we to separate?', p. 38 (see Appendix); cf. *Works* XIII. 229–30, where one sentence is omitted.

10. Tyerman, *Wesley* II. 388.

11. *Minutes* I. 59.

12. Ibid., I. 541.

13. Ibid., I. 542–7.

14. Bradburn, *The Question*, pp. 10–11.

15. *Letters* VII. 115; cf. p. 69.

16. Tyerman, *Wesley* III. 364.

17. *Arminian Magazine*, 1782, pp. 92–3, 152–3, 374–5; cf. *Letters* VII. 91–3, 98–9, 107–8.

18. Bradburn, *The Question*, pp. 11–12.

19. *Letters* VII. 206; cf. pp. 107, 114, 126, 136, 142, 170, 210, 219.

20. Ibid., VII. 170.

21. Ibid., VII. 136

22. *WHS* I. 127, VIII. 21.

23. Bradburn, *The Question*, pp. 12–13; cf. *WHS* XXXIV. 154–5.

24. *Journal* VI. 224, 437d, VII. 17: cf. above, pp. 215–16, for M'Nab's opposition to Rev. Edward Smyth's officiating there as a clergyman usurping his own responsibilities.

25. Ibid., VI. 310; cf. pp. 410–11, 413.

26. Ibid., VI. 403; cf. Bowmer, *Lord's Supper*, pp. 75–8.

27. *Letters* VII. 163.

28. Ibid., VII. 213.

29. Ibid., VII. 215.

30. *Minutes* I. 165, 179, 190, 203, 213.

31. *Letters* VII. 326; cf. *Journal* VI. 518, where he exclaimed, 'all who preach thus will drive the Methodists from the church, in spite of all that I can do'. Cf. Wesley's letter to Ann Tindall, 26 November 1785: 'I think the Doctor must be in a dream or out of his senses to talk of the Methodists separating from the church!' (British Museum Add. MSS. 43695).

32. *Letters* VII. 327.

33. Tyerman, *Wesley*, III. 478.

34. *Minutes*, 1786, p. 22; cf. *Minutes* I. 193.

35. *Arminian Magazine*, 1788, pp. 340–8, 397–403; cf. *Works* VII. 174–85.

36. *Arminian Magazine*, 1788, pp. 400–2; cf. *Letters* VIII. 177–9.

37. *Letters* VII. 349.

38. Ibid., p. 339.

39. *Journal* VII. 217.

40. *WHS* XIX. 116. This passage in Wesley's *Journal* was omitted from the second edition of 1794, probably because it could easily be interpreted as a complete condemnation of what was then being agitated as necessary Methodist practice.

41. *Arminian Magazine*, 1799, pp. 601–2; cf. *Letters* VII. 345–6, *WHS* XXXI. 119–20, and *Arminian Magazine*, 1788, pp. 498–9.
42. *Journal* VII. 232. Samuel Bradburn notes in his own copy, 'They had their desire soon after' (*WHS* XIX. 116–17).
43. Ibid., VII. 340.
44. *Letters* VII. 331–4.
45. Ibid., VII. 370; cf. *WHS* X. 153 for the italicization.
46. Ibid., VIII. 10; cf. *WHS* XXVII. 182.
47. Ibid., VIII. 58.
48. Ibid., pp. 58–60, 63.
49. Ibid., p. 65.
50. Ibid., p. 66.
51. *Minutes* I. 213.
52. *Letters* VIII. 223 (21 June 1790).
53. *WHS* XVIII. 22.
54. The original reads 'separation, such was'; another possible emendation would be 'separation; such was'.
55. *Arminian Magazine*, 1789, pp. 45–6, dated 'Bristol, Sept. 20, 1788'.
56. *Journal* VII. 481–2; *Arminian Magazine*, 1797, p. 313. In his own copy of the *Journal* Bradburn added opposite the last sentence: 'Wonderful logic!' (See *WHS* XIX. 117.)
57. *Letters* VIII. 125–7: Arthur Keen endorsed the original: 'Wesley/ Whitefriar/Ans[we]r to our Remonstrance. No. 2.' (Methodist archives, London).
58. Ibid., VIII. 136–7.
59. *Arminian Magazine*, 1797, p. 313.
60. *WHS* IX. 188–91.
61. *Works* XIII. 268–71; cf. *Letters* VIII. 139–43.
62. *Journal* VII. 512, 514, 516–17.
63. *Minutes of the Methodist Conferences in Ireland*, Dublin, 1864, Vol. I, p. 48.
64. See *WHS* VIII. 15–20, 42–8, 95–7; cf. *Letters* VIII. 216.
65. *Letters* VIII. 253.
66. *Minutes* I. 547; cf. *Letters* VIII. 172.
67. Transcript in my possession; whereabouts of original unknown. In London Wesley continued to hold services at both West Street and the New Chapel at 5.0 a.m. as well as 9.30 a.m. both summer and winter. See *WHS* XXIII. 103.

NOTES TO CHAPTER SEVENTEEN, pp. 304–323

1. *WHS* XXIX. 28.
2. Ibid., XVIII. 23–4.
3. Addison, *United Brethren*, pp. 196–7.

4. Ibid., p. 204.

5. Ibid., pp. 205-6.

6. Ibid., pp. 210-12.

7. Ibid., pp. 212-13.

8. Ibid., p. 221. This was probably while Wesley preached on the priest-hood of Melchisedec at Manchester on Sunday evening 9 April; see *Journal* VII. 154, and cf. *Letters* VII. 324, where in a letter of 6 April to Charles he says: 'I tell our societies everywhere, "The Methodists will not leave the Church, at least while I live".'

9. Addison, op. cit., pp. 221-4.

10. MS letter in the Moravian archives, London; cf. Baker, *Charles Wesley*, p. 131, and Jackson, *Charles Wesley* II. 402-3.

11. Wesley made no bones, however, about defending his own Anglican methods of public worship, and on one occasion addressed a large congregation at Dundee in this manner: 'I love plain dealing. Do not you? I will use it now. Bear with me. I hang out no false colours, but show you all I am, all I intend, all I do. I am a member of the Church of England; but I love good men of every church. My ground is the Bible. Yea, I am a Bible-bigot, I follow it in all things, both great and small. Therefore I always use a sort of *short private prayer* when I attend the public service of God. Do not *you*? Why do you not? Is not this according to the Bible? I *stand* whenever I sing the praises of God in public. Does not the Bible give you plain precedents for this? I always kneel before the Lord my Maker when I pray in public. I generally, in public, use the *Lord's prayer*, because Christ has taught me when I pray to say—[Luke 11:2]. I advise every preacher connected with me, whether in England or Scotland, herein to tread in my steps.' (See *Centenary of Methodism*, Dublin, 1839, pp. 180-1.)

12. Wesley F. Swift, *Methodism in Scotland*, London, 1947, p. 58; cf. *WHS* XII. 107-8, XVIII. 1-6, XXX. 17-18, XXXI. 14.

13. John Wesley's letter in the magazine stated: 'For these forty years I have been in doubt concerning that question: "What obedience is due to Heathenish Priests and Mitred Infidels?" '—to which Charles replied, 'That juvenile line of mine I disown, renounce, and with shame recant. I never knew of more than one "mitred infidel", and for him I took Mr. Law's word'. In his *Elegy on the death of Robert Jones, Esq.* (1742) he wrote a scathing criticism of the Anglican clergy, closing with the line '*Heathenish priests, and mitred infidels!*' See *The Poetical Works of John and Charles Wesley*, ed. G. Osborn, 13 vols, London, 1868-72, III. 122, and *Letters* VII. 284, 288.

14. *WHS* XI. 53; cf. ibid., XII. 107-8.

15. Ibid., IX. 112 (30 March 1786).

16. *Letters* VIII. 135-6; cf. Tyerman, *Wesley* III. 581-3.

17. E.g. letters 'To the Rev. Mr. Al. Suter, Aberdeen', and 'To Mr. Suter at the Preaching-house in Plymouth Dock', *Letters* VIII. 23, 137.

18. *Letters* VIII. 98 (12 October 1788), and one of 14 February 1789 in the muniments of Wesley's Chapel, City Road, London.
19. Ibid., VII. 346; cf. pp. 295–6 above.
20. Ibid., VII. 352; cf. p. 291 above.
21. *Sermons*, Vol. VIII (London, 1788), pp. 249–272; cf. *Arminian Magazine*, 1789, pp. 6–14, 62–8, where it is dated at the end, 'Witney, October 17, 1787.' See also *Works* VII. 202–213, especially p. 208.
22. Ibid., VII. 377 (25 March 1787).
23. Ibid., VII. 389–91 (18 June 1787), from *Arminian Magazine*, 1788, pp. 264–6.
24. Ibid., VIII. 47 (18 March 1788).
25. *Arminian Magazine*, 1789, pp. 46–9; cf. *Works* XIII. 264–7; cf. also *Works* VI. 282 for Luther on revivals.
26. Mrs. R. Smith, *Moore*, p. 95, and *Letters* VIII. 129.
27. *HAM* I. 121–3, 229–31, 425–8; cf. *WHS* XXXII. 96; XXXIV. 105–7. The quotation occurs in a letter to Beverley Allen.
28. *Letters* VII. 354, 371–2.
29. Ibid., VIII. 200.
30. Ibid., VIII. 260.
31. *WHS* XVIII. 25–6; cf. *Wesleyan Methodist Magazine*, 1845, p. 113.
32. *Journal* VII. 422.
33. *WHS* XVIII. 22; cf. *Minutes* I. 172. Wesley had earlier warned this preacher, William Moore, against associating with the separatists in Bath; see *Letters* VII. 123–4.
34. *Letters* VIII. 72.
35. Ibid., VII. 372.
36. Ibid., VIII. 58.
37. Ibid., VIII. 195; cf. pp. 177–9.
38. Whitehead, *Wesley* II. 498; cf. Lawson, *Wesley and the Christian Ministry*, pp. 90–1; the *substance* of the sermon, however, was relatively commonplace with Wesley.
39. *Arminian Magazine*, 1790, pp. 230–5, 286–90; cf. *Works* VII. 273–81.
40. See especially section 18, op. cit., pp. 288–9.
41. *Journal* VII. 523.
42. Ibid., VII. 524.
43. *Minutes* I. 585–9, 649–55.
44. Ibid., I. 533; cf. p. 596.
45. Ibid., I. 543.
46. *Journal* VIII. 342–4.
47. Ibid., VII. 525.
48. Ibid., VIII. 76; cf. VII. 514–15, VIII. 35. But note Henry Moore's astonishment at Wesley's avowal of supposed weakness, in his life of Wesley II. 379–80.
49. *Journal* VIII. 3–5.
50. *WHS* XV. 59.

51. *Journal* VIII. 102. Souvenirs made from this tree are extant.
52. *Letters* VIII. 205.
53. Ibid., VIII. 211.
54. Cf. above, pp. 198–9.
55. *Letters* VIII. 10–11, 78.
56. *Journal* VII. 339; cf. *WHS* XI. 93.
57. Licence dated 11 July 1787 in Methodist archives, London.
58. *Letters* VIII. 78.
59. Whitehead, *Wesley* II. 448; Moore, *Wesley* II. 381–2.
60. *Letters* VIII. 37, 280; cf. *WHS* XIX. 23.
61. *WHS* XV. 58, XVIII. 28.
62. Moore, *Wesley* II. 383.
63. Whitehead, *Wesley* II. 450; cf. Moore, *Wesley* II. 383–4.
64. The 1401 Act passed to suppress Lollardy, 'Concerning the burning of heretics'.
65. Moore, *Wesley* II. 384–5; cf. *Letters* VIII. 224–5, *WHS* XV. 58.
66. On 24 February 1789 Wilberforce called on Wesley, commenting that he was 'A fine old fellow'; see *Journal* VII. 471.
67. MS letter in Methodist archives, London, endorsed 'John Wesley/ Methodists Persecution'; cf. *Letters* VIII. 230–1.
68. *Letters* VIII. 58.
69. MS letter, 4 March 1786, in British Museum (Add. MSS. 43695); cf. *Letters* VII. 321, 324.
70. *Letters* VIII. 71.
71. Ibid., VIII. 72.
72. For a similar error in 1786 see *Letters* VII. 332.
73. *Arminian Magazine*, 1790, pp. 214–16; cf. *Works* XIII. 272–4.
74. See above, p. 232.
75. *WHS* XVII. 136–45.
76. *WHS* XXXIV. 153–8; cf. I. 42–6.
77. Jackson, *Early Methodist Preachers*, V. 60, 70–4.
78. *WHS* VI. 4–5.

NOTES TO THE EPILOGUE, pp. 324–5

1. Baker, *Representative Verse of Charles Wesley*, p. 370.
2. Cf. *Letters* VIII. 156, where Wesley agreed to try a proposed new evangelistic experiment.
3. *Journal* VII. 515, VIII. 3; cf. *WHS* XII. 108.
4. See above, pp. 313–14.
5. *United Methodist Free Churches' Magazine*, 1862, p. 360.
6. *Minutes* I. 31 (1746); cf. MS Minutes, p. 35.
7. *Letters* VIII. 112.

8. Ibid., VIII. 204.
9. *Memoirs of the Life of the Rev. Peard Dickinson . . . by himself*, ed. Joseph Benson, London, 1803, p. 67.
10. *WHS* IX. 112.
11. See p. 322 above.

NOTES TO THE APPENDIX, pp. 326–340

1. Because of illness Wesley had not been in Dublin since 1752. The 'serious man' may have been the banker William Lunell, who had been a leading Dublin Methodist, but had come strongly under the influence of Whitefield's Calvinism, which proved a disruptive element there.
2. Here as elsewhere the amanuensis has 'w^c' when apparently 'w^o' is intended. (Later examples are also noted '2'.)
3. As usual Wesley abridges and to a small extent paraphrases Article XIX.
4. Cf. Article XXVI, 'Of the unworthiness of the ministers, which hinder not the effect of the sacraments.'
5. Romans 12:21. (In this paragraph, as commonly throughout Wesley's writings, there are several scriptural references, including those to Heb. 10:34, Matt. 5:39, and Heb. 12:4; such reminiscences we do not normally document, but only direct quotations.)
6. I Peter 2:13.
7. Cf. Matt. 23:8–10.
8. Matt. 15:9, Mark 7:7.
9. II Chron. 20:3.
10. II Kings 23:1–25, II Chron. 34:29–33, 35:1–19.
11. See Nehemiah, Chapters 7–13.
12. I Cor. 14:40.
13. Mark 7:9; cf. v. 8. The Authorized Version reads 'reject the commandments of God'; in his *Explanatory Notes upon the New Testament* (published in the same year of 1755 as this document was prepared) Wesley translated ἀθετεῖτε as 'abolish'. His 'make void' here probably comes from the ἀκυροῦντες of v. 13, which the A.V. renders 'making . . . of none effect', and Wesley's *Notes* 'abrogating'.
14. I Peter 2:13.
15. Cf. Ezra 7:10, 25.
16. 'Word' is given as an alternative for 'law'.
17. Wesley speaks here of himself and his brother as ordained clergy, not of the preachers in general.
18. I Tim. 4:14.
19. Heb. 5:4.
20. I Cor. 14:35. Wesley correctly alters the 'women' of the A.V. to 'woman'. Cf. Acts 2:17.

21. This mistranslation of the A.V. was corrected in Wesley's *Explanatory Notes upon the Old Testament*, 3 vols, Bristol, 1765; see especially his note upon Leviticus 2:1. As opposed to the sacrifice of meat that of grain was bloodless, and the phrase 'unbloody sacrifice' was transferred also to the Lord's Supper in the early years of the English Reformation.
22. I John 2:1.
23. See the Council of Trent, Session 7, Canon 11; cf. *Works* X. 113–14; also pp. 136, 149.
24. With this paragraph (and a phrase or two from that preceding) Wesley began his 'Reasons against a Separation from the Church of England' in his *Preservative against unsettled notions in Religion* (1758). This well-known publication continued almost word for word the same as this manuscript to the end, except for an occasional omission. See *Works* XIII. 225–31.
25. Dr. Henry Pendleton, who preached against Lutheranism under Henry VIII, himself became a Protestant under Edward VI, but after boasting of his courageous fidelity once more became a Roman Catholic under Mary. See *DNB*.
26. Eph. 2:12.
27. Luke 1:79.
28. II Cor. 12:15, I John 3:16.
29. James 1:20.
30. See *Journal* III. 98–9, 117–20, 127–30, 409–14, 464–6, 507, V. 3. These are all examples, however, of persecutions of the Methodists by others, not of Methodists themselves using 'harsh methods'.
31. *A Letter to a person lately joined with the People called Quakers* (1748); see *Works* X. 177–88.
32. *Thoughts upon Infant Baptism*, Bristol, 1751, extracted from William Wall's *History of Infant Baptism*, and published anonymously. See Green, *Wesley Bibliography*, No. 149.
33. *Serious Thoughts upon the Final Perseverance of the Saints* (1751); see *Works* X. 284–98.
34. Eph. 4:14, 15.

SELECT BIBLIOGRAPHY

This is not a complete bibliography of the subject, but only a listing of some of the more important works to which reference is made in the text and notes. The following categories are omitted: the extensive manuscript material used, contemporary editions of Wesley's publications which are also available in his collected *Works*, articles in periodicals, chapters in composite works, and many books and pamphlets which illustrate peripheral points.

The first citation of any work in the text gives most of the details listed here. Thereafter the notes in general record simply the author's name and a title long enough only to distinguish it from other works listed here.

Abbreviations used

DNB	*Dictionary of National Biography*, q.v.
HAM	Bucke, Emory S. (ed.), *History of American Methodism*, q.v.
Journal	Wesley, John, *Journal* (Standard edition), q.v.
Letters	Wesley, John, *Letters* (Standard edition), q.v.
LQR	*London Quarterly and Holborn Review*, q.v.
Minutes	*Minutes of the Methodist Conferences*, q.v.
MS Minutes	Wesley Historical Society: Publication No. 1, q.v.
WHS	Wesley Historical Society: *Proceedings*, q.v.
Works	Wesley, John, *Works*, 14 vols, ed. T. Jackson, q.v.

ABBEY, C. J., and J. H. OVERTON, *The English Church in the Eighteenth Century*, 2 vols, London, Longmans Green, 1878.

ADDISON, WILLIAM G., *The Renewed Church of the United Brethren, 1722–1930*, London, S.P.C.K., 1932.

Arminian Magazine, ed. John Wesley, London, Fry, Paramore, etc., 1778–1797, continued as the *Methodist Magazine* (*1798–1821*) and the *Wesleyan Methodist Magazine* (1822–1913).

ASBURY, FRANCIS, *The Journal and Letters of Francis Asbury*, ed. Elmer T. Clark *et al.*, 3 vols, London, Epworth Press, and Nashville, Abingdon Press, 1958.

ATMORE, CHARLES, *The Methodist Memorial*, Bristol, Edwards, 1801.

BAKER, FRANK, *William Grimshaw, 1708–1763*, London, Epworth Press, 1963.

BALLEINE, G. R., *A History of the Evangelical Party in the Church of England*, London, Longmans, Green, 1933.

BAXTER, RICHARD, *Practical Works*, 23 vols, London, Duncan, 1830.

BEARDSLEY, E. E., *Life and Correspondence of the Right Reverend Samuel Seabury*, Boston, Houghton, 1881.

BENHAM, DANIEL, *Memoirs of James Hutton,* London, Hamilton, Adams, 1856.

BENSON, JOSEPH, *An Apology for the People called Methodists,* London, Story and Whitfield, 1801.

BOWMER, JOHN C., *The Sacrament of the Lord's Supper in Early Methodism,* London, Dacre Press, 1951.

BRADBURN, SAMUEL, *The Question, Are the Methodists Dissenters? Fairly Examined,* [London], np, 1792.

BROXAP, HENRY, *A Biography of Thomas Deacon,* Manchester, University Press, 1911.

BUCKE, EMORY STEVENS (ed.), *The History of American Methodism,* 3 vols, Nashville, Abingdon Press, 1964.

Certain Sermons or Homilies. . . . To which are added the Constitutions and Canons Ecclesiastical set forth in the year MDCIII, Oxford University Press, 1844.

CLARK, JAMES, *Montanus Redivivus,* Dublin, Saunders, 1760.

CLARKE, ADAM, *Memoirs of the Wesley Family,* 4th edn, revised, corrected, and considerably enlarged, 2 vols, London, Tegg, 1860.

CLARKE, J. B. B., *An Account of . . . Adam Clarke,* London, Clarke, 1833.

COKE, THOMAS, *An Address to the Methodist Society . . . on the settlement of the preaching houses,* Liverpool, M'Greery, 1795.

— and HENRY MOORE, *The Life of the Rev. John Wesley,* London, Paramore and Whitfield, 1792.

— *Sermon preached . . . on the death of the Rev. John Richardson,* London, Paramore and Whitfield, 1792.

— *The Substance of a Sermon preached . . . at the Ordination of the Rev. Francis Asbury to the office of a Superintendent. . . .* London, Paramore and Scollick, 1785.

CRAGG, G. R., *Reason and Authority in the Eighteenth Century,* Cambridge University Press, 1964.

CROOKSHANK, C. H., *History of Methodism in Ireland,* 3 vols, Belfast, Allen, 1885.

DAVIES, G. C. B., *The Early Cornish Evangelicals, 1735–1760,* London, S.P.C.K., 1951.

DAVIES, RUPERT, and GORDON RUPP (eds), *A History of the Methodist Church in Great Britain,* Vol. I, London, Epworth Press, 1965.

DICKINSON, PEARD, *Memoirs of the Life of the Rev. Peard Dickinson, . . . by himself,* ed. Joseph Benson, London, Story and Whitfield, 1803.

DREW, SAMUEL, *Life of the Rev. Thomas Coke,* London, Cordeux and Blanshard, 1817.

EAYRS, GEORGE, *John Wesley, Christian Philosopher and Church Founder,* London, Epworth Press, 1926.

EGMONT, JOHN PERCEVAL, First Earl of Egmont, *Diary,* 3 vols, London, Historical Manuscripts Commission, 1920, 1923.

EMORY, JOHN, *A Defence of 'Our Fathers',* 5th edn, New York, Bangs and Emory, 1836.

[ERSKINE, RALPH,] *Fraud and Fals[e]hood discovered*. Edinburgh, np. 1743.

FLETCHER, JOHN W., *Posthumous Pieces*, ed. Melville Horne, Madeley, Edmunds, 1791.

[GIBSON, EDMUND,] *The Case of the Methodists briefly stated; more particularly in the point of field-preaching*, np, 1744.

— *The Charge of the Right Reverend Father in God, Edmund Lord Bishop of London, at the Visitation of his diocese in the years 1746 and 1747*, np, nd.

[—] *Observations upon the conduct and behaviour of a certain sect usually distinguished by the name of Methodists*, London, np, 1744.

GREEN, RICHARD, *Anti-Methodist Publications*, London, Kelly, 1902.

— *The Works of John and Charles Wesley: A Bibliography*, 2nd edn, revised, London, Methodist Publishing House, 1906.

GREEN, V. H. H., *The Young Mr. Wesley*, London, Arnold, 1961.

HAMILTON, J. TAYLOR, *A History of the church known as the Moravian Church*, Bethlehem, Pennsylvania, Times Publishing Company, 1900.

HARMON, NOLAN B., *The Rites and Ritual of Episcopal Methodism*, Nashville, Lamar and Barton, 1926.

HOOKER, RICHARD, *Works*, ed. John Keble, revised by R. W. Church and F. Paget, 3 vols, Oxford University Press, 1881.

HURST, JOHN FLETCHER, *History of Methodism*, 8 vols, London, Kelly, 1901.

JACKSON, THOMAS, *Life of the Rev. Charles Wesley*, 2 vols., London, Mason, 1841.

— (ed.), *Lives of Early Methodist Preachers*, 4th edn., 6 vols, London, Wesleyan Conference Office, 1871.

JEWEL, JOHN, *Works*, ed. John Ayre, 4 vols. Cambridge University Press, 1845–50.

JONES, M. H. (ed.), *Trevecka Letters*, Caernarvon, Calvinistic Methodist Book Room, 1932.

[KING, PETER,] *An Enquiry into the Constitution, Discipline, Unity and Worship of the Primitive Church*, London, Wyat, [1691].

LAYCOCK, J. W., *Heroes of the Great Haworth Round*, Keighley, Rydal Press, 1909.

LEWIS, A. J., *Zinzendorf*, Philadelphia, Westminster Press, 1962.

LOCKWOOD, JOHN P., *The Western Pioneers* (Boardman and Pilmoor), London, Wesleyan Conference Office, 1881.

MACDONALD, JAMES, *Memoirs of the Rev. Joseph Benson*, London, Hamilton, 1822.

McADOO, H. R., *The Spirit of Anglicanism*, London, Black, 1965.

M'CAINE, ALEXANDER, *Letters on the Organization and early History of the Methodist Episcopal Church*, Boston, Norris, 1850.

McGARVEY, WILLIAM, *Liturgiae Americanae*, Philadelphia, Sunshine Publishing Company, 1895.

Methodist Episcopal Church, *Minutes . . ., composing a Form of Discipline*, Philadelphia, Cist, 1785.

— *Minutes of the Methodist Conferences annually held in America, from 1773 to 1794, inclusive*, Philadelphia, Tuckniss and Dickins, 1795.

Methodist History, Association of Methodist Historical Societies, Lake Junaluska, N.C., 1962–8.

Minutes of the Methodist Conferences, from ... *1744*, Vol. I (1744–98), London, Mason, 1862.

Minutes of the Methodist Conferences in Ireland, Vol. I (1752–1819), Dublin, Religious and General Book Company, Kershaw, 1864.

MOORE, HENRY, *Life of the Rev. John Wesley*, A.M., 2 vols, London, Kershaw, 1824.

MYLES, WILLIAM, *A Chronological History of the People called Methodists*, 4th edn, London, Cordeux, 1813.

OUTLER, ALBERT C., *John Wesley* (edited selections, in 'A Library of Protestant Thought'), New York, Oxford University Press, 1964.

The Oxford Methodists, London, Roberts, 1733.

PEASTON, A. E., *The Prayer Book Reform Movement in the XVIIIth Century*, Oxford, Blackwell, 1940.

— *The Prayer Book Tradition in the Free Churches*, London, Clarke, 1964.

PEIRCE, WILLIAM, *Ecclesiastical Principles and Polity of the Wesleyan Methodists*, London, Hamilton, Adams, 1854 (also 2nd edn, 1868, and 3rd edn, 1873).

PRIESTLEY, JOSEPH (ed.), *Original Letters by the Rev. John Wesley and his friends, illustrative of his early history*, Birmingham, Pearson, 1791.

RATTENBURY, J. ERNEST, *The Eucharistic Hymns of John and Charles Wesley*, London, Epworth Press, 1948.

REYNOLDS, J. S., *The Evangelicals at Oxford, 1735–1871*, Oxford, Blackwell, 1953.

RICHEY, MATTHEW, *Memoir of the late Rev. William Black*, Halifax, Nova Scotia, Cunnabell, 1839.

ROBERTS, GOMER M. (ed.), *Selected Trevecka Letters (1747–1794)*, Caernarvon, Calvinistic Methodist Book Room, 1962.

SCHMIDT, MARTIN, *John Wesley: a theological biography*, Vol. I (trans. Norman P. Goldhawk), London, Epworth Press, 1962.

SEABURY, W. J., *Memoir of Bishop Seabury*, New York, Gorham, 1908.

[SEYMOUR, A. C. H.], *The Life and Times of Selina Countess of Huntingdon*, 2 vols, London, Painter, 1840.

SIDNEY, EDWIN, *The Life and Ministry of the Rev. Samuel Walker*, 2nd edn, London, Seeley and Burnside, 1838.

SMITH, GEORGE, *History of Wesleyan Methodism*, 5th edn, 3 vols. London, Longmans, Green, etc., 1872.

SMITH, MRS. RICHARD, *Life of the Rev. Henry Moore*, New York, Lane and Tippett, 1845.

— *Raithby Hall*, London, Wentheim, etc., 1859.

STAMP, WILLIAM W., *The Orphan-House of Wesley*, London, Mason, 1863.

The State of Subscription to the Articles and Liturgy of the Church of England towards the close of the year 1773, London, 1774, see [WOLLASTON, FRANCIS].

STEPHENS, A. J., *The Book of Common Prayer, with notes, legal and historical*, 3 vols, London, Harrison, 1849.

STEVENSON, G. J., *City Road Chapel, London*, London, Stevenson, [1872].

— *Memorials of the Wesley Family*, London, Partridge, [1876].

STILLINGFLEET, EDWARD, *The Irenicum, a Weapon Salve for the Church's Wounds*, 2nd edn, London, Mortlock, 1662.

STOEFFLER, F. ERNST, *The Rise of Evangelical Pietism*, Leiden, Brill, 1965.

SWEET, WILLIAM WARREN, *Religion on the American Frontier, 1783–1840: Vol. IV. The Methodists*, Chicago, University of Chicago Press, 1946.

SWIFT, WESLEY F. *Methodism in Scotland*, London, Epworth Press, 1947.

SYKES, NORMAN, *Church and State in England in the XVIIIth Century*, Cambridge University Press, 1934.

— *Old Priest and New Presbyter*, Cambridge University Press, 1956.

— *William Wake*, 2 vols, Cambridge, University Press, 1957.

[TAILFER, PATRICK], *A True and Historical Narrative of the Colony of Georgia*, Charleston, South Carolina, [1741].

TAYLOR, JEREMY, *Works*, ed. R. Heber and C. P. Eden, 10 vols, London, Longmans, Green, etc., 1862.

TELFORD, JOHN, *The Life of John Wesley*, 3rd edn, revised and enlarged, London, Kelly, 1910.

THOMPSON, EDGAR W., *Wesley, Apostolic Man*, London, Epworth Press, 1957.

TIGERT, JOHN J., *A Constitutional History of American Episcopal Methodism*, 6th edn, Nashville, Smith and Lamar, 1916.

TOWLSON, CHARLES W., *Moravian and Methodist*, London, Epworth Press, 1957.

TYERMAN, LUKE, *The Life and Times of the Rev. John Wesley, M.A.*, 3 vols, London, Hodder and Stoughton, 1870–1.

— *The Life and Times of the Rev. Samuel Wesley, M.A.*, London, Simpkin, Marshall, 1866.

— *The Life of the Rev. George Whitefield*, 2 vols, London, Hodder and Stoughton, 1890.

— *The Oxford Methodists*, London, Hodder and Stoughton, 1873.

— *Wesley's Designated Successor: the life . . . of the Rev. John William Fletcher*, London, Hodder and Stoughton, 1882.

WARREN, SAMUEL, *A Digest of the Laws and Regulations of the Wesleyan Methodists*, 2nd edn, London, Stephens, 1835.

WESLEY, CHARLES, *Journal*, ed. Thomas Jackson, 2 vols, London, Wesleyan Methodist Book Room, nd.

WESLEY, JOHN, *A Christian Library: consisting of extracts from . . . the choicest pieces of practical divinity which have been published in the English language*, 50 vols, Bristol, Farley, 1749–55.

— *A Concise Ecclesiastical History*, 4 vols, London, Paramore, 1781.

— *Explanatory Notes upon the New Testament*, London, Bowyer, 1755.

— *Explanatory Notes upon the Old Testament*, 3 vols, Bristol, Pine, 1765.

— *The Christian's Pattern, or a Treatise of the Imitation of Christ. Written originally in Latin by Thomas à Kempis . . . Compared with the original, and corrected throughout, by John Wesley*, London, Rivington, 1735.

— *The Journal of the Rev. John Wesley, A.M. . . ., Enlarged from Original Manuscripts . . ., Standard Edition*, ed. Nehemiah Curnock, 8 vols, Bicentenary Issue, London, Epworth Press, 1938.

— *The Letters of the Rev. John Wesley, A.M. . . . Standard Edition*, ed. John Telford, 8 vols, London, Epworth Press, 1931.

— *The Sunday Service of the Methodists in North America: with other occasional services*, London, np. 1784.

— *Wesley's Standard Sermons*, ed. Edward H. Sugden, 2 vols, London, Epworth Press, 1921.

— *The Works of the Rev. John Wesley, M.A.*, 32 vols, Bristol, Pine, 1771–4.

— *The Works of the Rev. John Wesley, A.M.*, 14 vols, London, Wesleyan-Methodist Book-Room, n.d. This is almost identical with the London, 1872, edition re-issued by Zondervan, 1958. These editions differ from the Third Edition, ed. Thomas Jackson, 14 vols, 1829–31, only in the pagination of vols. XI–XIV, mainly because of minor additions and some consequent rearrangement.

— and CHARLES WESLEY, *The Poetical Works*, ed. G. Osborn, 13 vols, London, Wesleyan Methodist Conference Office, 1868–71.

[WESLEY, SAMUEL, ed. John Wesley], *Advice to a Young Clergyman*, London, Rivington and Roberts, 1735.

Wesley Historical Society, *Proceedings*, 1893–1967.

— *Publications*, Number 1: 'John Bennet's copy of the Minutes of the Conferences of 1744, 1745, 1747 and 1748, with Wesley's copy of those for 1746', London, 1896, with an appendix added in Vol. IV of the *Proceedings*, 1903–4, containing the MS Minutes for 1749, 1755, 1758.

— *General Index to the Proceedings, Vols. I–XXX and Publications I–IV (1897–1956)*, compiled by John A. Vickers, Leicester, 1960.

WHITEFIELD, GEORGE, *George Whitefield's Journals*, new edn, London, Banner of Truth Trust, 1960.

— *Works*, 6 vols, London, Dilly, 1771–2.

WHITEHEAD, JOHN, *The Life of the Rev. John Wesley, M.A.*, 2 vols, London, Couchman, 1793, 1796.

[WOLLASTON, FRANCIS,] *The State of Subscription to the Articles and Liturgy of the Church of England towards the close of the year 1773*, London, Wilkie, 1774.

WOOD, A. SKEVINGTON, *Thomas Haweis, 1734–1820*, London, S.P.C.K., 1957.

WOODWARD, JOSIAH, *An Account of the Rise and Progress of the Religious Societies in the City of London*, 5th ed, London, Downing, 1724.

WORKMAN, H. B., *et al.* (editors), *A New History of Methodism*, 2 vols, London, Hodder and Stoughton, 1909.

INDEX

(N.B. Only select matter in the Notes is indexed, not the authorities cited.)